WITHDRAWN

D1171992

The house in which Senator Borah was born, June 29, 1865, ten miles from Fairfield, Illinois.

Acme

William E. Borah in 1897.

Idaho Historical Society

Senator Borah speaking at Idanha Hotel, Boise, after his vindication.

Idaho Historical Society

Senator Borah in Boise, Idaho.

Johnson Studio, Boise

The senator's recreation.

International Newsreel

Borah's attempt to redirect the Republican Party.

College of Idaho—Borah Collection

Senator William E. Borah in 1936, speaking at the Shrine Hall in Brooklyn, after being hailed as a square dealer.

Wide World Photos

Senator Borah, dean of the U. S. Senate, introduces President Franklin D. Roosevelt to 15,000 persons in Boise, Idaho, where the presidential party stopped on the westward trip.

Acme

Mrs. William E. Borah.

Johnson & Son, Boise

Senator William E. Borah.

Blackstone Studios, Inc.

Mrs. William E. Borah, widow of the senator, by his statue at its presentation to Congress, in the rotunda of the Capitol.

Acme

BORAH

by MARIAN C. McKENNA

Ann Arbor: The University of Michigan Press

Designed by Stuart Ross

Library of Congress Catalog Card No. 60-15771
Published in the United States of America by
The University of Michigan Press and simultaneously
in Toronto, Canada, by Ambassador Books Limited
Manufactured in the United States of America by
The Haddon Craftsmen, Scranton, Pa.

Contents

Brother, thou hast possibility in thee for much: the possibility of writing on the eternal skies the record of a heroic life.

—THOMAS CARLYLE

I Prairie Lad

When
Swift down the shining iron track
You sweep, and fields of corn flash back,
And herds of lowing steers move by,
And men laugh loud, in mute mistrust,
I turn to other days, to men
Who made a pathway with their dust.
—Joaquin Miller

At Omaha station, the eastern terminus of the Union Pacific, a stocky young man of twenty-five, carrying a canvas telescope valise and some packages containing all his worldly possessions, stepped up to the ticket window and purchased a seat on the emigrant train to Ogden, Utah, where it was possible to change for various cities on the West coast. He was not yet certain of his destination. For an hour or more he waited in the station before his train departed for the West. When word was passed along to pick up his bundles and get under way, he found that he was exchanging discomfort for downright misery.

On that late October day in 1890 a chilling wind swept across the open railroad platform and through his threadbare overcoat. Carrying a guidebook under one arm, he appeared to be dressed in clothes he had slept in. His hat looked like a relic of school days. He wore a half-inch collar that had lost its gloss and no necktie. Shivering a little and straining under the load of belongings brought from his sister's home in Kansas, he noticed women with bundles and children hurrying toward the last of the three passenger cars. The central coach was occupied by men, and the foremost was for Chinese and Negro laborers.

In those days a coach on the transcontinental run was a long, narrow wooden box like a flat-roofed Noah's ark, with a stove and a convenience at either end, a passage down the middle, and transverse benches on each hand. The emigrant cars on the Union Pacific were remarkable for their extreme plainness and for the inefficacy of their lamps, which often went out or shed but a dying glimmer while they burned. The young man, settling himself on one of the narrow wooden benches, concluded that any reading in the heavy lawbooks he had brought along would have to be done by daylight.

Soon he felt the discomfort of the stuffy atmosphere, poisoned by numerous unpleasant odors. As the train pulled out of the station and rumbled away into the twilight, somewhere a German emigrant with a concertina favored the weary crowd with a selection; the roaring, banging, and clanging of the wooden coach half drowned his music.

A troubled, uncomfortable evening in the cars merged into an unhappy night. The benches were too short and narrow for anyone but a young child; however, the railroad company's enterprising "servants," as they were called on the posters, had devised a plan for giving a little nightly rest to travelers on the six-day trip to the coast. They prevailed on pairs of men to "chum together." To each of the "chums" they sold a board and three square cushions stuffed with straw and covered with cotton. The benches were made to face each other in pairs, for the backs were reversible. As the night progressed, the boards were laid from bench to bench, making a couch wide enough for two; thus the "chums" lay down side by side on the cushions with their feet toward the engine.

Naturally this plan could only be carried out if the "chums" agreed and the train was not too crowded. The white-haired official on the emigrant train made a most active master of ceremonies, introducing likely "couples" and even guaranteeing the amiability and honesty of each. The greater the number of happy couples, the better for his pocket. The price for a board and three cushions began at two dollars; but as the night wore on, it dropped to as little as fifty cents.

The stretch to Cheyenne across the Nebraska plains was about one hundred miles, most of which were covered at night. The young lawyer spent the first night stretched out on one of the narrow wooden benches and wrapped in his overcoat. Morning came with a freezing chill such as he had rarely felt. Only the third-class traveler knows the sensation of that first awakening: cramped limbs, incessant yawning, and the feeling of having narrowly escaped lockjaw. White mists hung thinly over the surface of the plain. Gradually it grew warmer, but he longed for a bath and a hearty breakfast.

Meals were to be had at wayside stations, but at best they were no bargain. The Pacific Railway offered the same greasy menus as the old-time stage stations. Ruefully the traveler noted the price of griddlecakes and molasses (seventy-five cents). At Cheyenne he limited himself to some crackers and five-cent oranges peddled by newsboys who also sold soap, towels, coffee, tea, sugar, low-grade books, lollipops, and cigars. Rarely was more than twenty minutes allowed for a meal on an emigrant train, and there was no one to shout the warning, "All aboard." Waits to allow express trains to pass were frequent. Emigrants were unaware that their cars were often attached to slow-moving freight trains, which made it impossible to predict the duration of passage within less than a day. Furthermore, delayed schedules required extra meals, which the strapped traveler could not afford. In those days a dollar was a steep price for ham and fried potatoes. As Emerson Hough wrote:

> The days of the adventurers are gone. There are no longer any Voices to summon heroes out on voyage of mystic conquest. It now costs not so much heroism, but so much money, to get out into the West, and it costs so much to live there.[1]

Making an observatory on top of a baggage car, the young Kansan, who as a boy had "ridden the rods" many a time, sat by the hour watching the line of rails stretch over the elevated plateau of Wyoming from horizon to horizon, "like a cue across a billiard board." On either side the broad plain ran on and on. In all that vast expanse of land and sky the twin threads of the single-line track, glistening in the sun, were the only indication of the presence of man. The passing train toiled over this infinity like a snail—

> In a land so far that you wonder whether,
> If God would know it should you fall down dead.

In spite of the emptiness, the traveler found a certain exhilaration in this spaciousness, this freshness, in the discovery of the whole arc of heaven and the unbroken line of the horizon. No longer did the locomotives run into buffalo as the herds crossed the rails or charged the train, yet he could not but reflect on the pioneers who had struggled across the old emigrant trails, painfully urging on their ox teams, weary by noon, with no landmark but the unattainable evening sun. Slowly the engine pulled up over the first range of mountains to Sherman, Wyoming, eight thousand feet above the sea. After descending the incline to the Laramie plains, the train made a thirty-minute stop for dinner at Laramie City.

Pulling out of Laramie, the traveler could see the mountains on either side recede as the rails cut through millions of acres of sagebrush. New ranges came into view. All day he traveled through these mountains, over the North Platte, past Rawlins, and hour after hour he saw the same unkindly world about him: tumbled boulders, cliffs that drearily imitated the shape of monuments, and at long intervals a creek running down through a canyon. At times there were no trees, patches of sward, or commanding mountain forms; over the whole landscape stretched the sagebrush, its grays darkening to black, and the only signs of life were a few fleeing antelope. The plains had a grandeur of their own, but here was desolation. Except for the air, which was light and stimulating, nothing in the region appealed to the wayfarer.

On the second night out, between troubled naps in the day coach, the young lawyer began a conversation with a salesman of sewing machines. The usual talk in the cars concerned hard times, new opportunities, and the hopes that lured men westward. The salesman drew from his pocket a map of Idaho which he spread before them. He pointed to the capital, Boise, as a likely place for the young lawyer to settle.

The next day he met another man whom he later identified as Nat Taylor and described as ". . . a gambler— 'a sport' as we called it then. He was expensively dressed. I was flattered when he took an interest in me. Boise, he said, was the place to stop. Great opportunities in Boise." The gambler even offered to lend him money and send him clients. "I live at Nampa," he said, "and I will get you some business. We'll see to it that you don't starve."

"Of course, I passed it out of my mind," the lawyer related. "I thought it was the last time I should ever see him."[2]

The train was now in Utah. All day they traveled through deserts of alkali and sand with stretches of bare sagebrush country that seemed little kindlier. On through this unwatered wilderness and haunt of savage tribes they pushed until they came to Ogden, where passengers heading for points on the West coast changed to trains connecting with the Oregon Short Line Railroad. Comparing his railroad folder with the money in his pocket, the lawyer from Kansas came to the sudden realization that he could not afford to go on to the coast. He had just enough cash to take him to some city in Idaho, leaving about fifteen dollars for food and shelter when he reached his destination. Remembering all the glowing stories he had heard about Boise, he bought a ticket to nearby Nampa and completed the journey with his gambler friend.

They left Ogden in the evening. In the twilight they saw the amorphous hills defiling past. The strain of the day caught up with them, but the young lawyer slept only fitfully. Most of the night he lay in the cold darkness wondering where the next night would find him, what his fate would be, and if he could succeed in Boise. More than anything else, he dreaded failure. In the morning he found southern Idaho identical with Utah. Down the long canyons rolled the train, its whistle awakening the echoes. One more day and night of desert, sagebrush, an occasional clump of trees, crossing and recrossing the Snake River, and they were in Nampa.

The Idaho Central from Nampa to Boise had been completed three years earlier in 1887. Here the young lawyer parted with the gambler and took "the stub line" east to Boise station, "a crude, weatherboarded shack on the south side of the Boise river." Horse-drawn cabs met the trains to take passengers from the station to the city. So it was that William Edgar Borah, a farm boy from southern Illinois who was educated in Kansas, crossed the plains and came to settle in Boise, because that was as far west as his pocketbook would take him.

Borah's paternal ancestors had migrated to America from Bohemia in 1760. The line has been traced back to the family of Katherina von Bora, a German nun who left her convent during the Reformation to become the wife of Martin Luther. Three Borah brothers settled in Lancaster County, Pennsylvania, and two of them fought in the Revolutionary War. Later they joined a group going to Morgantown, Kentucky, where, with their sons, they established a ferry in Butler County at a horseshoe bend in the Green River. There they worked their farms on the fertile river bottom lands. The little town, called "Borah," even had its own post office until a new wave of westward migration drained off the population.[3]

The moving frontier took the Borahs and other settlers across the Ohio River in 1820 to Wayne County in southern Illinois. John Borah had married Sarah Wilson. When their son, William Nathan, was but a child of two, they bought a farm in Jasper township, six miles northeast of Fairfield. The Illinois Central then sold land for ten or twelve dollars an acre with a 25 per cent discount for cash. The region in which they settled, near Cairo, was called "Egypt," one of the less fertile parts of Illinois; but it grew fair crops of corn and wheat, and its farmers could ship bacon down the Mississippi to southern plantations. Here the Borah children grew up and worked the land. William Nathan, the oldest son, purchased sixty acres of his own in time and brought Elizabeth West as his bride from Indiana in 1846. He fought with the Union army in the Civil War, returning to his farm after Appomattox just in time to be presented with a sturdy infant son, born on June 29, 1865, and named William Edgar.

He was the seventh child and third son in a family of ten. Hettie and Walter died. Oliver, Frank, Caroline, William, Susan, Sarah, Martha, and Alice all grew up to a life of hard work on the farm. Years later his sister Sue wrote to William: "You had no youth, only work . . ."[4] Sincere piety pervaded the Borah household, for both parents were devout Presbyterians. They attended the Cumberland Presbyterian Church, where on occasion "Uncle Billy," as their father was called, would substitute for the absent minister. He would select a text from scripture and preach extemporaneously, astonishing his listeners with his power of language. He knew the Bible better than most clergymen. At home he was a strict disciplinarian who taught his children habits of industry. He tempered his stern morality with charity and tolerance, but on certain matters he was uncompromising. He recognized only two worthy callings in life: the ministry, to which he himself had at one time been drawn, and farming.

His wife, Elizabeth, was a small woman with soft, liquid blue eyes and a weather-beaten face, accustomed to the hardships of life on a prairie farm. She moderated her husband's strict rule with a gentler kindness. Her son William later described her as "one of those patient, devoted farmers' wives who gave her life and soul's highest aspiration to home and family. She was a devout Christian."[5]

What Borah later said about General Grant applied equally to himself: "He was born neither to wealth nor want. His parentage was neither illustrious nor ignoble. All the days of his youth were commonplace."

For young Will Borah, who liked action, life on his father's farm was monotonous work. The farm year began with the spring plowing. Before the sun rose, he was out in the fields urging the plodding oxen on to greater efforts with Latin expletives, as had a youthful Daniel Webster two generations earlier. Will's maiden speech was made to a mule between two rows of corn in his father's fields.[6] After the plowing came harrowing, planting, weeding, and the unending struggle with pests. Haying was followed by the reaping and threshing of grain. While he toiled, the stories he had heard of the great world beyond the farm awakened in him the desire to achieve. As a young lad he was a dreamer.

In winter there were fences to mend, cattle to care for, mules to break (Will Borah was regarded by the "Elm Flat Kids" as the best mule breaker for miles around), and visits to the blacksmith's shop in neighboring Carmi, where the horses were shod, plows sharpened, and harnesses mended.[7] From dawn to dusk the Borah boys worked at their farm chores, for there was always something for them to do.

At Tom's Prairie School near Fairfield children were exposed to the erudition of a college-trained, though often inebriated, schoolmaster. Here Will Borah studied from Ray's *Arithmetic,* and in McGuffey's *Readers* he found the model orations he loved to recite: "Ye call me Chief," or "It is natural for us to indulge in the illusions of hope," and "Give me liberty or give me death." In grammar school he grew to like books better than anything else. He had his share of games, but he spent many more hours reading everything that came to hand: the Bible, *Pilgrim's Progress,* Franklin's *Autobiography,* and other classics. His family bought an occasional copy of the Chicago *Inter-Ocean.*

Once he ran into difficulty through reading *The Mistakes of Moses.* As he related it:

> . . . at the age when every boy knows just how the world was made and how man accidentally arrived upon earth, I secured . . . a little volume of Colonel Ingersoll's . . . I was perfectly fascinated with the story . . . I soon found out that [Moses] . . . had killed an Egyptian and hidden him in the sand . . . I was so glad to find these saints were human. One day while sitting under a tree reading when I ought to have been pulling weeds out of the corn, father came along and asked what I was reading. I closed the book and being in rather a close place . . . I concluded I would keep still . . . Father, thinking that my silence under such circumstances was an admission of guilt, reached over, took possession of the book, and I never read any more of that volume . . . I went my way disconsolate. I had no Ingersoll and the intellectual heavens were without a star.[8]

Borah adhered to the agnosticism of Robert Ingersoll until he read a life of Napoleon. Then the boy was deeply impressed by the general's declaration aboard ship, under a star-studded firmament, that there must be a God to have created this awesome universe; as a result his skepticism vanished.[9]

He soon exhausted what Tom's Prairie School could offer, but the next step was difficult. His father finally consented to further schooling for young Will because he thought the boy would study for the ministry, a calling for which he seemed to be well-equipped. With the money obtained from the sale of a few head of cattle he had raised, he enrolled at the Cumberland Presbyterian Academy at Enfield some twenty miles south of his home. He made the long ride on horseback each day and returned to his farm chores at night. Afterwards he studied his lessons by firelight.

At Enfield he delighted in debating. He was poor in mathematics but excelled in Latin. History and literature were his favorite subjects. Unfortunately for him, the principal would not tolerate boys who hitched rides on freight cars of the Illinois Central to spend the night in the neighboring town of Carmi. When his father learned the facts, he punished young Borah but at the same time wrote the principal requesting that he be allowed to finish the spring term. Borah did not return to Enfield the following fall, for his father was land-poor. The family always had enough food and clothing, but there was insufficient money to educate the children. Moreover, it was now clear that Will entertained no thoughts of becoming a preacher.

At one time he thought he liked acting well enough to make a career of it. A traveling Shakespearean troupe, passing through Fairfield, provided him with an opportunity to test his theatrical talents. Because he knew the part perfectly, he was invited to play Mark Antony in *Julius Caesar.* He accepted the offer on the spot, ran away from home, and joined the company on the road. However, his father pursued him and induced him to return home; acting had no place in a family of God-fearing Calvinists. Will Borah was to remain on the farm a few years more, but this episode indicated that he was restless and discontented. After his taste of education, he had made up his mind he would have more. At his father's house gathered the legal minds and political elite of the countryside. In this atmosphere of heated political discussions he developed a burning interest in legal matters. On family visits to the county seat nobody worried about his frequent disappearances. They knew they would find him at the courthouse. Sometime before he was sixteen he decided to become a lawyer. Later he remarked: "I can't remember when I didn't want to be a lawyer . . . There is no other profession where one can be absolutely independent."[10]

Occasional country fairs and political meetings added variety to life in southern Illinois. At the fairs the chief attraction for young Borah was racing, for he had always loved horses. Political meetings interested him even more. He described Fairfield as "a hotbed of politics, where one year the Democrats polled a tremendous vote and where the next year the Republicans had startling majorities."[11] Feeling ran high, and factional fist fights were not unusual. Borah's father was always in the center of these discussions. His son later remarked: "My father was a student of politics, both here and in other parts of the world. He often discussed public affairs with me, and I perceived that the mistakes of the great men of the Civil War period came from their blind partisanship. Very early I myself tried to rise above partisanship." Politically, Illinois was dominated by Civil War veterans, who believed that the Republican party had saved the Union and that the Democrats represented only sinful cities and ignorant emigrant groups. Will's political baptism came later during the campaign of 1884 when he delivered his first public speech for James G. Blaine, who ran unsuccessfully against Cleveland.[12] Blaine's running mate was John A. Logan, famed for his Civil War record and spread-eagle oratory. This hero of southern Illinois was Borah's boyhood idol and the source of much of his early faith in Republicanism.

The year 1883 marked a turning point in the life of Borah. A letter from his sister, Sue Lasley, who then lived in Lyons, Kansas, with her husband and their young son, inquired whether he would like to make his home with them. Knowing that he was anxious to study law, she pointed out the advantages in associating with her husband, Ansel Lasley, who had his own practice in Lyons. Will could attend high school in Lyons and perhaps earn enough money to finish his education at the state university.

It was an attractive offer and one not likely to come again. Although his father was not pleased with this turn of events, he realized that life on the farm was disagreeable to his son and decided not to stand in his way. So at eighteen Will Borah left to further his education. He later wrote: "I didn't know how I was to get an education, nor had I any definite plans, but I thought fate in some manner would take care of my case. My father had previously signed notes for another man and lost a considerable part of his property."[13]

There was nothing to keep an ambitious young man in Fairfield. Years later his brother Frank, then a lawyer in New Orleans, wrote Will: "Why anybody would want to live in that God-forsaken place, I do not know. . . ."[14]

Lyons, the Rice County seat, was a town of about one thousand people in the middle of the Kansas prairie. "Gingerbread" houses with bay windows lined the streets radiating from the courthouse green. The public square was surrounded by buildings of homemade soft brick with false fronts. Nine lawyers had their shingles swinging in the dusty breeze or nailed flat against an outside wall. When Will Borah arrived he began searching for the one which read:

ANSEL M. LASLEY: ATTORNEY

Lasley had come west from Ohio when he was sixteen. He had read law in Springfield, Illinois, in the firm of Orendorff and Creighton; had been admitted to the Illinois bar in 1877; and had begun his practice in Fairfield, where he met and married Sue Borah. After they moved to Lyons, he rented an office and bought a house at 500 East Lyon Street.

This small Kansas town had just a little more to offer culturally than Fairfield. A newly organized library had a small collection of books, mainly concerning religion, biography, and poetry, as well as files of the *Century* magazine, Chicago *Graphic*, and *Atlantic Monthly*. Borah became a frequent visitor.[15] During those first months he studied Latin, English grammar, and constitutional government in the high school. The following summer he took a course in teaching methods at the Rice County Normal Institute in Lyons. In the fall of 1884 he became a teacher in the neighboring Wabash school at $35 per month. He joined the Young People's Band of the Presbyterian church, and when the Rice County Teacher's Association presented a public program, he addressed their meeting.[16] Later he confessed that he became so engrossed in reading history and law that he never applied himself properly to teaching. His pupils were often forced to serve as a captive audience for his orations, and after the four-month term both Borah and the Wabash school had had enough. By teaching school in the winter and working as Art Gleadall's farm hand in the summer, he managed to save about $100, enough to enter the University of Kansas the following fall.

The university, with a faculty of twenty-four, was not yet twenty years old when Borah was admitted on September 11, 1885. The chancellor himself registered new students, and the total enrollment was about four hundred. Ashamed of the fact that he was a little older than the other students, Borah gave his age as nineteen. His preparation being unsatisfactory for college work, he was enrolled as a subfreshman and was assigned certain prerequisite courses.

The university town of Lawrence lies among rolling hills about thirty miles from the eastern border of the state. The university buildings occupy Mount Oread, overlooking the Kaw Valley, the Kansas River on the north, and the historic Wakarusa on the south. On a clear day students could see the smoke of Kansas City. Of special interest to Borah was the library, which boasted a collection of about eight thousand books and periodicals, "singularly free from trash," according to the catalogue.[17]

The university was coeducational. The students lived in boardinghouses and fraternity houses or roomed with faculty members. Borah rented an inexpensive room in the home of Lewis Dyche, professor of archaeology. As tuition fees exhausted most of his money, he had to wait at table in a New Hampshire Street boardinghouse. Many years later he told a reporter: "I took any job that offered. I waited on tables, cut the grass, chopped wood, worked in the fields, tutored at night. I snatched what time I could, ten minutes here . . . an hour there . . . for my studies." His diploma in the 1890's, as Senator Norris once said, represented not only study but corn husking, wood splitting, timber clearing, and self-denial.[18]

Along with the hundred other students admitted as subfreshmen Borah spent his first year taking courses in Latin (a term each of Cicero and Virgil), natural philosophy, and English. He spent many hours in the library reading indiscriminately and later confessed he was always much more of a reader than a student. Probably because of lack of funds he dropped out of college after completing the fall term and the first half of the spring semester.[19]

The next autumn he qualified as a freshman in what was then called the Latin scientific course. He completed work in advanced Latin (Livy), history, elocution, English, American literature, and the history of the English language. Two of these courses were normally on the sophomore level, and one was on the junior level. Despite all his outside work and reading, he applied himself to his studies and received the highest attainable grades. During the spring term he took trigonometry, chemistry, botany, and German. He joined the Orophilian Society but rarely participated in the formal debates, for he had little time. At least twice a year, however, freshmen were required to give declamations "in the hall."

In those days the university could boast of gifted students like the redheaded, quick-witted, mandolin-playing William Allen White admitted in 1886. He was three years younger than Borah and not nearly so sober and earnest. White later described Borah during his college days as a "thick-necked, starry-eyed boy with an Irish twitch when he smiled . . . a twitch that looked as though he was scaring away a fly on his nose and lower jaw." He observed that Borah was indifferent to the opinion of others, anxious to get on in the classroom, not exactly a grind but a man who had years to make up and a purpose to attain, one of those older students who, like a big Newfoundland dog among smaller and more agile pups, is good-natured as long as he is not disturbed.[20] Although these two were only acquaintances in college, the years were to bring them together as close friends. Other students later achieved prominence: Fred Funston emerged from the campaign in the Philippines a major-general; Herbert Hadley became governor of Missouri; and Vernon Kellogg served with the relief committee in Belgium during World War I.

When a newspaper writer later observed that White, Funston, Borah, and Hadley all had the common quality of personal honesty, White replied:

> I think that the thing we all had . . . was a tremendous desire to be free. Looking back in those days it was obvious that we all were battling against conventions . . . we were militant in our letch to be free . . . I was . . . just as irregular educationally as I have been politically. And it was just because I didn't subscribe, I didn't conform . . . Our meeting place was in the classes of James H. Canfield . . . he was a free man who preached freedom and nurtured independent thinking and made us more or less rebels, all of us . . . let's say it was the love of freedom, the thing called independence, that we got out of K. U.[21]

Borah did not neglect the social opportunities offered by a fraternity. In the fall of 1886 he was pledged to Beta Theta Phi, which passed over his friend Will White because he was "too damned fresh." According to a tradition still remembered at the university, his fraternity brothers decided one evening to have some fun at the expense of a local farmer. They planned to steal some turkeys which their girl friends would roast for a feast. When Borah learned about this, he aired his objections to a plan which he called unworthy of students and gentlemen. The raid went on as scheduled, though it was nearly foiled by a watchdog which was tackled by a theology student who also played football. When the boys returned triumphant with their spoils, Borah refused to join them in eating the turkeys.

The raiders decided to prolong the fun by having a townsman impersonate a farmer and call on Borah. The stranger inquired if the puzzled student was "Borer," a member of the "bite-a-piece-a-pie club." After Borah affirmed these rough estimates, the "farmer" then related how he had been robbed of six fine turkeys by this group. Even though "Borer" had not been with them, the "farmer" insisted he knew about the robbery and therefore shared in the guilt. He ordered Borah to pay five dollars for the turkeys or he would have them all arrested. Borah thought about the difficulties of satisfying the police and finally decided reluctantly to give the man five dollars, even though it meant almost a month's board. That night there was another feast in the fraternity house at Borah's expense. Each year since then, at Christmas time, the fraternity holds a "turkey pull" commemorating this affair.[22]

Some of the faculty members at Kansas University in the eighties would have been an ornament to any college. James H. Canfield taught history and economics and was probably the most inspiring teacher Borah had. Discussions of social and economic problems enlivened his classroom. In Republican Kansas he stood out conspicuously as a rebel and a passionate exponent of free trade. Time after time Republican wheel horses tried to force the university trustees to discharge him. He was considered a dangerous radical for allowing students to write papers on such subjects as communism, the distribution of wealth in the United States, the ethical relations of capital and labor, and the management of railroads.

Canfield worked hard at teaching. He had two long tables in his room and a small one connecting them. Here his pupils sat facing him. White, who sat opposite Borah, later described him as a "solemn, shrewd, rather silent Beta, who cracked few jokes but understood them all." In these informal round-table discussions every student was given an opportunity to express his views, and the classroom was sometimes a babble of clamoring voices. White recalled that Borah took a prominent part. "Professor Canfield encouraged it and we all used to like to wrangle with Bill somewhat to hear his booming voice. He loved the debate . . . which the classroom brought out." When Canfield left the room, he was usually wet with perspiration and utterly exhausted. Years later the senator paid tribute to him as the teacher who had exerted the greatest influence over him.[23]

White and Borah used to walk down the hill from the university together with their heads "in the stars" and their feet on the board sidewalk. They talked seriously, for Borah, the student, was always serious. He had little humor then and less time for the gayer phases of college life—"girling," group singing, poker with matches, hard cider, and baseball. At the big affairs Borah usually had to be "doled out" to a sorority girl. He seemed to be in a hurry to get into the serious side of life.

The winter of 1886-87 was severe throughout the entire West. Borah continued to work hard, washing dishes, chopping wood, and setting type in the Lawrence *Journal* plant. Often he came to breakfast red-eyed and weary after setting type all night. Frequently he went without lunch or dinner, using every spare moment to study or tutor some other student. That spring his health broke down completely, and a medical examination showed he had tuberculosis. In March he left the college and was forced to seek help from his sister and brother-in-law in Lyons, where the slow process of convalescence began.

Sue Lasley nursed him expertly; realizing that his condition was partly the result of malnutrition, she fed him large quantities of vegetables and fruit. They built a veranda on the south side of the house near the garden, where he rested or dozed. Occasionally Ansel or Sue read to him. When his strength returned, he began reading law at home and continued his preparation in Lasley's office. By fall he was making a special study of evidence in anticipation of becoming a trial lawyer. His recovery was so complete that he was never troubled by any trace of the disease in later life.

The requirements for the practice of law in frontier towns such as Lyons were elementary. On September 16, 1887, Borah passed the easy bar examination and was admitted to practice in Rice County. It was with great pride that the twenty-two-year-old lawyer viewed the newly painted sign on the office door:

LASLEY AND BORAH: ATTORNEYS AT LAW

Local pranksters took pleasure in teasing him about his new position. The following appeared in the local paper:

WANTED: A young man out of employment desires a rich widow with weak lungs and a bad cough, to take him to raise; object—not matrimony but grub. Apply at office of Lasley and Borah.[24]

The mayor of Lyons appointed Borah city attorney in 1889.[25] His job was to advise councilmen on legal matters, check the actions of previous councils, draft city ordinances, and file suits for and answer those against the town. Once he went to Colorado on city business. This experience gave him confidence and taught him about municipal government.

The late 1880's brought extremely hard times to the West. Farm prices were low, and nine out of every ten farms were mortgaged. Both interest rates and resentment ran high. During such difficult times cases were hard to find, especially for a fledgling lawyer in competition with half a dozen of the best attorneys in Kansas practicing in Lyons.

One of the earliest cases Borah took involved a judgment against a hardware store in Lyons during those years when people had little or no ready cash. The store bought its stock from the Simmons Company in St. Louis. When the Lyons merchant found himself unable to pay for a large order, an attorney named Foley brought suit for the Simmons Company. Borah, representing the Lyons merchant, attempted to delay the suit until trade picked up and a payment could be made on the bill. It was then customary for the defendant to file an answer to the charges against him in court, and the plaintiff had to go to the courthouse to read it in order to find out what it contained.

The answer in this case was frivolous. The defense claimed that the barbed wire sold to the merchant was guaranteed to be of the best quality, but when strung across the plains, the wind swept the barbs off the wire. After impugning the quality of other products sold by the Simmons Company, the answer charged that the attorney for the plaintiff was Canadian by birth and had no right to plead in the courts of the United States. Foley was a fiery fellow. When he read this answer, he lost his head and got a revolver. Borah, forewarned, had to leave town and stay away until Foley calmed down.[26]

By the fall of 1890 Borah decided that he could not live on optimism. Lyons had little to offer a young man who felt he was destined for eminence. In those days almost every lawyer was a jury lawyer, and the county courtroom was the practice field for the stump. Lincoln had discovered that he could make a good speech, which led him, after various attempts at other occupations, to choose the bar as a career. Borah had also discovered by then that he, too, could make a good speech. While the Lasleys moved to Chicago, he decided to go west to seek fame, fortune, and an opportunity to grow up with the country.

II Frontier Lawyer

Room! room to turn round in, to breathe and be
free,
To grow to be giant . . .

—Joaquin Miller

At the beginning of the century Idaho was still primarily a mining area, its mineral and cattle interests much stronger than the farm and labor groups. It was settled by pioneers—originally a backwash of the first wave of gold seekers who had previously passed through on their rush to the Pacific coast, and then by native stock from the Midwest and New England who journeyed over the Oregon Trail and cut northward. As a territory it had few urban areas and did not attract many foreigners. After 1870 the railroads brought greater numbers, who demanded the advantages and protection of statehood. With an area of 83,557 square miles and a population of 88,000 Idaho was admitted to the Union July 3, 1890, just a few months before Borah arrived.

Geographically, Idaho is an incongruent state whose unusual boundaries inscribe a great rectangle on the western slope of the Rocky Mountains. The base of the rectangle rests on Utah and Nevada. Atop is superimposed a jagged wedge running far to the north between Montana and Washington to the Canadian border. This land of peaks, canyons, lava beds, sagebrush barrens, fertile valleys, and towering forests offers great geographic diversity. The most beautiful scenery is at the very top of the panhandle with dense forests, high mountains, and racing streams in the country of the Kootenai River, Lake Pend Oreille, and Lake Coeur d'Alene—an American Switzerland, Vardis Fisher has called it.

The northern and central parts of the state are also mountainous, while the arid plains in the south form the principal agricultural area. The heaviest concentration of population is in the southeast, where streams of influence from Mormon Utah, mining Montana, and pioneer Oregon have coalesced. Gradually Idahoans turned from mining and lumbering to livestock and agriculture. The former are still important industries, but agriculture is by far the most important economic activity. Southeast of Lewiston in the arid lands of low-lying valleys volcanic lava ash, rich in phosphorus and potash, has created a soil remarkably fertile when irrigated. Inadequate rainfall here forced the creation of a new kind of civilization and prolonged the pioneer spirit among the settlers. The chance which brought the young Borah, empty-handed, to see what this country could offer made him free as few other places could and helped to determine his singularly unhampered political course.

Boise, the capital, was built on what was once a sagebrush plain, almost a desert, at a time when there was no railroad within three hundred miles. It lies in a broad crescent-shaped valley on the north side of the Boise River and owes its name to the French explorers in Captain Bonneville's expedition who, on first glimpsing the willow trees lining the river after days of weary travel across the arid Snake River plains, exclaimed: "Les Bois! Voyez les Bois!" Here the city was founded in 1863.

With two thousand people Boise in 1890 retained its frontier spirit. The buildings in the business district were of brick and stone, for a city ordinance prohibited wooden structures. Three hotels and twenty stores lined the wide, tree-shaded streets; a four-story elementary and high school stood on the present capitol grounds; the town also had a courthouse, a small electric lighting plant, telephone service, a theatre, literary clubs, a library, and a daily newspaper with AP dispatches, which now and then advertised land enough in the neighborhood for all those who chose to come to this "bright spot of the West."

When Borah arrived, Boise was a "wide open town" which needed law and order more than it wanted them. The city was generously sprinkled with gambling places, saloons like "The Naked Truth," bawdy houses, and dance halls. Here was a town for miners and cowboys to spend their money, "where men played three card monte, 'chuck-a-luck,' rondo coolo, faro and in a hundred other ways gambled the day and night away, where vice of all kinds flourished unashamed and 'six shooter' justice sent some of the worst sinners the world ever saw to the 'boothill' graveyards."[1]

Milder forms of amusement were soon available for those with the disposition and leisure to enjoy them: dancing clubs, literary societies, the Sonna Opera House, Pinney's Columbia theatre, and an annual strawberry festival, masquerade ball, and Fourth of July celebration. Outside the city limits was a race track. The public reading room afforded "young men . . . a place to devote their minds to mental cultivation during their leisure hours instead of doing worse . . ."[2]

Here a lawyer had to do more than quote statute or Latin phrase. An enactment rarely carried undisputed authority unless it conformed to local common sense. Just out of territorial embryo the state was accustomed to the informal justice of a sheriff's posse or a vigilance committee. A lawyer not only had to know his business but had to make these frontiersmen see the reason for law. Such training often produced a great attorney.[3] During his first days in Boise Borah became convinced that before Idaho could become a peaceful, prosperous state, much legal pioneering would have to be done. He visited the county court where he watched a tipsy advocate wrestle with the intricacies of civil law. A sober lawyer, he mused, might go far here.

A dozen other lawyers were then practicing in Boise. Borah learned that none of them needed a clerk or assistant, but he was determined to succeed. With the few dollars he had left or could borrow, he rented one room over the brewery on Main Street, which served as an office during the day and a bedroom at night. He equipped it with a desk, two kitchen chairs, an old leather couch, an oak table with carved initials, a tin cuspidor, and pictures of Lincoln and Marshall. Here he began to practice, "not as a full fledged lawyer," he later admitted, "but as one licensed to prey on the public." He was examined by Justice Isaac N. Sullivan of the State Supreme Court and was admitted to the Idaho bar February 18, 1891.[4]

Later Borah wrote: "The first year in Idaho was the most melancholy of my existence. I battled desperately for a living, and many times was on the point of surrendering. I was an utter stranger in Boise, and the town was full of attorneys, all of whom had plenty of friends and acquaintances. But I kept on; I don't know why or how, and in the second year came brighter days and prospects. Little by little I built a respectable business."[5]

During territorial days a number of Chinese had come inland to work in the placer mines. After this means of livelihood was no longer available, those who were not driven out opened laundries, worked truck gardens, peddled vegetables, or served as domestics.

Borah's first case came to him through the gambler from Nampa, who telephoned him to hurry over. A murder had been committed. The switchboard operator had raided the icebox in the hotel kitchen late one night, and the Chinese cook had chased him with a carving knife. Enraged, the operator shot the cook in the back as he left the kitchen. Borah's job was to defend the operator. The preliminary hearing was conducted before the elderly Judge Long. When the prosecutor charged the operator with murder in the first degree, the judge advised: "It is not murder to kill a Chinaman. You can't charge a man with anything but manslaughter for killing a Chinaman." The prosecutor rejoined: "In view of the known facts, I am compelled to insist on the charge as I made it. The law will permit nothing else."

Borah had been prepared to argue self-defense, but when he saw that the court intended to discharge his client anyway, he refrained from cross-examining or making any argument. The charge was changed to manslaughter, and the telephone operator was acquitted. As they left the courtroom, Borah told his client: "I don't know much about the courts in this part of the country, but anywhere else, if you shot a human being in the back and killed him, you surely would have been punished. I advise you to get out of Nampa as quickly as possible." And he did.[6]

With his fee of thirty-five dollars Borah subsisted until another client appeared. "My second case," he related, "came to me because the other lawyers in Boise had declined to take it. It was a claim three or four years old against a railway for the killing of some livestock. The railway was new and popular and damage suits were unheard of in Idaho. I settled the case to the satisfaction of my client, and after that I was employed in criminal practice and in litigation between sheep and cattle men."[7]

During that first year he took any case that came his way. Alfred A. Fraser shared an office with him for a few months until in February, 1892, Borah and Stewart became associates. Inserting a notice in the newspaper,

STEWART AND BORAH: ATTORNEYS AT LAW

they rented office space over Himrod's store in the Brodbeck building. Judge George H. Stewart had presided over several cases argued by Borah and was impressed with his ability, but their association was in no sense a partnership.

Another case involved a powerful lumberjack who sued a Boise mechanic, Jim Lusk, for assault. The six-foot French Canadian charged that Lusk, in an argument over a woman, struck him on the head with a fourteen-inch spanner and the blow resulted in complete loss of memory. As the trial proceeded, Borah, representing Lusk, asked the two men to stand before the jury. Borah's client was dwarfed by the towering lumberjack. As he was about to begin his cross-examination, he handed Lusk a small bicycle wrench and asked him to demonstrate how he would strike such a tall man with this instrument. Before Lusk could attempt anything, the Canadian shouted: "But that's not the wrench he struck me with." Borah asked eagerly if he were certain. Lusk's wrench, he replied, was at least a foot long; he had seen the defendant using it on a wagon wheel. "Anyway," Borah remarked, "your memory has improved." With little further effort he secured a verdict of not guilty for his client.

As his legal business increased, Borah was soon able to afford a room with the Agnew family at 752 Idaho Street. James Agnew was the proprietor of the livery stable and one of Boise's chief funmakers. Later Borah lived with the Gowdy family and once wrote: ". . . I remember so well . . . Nellie Gowdy, almost as dear to me . . . as one of my own sisters. You know I lived in their home and if ever there was a perfect home, that was it, or it would have been if . . . not . . . for the roomers they had . . ."[8]

He now dressed in long coat, tight-fitting ranch trousers, waistcoat, string tie, watch fob, and a wide-brimmed slouch hat. His dapper appearance was in great contrast to his down-at-the-heel aspect of a few years earlier when the stagecoach brought him into Boise. He presented himself one day at the local bank to cash a check. The teller hesitated, asked him to wait, and sent for the president. From behind a door the official scrutinized Borah and concluded: "Why, that man's a gambler. I wouldn't cash his check."[9]

Within a year or two Borah had so many clients and such a reputation that young lawyers asked to work for him and read law in his office. Somehow he found time to help them. Charles Koelsch, later to become judge of Ada County, came to Boise from Wisconsin for his health and read law in Borah's office. Charles Cavanah made the journey from Texas in 1894; with John Blake he secured a desk in the three rooms on Seventh and Main streets, forming the nucleus of the firm Borah, Cavanah, and Blake, an association which endured until 1907.

By 1892 Borah was active in state politics. He served as part-time secretary for William J. McConnell, elected governor in 1892 and re-elected in 1894. McConnell had migrated from Michigan in 1860. He drove a team of oxen across the plains and settled in north Idaho, where he established a merchandising firm in Moscow, and soon organized the first group of vigilantes in southern Idaho. He arrived in Boise late in December 1892 accompanied by his young daughter Mary, who also served as his secretary. They lived at the Sherman House on Seventh and Jefferson streets.

It was inevitable that Borah should soon become acquainted with "Miss Mamie." They were often seen together at political meetings and public functions or riding in the hills. Mary McConnell was a vivacious, blue-eyed blonde, sociable and attractive, the prize catch in Boise's young social set. After a long courtship they were married in Cyrus Jacobs' home on Sunday, April 21, 1895, with Justice Joseph W. Huston of the State Supreme Court performing the ceremony.[10] Borah's best man was Frank Black, and Mamie Jacobs was the only bridesmaid. The couple took the morning train, a rickety passenger-freight called the "Cannon Ball," to Caldwell, where Borah had to argue a case next morning. At the Caldwell Hotel they were given a reception by friends and were serenaded by the Caldwell Cornet Band.

In 1898 the Borahs bought the house at 1101 Franklin Street. Like others designed by the Boise architect, John Tourtellotte, it was of white clapboard with a cut-stone foundation and Victorian embroidery of gables, turrets, and pinnacles. It had a large living room, separated by sliding doors from a bright front room facing Franklin Street; Borah lined this room with bookshelves and used it for a study. A small veranda screened by climbing roses and syringa bushes made an ideal retreat in warm weather. From the house to his office in town was a walk of ten or fifteen minutes. A streetcar ran along Eleventh Street into the city, but he rarely used it. There was a carriage house on their corner lot; however, they kept their horses at Agnew's livery stable.

Mrs. Borah attended to their social obligations, for her husband was absorbed in his work. Returning from his office, he would often shut himself in his study to prepare for a new case or read. Occasionally he stayed in town and worked on briefs far into the night. At home he would emerge from the study long enough to eat dinner, and then return to work again. Judge Sullivan once remarked that Borah's studious and temperate traits were a matter of comment among Boise citizens.

One evening Borah came home to find the house filled with Mrs. Borah's friends playing bridge. He muttered a few words of greeting and withdrew to his study. When the ladies finally left, he chided his wife for delaying dinner. "Well, William," she chirped in her high voice, "perhaps if you hadn't been so loquacious, they might have left sooner."

From a cash-and-carry, police-court practice Borah graduated to the attorneyship of large corporations like the Barber Lumber Company and the Mammoth, Hercules, and Sunshine Mining companies. As his corporation activities grew, more and more cases had to be argued in courts outside Ada County. It was often necessary for him to travel hundreds of miles through Oregon and Washington into north Idaho, where the big lumber and mining companies were located. After 1900 he turned almost exclusively to corporate practice, but by that time his reputation as a successful criminal lawyer was well-established. One of the cases which won him notoriety grew out of the struggle between cattle and sheep interests in the Northwest. Idaho's rangelands attracted large herds of sheep brought in from Utah. When they encroached on former cattle territory and spoiled the land for future use by cattlemen, ranchers attempted to take the law into their own hands. Range wars killed nearly as many men as saloon brawls during the nineties. At first cowboys threatened the sheepherders; later they shot their sheep. This disorder reached a climax in 1896 when two sheepherders, John Wilson and Dan Cummings, were murdered with a .45 revolver firing .44 cartridges.

Suspicion centered on "Diamondfield Jack" Davis, a gunman from Nevada. Tall, powerful, and unscrupulous, he was known as a desperado throughout the Rocky Mountain West. During a labor war in Goldfield, Nevada, he was so girded with firearms that he was unable to rise from his chair. He rode range for the Shoe Sole Brand, a large cattle outfit, and also for the Sparks Harrell Company of Nevada. When Davis was arrested, James H. Hawley and K. I. Perky of Boise were employed to defend him; John C. Rogers of Albion was the Cassia County attorney; and Borah was employed by the county to assist Rogers as prosecutor.

Davis' trial began in April before Judge Charles Stockslager of Cassia County and lasted thirteen days with continuous night sessions. Peaceful Albion was tranformed into an armed camp. Sheepmen sympathized with the prosecution; cattlemen were hot partisans of the accused. The antagonists milled around the courthouse, crowded local bars, and made the courtroom atmosphere so tense that at each session men had to be searched and relieved of weapons.

In the interval between Davis' arraignment and the first day of his trial Borah hired a horse and rode through the Snake River Valley to Wells, Nevada, stopping at a number of ranches where he spent the night trading stories with cowboys. No one recognized him. Where courtesy demanded an explanation, he said he was looking over the country with the hope of buying a ranch. The cowboys talked freely.

At one of the Sparks Harrell ranches a foreman named Harris recounted his adventures with Jack Davis, whom he disliked intensely and who had stayed at that ranch two or three nights in February. Harris recalled how he had watched Davis, who carried a .45 loaded with .44 cartridges, lying in bed shooting at the rafters overhead. Borah examined the bullet holes. He learned that one night Davis had changed into dark clothes and explained that he had work to do after dark. Returning a day later on his foam-stained horse, he had spoken exultantly about doing business with sheepherders. Other cowboys confirmed Harris' story; they had seen Davis riding along the river near Goose Creek with a companion. He had even boasted to one of his friends that he had killed two sheepherders. After gathering this evidence Borah rode back to Albion.[11]

No one except Davis was more surprised than these cowboys when they were summoned as witnesses in his murder trial. Harris was the first to be called to the stand. He failed to recognize Borah and denied any knowledge of the crimes. When suddenly he found himself confronted by the boyish-looking stranger who had been his guest, he sat dumbfounded. He no longer saw any point in delaying the inevitable and told the jury what he knew. As he spoke, Davis lunged toward him but was restrained by Borah and a court officer. The other witnesses corroborated Harris' testimony.

Two days later Borah delivered his closing argument, reminding the jury members that with them alone rested the power to enforce law and protect life. In vivid terms he described the murder and the murderer, ". . . cool, calculating, cautious, cowardly, he steals upon his victim . . . and from ambush shoots him like a dog . . ."

> Look upon the scene again and tell me is there a single touch of humanity to relieve it of its awful hideousness. Oh God, if I could but paint the feelings of those dying boys . . . crawling in their blood and writhing in the agony . . . of death, if all could but catch one glimpse of that vision . . . then we could properly say this is not murder, the term is too soft, it is studied, planned assassination.
>
> Gentlemen, I appeal to you as citizens . . . in the name of our homes and our lives, in the name of law—has not the state proven enough? Have you doubt under this evidence who killed those boys? I don't believe you have, and so believing and trusting well in your faithful purpose upon the part of the state, I rest its cause with you.[12]

On April 24 the jury found Jack Davis guilty of murder in the first degree and sentenced him to be hanged. Minutes before the hanging, the gallows up and the noose dangling, he was granted a stay of execution. His sentence was later commuted to life imprisonment. Powerful cattle interests obtained his reprieve but lost their motion and two subsequent appeals for a new trial.[13] They persisted in applying pressure until finally in 1901 Governor Frank Hunt granted Davis a full pardon based on the testimony of a man who said he killed the two men in self-defense.[14] Borah never believed his story, and the governor was criticized all over the state.[15] It was estimated that Davis' defense and appeals cost the cattlemen over $150,000.

The record stood, nevertheless, that lawless cattle interests had been defeated in an Idaho court. In public opinion Davis remained a murderer, whose conviction Borah had obtained under melodramatic circumstances. Once more he had demonstrated the courage and resourcefulness which made him a leading trial lawyer in the Northwest.

Idaho's rich timber and mineral resources invited development by large eastern and western mining corporations. As Butte is the great storehouse of copper in Montana, the Coeur d'Alene area is Idaho's source of lead and silver. This isolated region was the scene of mining disorders between 1892 and 1899 which attracted national attention to Idaho.

The Bunker Hill-Sullivan Mining Company operated the most extensive lead reduction works in the area with mines at Wardner and a mill at Kellogg. The Western Federation of Miners, a well-established labor organization with an almost lurid history, was well-organized in Coeur d'Alene and even had a local group of two hundred fifty men in the Bunker Hill Company; but although the union won its terms from all other employers, the Bunker Hill Company stubbornly refused to grant union recognition.[16]

A strike was called. All work in and around Wallace came to a halt. Early on April 29, 1899, a group of miners took possession of a Northern Pacific train connecting Burke with the other mining camps in the canyon below. They ran the train to Gem, where they loaded sixty boxes of dynamite. At Wallace more union men were taken on and the engineer was ordered to proceed to Kellogg, where about one thousand armed and masked men got off and marched to the Bunker Hill-Sullivan mill, put the guards to flight, deposited the dynamite under the machinery, and in seconds blew the quarter-million-dollar mill to fragments. Office buildings, houses, and stores were set aflame; everything was demolished. Then the men marched back to Kellogg. Nearly all the company employees escaped, but on the way to the station Jim Cheyne, a hired strikebreaker, and two others were captured by the miners' pickets, subjected to indignities, and then ordered to run. A fusillade of bullets followed them, wounding Cheyne, who died three days later in a Spokane hospital.[17] The mob boarded the train and ordered the engineer to run it back up the narrow canyon to Burke. The miners returned to work as if nothing untoward had happened.

Governor Frank Steunenberg, serving his second term, was an honorary member of the Boise Typographical Union and was regarded with favor by labor until he called in federal troops to quell the disorders and declared martial law in Shoshone County. Within a week more than one thousand arrests were made, many without warrant, and the prisoners were herded into "bull pens."[18]

When a special grand jury convened, numerous indictments were found against members of the miners' unions. Among those indicted was Paul Corcoran, secretary of the Burke local, described as a "man of some means and high standing in the community." He was charged with the murder of Jim Cheyne. To prosecute him the state selected James H. Hawley, James Forney, and Borah. In retaining them, Governor Steunenberg said: "I want not only men of brains but lawyers with the milk of human kindness . . . I want no prosecutor who would present evidence simply to convict . . . I want both sides presented to the jury and do not want a lawyer who will seek to make a reputation as a prosecutor at the expense of these unfortunate men. I want lawyers like the presiding judge, who can and will be as fair to an underdog as to the richest and most influential citizens in Idaho." George H. Stewart, judge of the Third Judicial District, presided at the trial. The Western Federation of Miners, which assumed the conduct of the defense, retained Patrick Reddy, Frederick G. Robertson, and Walter Johnson.

The state held all persons, jointly engaged by a previous understanding, responsible for all the consequences of an unlawful act committed by any member of the conspiracy. Corcoran was the only prisoner tried for murder, seven others having escaped. He was a man of family and previous good repute. The object of the prosecution was to show union members and others that the law was supreme and would reach anyone, even a prominent member of the union.

The trial began at Wallace on July 8, 1899. There was difficulty empaneling an impartial jury because nearly the entire population of Shoshone County lived on the south fork of the Coeur d'Alene River. There was greater difficulty securing witnesses because men were either sympathetic to the union cause or were afraid to testify; none would have spoken had it not been for the presence of federal troops. The conductor of the train which carried the miners to Kellogg refused to identify anybody. He was offered a position on any road in the East at a good salary, but he informed Borah that union men would follow him to the end of the earth and kill him if he identified any of them.[19] Impartial jurors were finally drawn from the sparse population on the north fork of the river.

Under cross-examination by the prosecution Corcoran insisted he was at Burke, several miles away, when the shooting occurred. Defense witnesses corroborated this. A butcher at Burke testified that the accused had bought a chicken from him that day. Borah produced the butcher's account book, showing that the chicken had been purchased on another day.

Witnesses for the prosecution swore that they had seen Corcoran at Kellogg, and at Gem and Burke on the return trip. From the door of their house Mr. and Mrs. Colburn saw Corcoran riding atop a box car, holding a rifle across his lap. At Burke witnesses had seen him jump from the car to the platform while the train was still moving, and a woman swore she recognized him as Paul Corcoran.[20]

To the astonishment of the state, the defense put on the stand witnesses, including railroad engineers, who swore that it would be impossible for a man to sit on a freight car traveling at normal speed along the tortuous curves and rough roadbed to Burke. The brakeman declared emphatically that with all his experience he couldn't be hired to attempt such a thing. He also swore that the jump to the platform would have broken a man's legs. Hawley and Borah were temporarily stumped by this testimony.

The night before they were to introduce their rebuttal, Borah decided on an experiment—to ride the freight car. Hawley protested and insisted that someone else be assigned because if Borah failed, the case would fall to pieces without him; however, Borah assured him he was familiar with freight cars. Asked why he rode them, the once truant schoolboy explained simply: "There were times when I wanted to be somewhere else."[21]

The railroad company was induced to make up a train with the same trainmen and engineer who had taken the rioters to the mill. Borah, Hawley, and four others boarded the train at Kellogg and began the trip to Burke. The engineer had agreed to maintain the same rate of speed, never exceeding thirty miles an hour. Borah, perched atop a box car with rifle in hand, steadied himself for six miles over the winding track which dropped off into the steep canyon below. When the train reached Burke, he jumped to the platform without even twisting an ankle! The next day in court four former defense witnesses swore that Borah had performed this dare-devil feat. Their evidence marked a turning point in the case. "It convinced the jury," Borah recalled with satisfaction. "They slept while the defense put forward its case."[22]

After three hectic weeks Borah delivered the closing argument for the prosecution on the afternoon of July 27. The Miners' Federation had centered its attack on him. Charged with being relentless in this case, Borah replied: "I would that I could be as remorseless for justice as the man who planned this hellish expedition was remorseless for crime."[23]

He denied that the prosecution was attacking labor unions. The state had no complaint against unions unless they transformed themselves into criminal organizations which shot down innocent men and dynamited private property. He maintained that if the members of a church should meet around the altars of worship today to formulate a plan to rob a bank tomorrow, the sanctity of the organization would not shield them. Union recognition was the sole cause of the disturbances. It followed that the Western Federation of Miners was the only organization which would or could act against this company on such motives as hate, revenge, or intimidation. If, as the defense maintained, the workers went down the canyon that day only to destroy the mill with no intention of taking any lives, "why then were they all heavily armed?" and "why were they careful to take along . . . a physician equipped with instruments and bandages?" Borah proceeded to show that a conspiracy existed, that Corcoran was a part of it, and that he went to Kellogg to engage in acts which resulted in murder. Appealing to the jury's sentiments as Idahoans, he asked:

> What is this splendid fabric which the restless energy and indomitable courage of the old pioneer has carved from the wild waste of the great Northwest and set as a gem in the crown of our common country? Is it . . . a commonwealth where men can dwell together in peace and safety . . . Has it power to punish a crime?
>
> Or is it but a miserable pretense; a shameless, deluding mockery, where anarchy rules with a ruthless sway, and the most revolting of crimes go unwhipped before the altar, where murder walks the streets of your town, selects its victim with indifference and slays him with

impunity, yes, more, in the very presence of death the officers of the law laugh hyena-like above the prostrate victim and dance above the bleeding form like spirits incarnate from the crypts of hell.[24]

On July 27, 1899, Corcoran was found guilty of murder in the second degree and was sentenced to seventeen years in the penitentiary. On appeal to the State Supreme Court the conviction was sustained. Corcoran served less than seventeen months, however, for in 1901 he was pardoned by Governor Hunt, who was accused of courting the labor vote for the Democratic ticket in Idaho's northern counties.

The "bull pen" prisoners were released, but only after they had made their classic attempt to escape by a two-hundred-foot tunnel. The troops were later removed, and a House committee began an investigation into mining conditions in the district. Two results followed: the Western Federation of Miners was almost completely disbanded in the Coeur d'Alene area, and the labor leaders of the disturbances were compelled to locate in other parts of the United States.[25]

A disturbing incident occurred in May 1903 at Nampa when the Boise baseball team won a league contest, 7 to 0, primarily because the Nampa batters could not find Pitcher Bailey who held them to three scattered hits. The game had an unfortunate ending; a fight developed between the two teams after a small boy was knocked down and Jim Quarles, a Boise bootblack, protested to a Nampa player for hitting the boy. Quarles was knocked down, kicked, and hit over the head; he barely managed to escape. John Grogan, a special officer in Nampa, pursued Quarles and his companion Williams, firing wild shots after them. Quarles then drew a pistol, fired one shot, and hit Grogan in the chest. He was taken to the hospital in critical condition. When they realized Grogan was an officer (he wore no badge), Quarles and Williams gave themselves up and were marched to the Nampa jail followed by an angry crowd restrained only by the pistols of the officers.

Shortly before midnight an infuriated mob forced their way into the jail, but a lynching was prevented by a force of special officers who held the mob at bay while Mayor Sutherland pleaded with them to allow the law to take its course. Meantime the *Statesman* office at Boise notified Borah and Governor Morrison. A special train took them to Nampa, where they were met by the Canyon County sheriff and a posse.

Borah and Sheriff Agnew of Boise made their way through the menacing crowd to the jail and presented Nampa officials with an order from the governor, who was waiting in the train, to remand the imperiled men into Sheriff Agnew's custody for removal to Boise. The mob tried several times to break in while the papers were being served. James Wells, a burly barber in the Dewey Palace Hotel, appeared to be the leader of the mob. In an ugly mood he told Borah: "We don't want any Boise niggers around here intimidating our citizens and shooting our officers. That man Grogan has a wife and five children. We just won't stand for it, that's all." Borah tried to reason with him; finally he quieted down and walked away sullenly. Borah also harangued the mob, reminding them of their duties as citizens and leading them to believe that the special train, with drawn blinds, was packed with state militia awaiting orders from the governor, who never showed himself. Councilman Callopy, who had been on his feet all that night, deputized a number of the mob to act as a guard for the prisoners, who were then led, unmolested, from the jail to the waiting train. Once safely aboard, Quarles, who had served with a colored regiment in the Spanish-American War, sighed in relief and said: "Why Mr. Sheriff, your voice sounded to me like the voice of an angel when I first heard it outside that jail door."[26]

In labor accounts of these events Borah's role was slightly exaggerated. No one deserved all the credit for preventing the lynching of the two Negroes. Publicists later overemphasized his role in the Nampa riot to counteract unfavorable criticism stemming from his opposition to the Wagner-Costigan antilynching bill.

Even though his practice was thriving at the turn of the century, Borah contemplated leaving the West to resettle in some large eastern city where a greater variety of cases would give his legal talents wider scope. A letter from Fred Dubois, one-time Democratic senator from Idaho, reveals that he was busy in 1899 exploring the ground for Borah in the East and trying to find a position which would net him at least five thousand a year. Dubois thought that New York City offered the best opportunity.[27]

It was not that Borah had outgrown Boise. He had more business than he could handle and an income in five figures, but a career as a lawyer did not wholly satisfy him. Throughout life he was indifferent to money, except that he resented wasting it. He had already decided to enter politics, a normal course for ambitious lawyers in the West; thus when no attractive offer came from the East, he concentrated on winning public office in Idaho, which had witnessed his legal prowess and now awaited a demonstration of his skill at the game of politics.

III Young Man Eloquent

The profession I chose was politics; the profession I entered was law. I entered the one because I thought it would lead to the other. It was once the sure road; and Congress is still full of lawyers.
—Woodrow Wilson

Since coming to Idaho, Borah had labored to make Boise a law-abiding city and had thus commended himself to its citizens. His early ventures into politics indicated a steady growth in prominence. In 1891 he was nominated by Republicans for the position of city attorney, but he withdrew because he had not yet reached the required age.[1] The following year he served as chairman of the Republican State Central Committee until the pressure of his growing practice forced him to resign. He attended the state convention which named delegates to the Republican national convention, adopted a free-silver plank, and approved the McKinley tariff.[2] At Moscow a few months later he was temporary chairman of the state nominating convention. The Republicans elected their state ticket in November 1892, although James B. Weaver, the Populist candidate for president, carried Idaho.

At the Republican national convention of 1896 in St. Louis, William McKinley was nominated and a gold-standard plank was adopted. Senator Henry M. Teller, after making the final appeal for silver, walked out, followed by the Colorado and Idaho delegates.[3] The Republican party in Idaho and other mountain states split into two factions; Borah joined the majority which repudiated the action of the national convention, enthusiastically organized themselves as Silver Republicans, and supported William J. Bryan for the presidency. In Silver City Borah addressed a Democratic meeting, explaining that he did so only because of his interest in silver; he said he was a Republican by conviction and intended to remain one. He did not even want to surrender the name Republican by giving it a prefix and held out to the last to make no changes except to insert in the platform an endorsement for the principles of bimetallism. In a dingy room of the Capitol Hotel in Boise the leaders assembled to launch the new party; there Borah drew a picture of the lawlessness of corporations and their abuses, and hoped the doctrine advocated would bring them to their knees. "On no other principle do I disagree with the Republican Party, and when that issue is settled, I and my friends are ready to resume allegiance to the old party."[4] In August the Silver Republicans of Ada County held an indignation meeting in which they denounced regular Republican state officers from Governor McConnell, Borah's father-in-law, down the line. When Borah spoke, he was hissed. The Silverite told the hecklers that the meeting was based on principles which Republicans had defended for years and suggested that McKinley be read out of the Republican ranks. He called upon the audience to stand by silver and "that brilliant leader, William J. Bryan."

When the Silver Republican convention met in Idaho, Borah was chosen chairman and Senator Frederick Dubois was floor leader. Borah was proud to preside over a body of men who believed in principles rather than partisanship. He described the evils of monometallism and argued for the restoration of silver to its ancient place as primary money. Acknowledging that defiance of the national platform seemed to many honest Republicans an act of treason, he stated: "Republicans, you who support the St. Louis platform, do as you think best, but if you succeed in fastening this badge of suppliant cowardice upon our party, this brand of un-Americanism, you have not only betrayed the principles for which the sainted Lincoln died, but you have written the epitaph of his party."[5]

In this early speech the rugged nationalism so characteristic of Borah's entire public career was clearly evident, accompanied by an ingrained antagonism to Great Britain common among westerners:

> . . . next November, the American people will send forth a new Declaration of Independence which will say to England, we would like your cooperation in the elevation of humanity, we would like you to join us in bringing back the happiness of mankind, we recognize the force of your imperial genius and your prowess among the nations of the earth . . . but since you have refused to listen to the appeals of twenty years, we shall try it alone.[6]

In the contest for Idaho's single congressional seat that year the Silver Republicans, stalwart Republicans, and Populist-Democrats

(Popocrats) all had candidates. Senator Dubois persuaded Borah, then thirty-one, to run for congress on the Silver Republican ticket; he finally yielded, knowing that with the silver vote split he had little chance of winning the seat. Borah opposed fusion as earnestly as dropping the Republican label, but the convention endorsed the presidential electors of the fusion ticket and Dubois carried the day with "free silver" as the slogan. Borah campaigned energetically, asking for the return of Dubois to the Senate and giving only secondary attention to his own candidacy. The regular Republican organ commented acidly:

> Mr. Borah . . . looking on enviously at the reputation Mr. Bryan has been making as a "Willie Boy," could resist the temptation no longer, and has accepted the nomination for Congress with the understanding that he should be allowed to make seventeen speeches a day from now until November and be billed as the boy candidate who has never been old enough to accept a nomination.[7]

Nearly everyone in Idaho except a few postmasters voted for silver that year. McKinley polled only two votes in the entire state! Regular Republican candidates for state offices were snowed under. According to the *Congressional Directory* for 1897 their nominee for the congressional seat, John T. Morrison, received only 6,054 votes. Although Borah ran ahead of the other silver candidates on his ticket, polling 8,984 votes, he lost to the Populist-Democrat, James Gunn, who received 14,487 votes. Dubois was defeated.

Silver Republicans and Democrats again fused in the state elections of 1898; at this point Dubois joined the Democratic party and Borah broke with the Silver Republicans. While he had previously sacrificed his political affiliations in the hope of accomplishing something for silver, he was no longer willing to continue this detour for mere office-getting. He refused to take part in the campaign. Once he came to the realization that free silver could not be won through such men as Teller and Bryan, without embarrassment or apology Borah joined the steady drift back to the Republican fold where he was welcomed. In the campaign of 1900 he made eight speeches for McKinley, but Populist sentiment again enabled Bryan to carry Idaho. After that campaign free silver was a dead issue.[8]

Calling for a union of reform forces to battle for the protective tariff and expansion, Borah extolled our *opéra bouffe* war with Spain as a brilliant military performance in defense of an oppressed people of another language, climate, and inferior race. With some reluctance he would have assumed responsibility for the new territory acquired as a result of the war, which gave rise to America's experiment in colonialism. Of imperialism he then said: "This is a term cunningly coined and persistently applied with the hope upon the part of those doing so that they will stay the wheels of progress by an unpleasant and misapplied epithet."[9] Borah found no constitutional bar to the annexation of the Philippines; rather he drew a historic comparison between it and the Louisiana Purchase. Predictions of 1803 that no system of government could unite so vast a territory, binding together trappers, Indian fighters, men who built ships, and those who read Greek on the shores of the Atlantic, "especially those who loitered around Boston," had not materialized. Perhaps dire forebodings about the Philippines would prove equally inaccurate. In future years Borah became an impatient champion of speedy independence for the Pacific Islands. Unlike other zealous nationalists, like Albert J. Beveridge and Theodore Roosevelt, Borah did not overestimate the imperialist appetite of the American people.

The year 1902 marked a turning point in Borah's political career, for he then began to seek public office in earnest. Because law no longer satisfied his growing ambitions, he began to consider seriously the game of politics and played it to win. Years later he explained to a newspaperman that having exhausted the possibilities of legal practice in a sparsely settled state, he had to make a new move and running for high office seemed to be the answer.[10]

He became one of the young leaders of the Republican party revitalized by Theodore Roosevelt. Borah considered it a happy stroke of fate which brought this energetic reformer to the White House. He had tremendous confidence in the President, whose interest in western affairs and position on the trusts appealed to him; in turn, Roosevelt influenced him more than any other president. At the Republican State Convention in Boise on August 20, 1902, Borah asked:

> Why should this young commonwealth . . . reject the leadership of the aggressive Roosevelt, who is in sympathy with that eager, restless, un-

tiring energy which has made this trans-Mississippi empire and who proposes from his exalted place to defend our interests? No man, since Lincoln left his Western prairie home in Illinois, has understood so well or has been so anxious to give to the West all which is hers as the present leader of the Republican Party. Idaho will get in line to give him her electoral vote in 1904.[11]

At that convention Borah was chairman of the platform committee. The document adopted bore a strong resemblance to any respectable Bryanite declaration of principles, calling for the direct election of senators, government ownership of the railroads, restrictions on the trusts, tariff protection, and the placing of all trust-made articles on the free list. When the platform was published, the Democratic press gleefully denounced Borah as the "Tom Platt of Idaho politics,"[12] pointing out that Republican congresses had for years blocked legislation for the direct election of senators and shown little disposition to restrict trust activities. Borah was branded as "a secret chamber politician . . . and beyond all . . . a moral coward."[13] He had not entirely forgotten his Kansas training or the Populist cause, and probably saw the possibility of winning support from political mavericks like himself, who were torn between loyalty to the Republican organization and progressive ideas.

His aspirations for the Senate were no longer a secret. Helping to weld together the divided party, he stumped the state and organized local meetings in which he and his aides instructed some fifty Republican candidates for county nominations. A Boise gathering rose en masse and proclaimed its loyalty to him in reply to his challenge: "Those who are with me, I want them to declare themselves here and now." The old guard Republicans were startled by his activity, and it soon became evident that his forces would control the approaching state elections. Both sides spent money freely. On the eve of the primaries it was reported that Borah "for once in his life has opened a barrel." The Democrats had to walk to their polling places because the Republicans hired all the carriages in town.[14] In the September primaries Borah's followers carried every precinct in Ada County by majorities which gave them the lead in the coming state election. It was now accepted that Borah dominated his party and had delivered the death blow to the old guard in the state machine.

The rapidity of his rise was remarkable. He had been a regular Republican only three years, yet Democrats were already referring to him scornfully as "the party boss." Men who had grown gray in the service of Republicanism were thrust aside to make way for the young Boise attorney. As was expected, in November the Republicans won all state offices and a strong majority in the legislature. Borah was the popular choice for senator; his supporters carried him on their shoulders as though he had already won the seat.[15] One delegate remarked: "The contest appears like a walkaway for the Boise reformer. His opponents might continue to combine, but it will avail them nothing. The break to Borah seems not far distant. He has friends in the enemy camp who are only awaiting the proper time and then watch the stampede to get on the Borah bandwagon.[16] After engaging campaign headquarters in the Idanha Hotel, he left for north Idaho to assault the stronghold of Weldon B. Heyburn, the other Republican candidate for re-election to the Senate. Heyburn was so regular that he had adhered to the McKinley wing of the party in 1896, even though he came from Wallace in the heart of Idaho's silver country.

Since 1894 Borah's supporters had been urging him to try for a seat in the Senate. Intelligent and discriminating, free from embarrassing political entanglements, identified with no questionable political methods, eloquent, and of unchallenged integrity, he could be expected to attend to public affairs with diligence. Moreover, he would be content to allow the state to manage its own political affairs. No other candidate aroused such enthusiasm, especially in Ada, Canyon, and Owyhee counties. Idahoans could search their state thoroughly and still not find an abler man for the office. The people were eager to hear this "young man eloquent."[17] However, seasoned politicians still regarded him as an outsider, a newcomer, an upstart, and in those days it took more than the favor of the people to place an individual in the Senate.

Influence outside the state was brought to bear on the Republican organization to support Borah in this campaign. During September 1902 his friend from college days, William Allen White, by then a prominent Kansas journalist, visited southern Idaho to gather material for a series of articles on the mining region around Thunder Mountain. At this time White renewed his friendship with

Borah. A month later White sent the following letter to Senator Mark Hanna of Ohio:

Your friend ex-Senator Shoup and my friend, W. E. Borah . . . are the leading candidates for the Senate from Idaho at the coming election. Borah has twenty-five votes tied up good and tight. He needs three more to nominate him. Shoup has five votes and the prestige of his former service.

White explained how a mutual friend, Perry Heath of Salt Lake City, had persuaded politicians and the Republican committee in Idaho that Hanna was particularly interested in George Shoup's election. White wrote: ". . . you don't realize how much advantage this fact gives a man out here in the West where your judgment is regarded by Republicans as final in matters of policy . . . I feel sure that you would not allow the impression to prevail that you would let the fact of your personal preference and the weight of your place as Republican National Chairman weigh in any man's favor in any contest outside of your home state. Yet in Idaho, all unknown to you, that is exactly the situation." He advised Hanna:

. . . if you could find the opportunity to declare that the National Committee has no interest in the Idaho senatorial election further than . . . the desire to see a Republican win, it would be only fair to all the candidates. Such a note might be addressed to Judge D. W. Stanrod, the National Committeeman from Idaho . . . or . . . to me and I would see that it was published in Idaho . . . Now about Borah: He is . . . shrewd, levelheaded and true. You need not fear him. He admires you as much as I do, and I believe that is the limit. He would be your friend and would listen to you . . . I vouch for him . . . I am sure that you would not stand in the way of a young man. It is in the interest of fair play that I approach you on this Idaho situation. It seems to me that I am asking nothing that you cannot honorably give . . .[18]

Senator Hanna agreed to White's request.

When the Idaho legislature convened in January 1903, the Republican candidates for the Senate were Borah, Heyburn, Judge D. W. Stanrod, an Oneida County attorney, and ex-Senator Shoup. On January 8 the first Republican caucus, behind closed doors, agreed to ballot for three consecutive nights, a majority of twenty-six being necessary to nominate. On the first ballot Borah received eighteen votes, Heyburn fifteen, and the others a total of seventeen. Borah showed such strength that his rivals became alarmed. Scarcely ten minutes later they began to plan a combination. Judge Stanrod, in council with other members of his party, decided to withdraw; the same afternoon Shoup announced his retirement from the contest. This left Borah and Heyburn to fight it out.

It was reported that while the second caucus was in session, Heyburn supporters appeared outside with money to wager on him. A Lewiston man was said to have deposited $1,500 with the clerk at the Idanha Hotel. Though Borah's followers were confident of victory, rumors spread that at a secret caucus in Heyburn's headquarters late that afternoon twenty-eight legislators signed pledges to vote for him.[19] At the second regular caucus Borah received only four votes from the former Stanrod-Shoup forces; the majority went to Heyburn. At the final caucus that evening Heyburn received twenty-eight votes and Borah twenty-two. Borah accepted defeat gracefully, commenting: "I am still a Republican. The party's choice is satisfactory to me."[20]

The chief cause of Borah's defeat was the enmity of the old guard, who thought his platform altogether too radical. He was regarded as unreliable because of his defection in 1896 and too inexperienced to represent Idaho in the national legislature. Lyttleton Price, Borah's campaign manager, was clearly incompetent. Moreover, Borah still had some things to learn about campaigning. He vociferated too much; his concern for the reputation of Idaho was altogether too profound; his staging was overdone. Above all, in 1902 he trusted the people too little and the politicians too much. However, he was still young and eager to learn.

Just what pressure was brought to bear to secure those twenty-eight signatures on the combination pledge so quickly in secret caucus has never been established. It was reported at the time that the inducements were substantial. Within forty-eight hours after his defeat Borah was told that six or seven legislators had been bought for Heyburn at $750 a head. One man is said to have later confessed this to Borah and wept. It now appears that these charges of bribery had little foundation in fact, grew feeble, and were quietly dropped. They were probably put forward to relieve the stress of mind and furnish some excuse for the ignorance of Borah's friends. When the official vote was being taken in the legislature, twenty-two former supporters of Borah wanted to desert Heyburn; Borah insisted that they stand by the party's nominee: "Your names and my name are upon that caucus agreement. We are bound by its letter and spirit . . . In addition, we are all Republicans anxious to maintain the party in power."[21]

James Hawley, the Democratic candidate for the senatorship, who received a pledge of seventeen votes in the legislature, urged Borah to accept his votes to satisfy the public; however, Borah held that no failure by the members of his party to keep faith with him justified this. In declining Hawley's offer, Borah told the legislature:

> The contest is over, and your duty is done as you understand it. So far as I am personally concerned, I shall push this incident from me as an event of years long gone by. It will be recalled only when I wish to think of the dearest of friends and reflect upon the most unselfish loyalty ever known in Idaho politics. The first few minutes after the news came of my defeat it seemed unbearable. I stood by the open grave of a great hope . . . I confess to you that I was moved, but these moments, burdened with their disappointments, have gone, and with them, all unmanly and bitter feelings.[22]

Returning to his law practice, Borah resolved that this setback would not end his political ambitions. In 1906 he would make an even more strenuous campaign to succeed Senator Dubois, reelected for a second term in 1900. Meanwhile he would concentrate his efforts on changing the nominating procedure. He would put his name before the people whether they had a primary law or not, and his campaign slogan would be "King Caucus must go!"

At the Pocatello convention in May 1904 Borah made a rousing speech endorsing Theodore Roosevelt for the Republican nomination. It was this speech, one of the best of his life, that completely alienated him from the old guard in Idaho. He also attended the Chicago convention that year with Senator Dubois in order to confer with Senator Lodge, Spooner, and Gallinger upon a possible plank in the national platform on polygamy.[23] The plank was never adopted, but Borah had his first meeting with national statesmen.

Concerning his candidacy for the Senate, Borah told an interviewer: "I like politics and I will probably take an active part in them as long as I live, but I have come to like that freedom which one enjoys when he can say what he thinks and do as he wishes without feeling that he is endangering his throne . . . In other words, if I can be Senator with a certificate of the confidence of the people of my state I would like it but if it must be as it is so often secured, let somebody else have it. I don't want it at that price."[24]

In October 1904 he told another reporter: ". . . while I will be a candidate, I am not disposed to go farther than to fully and fairly submit the matter to the people. I don't want to engage in the usual tactics of caucus and trade. I haven't the time nor the desire. If Senators were elected by popular vote, I would be in a position to say positively I would be a candidate. In these days when the whole world knows that the United States Senate is the blockade on all great questions, I am utterly opposed to any man holding a place in that body who is not willing to submit his views and candidacy to popular approval."[25]

A fuller statement came early in 1906. He announced that he was submitting his name at the primaries on condition that the county convention demand that the state convention make the nomination of the party's candidate rather than offer a mere endorsement. Borah's enemies opposed this change, but the plan soon met with wide acceptance and his followers scorned the objections of the State Central Committee. The matter was for the people to decide at the primaries.

Senator Heyburn, in a letter to Borah, gave his opinion that the plan was unconstitutional. He received a stinging rebuttal from Borah:

> You say in effect that such a proceeding is unconstitutional. Into this domain of constitutional discussion which is a peculiarity of yours, I hesitate to enter . . . only may I ask you what part of that document so often referred to in high sounding phrases for the purpose of misleading some who think there is an occult force in its provisions which only the eminently wise can detect, prevents a political convention from endorsing its choice for the United States Senate? Everyone knows that as a legal proposition it does not bind the members of the legislature, and everyone knows that the will of the people, thus expressed is generally accepted by their routine servants. Public opinion is one thing to which even the Senate of the United States will yield.[26]

In a pamphlet written and distributed before the convention Borah further explained his plan, which he believed the nearest approach to the election of senators by popular vote to be had under existing conditions. Borah much preferred the constitutional amendment which the public had long petitioned, but these efforts were frustrated by the same influences opposing his convention plan. Those who referred to the procedure as unrepublican were reminded of Lincoln's request for the endorsement of his party in the state convention as the Republican candidate for the Senate in 1858. What Borah sought was the kind of resolution passed by that memorable convention, "the wisdom of whose action has never been impugned or questioned."

> Resolved, That Hon. Abraham Lincoln is our first and only choice for United States Senator to be created by the expiration of Mr. Douglas' term of office.

This resolution made Lincoln the choice of his party, and in those days, wrote Borah, no demagogue dared to insult the manhood of the party by intimating that the resolution was not binding on every party member.

Concluding that there were perhaps reasons why he should not be endorsed by the state convention, Borah saw no reason why the Republican party should not take the first step toward election of a senator by direct vote. "The Republicans in Idaho defeated the primary election law. Shall we now oppose the convention plan?" he asked. "From one end of this land to the other the people are making a bold effort to get in close touch with their representatives and this contest will not cease until they shall have realized fully their desires."[27]

In July 1906 the delegates to the Ada County convention were chosen. By nightfall it was apparent that the county was solidly for Borah.[28] Two days later the delegates voted as a unit for him. ". . . For this high office Ada County presents a favorite son in the person of William E. Borah. We believe he has the qualities of character and intellect to eminently fit him for this exalted station and that in his selection Idaho will have a representative in the Senate . . . the equal of any state in the union. We commend him to the convention as the unanimous choice of his friends . . . who know . . . his magnificent equipment for the responsibilities of this great task."[29] After July 22 there was little doubt Borah would have his majority in the state convention, though he was opposed somewhat in the northern counties.

The state convention met at Pocatello in August. Borah had one hundred twenty-four votes pledged, but could not muster a majority that would abide by a caucus decision. The contest found him opposed by James H. Brady, chairman of the State Central Committee, James H. Beatty of the Federal District Court in Idaho, and Judge D. W. Stanrod of Pocatello. The regulars supported Frank Gooding for governor. Borah had the support of three of the Mormon counties in southern Idaho, putting him in a strong position with the Gooding faction. Borah and Gooding appealed to the county delegations in which each had the strongest support, and an agreement was worked out on July 31 by which Gooding would be nominated for governor and Borah would be nominated for the Senate. Brady decided to retire from the race, and it was agreed that the Gooding bloc would name the state ticket with no interference from Borah's followers. This arrangement irritated some of the delegates, but they had no practical means of offering a protest and the bargain went virtually unchallenged. The next day the convention made the nomination by acclamation. Edgar Wilson, a Boise lawyer, put Borah's name in nomination. One after another, chairmen of the county delegations seconded the nomination until Frank Gooding moved that Borah be declared the unanimous choice of the convention. This was greeted with a roar, during which Borah ascended the platform to accept the honor.[30]

The campaign which followed developed into a pitched battle between Borah and the Democratic candidate, Senator Fred Dubois, who was up for re-election. Dubois, still in control of his party, was able to dictate the platform and continued his anti-Mormon campaign begun several years ago. As a result practically all Mormon voters in the state cast their ballots for Gooding and Borah; thus the Republicans won an easy victory.

The Idaho legislature convened in January 1907. When, on January 15, Borah and Dubois were nominated, the president of the Senate directed the secretary to call the roll which showed that Borah had fifteen and Dubois six votes. In the House Charles

Cavanah, Borah's old law associate, in an impressive nominating speech predicted: "He will carry into the United States Senate a trained mind, disciplined by the sternest culture of his faculties, disdaining any plaudits which are not of honest reward, or robust reasoning on generalized facts . . . These splendid qualifications are embodied in your countryman, friend and unanimous choice of the Republican party of Idaho, the Honorable William E. Borah."[31] Borah received thirty-eight votes and Dubois twelve. The following day a joint session of the legislature confirmed Borah's election. He received the vote of every Republican member. The entire chamber and gallery were crowded with spectators when a committee of three conducted the senator-elect to the chamber. There were loud cheers as Borah mounted the rostrum, a handsome figure, erect, flushed with excitement, looking down on the delighted faces of his friends:

> You have given me a great honor and deeply and sincerely I thank you . . . Indeed it is an unqualified honor to represent the State of Idaho in the Senate of the United States in this important period of her growth and development . . . I understand they have an unwritten law under which a man is supposed to be dead for two years . . . If they put me down in the cellar where they did La Follette, and you do not hear from me, you will understand . . . I shall always endeavor to act to the best of my ability whenever and wherever Idaho's interests are involved . . . wherever I can act in accordance with the demands of the national welfare.
>
> I now thank you all, the citizens generally, for the support which you gave me in the campaign, the members of the joint assembly for faithfully executing their trust, and hope to see you later this evening at the Idanha where there will be something doing.[32]

The reception at the Idanha Hotel that evening surpassed all precedents in its gaiety. Costumes ranged from full dress to homespun; Borah himself appeared in a dark business suit. That night the drinks at all Boise bars were on him.

For Borah the open grave had been transformed into an open door. The caucus system of nominating candidates had given way to nomination by the state convention, which, if it did not morally obligate the legislator to vote for the candidate named, certainly put him under strong pressure to do so. Even many of the Democrats were happy to see the man who had been an outstanding advocate of some of their principles win the Senate seat. They admired his freedom of political action and had favored him above all other Republicans.

However, in some quarters the results were disgruntling. Judge Beatty, who ran a poor third in the race, was bitter. With some rancor he remarked: "I sought election only as the law provides—through the legislature. He [Borah] having failed thus, resorted to the state convention, where by combination and division of spoils with those he had denounced as corrupt, he succeeded."[33] There was a particle of truth in the charges Beatty made. The final bargain between Borah and the state machine backing Governor Gooding at the convention was arrived at in a caucus agreement, though Borah had campaigned on the slogan "King Caucus must go!" Sixty or more of the Borah delegates had protested this bargain, but found themselves powerless against the machine driven by Gooding and Brady. Borah's offer to withdraw from the race was futile, for that would have left his followers with no candidate at all. He evidently made a sharp distinction between caucuses for nominating candidates and caucuses for other purposes. Borah adopted a strategy, including bargaining, designed to win him the Senate seat. At least there was no secret caucus, bribery, or sale of votes.

The future senator was powerfully aided from beginning to end by Calvin Cobb, editor of the Idaho *Statesman;* he had been quick to recognize Borah's potentialities and his magnetic pull on the voters. He commented editorially on Borah's triumph:

> There was no turmoil, no bootlicking, no guerilla warfare, no trades in jobs, no barter or sale of men's honor . . . it was as calm a proceeding as a vote to pay a bill . . . no frills or feathers, no waste of words or money or temper. There was no promise of jobs, no hopes of rewards to come in the vote so cast. It was the voice of the people of Idaho speaking.[34]

Soon after Borah's election to the Senate and before he took his seat, he was involved in two dramatic trials, one of which raised grave doubts whether he would ever be able to go to Washington at all.

IV Borah Versus Darrow

Nothing astonishes men so much as common sense and plain dealing.

—Ralph Waldo Emerson

After the Wallace murder trial Borah's reputation spread rapidly throughout the Northwest, and other mining and lumber corporations in north Idaho sought his services. His disdain for criminal cases, coupled with the more attractive fees offered by the big corporations, hastened his transition from criminal to corporation law. His expanded practice after 1900 apparently netted him an annual income of about $30,000.

From 1899 to 1905 there was relative peace in the mining regions of Idaho, but hatreds smoldered just beneath the surface. Radical labor factions were bitterly antagonistic to Governor Frank Steunenberg for the position he had taken against law-defying elements. He occasionally received anonymous letters threatening his life, but these rarely disturbed him or deterred him from the performance of his official duties. When his second term expired, he returned to Caldwell, a town about thirty miles west of Boise; there he resumed his activities as a rancher, speculator in timber, and president of the Caldwell Bank.

On the cold, snowy evening of December 30, 1905, Steunenberg came home at dusk after a meeting with friends at the Saratoga Hotel in Caldwell. As on countless other evenings he walked up to the old wood and woven wire fence and swung open the side gate. In doing so, he set off a bomb; the explosion horribly mangled his body. He was carried into the house, where he muttered a few labored words to his wife: "Who shot me, Mother?" Twenty minutes later he was dead.

In Boise the news caused intense excitement. Headlines screamed:

FORMER GOVERNOR STEUNENBERG VICTIM OF BOMB OF INFAMOUS ASSASSIN[1]

A special train rushed Governor Frank Gooding, Attorney General Frank Martin, Borah, and other close friends to Caldwell. The mutilated remains of his friend, the blood-stained snow, the shattered gate, and the fragments of garments blown fifty feet away made a lasting impression on Borah. As governor, Steunenberg had treated him like his own son, calling him William and helping him rise in Idaho. He had been both friend and counselor. For these reasons and because of his ability as a speaker, Borah was asked to deliver the funeral oration at Caldwell on January 3, 1906. He told the mourners of the qualities which had made Steunenberg great in the eyes of his fellow men. He was "of the granite hewn."

But there was another side to his nature—the one which makes our grief so unspeakable now. How full and rich, how unselfish and complete his friendship, of which he gave so generously to all! This man of unbending will, of iron determination, was as faithful and considerate as a woman. His countless acts of friendship, his devotion to the richest passion which sheds its perfume in the human heart, are testified to by the grief and tears of those gathered from every part of the State.

But in the midst of this awful tragedy let us strive to be just. This crime, when fastened upon its author, will place him or them beyond the pale of human forgiveness or pity. Therefore let us not place it unjustly or upon suspicion. Let us not believe it is the crime of any class or any portion of our citizens, or that it finds sympathy with anyone other than the actual perpetrator. Let us hope that when mystery yields up her secret it will be found that it is some one irresponsible toward all others . . .[2]

Governor Gooding ordered mounted police to surround Canyon County. All trains were stopped and searched. It was believed that the murderer could not have gone far from the scene of the crime. Within a few days detectives became suspicious of a stocky man with a black valise registered at the Saratoga Hotel in Caldwell. Pieces of plaster and chloride of potash useful in making a bomb were found in his room, and his valise contained other suspected materials. He was arrested on New Year's Day and eventually removed to the penitentiary at Boise. Although he called himself Tom Hogan, he was later identified as Harry Orchard, a figure in the Coeur d'Alene disturbances of 1899 who had disappeared immediately after the riots.

The state employed James McParland, the Pinkerton detective from Denver who had gained prominence in the "Molly Maguire" labor troubles in the Pennsylvania coal fields. He alone visited Orchard over a period of months, during which he secured the confidence of the prisoner. Capitalizing on Orchard's latent religious sentiments and the remorse induced in him by prolonged solitary confinement, the detective pointed out the possibilities of immunity if Orchard would co-operate with the state in prosecuting the real murderers, the men who had hired him to kill the ex-governor. At last, in February 1906 Orchard made a full confession of all the crimes he had committed in his fantastic career. His motive, he said, was "to make himself right with God and man."

Shortly after signing his confession, Orchard was visited by James Hawley, one of the state's prosecutors in the forthcoming trial, and later by Borah, also appointed by Governor Gooding as special counsel for the prosecution. No record of their interviews with the prisoner exists, but evidently Hawley promised to do all he could to see that Orchard was dealt with leniently. Orchard alleges that Borah also promised clemency, though later Borah vehemently denied this. He was so intimate with Steunenberg that it is difficult to conceive of his showing anything but bitter hostility. In an interview with Orchard some years ago the author found him reluctant to discuss his relationship with Borah. He admired Hawley because he was a man of his word, but he admitted a dislike for Borah and said he did not wish to "blacken the man's name" after he had been long dead. During the Haywood trial Borah had made repeated denials of any bargain, but Orchard insisted on his version.[3]

Orchard's confession implicated William Haywood, secretary of the Western Federation of Miners; Charles Moyer, its president; and George Pettibone, another union official. A Canyon County grand jury returned a joint indictment of them, and Idaho authorities ordered extradition. The three men were taken from the union's headquarters in Denver and brought to Boise, where they were to stand trial. Since the state had the strongest evidence against Haywood, he was tried first.

Attorneys for Haywood were Edmund Richardson of Denver, Edgar Wilson and John Nugent of Boise, and Fred Miller of Spokane, all serving under Clarence Darrow, the noted Chicago trial lawyer and liberal, who headed the counsel for the defense. Thus, the Haywood trial brought Darrow and Borah together in a dramatic courtroom battle.

O. M. Van Duyn of Canyon County, W. A. Stone of Caldwell, and Charles Koelsch of Boise served as counsel for the state, while Borah and James Hawley of Boise were special prosecutors. Again it was the team of 1899, Borah and Hawley. By entering the case, Borah was placing himself in opposition to a well-organized labor movement with a membership of hundreds of thousands; thus he faced a menace of the same physical injury that overtook Steunenberg. Few men in Idaho were more likely to be the target of an assassin. Perhaps this explains the fact that he charged the state the rather high fee of $5,000.[4]

The case was delayed by habeas corpus proceedings, and the defendants remained in jail almost six months before the trial. Haywood tells us Clarence Darrow often came to the jail depressed and worried. The defense had no idea what procedure the state would follow in trying the case, nor did they know the nature of the confession made by Orchard, who was under heavy guard in the state prison. The air was heavy with pessimism. Pettibone expressed sympathy with Darrow, saying he realized it would be hard for him to lose this great case, but "You know," he added, "it's us fellows that have to be hanged!"[5]

The trial of "Big Bill" Haywood was the talk of the West. Boise swarmed with visitors anxious to witness so remarkable a courtroom drama: lawyers, tourists, at least one psychologist (Hugo Munsterberg of Harvard), and the representatives of leading newspapers. Every phase of the case would be reported in minute detail. Thus Borah made his debut on the national scene, simultaneously, as it happened, with the lawyers who prosecuted Harry Thaw, the slayer of Stanford White. To be sure, the Thaw trial was primarily sensational, while the Boise case involved much class feeling. A colossal feat of propaganda had been accomplished to arouse national interest and acquaint the people with the capital-labor situation in the West. Mass demonstrations like those held in New York impressed the public and helped focus the anxious attention of all classes on Boise. Despite Borah's insistence that the only issue involved in the case was Haywood's guilt, the labor press was doing its utmost to lead the world to think that labor, not Haywood, was on trial.[6]

Haywood's trial began on May 9, 1907, with Fremont Wood as the judge. The courtroom was filled, and hundreds stood outside on the lawn. After more than three weeks of examination and elimination a jury was finally empaneled. Most of the jurors were ranchers, but the prosecution had somehow succeeded in qualifying Mr. Robertson, with whom Steunenberg had once made his home.[7] All swore they were impartial and would "a true deliverance make between the State of Idaho and the prisoner at the bar."

At this point Orchard's confession was published in several newspapers, including the Idaho *Statesman*. An investigation by Charles Koelsch proved that no improper motive actuated anyone connected with the newspapers concerned.[8] There is little question as to which side profited most by this disclosure, for it gave the defense foreknowledge of the state's most important piece of evidence. With upwards of a million dollars at their disposal from the coffers of the Western Federation of Miners, the defense lawyers at once engaged a crew of investigators who checked every detail of Orchard's story and interviewed every person mentioned. They based their cross-examination on this careful work and prepared opposing witnesses to counter or disprove the state's evidence.[9]

The parallel between the Haywood case and the Corcoran case is striking. Conspiracy would be the charge. It was not contended that Moyer, Haywood, or Pettibone actually planted the bomb that killed Steunenberg, but the state was confident of its ability to prove that the trio concocted the plot and hired Harry Orchard to carry it out.

Every trial has its high points. After the prosecuting lawyers laid their foundation with the testimony of several minor witnesses, they brought in their star witness. All eyes were turned toward the center aisle of the courtroom as a line of deputy sheriffs made their way to the judge's desk. In their midst was a short, stout man with a red face, small nose, wide forehead, bright blue eyes, and a ready smile. Most of the spectators were astonished. Was this the confessed assassin of eighteen men? In appearance he resembled a cheerful milkman. Upon the jury's faith in his sincerity depended the verdict in one of the greatest criminal cases ever tried in United States courts.

Orchard underwent a severe cross-examination which lasted intermittently for six days; it was conducted by Edmund Richardson, a Denver attorney who knew his case thoroughly and was moreover a man of great force, legal ability, and resourcefulness. Though he failed in getting Orchard to contradict himself, it was not for lack of earnest effort. There was no legitimate tactic in the art of cross-examination which he did not use again and again. Orchard, cool and deliberate, always had his answer ready. When Borah's turn came to examine Orchard, he asked few questions but merely told him to narrate his story to the court. If the cross-examination did nothing else, it established that Orchard was sane to the point of bleakness.

The state made every effort to corroborate Orchard's testimony, for an Idaho statute bars conviction on the testimony of a single accomplice, no matter how credible. Witnesses were produced who supported much of what Orchard said concerning his activities for the Miners' Federation, but this was corroboration of collateral material and its legal competency was questionable. Darrow's line of defense was to parade the whole succession of crimes that Orchard had committed and to expose Orchard's simulation of a Christian conversion as a desperate effort to obtain pity. The attorney charged that a bad conscience was driving Orchard crazy and had impelled him not only to tell his own guilty secrets but to try to lay the blame for these crimes on others.[10]

Another high point in the trial was reached on July 12 when Bill Haywood took the stand. Under fierce questioning by Borah, he flatly denied any connection with Orchard or knowledge of his movements. Newspapers called it the cleverest cross-examination of the trial.[11] Borah's object was to trap Haywood into furnishing him with material on which he could subsequently base an argument. The two were in many ways evenly matched: Borah, highly skilled in interrogation and in the adroit management of reluctant witnesses; Haywood, keen and cautious, shrewdly fighting for his life. Throughout Haywood's examination Borah remained for the most part respectful and courteous and never tried bullying tactics. He led his witness many times to a point where attorneys for the defense feared some damaging admission, only to have Haywood dexterously evade him by an apparently frank explanation. Haywood instinctively detected the drift of Borah's most artful queries, scenting the construction the prosecuting attorney was seeking to place on his answers.

Time and again Borah tried to establish an intimacy between Haywood and Orchard, which Haywood repeatedly denied. The witness was shrewd enough not to betray bitterness against any of the men Orchard accused him of conspiring to assassinate. When pressed to acknowledge his deep hostility toward ex-Governor Steunenberg, he ingeniously replied: "I regarded him as opposed to our organization and false to his oath as governor, but I did not feel any differently toward him personally than I do toward you. I regarded him just as I regard you, Senator Borah."[12]

When Borah showed his witness an editorial in the *Miner's Magazine,* in which Steunenberg was characterized as a "hireling and traitor," and asked him if it expressed his views and those of the organization, Haywood repeated: "I didn't regard Steunenberg personally any different from the way I regard you, Senator Borah, or Bartlett Sinclair, or any of the others who were mixed up in that trouble." This nettled Borah, who then fired questions at Haywood with a rapidity that was bewildering.[13] The cross-examination raised serious questions, particularly in regard to Orchard's means of livelihood while in Denver. In his autobiography Haywood relates:

> Borah, in his cross-examination, did not have things all his own way. He faced me with his bulldog expression and the deep dimple in his chin, and asked about the resolution I had written in Silver City:
>
> 'You felt very bitter against Governor Steunenberg?' 'Yes,' I answered, 'I felt toward him much as I did toward you and others who were responsible for martial law and the bull-pen in the Coeur d'Alenes.'
>
> 'So I have understood,' the Senator remarked. Just what he meant I could not make out.

Haywood wrote that during the cross-examination the setting sun was shining through a window facing him. He asked the judge, "If your Honor please, will you kindly have the shutters closed on that window? The sun is shining in my face and I cannot see the senator's eyes."

"It was not my intention to disconcert the senator," he relates, "but I was told afterward that he [Borah] said he had never heard of a man on trial for his life who was so anxious to see the prosecutor's eyes." Borah was reported to have said: "It doubled me up like a jackknife."[14]

In the opening argument for the defense Darrow made one of the longest and most forceful speeches of his career; it lasted eleven hours. Dressed in a slouchy gray suit, he walked up and down before the jury and made wild gestures. Sometimes he was aggressive, his great voice rumbling; then he would assume a pleading attitude, displaying an astonishing mastery of detail, all without notes. He called the trial an inquisition conducted by mine owners in Idaho and Colorado who had subverted the state. He gave a history of the labor movement, talking in denunciatory vein about wage slaves, the twelve-hour day, mine fires, cave-ins, explosions, arsenic fumes, paralysis, and industrial evils generally. The Western Federation of Miners had been formed to protect helpless and hopeless workers, and he recited its achievements. At times he spoke more for labor than Haywood, as if the Western Federation were on trial.[15] Labor unions are often brutal, he said, "but I don't care how many brutalities they are guilty of; I know their cause is just." Borah at once rose to object: "This is merely a murder trial," he said. "We are not fighting organized labor." Then Darrow shifted his argument to Harry Orchard. Darrow did not want a verdict of manslaughter or any other compromise, for either Haywood was guilty and should be hanged or he was innocent and should be acquitted. The Chicago attorney used his heaviest weapon when he attempted to demolish the credibility of Orchard's testimony. Over and over again he asked the jury if they would take a man's life on "the rotten testimony" of a depraved killer. "Where is the evidence?" he asked. The state's case, he charged, was nothing but Orchard from beginning to end.

Darrow treated Orchard's alleged conversion cautiously, admitting his own agnosticism. He questioned Orchard's sincerity, noting that he had confessed first to Pinkerton detective James McParland and later to clergyman Dean Hincks. Later Darrow wrote: "In all my experience, I never had a better opportunity, and when I had finished I felt satisfied with the effort I had made."[16]

Borah followed Darrow with the closing argument for the state on the evening of July 25. More than a thousand people tried to gain admission to the crowded courtroom that evening. Darrow later observed that there was a marked contrast between the audience during his plea and that which heard Borah's argument. When Darrow spoke, the courtroom and lawn outside were packed with workingmen, socialists, radicals, and idealists from every section of America; however, Borah made his final address to the elite of Boise and all the state. They were dressed as though attending a social event, which indeed it was. The common people had been given their opportunity in the afternoon. The room had been thoroughly aired, if not fumigated during the recess, Darrow reported. "As I looked over the assembly," he commented, "I was reminded of Byron's description of the ball in Brussels on the eve of the battle of Waterloo."[17]

Mrs. Steunenberg, the murdered governor's widow, made her appearance in court for the first time. Seated beside her was her young son Julian. Governor Gooding, a number of the executive staff, and members of the state judiciary were in the courtroom. Haywood was surrounded by his counsel, and beside him sat his invalid wife. Ethel Barrymore, currently appearing in a Boise production of *Captain Jinks of the Horse Marines,* arrived accompanied by Mrs. Borah.

Detective agencies exploited the situation fully. They kept the atmosphere tense with excitement during the trial in order to drum up business and collect fat fees. Once, when their dismissal was being considered, they planted dynamite on a hillside creating a great explosion. An increased guard was proposed for the special prosecutor. Borah protested to Governor Gooding: "These people would not be interested in killing a prosecutor when a governor is available. Their scheme contemplates murder not oftener than once in six months. There is consequently no use to put guards around my house until some months after you have been done away with." Not seeing the joke at all, Gooding swore loudly.[18]

Much of Borah's speech that hot July evening was in reply to Darrow; there was little attempt at oratorical display. Standing apart from the jury, he talked in deliberate fashion, beginning in a conversational tone which carried scarcely beyond the jury box. Every sound in the room was hushed. In his opening words he said that the state wanted no vicarious atonement. "We do not want the defendant in this case to suffer by reason of the crime of Harry

Orchard if he was not in fact connected with it, aiding, abetting and assisting in its perpetration."

Then Borah denounced Darrow's statement that the jurors' minds had been poisoned against the defendant. "Have you heard anybody in Boise asking for the blood of William Haywood?" he asked. No man, he insisted, ever sat in a courtroom where there was greater fairness or more determination to see that justice was done. While the prosecution was not fighting organized labor, neither were they there to consent that organized labor should be a shield to crime. The great question, he told the jury, was that of Harry Orchard's truthfulness. He ridiculed the inconsistencies of Darrow's speech, in which he had first implied that Orchard was a homicidal maniac and then treated him as a Pinkerton detective. If Orchard were any kind of a maniac, the fact was not revealed in the astute cross-examination by Mr. Richardson. Nor could the jury but admire the method in Orchard's madness in that he always chose an enemy of the Western Federation of Miners for his next victim.

When he took up Orchard's alleged regeneration, he called attention to the fact that the question of religion had not been introduced into the case by the state. Borah went on to relate his own youthful experience as skeptic and agnostic. Stepping close to the jury box and turning halfway around so that he could see Darrow, who sat behind him, he said in a low, conversational tone: "Mr. Darrow . . . was generous enough to give us a discourse on religion incident to a discussion of the evidence in this case. I hardly think he is an expert on the subject." Then with a swift sweeping gesture at Darrow his deep voice rang through the courtroom: "I say to you tonight, that I am not a religionist, neither am I a hypocrite, but it is too late, in this, the morning of the twentieth century, to write upon the divine brow of the One who died on Calvary, 'imposter'; too late to write above that bowed head, 'false prophet'. While some may not know, millions do know that their Redeemer liveth. It is too late to argue against the teachings of Him who said: 'This day thou shalt be with me in paradise.'" In the most dramatic part of his delivery he continued:

Orchard may not have religion, I do not know, but I do know that twenty centuries of Christian civilization . . . thousands and thousands of the best men and women who ever walked upon this earth tell us and teach us that there is a divine power which can reform men's brains . . . make better men's hearts . . . In the night of despair, when the stars of hope are dead, every sinner of us, the bravest and the frailest, turns at last to that old book which our mothers loved. It is the only book on earth when we are face to face with the trouble which human aid can not alleviate. When some great sorrow presses us to earth and we are locked in with our own sufferings, how quickly memory carries back over the years and we are landed again at the old homestead. In the twilight sits a saintly form, bent and gray, and on her lap rests the book—it is mother and her Bible. There is the picture, memory will never lose it, it is the anchor of the moral world . . . all the mockery and blasphemy and scorn of atheism can not cloud its beauty . . . God never intended it should be destroyed . . . And if Orchard, poor, miserable wretch, his hands red with the blood of more than a score of innocent men, his soul steeped in the very fumes of hell—if he saw that picture and was drawn to it again he simply saw what every criminal sees when he stands looking out from behind the prison bars at the near end of life. Oh, I learned long ago not to mock at any man's religion. It is at last a secret between himself and his God.

He reached a climax when he answered the charge that the state had promised Orchard immunity in exchange for his testimony. With blazing eyes he turned on the counsel for defense. In behalf of the state, its people, the governor, and himself he disclaimed all intention or desire to give Orchard immunity. "Trading in blood? You may turn *him* [Haywood] loose, but you will never get twelve men in this State of Idaho who will turn Harry Orchard loose, and you will never find a man in this State who will, as Governor, turn him loose." Then, his face pale and his voice quivering with emotion, Borah raised his right arm and said: "And I trust that if ever I compromise with the man who planted that bomb at Steunenberg's gate, that the great God will wither my right arm until it falls from its socket." After allowing for the full dramatic effect, he continued: "There is only one place for that man Orchard and that is in the penitentiary until the time comes for him to go hence. And I want to say to you that the man who intimates that I would compromise with Harry Orchard does not understand the kind of blood that circulates in my body. He does not know the love I bore the dead."

After speaking for an hour and a half, Borah announced his

desire to stop because it was too hot to proceed. He told Judge Wood that he expected to conclude his argument on the following day. The court adjourned and the sweltering spectators hurried outside for a breath of air.

The next morning at nine o'clock Borah continued his argument for the state. He was again in excellent voice, making it possible for parts of his speech to reach the crowd outside. He dealt almost exclusively with an analysis of the evidence. Repeatedly he exposed the errors of the other lawyers by citing verbatim testimony on points raised by them. Instead of beginning with the explosion of the Bunker Hill-Sullivan mill, he commenced with the murder of Steunenberg and then moved backward to trace Orchard's career of crime. He reminded the jury that every consecutive act of Orchard was influenced by Denver and every crime he committed had originated in Haywood's office. Fresh from every misdeed, Orchard had hurried back to Denver. Then, smiling, Borah leaned toward the jury to ask: "Why? Why always back to Denver, unless there it was to find the protection and pay of his employers?" Borah continued to press the state's charge of conspiracy, reviewing the testimony of each witness and using it to establish the veracity of Orchard's statements. So adroit was his treatment and so familiar was he with the record that he gave the story all the interest of novelty.

Only one organization, he argued, had any interest in the assassination of Steunenberg—the Western Federation of Miners. Only one body of men had ever been assailed by the governor. Only Haywood, Moyer, Pettibone, and their associates regarded him as an enemy. Borah pounded allegation into the jury—the Federation's hatred of Steunenberg as the representative of organized wealth. Whenever his discussion wandered afield, he always brought it back to emphasize Haywood's bitter animosity toward the former governor. Borah used his material well. The case was weak so far as direct incriminating evidence was concerned, but by his forcefulness he made it seem strong.

Selecting only the evidence of witnesses for the defense and leaving Orchard's confession aside, Borah wove together the movements of five men: Haywood, Moyer, Pettibone, Orchard, and Simpkins. Without departing from the record, he brought these officers and members of the Western Federation of Miners into a close-knit group. At first this was done cautiously, quietly, almost monotonously. Then Borah's voice and manner changed as he sprang into action:

> . . . Watch these five men! In a little over thirty days Frank Steunenberg is to die . . . they are in touch with one another; you will find out . . . Watch them! Do not expect the State to prove all they said, but watch their actions. One conspirator is today a self-confessed murderer [Orchard]; another conspirator a fugitive from justice [Simpkins]; another conspirator down here in jail and afraid to testify [Steve Adams]. No evidence? What more do you want?

For a few seconds there was dead silence in the courtroom. Then, relaxing, Borah continued. He brought Davis, Copley, Adams, and Easterly, all officers or members of the Western Federation of Miners, into touch with Orchard. He drew picture after picture of the men associating together at various times:

> Mr. Darrow may say of me, as he did of Hawley, that I am crazy; but I have lucid intervals, and I say to you that if you will start with Harry Orchard . . . and trace his testimony and watch the actions and read the letters and telegrams, watch the movements, the concerted actions, of all these five men, you will find that there is a complete and absolute conspiracy proved beyond a reasonable doubt and that conspiracy had for its object, among other things, the murder of Frank Steunenberg . . .

At this point Borah asked for an adjournment.

The court convened that evening at seven. As on the previous evening every seat in the room was taken, and men stood two and three deep all around the walls. An overflow crowd, unable to gain admission even to the corridors, again stood outside on the lawn to catch phrases and sentences through the open windows of the courthouse. Reporters paid close attention to the effect of Borah's words on the key figures of the trial. Through part of his argument Mrs. Haywood wept quietly. At one point Haywood's mother was overcome and had to be led from the courtroom. Mrs. Steunenberg was also forced to leave the room before Borah had been talking an hour and a half. The jurors sat straight in their chairs, their eyes fixed on him, almost spellbound by the swift logic of his argument. Haywood showed the least emotion of all during Borah's speech, but at its high points his cheeks blanched. His lips were firmly set, and his eyes followed every move and gesture of the speaker as if fascinated. Darrow's face was grave. At first he had tried to wear his usual half-derisive smile, but it soon faded as Borah began to talk more forcibly. Richardson's face wore a worried look, and he gazed fearfully over the faces of the jury to read the effect that Borah was making upon their minds.

In a last burst of eloquence Borah brought to a close his long argument, which altogether had consumed nearly nine hours in its delivery, as he warned the twelve jurymen of their solemn duty:

> I have no doubt that many times during this trial you have been much moved by the eloquence of counsel for the defense . . . But as I listened to the music of their voices and felt for a moment the compelling touch of their hypnotic influence, there came back to me all the more vividly, when released from the spell, another scene—there came to me in more moving tones other voices. I remembered again the awful night of December 30, 1905, a night which added ten years to the life of some . . . in this courtroom now. I felt again its cold and merciless chill, faced the drifting snow and peered at last into the darkness for the sacred spot where last lay my dead friend, and saw true, only too true, the stain of his life blood upon the whited earth. I saw men and women standing about in storm and darkness, silent in the presence of the dreadful mystery, and Idaho disgraced and dishonored—I saw murder—no, not murder—a thousand times worse than murder, I saw anarchy displaying its first bloody triumph in Idaho . . . As I thought over that night, again I said to myself, Thou living God, can time or the arts of counsel unteach the lessons of that hour? No, no; for the sake of all that good men hold near and dear let us not be misled, let us not forget, let us not be falterers in this great test of courage . . .[19]

Counsel on both sides commended his great effort. Mrs. Haywood shook his hand from her wheel chair and thanked him for his fairness. Later her husband told members of the press: "Well, I have heard the best of them in the country but Borah beat them all." Clarence Darrow, attorney for the defense, said: "Senator Borah's speech to the jury was the fairest and ablest I have ever heard from counsel in a great murder trial. Mr. Borah might have said more without being outside the record, but it was noticeable that he omitted some things in order to avoid the slightest tinge of unfairness."[20] Later he wrote that few men he had ever met in a courtroom contributed so much industry, learning, and natural ability to a case as Mr. Borah.[21] A remarkable tribute was paid Borah's speech in the editorial column of the Idaho *Statesman:*

> As the country reads the report of that address this morning, it will be realized in every town and hamlet that the man by whom it was delivered is one of the great ones of the land. We might as well recognize that fact. He is no longer ours; he belongs to the nation.[22]

Judge Wood's instructions to the jury were lengthy. Out of sixty-four paragraphs in his charge, some forty or forty-two dealt with the subject of reasonable doubt. Under those circumstances it seemed to the New York *Times* correspondent, Oscar King Davis, that only a superhuman jury would not have concluded that the judge charged that a reasonable doubt existed in this case. Judge Wood reminded the jurors that the statutes imposed a bar to conviction on the testimony of an accomplice alone, no matter how credible to the jury, unless there was clear and independent corroborative evidence. Such corroboration had to connect Haywood with the crime charged against him and not with other crimes not alleged in the indictment.[23]

The case went to the jury around ten o'clock that Saturday night after continuous sessions which had lasted nearly three months. Haywood and his attorneys did not expect an acquittal. The most they anticipated was a divided jury; one or two jurors would hold out against acquittal, producing a compromise verdict, which Darrow did not want, or a hung jury, which would mean retrial. The long wait was extremely trying to the lawyers in the case and to the men whose lives hung in the balance. A few of the attorneys went to Edgar Wilson's office; others gathered in Borah's. Richardson announced that he had performed his duty and could sleep as well as if he had never been in the case, so he went to bed. Some of the spectators walked the unpaved side streets of the city, where on every corner little knots of men stood discussing the case. All night long a light burned in the jury room.

At seven the following morning the lawyers were notified that the jury had reached an agreement, and Judge Wood was summoned. By eight the courtroom was packed, the judge had arrived, and the lawyers were in their places. The room grew still as death when the verdict was handed to the clerk of the court, who read: "Not guilty." There was no cheering. The prosecution was stunned, for few had expected this outcome. Haywood's countenance broke into a broad grin after the initial shock, and his wife wept. The crowd hurriedly disbanded into small groups outside.

After the eloquence of Darrow acquitted Haywood and later Pettibone, the charges against Moyer were dropped. A year later Orchard was tried and convicted of murder in the first degree, but his sentence was commuted from death to life imprisonment for turning state's evidence. He lived for many years in a small cabin inside the walls of the state penitentiary at Boise, a devout Seventh Day Adventist and a benign "lifer," tending chickens, turkeys, and a vegetable garden until his death in 1954 at eighty-eight. Haywood was convicted in 1917 for systematic sabotage in vital war industries, forfeited his bond, and escaped to Russia, where he died in 1928.

Contrary to popular legend the Haywood trial had no bearing on Borah's election to the Senate because his election was assured when the state legislature was chosen in November 1906 and the trial took place in May 1907. Perhaps Borah went into the case as an "obscure country attorney," but he emerged a national figure.

V Borah on Trial

His enemies shall lick the dust.
—Psalms, LXXII, 9

When the West was young, it was tacitly understood that pioneers could help themselves to whatever natural resources they needed for survival and comfort. This policy the government felt compelled to pursue in order to encourage the opening of the West to settlement. Under the first successful land sales law, that of 1820, huge tracts were sold at a minimum price (rarely exceeded) of $1.25 an acre. The Homestead Act of 1862 made land free in farm-size allotments to actual settlers. Because this law could not properly be applied to rough and semiarid areas, Congress passed a succession of other enactments to promote the development of the Far West. They included the Desert Land Act of 1877, the Timber Culture Act of 1873, the Timber and Stone Act of 1878, and the Reclamation Act of 1872. Under Presidents Harrison and Cleveland large national forest reserves were created, and President Roosevelt greatly enlarged them. The growth of Idaho was to no small extent shaped by these steps of the national government.

The Timber and Stone Act provided that one hundred sixty acres of timberland on the public domain, unfit for cultivation, could be bought by a citizen for $2.50 an acre. To comply with the law, the settler had to file an affidavit which declared that the land was for his exclusive use and benefit and that no prior agreement had been made by which the benefit of the purchase could be obtained by any other person. From the outset the law was unpopular in the West, where powerful interests wished to obtain government land in larger tracts and many people deplored what they thought was a federal policy of locking up natural resources. Among the outspoken opponents of the law was Borah.

Meanwhile large lumber companies which relied on public indifference or support had found ways to subvert the government's land policy to their own advantage. They sent out "timber cruisers" to search the public domain for valuable stretches of accessible forest; then they took fraudulent steps to obtain title. The favorite method first used by companies was to urge their employees to take up claims. Officials later began to advertise for persons with timber rights who were willing to file for them. Each married couple was eligible to file for three hundred twenty acres. The companies furnished the necessary data and made out papers to be signed, so that the pliable claimant never had to leave office or home to become locator and ostensible owner of one hundred sixty acres of raw timber. The company not only furnished the money to perfect title but also paid the claimant a bonus—perhaps $100. Tracts amounting to one hundred thousand acres or more, worth more than four times what was paid for them, were thus in some instances obtained by a single company.

A peculiar feature of this abuse was the open way in which these transactions were conducted. Members of Congress from western states were indifferent. Some even maintained that the practice offered a good way for their constituents to make a few dollars by exercising their "citizenship rights." By 1900, reports of special agents sent out by the Department of the Interior demonstrated the extent of the thievery by which eastern lumber companies had obtained vast areas in Oregon, Washington, Idaho, and California under laws intended to promote the settlement of homesteaders. The secretary of the interior, Ethan Allan Hitchcock, thought the solution to "the greatest scandal of our time" was the repeal of all land laws except the Homestead Act. A Canadian commission sent to the United States to study the land laws reached the same conclusion.

Borah joined those who condemned the Timber and Stone Act as "a piece of infamy," because it forced a man to swear that he did not take the land on speculation, which was construed by the Department of Justice to mean that he must not take it "with a view to selling it." Speculation was one thing, said Borah, but a perfectly legitimate business transaction was quite another. Every man who buys a commodity for the purpose of selling it is not, in any strict legal sense, a speculator. These timber claims were perfectly legitimate, and it was not within the province of Congress to stigmatize as criminal those engaged in making them.[1] He said:

There is not a man in the department of the Interior . . . but who knows full well that ninety-nine men or women out of a hundred take up these

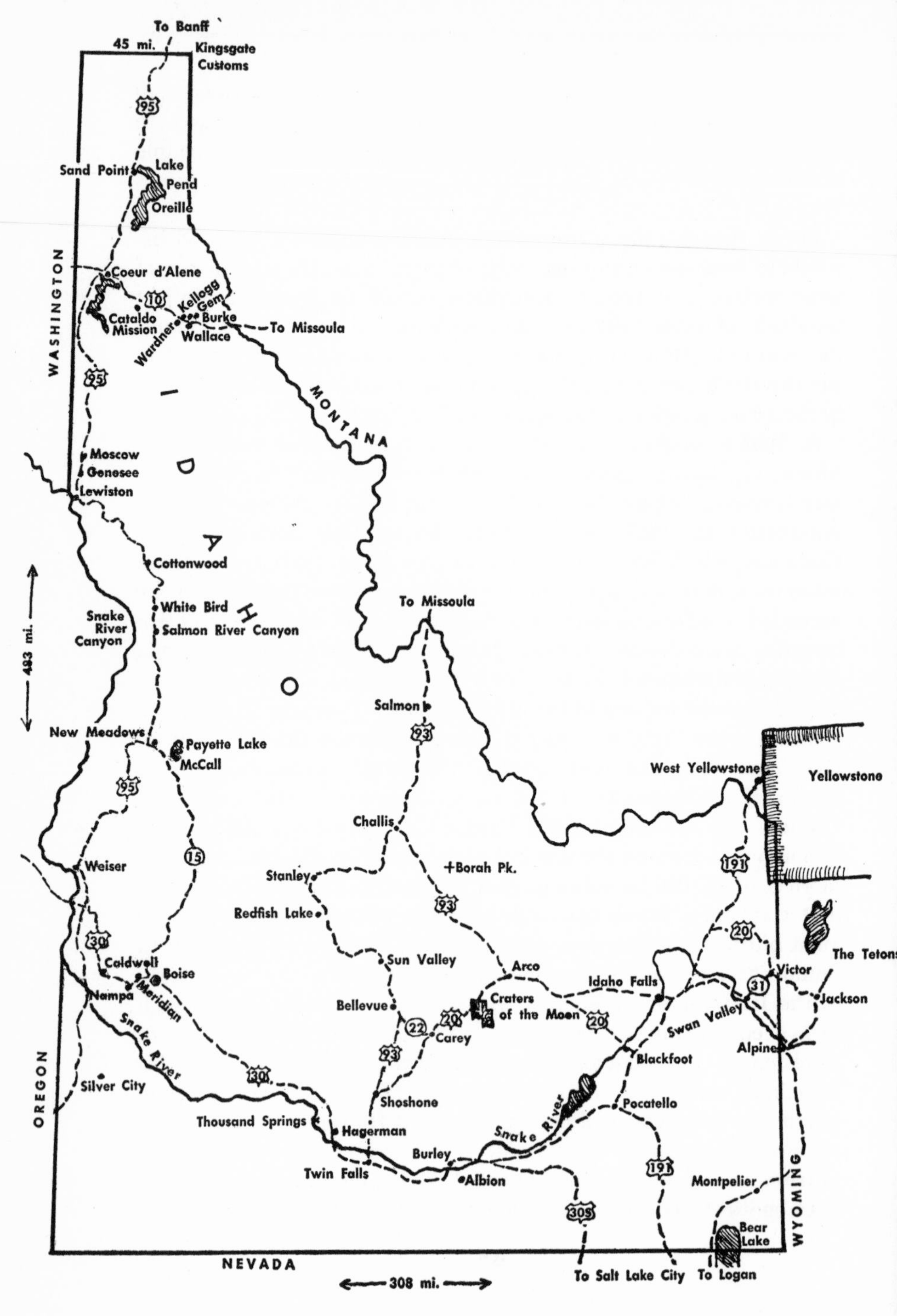

To Banff
45 mi.
Kingsgate Customs
95
Sand Point
Lake
Pend
Oreille
WASHINGTON
Coeur d'Alene
10
Cataldo Mission
Kellogg
Gem
Burke
Wardner
Wallace
To Missoula
95
MONTANA
I
D
A
H
O
Moscow
Genesee
Lewiston
Cottonwood
White Bird
Salmon River Canyon
Snake River Canyon
483 mi.
To Missoula
Salmon
93
New Meadows
Payette Lake
McCall
95
West Yellowstone
Yellowstone
Challis
15
Weiser
Stanley
+Borah Pk.
191
Redfish Lake
93
30
20
The Tetons
Sun Valley
Caldwell
Boise
Arco
Idaho Falls
Victor
Meridian
Nampa
Bellevue
Craters of the Moon
31
Jackson
22
20
20
Swan Valley
Carey
Alpine
Blackfoot
93
Snake River
30
OREGON
Silver City
Shoshone
Pocatello
Thousand Springs
Hagerman
Snake River
Burley
191
Twin Falls
Albion
Montpelier
WYOMING
305
Bear Lake
NEVADA
To Salt Lake City
To Logan
308 mi.

claims with no other view than to sell them as soon as they get title. Notwithstanding this knowledge, the government continues to issue final receipts and thus connives in the doing of that which it afterwards seeks to visit upon someone as a fraud.[2]

Borah thought the government should establish a rule which would at least not entrap men into wrongful acts. He admitted that some instances of actual wrongdoing should be punished, but in hundreds of other instances the people would not think of taking the land unlawfully. "I do not justify any man in wrongdoing, but I say this deliberately, that the government has blundered shamefully in the administration of the Stone and Timber Law."[3]

In 1902 a company was organized by James Barber and Sumner Moon, who held large interests in the Northwestern Company. Former Governor Steunenberg of Idaho sold out his interests in other enterprises and took shares in what became the Barber Lumber Company, which built a large mill on a new site, Barber, about five miles from Boise and had plans for another. By 1905 its capital stock exceeded a million dollars.[4] Lands acquired by entrymen for this company were deeded to three dummies designated in 1902, 1903, and 1904. Additional deeds, about two hundred forty in all, were recorded at the request of the attorney for the company in 1903 and 1904. Between April and July the three dummies deeded all their lands, over fifty thousand acres in Ada County alone, to the Barber Lumber Company.

Borah was attorney for the Barber Company from 1903. Frank Steunenberg drew on the account of the company as agent, received more than $30,000 for services, and was said to have retained Borah as his attorney. Borah had nothing to do with deeds filed prior to 1903, but he passed on some deeds of entry, along with the deeds of dummy trustees to the company after that date.[5]

The land frauds division of the attorney general's office, which had been strenuously active in exposing frauds in the western states since 1900, began an investigation in Idaho in 1905. On March 11, 1907, while the Haywood trial was pending, a federal grand jury convened at Boise. Its proceedings were kept secret, but rumors spread rapidly that the jury had voted twelve to ten for the indictment (under Section 5440 of the Revised Statutes) of more than one hundred men implicated in timber frauds and that Borah was among them.[6] Frank Steunenberg, already deceased, was included. It was rumored that during the Coeur d'Alene riots Steunenberg had gone to Spokane and accepted a bribe of $50,000 from the Mine Owners' Association. His connection with the Barber Lumber Company was given publicity, and dark hints were circulated of timber frauds perpetrated by him and his friends.

It seemed more than a coincidence that both the murdered man and the prosecutor in the trial of his assassins should be indicted on the eve of the Haywood trial. Christopher P. Connolly, a newspaperman, later published an affidavit in which a reputable citizen of Salt Lake City swore that shortly after the grand jury adjourned, one of the attorneys for Moyer, Haywood, and Pettibone told him that the indictment of Borah had cost his clients $15,000.[7]

Governor Gooding, who was determined that Moyer, Haywood, and Pettibone should be vigorously prosecuted, declared that the indictment was part of a scheme of the Western Federation of Miners to keep Borah out of the prosecution of Haywood and asked President Roosevelt to have Borah's trial postponed until after the Haywood trial. Roosevelt acquiesced, and the delay had an important effect upon subsequent proceedings. The prosecuting attorney in Boise was loud in his objections to postponement and in his assertions that if he could get Borah in court, he would convict him.

In January 1907 Borah had been elected by the Idaho legislature as United States senator. He was to take his seat on December 4. The question now was whether he would go to the national Capitol or to the penitentiary! He probably knew by the end of March that his name appeared in the indictment. He wrote in April to the Barber Company's attorney in St. Paul:

> As I telegraphed you . . . the rumor is that Barber, yourself, Carson, Moon, Chapman, myself and all other relatives and kith and kin of each and all whom they can hear of have been indicted. I am satisfied it is true although they have refused to exhibit their indictments. Of course you know how utterly villainous this is in view of the exceptionally strict integrity with which the Barber Lumber Company did business in this state. I am satisfied we will have to confront it.[8]

It soon became evident that the indictment was part of a well-contrived plot by Borah's political enemies to blacken his name and deprive him of his new political honors. He was being attacked by a small but powerful clique of federal officials, who probably never anticipated that he would be convicted but fully expected that the suspicions aroused would ruin his political future. The group consisted of three prominent men: James H. Beatty, Norman Ruick, and Ruel Rounds. They had all opposed Borah at the Pocatello convention in 1906. Beatty, a federal judge who had reached retirement age and was about to resign from office, had been an aspirant for the senatorial nomination but lost to Borah. He had openly criticized the methods Borah used to secure the nomination for himself. Explaining the indictment to a friend, Borah wrote: "We had retiring from the bench a superannuated imbecile who was filled with venom and spleen over his political disappointments which no one ever took seriously except himself."[9] Norman Ruick was United States district attorney, an ideal position in which to secure the indictment against Borah. Ruel Rounds was the United States marshal, who stood ready to select a jury packed with Borah's enemies; Beatty would be the trial judge while Ruick prosecuted the defendant.

Previously Ruick had been indicted for perjury and extortion but escaped trial on a technicality. One of the first to appreciate the value of the timberlands in the Boise Basin, he organized a railroad company which planned a line from Boise through this wild, undeveloped country to the timberlands; after the Barber Lumber Company was organized, he approached it to promote his railroad scheme, having already secured a franchise and right of way. He wanted a twenty-year contract for hauling timber and suggested methods by which the company could acquire still larger tracts in the Boise Basin. E. E. Garrett, registrar of the land office at Boise, was a director in Ruick's railroad corporation, a fact which he did not allow to escape the representatives of the Barber Lumber Company. One of the first duties of Borah, as attorney for the company, was to pass upon Ruick's proposition. He rejected it. Scarcely six months later Ruick secured an indictment against the company from a federal grand jury.

Grand juries, under the law, had to consist of not less than sixteen nor more than twenty-three persons. At the suggestion of Attorney Ruick, Judge Beatty issued a venire for twenty-three. Shortly thereafter Marshal Rounds asserted that he was unable to find most of the persons whose names were on the list. Oscar King Davis, a noted newspaperman covering the Haywood trial for the New York *Times*, later was ordered by Theodore Roosevelt to make a private investigation, which revealed that all the men whom the marshal said he could not find might have been reached by telephone in one afternoon.[10]

The original venire of grand jurors was drawn from the regular jury list, but the special venire to fill an incomplete panel was left to be selected by the United States marshal from the body of citizens. In this instance Judge Beatty ordered Marshal Rounds to summon ten additional jurors in place of those reported "not found." By a singular coincidence the ten jurors who responded were friends of the Beatty faction which had fought Borah at Pocatello. Ruick was reported to have exerted undue influence on the grand jury, but at that time no one, least of all Borah, had any knowledge of what was being done.

When ex-Governor McConnell was questioned by reporters on the rumors concerning his son-in-law, he replied: "The truth is that Senator Borah has been an attorney for a lumber company. He has never taken any timber land himself and he has seen to it that neither his wife nor his secretary took any. He is a lawyer of high standing at the bar, and it is not to be presumed that he advised his clients to violate the law."[11] The socialist press took another view:

> Borah, the indicted Senator, is the central figure in the prosecution of Moyer, Haywood and Pettibone. Borah was awarded the senatorship because of his acting the dirty tool for the mine owners in the kidnapping conspiracy . . . The part of the evidence we already have is sufficient to prove him a pervert and a moral monster. Yes, it is Senator Borah, the Joe Bailey of Idaho, the Silver Bugle of the mountains, the town bull of Boise.[12]

The delay in Borah's case caused by the Haywood trial enabled Oscar King Davis and other newspapermen to make their investigation for Theodore Roosevelt before the Haywood trial ended, showing how the grand jury had been packed. Roosevelt was urged to take action on Borah's behalf but hesitated because of the possible effect on the Haywood trial: "I could do no worse thing for the cause of justice in this particular . . . case than to seem to shield a United States Senator . . . concerned in the prosecution."[13] He merely intimated he would send a special investigator and if Davis' charges were substantiated, he would dismiss Ruick. His one official act at this point was to order Attorney General Bonaparte to replace Judge Beatty with a temporary appointee, Frank Dietrich.[14]

Borah appeared only mildly concerned, but he realized the gravity of the situation and the danger to his position. He made an effort to rally support from every quarter possible. One politician suggested a meeting ". . . at Boise or some other convenient point with a delegation of eight or ten others of the best Republicans over the State . . . to formulate a plan of action and proceed to Washington at once . . ."[15] From Washington, Senator Jonathan Bourne of Oregon wrote: "I make it a point to see the President almost daily and can assure you that this talk of your enemies has in no way weakened the confidence that the President feels in your integrity. He this morning authorized me to say that absolute justice should be done you and that he would stand by you for everything that is right . . . On account of references herein I think you will see the justice of my request to destroy this letter after perusal."[16]

Replying to Bourne, Borah wrote that he would not presume for a moment to go to the President for a favor. "I know him too well for that." However, he added:

> It seems to me that before the indictment is brought out and I am compelled to submit to this humiliation before the public that I might be permitted to have a word with an unprejudiced Department of Justice. I do not know what they have proved, but I do know that there is not a single fact but what I am ready to meet and explain and give in full details concerning the same.

More than once, in this letter and others, Borah seemed to reduce the question of his guilt to the fact that he stood to gain nothing from the Barber Lumber Company's dealings: "I have not a thing in the world, so far as I am individually concerned, to conceal. I have a check to cover every dollar paid out by me for the company. I have my written opinions delivered to the company under what conditions they could buy. I have my letters which anyone can see." Borah was among those who were instrumental in preventing the grand jury from seeing the books of the Barber Company. He told Bourne he had visited Secretary of the Interior Garfield and reminded him that he intended to retire as legal counsel from all those companies which might have business before the department, among them the Barber Lumber Company. Returning to Boise, he was called in to consultation with the new legal counsel employed and concluded that the government was "attempting to get those books solely for the purpose of preparing a civil suit to attack the title . . . as lawyers we had to judge of our rights. We did not believe they were entitled to the books."

Borah went on to show, however, that the grand jury did get the books, so far as his record with the company was concerned. "They also got . . . all my bank accounts . . . I asked permission in addition . . . to show my checks which I was denied before the grand jury."[17] In another letter Borah wrote: "Of course, there is so much feeling . . . politics, corruption in the matter that they will do anything in the world they can but I am not fearful of the result. They will never trace a dishonest dollar to my credit."[18]

Calvin Cobb, owner of the Idaho *Statesman,* was another Borah ally; however, the files of the Department of Justice show that he had close ties with the managers of the Barber Lumber Company and had used his influence for it in various ways. His son, Lyon, worked for the company, and a considerable amount of the bonds of the *Statesman* company were held either by the Barber Lumber Company or its principals.[19] Immediately after the grand jury returned its indictments, Cobb left Idaho, hurried to Washington, and had several talks with the President.[20] Shortly afterwards federal Judge Marsden Burch released a statement that the federal courts stand apart from the Department of Justice, which cannot interfere with their procedure. All indictments in Idaho would have to take their normal course. Borah himself shortly called on Roosevelt in Washington, but merely "to pay his respects."

Borah made his strongest appeal for help to his old college friend, William Allen White, who wrote in reply:

> As I see your situation, it is this: a vindication from the president by a dismissal of the proceedings, or a verdict by a jury, is needed to give you the confidence you believe is needed to continue in public life. Of course, if you were to have a trial anywhere else in the world than in Idaho just at this time, I should say take the jury, win your verdict and then go with me to T. R. and appeal to him as a man to give you the

recognition you have a right to expect. I know Roosevelt well enough to believe absolutely that in a month he would make his confidence in you so plain to Washington, and to Idaho that in a year the whole episode would receed [*sic*] into the distant past, and in five years would be only a memory.

White concluded that Borah's chief danger was the possibility someone who hated him would "hang" the jury. "The first thing to do is for me to try with all the earnestness I can to show the President how unjust it is to force you to trial on a matter that can be explained to him and to the attorney general [Bonaparte] . . . But I am satisfied that the attorney general is your stumbling block. Ruick and the judge [Beatty] made an impression . . . on . . . Bonaparte, I fear, but I have heard that he does not consider the evidence sufficient for a conviction. That, I believe, is the Washington situation . . . it is embarrassing all around . . . But I am willing, if you think best . . . to try a strong direct appeal to the President . . . I do want to help and I want you to lean on me."[21]

It appears from what Borah wrote to White and Bourne that he really wanted an exoneration from Roosevelt. Failing this, he was determined to go ahead, stand trial, secure an acquittal, and resign his position as senator. He poured his heart out to White:

Just entering the senate and public life I feel that I am on slippery ground where hundreds have slipped and fallen, and I don't know! I feel that I cannot succeed in public life if I am to enter with the condemnation of . . . Roosevelt's great administration upon me . . . though I should have the verdict of a jury it would be of little avail in my struggle for position, in the face of the fact that the administration thought me sufficiently guilty to deserve prosecution. The public could well say why did they prosecute him if they did not believe him guilty? For everybody knows that the government does not prosecute men unless the Department believes them guilty . . . I feel if I cannot satisfy the President and the Attorney General of my absolute innocence that I must resign from the Senate. Of course, I will not resign until a jury passes on the matter but will do so then.

Borah then appealed to White:

> Good friend, what do you think? Are you so situated that you could see the President within the next few weeks for me and find out what they propose to do? As I have said before, I have nothing to conceal from them nor do I want immunity. I simply want to satisfy them of my innocence and then I want a complete exoneration. Don't you think I am entitled to it?[22]

Borah's thinking was a little confused, for he was asking special treatment from Washington. He could not understand why, if the President believed him honest (as his friends repeatedly assured him he did), his career should be jeopardized by a federal trial.

After the Haywood verdict in July Borah made a hurried trip to Manitou, Colorado, the summer home of William Allen White, and appeared at his door one morning looking wan and anxious. He protested his innocence and told White his enemies in Boise had him framed. After rehearsing the facts, he asked his friend to go to the President at once and speak for him.[23] Although he was busy writing, White dropped everything and wired Oyster Bay for an appointment. Accompanied by James Hawley, Borah's counsel, and Christopher P. Connolly, a Montana lawyer who had been in Boise conducting a private investigation, he traveled to Oyster Bay for a conference on August 9, 1907. Others present were Attorney General Bonaparte; William Loeb, secretary to the President; John W. Yerkes, a Washington lawyer consulted by Borah; and Joseph G. Dudley, lawyer for the Barber Lumber Company.

Almost the entire day was spent reviewing Borah's case. Walter Johnson recounts that White first asked T. R. to have the government drop the entire proceedings against Borah.[24] However, before the talks had proceeded five minutes, Roosevelt decided that it was unwise to dismiss the action, not only for Borah's sake but because the claim would later be made that the case had been dismissed to secure his future support in the Senate.

As White suspected, Bonaparte proved antagonistic to Borah. All he knew of the circumstances involved came to him in the reports of federal officers in Boise. He argued that as an attorney for a lumber company Borah knew that at least some of the claims had been bargained for in advance and believed he had taken affidavits to shield himself against a future accusation of conspiracy. If such affidavits were proof of guilt, Connolly interjected, then every lawyer in the West was guilty. He explained what the confidential relationship of an attorney means and said that any lawyer might become entangled in the affairs of his clients with the very best of intentions without any stain upon his own character.[25]

Roosevelt finally instructed Bonaparte to have Borah severed from the original indictment and tried separately. He was to have an immediate trial at the next term of court in September. Borah's friends received the promise that Judge Dietrich and not Marshal Rounds would draw the jury for the trial. Roosevelt also gave his word that grand jurymen who would make affidavits as to what Ruick said to them about Borah would be offered immunity. If any improper act was proven, Ruick would be removed. White had the President's word that if Borah was acquitted, he would write the senator a letter for the people of Idaho that would leave no doubt as to his attitude.[26] The President thought that the trial might be so conducted that the judge would prevent the packing of the jury. This was a most important point, but Connolly recalled that Attorney General Bonaparte was not quite sure just what power the President or the federal judge would have in this respect.[27]

Borah was sorely disappointed in the results of the meeting. He evidently entertained hopes for a dismissal; Davis tried to console him by pointing out how effective a verdict of not guilty would be: ". . . it will be about the best that could be done."[28] Borah was unconvinced. He maintained that there was a direct connection between the conspiracy to ruin him and the Haywood case, although the government found no evidence to support this contention. Borah wrote: ". . . we have proof entirely satisfactory to us that Mr. Ruick has been handed a nice sum of money by the Western Federation of Miners to bring this thing on at this particular time . . ."[29] Borah hired Pinkerton detectives and had Ruick "watched."

When Ruick received instructions from Washington to prepare Borah's case for September regardless of the difficulties involved, he protested vigorously and called the whole proceeding rankly unjust to himself. Whereas he had earlier boasted he would convict Borah in an hour if he could only get him into court, he now complained that his witnesses were scattered, that it would take months to get them together, and that he needed more evidence.

When more pressure was put on him, he wired the attorney general suggesting that the indictment be dismissed.[30]

This raised grave questions regarding Ruick's sincerity. It appeared that he was maneuvering to strengthen the impression that the administration would intervene on Borah's behalf. Roosevelt became impatient and wrote Bonaparte: "I am not in the least surprised to learn that Ruick intended to state in open court, when dismissing the indictment against Senator Borah, that I was responsible for the inability to prosecute him . . ." It would be awkward to bring in a new prosecutor at this late date, but it seemed imperative to get rid of Ruick, whom Roosevelt called a "sharp scamp, guilty of trickery all along."[31]

Borah had good reason for feeling downcast. As late as August 30 he had seen no copy of the indictment; he feared that even one unfriendly juryman would hang the jury and that his enemies would do what he personally knew they had tried to do earlier—induce someone to testify falsely against him. He spent sleepless nights turning these dreadful thoughts over and over again. At the very least he thought he should receive a copy of the indictment and a prompt trial. "There is a decent way," he said, "to prosecute even a man charged with land stealing."

Actually he had good friends who stood by him. In addition to those in Idaho, Senators Spooner and Bourne were untiring in their efforts in his behalf. White, Connolly, Davis, Yerkes, Dudley, and even Loeb came to his aid more than once and with useful results. Former Senator Dubois gave at least the appearance of friendly support.[32] Bourne was one of many friends who wrote Borah not to resign his seat. Except for the mental strain incident to prosecuting Haywood, Bourne was convinced such an idea would never have entered his mind. "Such action," he wrote, "would be suicidal . . . misconstrued by your friends and distorted by your enemies. Whenever an individual knows in his own heart that he has done nothing wrong, he should realize that time will inevitably rectify any temporary accusation and procure . . . the admiration and sympathy . . . of all his fellow men whose friendship and respect are worth enjoying."[33]

A letter from William H. Taft, then traveling through Yellowstone Park, reveals that Borah solicited his help. Taft wrote: ". . . I have seen enough . . . to be convinced that you have been made the object of an outrageous conspiracy . . . I highly appreciate your delicacy in not coming to see me, although I should have been very glad if you had, because I should like to express to you in person what I feel in respect to the matter."[34] The kindhearted Taft favored dropping the case against Borah, but his advice was not accepted. He predicted acquittal for Borah and "a most useful and therefore most successful career in the Senate."

Though Borah may not have realized it at the time, under Roosevelt's personal direction the entire court machinery was set in fresh motion at Boise. Orders went to Judge Dietrich to empanel an impartial jury and begin an immediate trial. Sylvester Rush of Omaha and Marsden Burch of Denver agreed to assist in the prosecution as special counsel, along with Miles Johnson and F. M. Goodwin. Judge Dietrich was replaced by Judge Edward Whitson of Spokane. All the other court officers came from districts outside Idaho and, as Davis said, the stage was set for a square, honest, and disinterested trial of the case.[35]

Borah's attorneys were James Hawley, Alfred A. Fraser, a former associate, and Samuel L. Tipton, all of Boise. The trial was set for September 23, 1907. By the twenty-fourth the empaneling of a jury, mostly farmers and stockmen, was completed.

Marsden Burch made the opening statement for the government. The trial proceedings produced some of the strangest witnesses that ever took part in a prosecution. Into the limelight came Albert Klanop Nugent, who on cross-examination by the prosecution admitted perjuring himself in taking out timber claims. He also asserted that he was promised immunity by a federal officer if he would testify; that he had, at the request of a federal officer, sworn out a complaint against a man he did not know; and finally that his understanding was that he should swear to any complaint against any person regardless of his knowledge of the person's guilt. Then he swore that he had forgotten with which official he had made the bargain! He admitted that he did not know Borah and also that he knew nothing connecting him with land frauds. The government's second witness also acknowledged committing perjury in taking out timber claims.[36]

Borah permitted the prosecution to manage its case practically as it pleased, declining to cross-examine. The government called forty witnesses and the defense cross-examined only two, entering no objections on direct examination, allowing a vast amount of wholly irrelevant evidence, and omitting the motion to dismiss, which the judge evidently expected. After the case was before the court two or three days, Judge Whitson leaned over the bench and said to the prosecuting attorney: "When are you going to connect the defendant with any of this?"

Hawley surprised the jury by calling Borah to the stand as the only witness for the defense. He made a good witness and explained frankly, but with some show of feeling, all his transactions with the Barber Lumber Company. He explained that he had become general counsel for the company January 1, 1903; that he had known Steunenberg fairly well from the time he first came to the state, and after 1899 intimately; but that he had never acted as attorney for Steunenberg.

He declared that he had nothing to do with the timber entries of 1901 and 1902. He knew that the company wanted to get as much timber in the Boise Basin as possible and was using scrip to get it, but Steunenberg had charge of this and Borah knew only what Steunenberg told him. John Blake had desk room in Borah's office at that time and attended to some of the entries for the Barber people. Borah admitted that the recording of deeds was handled through his office but asserted that he never made any deeds for entrymen. He established the rule that no purchases should be made until the patent was received. He had no stock in the company, and his compensation had always been on a fixed salary basis; he made no timber entries, nor did his secretary or any relative. The matter of examining and recording deeds was routine, handled by clerks and stenographers in his office. He said fictitious names were used because company officers told him if it became known that a corporation was in the field, the price of lands would be doubled. Under cross-examination by Attorney Rush, he began to tell about the railroad scheme Ruick proposed but he was not allowed to finish his story. A ripple of laughter in the courtroom caused Judge Whitson to threaten to clear the court.

After Borah's examination Hawley astonished everyone by announcing: "We rest, your honor." The defense waived its argument and the government began summing up. The jury, which received Judge Whitson's instructions in writing, was out less than fifteen minutes. The verdict was handed to the clerk of the court, who after droning through the long list of men named on the original indictment, at last read: "We, the jury, find the defendant NOT GUILTY." The crowd broke into loud cheers, which Judge Whitson made little effort to quiet, mildly remarking: "I assume you all know that your conduct is highly improper. I will not attempt, however, to punish you for contempt of court." So ended the Borah trial.

On the streets outside the courthouse a parade was forming. By eight o'clock that evening Main Street was crowded with people from the corner of Sixth Street to the Idanha Hotel. A fire alarm was turned in, and Boise's horse-drawn engines clamored up side streets to join the procession, as did the town militia. Bells clanged; steam whistles shrieked. The marchers were laden with noisemakers, Roman candles, firecrackers, torpedoes, and red fire. Amid intermittent explosions they moved up the main street, passing Borah's office behind a brass band playing "Hail to the Chief," which was almost drowned out by the shouting. A group carried Borah on their shoulders and deposited him on the steps of the Idanha Hotel, where he spoke briefly from the balcony. Thanking them, he said:

> The humiliation which I suffered no tongue can tell. I felt that the State which had honored me had been brought into conspicuous shame. I felt that the loyal friends who had supported me had been compromised. For these reasons this ordeal has been enough for any man to bear. Now, if I can very quickly do something to honor my state and gratify my friends, it will indeed be happiness to me. Again, I thank you. You cannot realize how full my heart is and how devotedly I would dedicate myself to your interests and . . . welfare.[37]

The demonstration, with street dancing and fireworks, lasted far into the night. Boise had been waiting for a chance to celebrate, and this was it. As William Allen White wrote: "The whole town got gloriously drunk." It was a great night. Nobody paid for a drink that night except Borah, and every bar in town was crowded except the one his enemies frequented.

White tried to persuade Borah to write an account of the case for *McClure's*, for the facts had been garbled in many eastern newspapers. The Kansas editor wrote:

> . . . You are going to go considerably farther in this world than a sage-brush senator ordinarily goes. It may be a little disagreeable for you to have this thing rasped into your raw back just now, but in twenty years . . . when you are a candidate for vice-president or when the Senate committee on nominations is looking up your record to confirm you as . . . member of the cabinet or ambassador to England, it will be pleasant for you to refer your friends and your enemies to the final decision of the fourth estate of this government as recorded in *McClure's* magazine for January, 1908.[38]

Borah took his Senate seat in December. The following June Ruick was removed from office, and the government requested the resignation of Ruel Rounds.[39]

On the whole Borah had conducted himself well throughout the trying ordeal. His actions were certainly not those of a guilty man. He interposed no technicalities and refused to make any use—as his counsel believed he might have done—of the statute of limitations. His conduct was in marked contrast to that of the defendants in the Oregon land-fraud cases, where lawyers resorted to all kinds of tricks and a number of important witnesses suddenly disappeared.

From the purely legal standpoint, obviously no evidence was adduced at the trial to show that Borah was aware that the timber claims, acquired in 1901 before he became attorney for the Barber Lumber Company, were fraudulent. Nor was there any evidence to show that the deeds which he placed on record for his clients were tainted with fraud. If Borah was a part of a land-fraud conspiracy, it was not shown in the government's case. The evidence regarding titles that merely passed through his office was too meager to convict him. The government never had a case against Borah, and the Department of Justice might as well have dismissed the indictment against him. Those responsible for the indictment suffered far more than Borah, as there was no doubt in anyone's mind that they acted out of sheer partisanship and personal hatred.

The question whether Borah was in any way morally guilty is more difficult. He must have known the Barber Lumber Company bought a quantity of tainted scrip and was acting in defiance of the law. As the company's attorney, he could plead his privilege in that capacity. His position as counsel divested him of any criminal responsibility. From the very beginning he emphasized a lack of financial interest in the company's schemes, and his plea was largely successful because neither he nor his wife had ever owned any stock in the company.[40] However, was his record morally unsmirched?

Shortly after the trial Assistant Attorney Burch, chief of the land-frauds division in the West, enumerated the major reasons why he thought the government had lost its case against Borah. First of all, Borah's personality counted. His wide acquaintance and strong personal following were very important in saving him from conviction; he knew nearly all of the jurymen, and some of them were his personal friends. Once the prosecution had exhausted its challenges, it had no alternative but to accept the talesmen named. Borah, renowned as a brilliant trial lawyer, suave, eloquent, and magnetic, had just finished his campaign for the senatorship, in which he had shown his flair for practical politics. He was "a good mixer," equally at home in church or saloon. In particular, he was the pride of Boise —the town's first citizen and its leading attorney.

Moreover, the notion prevailed in the West that a lawyer could do almost anything he desired. People had the idea that he was like a father confessor in the Roman Catholic church, privileged to protect confidences (the matter of privilege is actually based on old English common law, which grants the right of silence to clergymen, lawyers, and physicians). Borah was hired by the company at a very high salary, Burch charged, because of his ability to advise the company as to the best way the law could be evaded. The law being plain, no high-priced attorney was necessary if the intention was to abide by it.

In the third place, there was a prevailing belief, distinctly favorable to the man on trial, that it was perfectly legitimate to beat the government out of public lands. Uncle Sam was viewed as a powerful absentee landlord whose benevolence was by no means proved and might well be doubted.[41] The practice had been winked at for over a century. Whereas it was wrong to steal from an individual (lynching was the punishment for horse theft), larceny of government timber was an altogether different matter. So many people were involved in these thefts and the pioneers were so accustomed to taking what they needed that they could hardly condemn even the men who took egregious quantities.

It was also generally believed that the Barber Lumber Company was a very wealthy concern which intended to erect mammoth mills near Boise, giving hundreds employment. Finally, the proximity of the case to the Haywood trial, in which Borah so brilliantly distinguished himself, also put the government at a disadvantage. First the prosecutors were forced to hold their case in abeyance until Haywood was tried, and then they were told to prosecute swiftly when their case was in no proper shape.[42] However, this summary of reasons for Borah's acquittal has a distinctly ex parte flavor. The principal reason was that the government case was prepared by men with mixed motives, in part improper, and thus lacked strength.

The government spent thousands of dollars and employed an army of lawyers who prepared tons of transcripts in their civil and criminal suits against the Barber Lumber Company and the Kettenbach bankers of Lewiston, but by 1909 the indictments against Barber, Moon, et al. were all dismissed. The statute of limitations had run out. They resumed their operations at once in the big mills along the Boise River. Borah came out of the whole affair with enhanced credit and went to the Senate in December 1907 with a prestige which is granted to few men in so short a time. The Lewiston *Tribune* summed up the episode when it said:

> Mr. Borah has won other hard fights, he may have others to win yet, but there is none that can mean so much as this has.[43]

VI Borah Goes to Washington

. . . The Great West nursed him on her rugged
knee.
The strength of virgin forests braced his mind;
The hush of spacious prairies stilled his soul.
Up from the log cabin to the Capitol,
One fire was on his spirit, one resolve—
To send the keen axe to the root of wrong,
Clearing a free way from the feet of God.
—Edward Markham

In March 1907 just before the Haywood trial Borah went to Washington "to look over the ground" and present his credentials. He visited the ornate Senate chamber and saw its green carpet, mahogany desks (each one with its cuspidor), waste basket, and chair with leather seat and back. He saw the galleries with their niches containing busts of past vice-presidents and the rostrum with its center chair for the president of the Senate. Soon he would be a part of all this. When Gilson Gardiner asked him what he thought of it, his cryptic reply was "bully."[1]

In Washington Borah was an object of interest and curiosity with his ten-gallon hat and quick step, which George Ade once described as "the walk of a man going for the doctor." He told reporters that as far as he was concerned, his state came first. "A senator is the voice of the state in an assembly of states," he said. "On general matters, the voice of Idaho, as far as I determine it, shall be for what a great majority of the people want. And by the people I mean the People, and not the associated special interests."[2] Already he was talking like a Progressive.

The first news that greeted him in the capital was a headline proclaiming his indictment in Idaho. It was a depressing prelude to his career. While government officials investigating land frauds were predicting that Borah would never take his Senate seat, Senator Spooner of Wisconsin went on record saying: "Mark my words. Borah is destined to be one of the great men not only of the Senate but of the country. Mind that you keep your eye on him."[3]

Borah returned to Idaho to begin the prosecution of Haywood, to be followed by the criminal proceedings against Moyer and Pettibone. During these months Mrs. Borah was busy supervising the packing of their belongings preliminary to moving to Washington. She came east in the fall of 1907 and set up house in Stoneleigh Court, a quiet, attractive apartment hotel with a rear view overlooking the wooded grounds of a convent. They celebrated Thanksgiving together just before his departure for Idaho. Mary Borah spent her first Christmas in Washington alone amid unfamiliar surroundings. It was a lonely beginning.

A year later the Borahs moved to apartment No. 21 at 2139 Wyoming Avenue, where they were to remain until 1930 when they acquired the larger apartment at 2101 Connecticut Avenue, which became their permanent residence. They chose Washington's fashionable northwest which already had the district's largest population and the most picturesque scenery. The landscape is full of variety. Great woods crown the summits of steep slopes, concealing the ravines and leaning over the brawling waters of Rock Creek, which falls into the Potomac a little farther south. In the park, reminiscent of Boise, Borah spent many hours walking or horseback riding along the winding paths.

In 1907 Washington was not yet the ten square miles of massive buildings and wide avenues visitors today behold, but there was much talk of expansion. Potomac Park, now a place of beauty, was still a swamp. There were as yet no Senate and House office buildings. Borah's office was in the cavernous basement of the Capitol. The Union station had not yet replaced the dirty, grayish Baltimore and Ohio terminal. Many of the street-cars had trailers; their operators stood at their posts unprotected in all kinds of weather. Every hour of the day echoed to the sound of horses' hoofs.[4]

The Borahs sold their house in Boise after moving to Washington and never maintained another residence in Idaho. When they went home for the summer, they lived in a hotel or rented the home of a friend. Soon after arriving in the East, Borah bought an electric car for Mrs. Borah to drive about town. Later they owned a 1931 LaSalle and hired a chauffeur, but the senator rarely used the car and never learned to drive.

Their apartment was on the seventh floor. Into their seven rooms Mrs. Borah eventually crowded a collection of Chinese and Japanese treasures. They were the gifts of Chinese friends in Idaho or were purchased from antique dealers in Washington. Everywhere were elephants by the hundreds—even a procession of them over the front-door ledge. Old ebony chests, brocade coverings, lacquered boxes, Chinese paintings, scrolls, oriental screens, temple chairs, carved teakwood tables, and a grand piano which was decorated the year round with blossoms filled the spacious living room. All about were flowers and plants; canaries filled the air with their song. It was aesthetic and restful. After a while Mary Borah made friends and was content in her new home.

One large room, the senator's study, was crammed with books, pamphlets, autographed photographs of prominent people, and cartoons depicting some phases of his political activity. On Mrs. Borah's bedroom wall was a large oil portrait of her husband and in the living room a painting of Idaho's highest mountain peak, afterwards named Mount Borah. Mrs. Borah had the aid of one servant, Daisy.

The average day for Borah began at seven. Sometimes he went for a walk, but more often the day began with riding horseback, exercise to which he had been accustomed in the West. His doctor recommended this activity as an outlet for his enormous energy and a means of preserving his health. The best time to ride, he was told, was before breakfast. A glass of hot water, milk, or buttermilk before the ride, a shower and a hearty breakfast afterwards, was an ideal health program to follow. Riding in winter appealed to him just as much as in the spring or fall. In sun, rain, or snow Borah could be seen almost any morning on horseback cantering along the wooded paths and streams of Rock Creek Park. This solitary equestrian figure became almost as much a part of the Capital scene as the Washington monument. Since boyhood Borah had loved good horses; he understood and admired them. He evidently believed that to be a leader of men one must turn one's back on men: for him one horse was a pleasant change from four hundred congressmen. He rode a chestnut stallion called "Jester," whose picture, hanging in the study, was inscribed: "Jester is a philosopher." After this mount was sent to pasture, a Maryland breeder presented Borah with a registered bay called "Al Smith"; Borah renamed the horse "Governor."

Usually he rode alone. Few men in Washington could match his strenuous pace. Had T. R. lived, they might have become congenial riding companions. Occasionally Henry Stimson joined him for a canter near "Woodley," his Washington home; and when C. C. Anderson was in town from Boise, they rode together. In the twenties Sir Arthur Willert, Washington correspondent for the London *Times*, accompanied Borah and left us this description of his companion: "He looked as a priest dressed for riding might look. Black, broad brimmed hat, black leggings, and . . . almost black breeches or trousers with the gaiters around them . . . anyhow unusual and the outfit set into relief that white, round, rugged, stony set good-natured face."[5]

Returning to the apartment, he would don the fluffy boiled shirt of the era with its detachable collar, a bow tie, and a roomy dark sack suit, often with trousers and coat unmatched. His shoes were always highly polished, accenting his small feet. Gathering up books and papers, he boarded a streetcar for "the hill." He never used taxis. Sometimes Mrs. Borah would drive him to the Capitol in her "electric" and take her seat in the gallery to follow the debate. On the Senate floor her husband cut a dashing figure. His round, smooth-shaven face was topped by dark brown hair parted in the middle and brushed back smoothly from the forehead and temples, falling profusely to his neck, western style. He was slender in his early forties, and his intense blue eyes conveyed a remarkable vitality.

His office was staffed entirely with Idahoans, none of whom were relatives. He brought his secretary, Cora Rubin, from Boise; she served during his entire career. If he had a statement for the press, she rushed from his inner office after dictation and came back directly with ten or twelve carbon copies. As years passed, she became the Cerberus who guarded the office door. With unflinching eye and straight face she would profess her ignorance of his whereabouts. It was embarrassing when in the midst of her protests the senator would pop his head out of the office to ask her a question. Appointments were limited; for days at a stretch he made none at all.

Morning hours were spent in correspondence. At noon he went to the Senate, where his attendance record was excellent. Frequently he joined in the debate; and when he delivered a prepared speech, reporters scurried to the press gallery to hear him. After a light lunch in the Senate cafeteria (usually soup, crackers, milk, and apple pie) he would take a short walk in the small park on the Delaware Avenue side of the Capitol and return to his office for appointments or work on legislation, speeches, or committee assignments. In the early twenties he was a paying member of the Senate Exercise Club ($10 per month), which employed a good osteopath, physical director, and masseuse in the gymnasium on the first floor of the Senate office building. There is no indication, however, that Borah took pleasure from his daily routine of exercise. He seems to have made a calculated effort to observe medical advice and preserve his health. Beyond this, he wrote a friend: ". . . I do not get very much out of life . . . the keenest exhilaration I do get is in trying in a humble way to help in these great matters of public concern."[6]

Those who came to talk with him learned that he was no misanthrope. Life to this midwesterner of Calvinist upbringing was real and earnest with much to be done "before the grim reaper cometh." He was a serious man full of serious thoughts. His sympathies were broad and he had an elusive charm, more apparent in the early years of his political career than later. Temperamentally, it was his habit to dwell on the dangers that beset the republic, dangers sometimes very real, so that an hour in his presence was sometimes depressing. Yet he maintained a freshness and belligerence of spirit, which puzzled both those accustomed to the party yoke and those whom experience had taught the art of compromise. Borah disliked compromise and hated the discipline party organization entails, in spite of the respect he had for organization. He firmly believed a public man should not be bound by his party on big or fundamental issues; in this view he was nearer to the English M.P. than he would have been willing to admit.

Clinton Gilbert reports that a conservative Republican senator once told him: "Borah is the ablest man who has been in Congress in many years. He is the quickest man on his feet I have ever seen. No one else is his equal in debate." As chairman of the Foreign Relations Committee, Borah spent many hours of the day at his roll-top desk in a corner of the committee room, where he was but a few steps from the Senate chamber. There, or in his high-ceilinged office, he read, dictated letters (sometimes he received as many as four hundred a day), chatted with friends, consumed quarts of mineral water, ate his lunch, and napped on the leather divan. The committee aide, Patterson, brought his lunch to the committee room and guarded the door while he ate or slept. There were few congenial Senate luncheons for the sensitive Borah after he quarreled with Hiram Johnson of California, who allegedly called him "the spearless leader."[7]

Borah was long the most outstanding speaker in Congress, his oratory being both intellectual and emotional. Although he resembled Bryan in power and persuasiveness, he never allowed his heart to dominate his brain as the Nebraskan did. The Idahoan was adroit in debate; he argued but never quibbled. Always courteous, the fairness of his manner disarmed his adversary. He never stooped to ridicule, sarcasm, or abuse. His compelling logic and sound arguments were couched in the simplest of language. One of the secrets of his success as a debater came from his careful preparation of a rebuttal for the chief objections which might be brought against his position. Seldom did he gesticulate; when he did, a favorite gesture was the outstretched hand, palm upward. Of mannerism there was nothing. He stood quietly behind his desk and directed his sentences and the shafts of his dark glances at his adversary. At other times he faced the front of the chamber, addressing himself straight to the rostrum. Even his frequent "Mr. President" had a poetic lilt.

His preparation for a speech was extensive and complete. He began by exploring his subject through wide reading and correspondence. His great anti-League speech was based on information in letters from Albert Beveridge, Governor Stokes of New Jersey, James M. Beck, George Harvey, Frank Munsey, and Daniel Cohalan, to name but a few. He would gather notes from pamphlets, newspaper clippings, articles, general reading, and petitions; these were arranged in file envelopes for ready access. For his speeches he made outlines and used meager notes, rarely going to the trouble of preparing a manuscript except for special public addresses, and sometimes not even then. Once having prepared a Senate speech, he would await a moment when the trend of debate warranted his remarks. Much of his success was to be found in the felicity of his timing, and his protests often had an uncanny effectiveness in arousing popular support.

He had a prodigious memory. The rumble of his great voice resounded in the corridor of the office building as he committed a passage or quotation to memory. He also used such occasions to polish his enunciation. The models for his style were Burke, Pitt, Fox, Daniel Webster, Wendell Phillips, and Lincoln. He studied their oratorical works with care and adapted some of their allusions and exclamations to his own use. There were few thrills at the Capitol comparable to seeing and hearing Borah on the Senate floor. Word from the press gallery that "Borah is up" sent hordes of reporters scurrying to their perches and crowds of visitors to the gallery. People would wait outside the doors on the chance of getting the seat of someone obliged to leave. Alice Longworth often sat listening in the front row of the senators' private gallery. Mrs. Coolidge was there occasionally, e.g., when Borah spoke on Russia. Even a diplomat or two would venture into the gallery. It was a treat to hear him.

Idaho took a tremendous delight and pride in his success as an orator. To the folks back home a Borah performance was described, with slight exaggeration, as follows:

> Bill gets up on his feet in the Senate, tosses his head a mite, gives a sort of hitching twist to his hands as if his cuffs were too small for him or something like that, and says a few words about the last line of the fifth paragraph of the seventh section of the third whereas of the treaty between Poland and Afghanistan, and the next thing you know the Bank of England is hollering for help and Syria's sent an ultimatum to Tierra del Fuego.[8]

Before making a public address, Borah followed a few simple rules. He never worked on a speech the evening it was to be given. He ate a light supper and rested for an hour or so before speaking. When traveling, he always had his trousers pressed. After the speech had been delivered, he never could sleep within less than two hours. "It takes that time for me to cool off," he explained. Speeches were a burden, but evidently he enjoyed the stimulation of an enthusiastic audience. He confessed that he was ambitious to speak in every state of the Union.

Once during a Liberty Loan drive in World War I Borah was invited to the home of Mr. and Mrs. Robert Huse of Elizabeth, New Jersey, where he was to have dinner before his speech. The Huse household was agog for the occasion; the servants had polished the family silver and Mrs. Huse had supervised the preparation of an elaborate repast. The senator arrived around four in the afternoon and promptly announced that he wished to nap. He was shown to the guest room with its eighteenth-century, canopied four-poster bed, removed his coat and vest, lay down with his high shoes on, and fell asleep. This shocked the household, including the servants. At dinnertime he was awakened and after some polite conversation was escorted into the dining room where the roast was about to be served. He abruptly announced that he would take a shredded-wheat biscuit with hot water and no sugar. Such was his meal, and it made quite an impression on everyone present.[9]

As forensic displays, his speeches were far superior to the generality of those delivered in or out of the Senate at that time. No one could get the ear of America better than Senator Borah; he was listened to even when he was not understood, for there was in his speeches a genuine sincerity and idealism that has always appealed to the American heart. Americans are incurably fond of ideals, and Borah spoke to their faith in Washington, Jefferson, and Lincoln, or rather to that faith purged of material considerations.[10] It was the beacon of his soul, and Americans responded warmly to his appeal.

The days varied, but Borah generally left the Capitol around six. After dinner he shut himself in his study and spent the evening reading every kind of book and document that interested him. Rarely did he leave the apartment at night, preferring books to the busy social life of Washington; this Spartan style of living also safeguarded his health. Occasionally the Borahs attended a movie; he preferred westerns, especially if Bill Hart played the lead. He accepted few invitations to public affairs. This antipathy to social entertainment became so well-known that finally his name was removed from the White House guest list for all but the most important functions. Visitors from Idaho were sometimes entertained at the apartment, where Mrs. Borah capably assumed their social obligations.

Often Borah returned home laden with volumes borrowed from the Congressional Library. After 1920 his taste in reading ran toward foreign affairs. He made many additions to his own collection from the stores and stalls of Washington and maintained a steady diet of newspapers and periodicals as well. He took major

New York and Washington papers, numerous Idaho dailies and weeklies, and a few magazines such as the *Nation, Outlook,* and *New Republic,* while he sampled other important periodicals on the newsstands. A typical list of books he had on loan from the library at one time in April 1925 included:

Byrne, *Marco Polo;* Moore, *International Law;* Ghandi, *Freedom's Battle;* Gandhi, *His Life;* Rolland, *Mahatma Gandhi;* Nathan, *Renaissance of International Law;* Thayer, *John Marshall;* Gillette, *White House Cook Book* (for Mrs. Borah); Johnson, *American Foreign Relations;* Ashley, *Twice Fifty Years of Europe;* Lincoln, *Writings;* Jordan, *Stability of Truth;* Kipling, *Verses;* Beard, *The Supreme Court;* L'Espagnol, *World Struggle for Oil;* Price, *Truth about Allied Intervention;* Walling, *Russia's Message.*[11]

Borah had adapted himself well as a young man to the uproaring whimsies of a frontier community and then to official Washington, while keeping a firm rooting in the classical verities. Shyness and introspection fashioned him into an intellectual recluse. Contemporaries remarked that his mode of living bordered on the monastic. A scholar in politics, he took pleasure in reading and studying of the widest range and acquired the equivalent of the higher education denied him by poverty and illness. History, biography, the classics, and constitutional law provided a steady fare. He could quote from memory long passages of Shakespeare, Milton, and the Bible. After he came to Washington, he taught a young men's Bible class. His favorite passage was the scholar's creed John Quincy Adams read to his Harvard classes; Borah memorized it and often quoted it for friends:

At no hour of your life will the love of letters ever oppress you as a burden, or fail you as a resource. In the vain and foolish exultation of the heart, which the brighter prospects of life will sometimes excite, the pensive portress of science shall call you back to the sober pleasures of her holy cell. In the mortification of disappointment, her soothing voice shall whisper serenity and peace. In social converse with the mighty dead of ancient days, you will never smart under the galling sensation of dependence upon the mighty living of the present age; and in your struggles with the world, should a crisis ever occur, when even friendship may deem it prudent to desert you, when even your country may seem ready to abandon herself and you, when even priest and levite shall come and look on you, and pass by on the other side, seek refuge, my unfailing friends, and be assured you will find it, in the friendship of Laelius and Scipio; in the patriotism of Cicero, Demosthenes and Burke; as well as in the precepts and example of him whose whole law is love, and who taught us to remember injuries only to forgive them.[12]

Borah's favorite novelist was Balzac, whose characters impressed him as being real and lifelike. He read all the works of Dickens and Thackeray; Dickens he found given a little too much to caricature, and Thackeray was a little too English for him. His taste in poetry, he admitted was rather old-fashioned. He never took any interest in free verse. The three poets he most admired, whose works he read and reread so often that he could quote pages from them, were Shakespeare, Milton, and Dante.[13] He told an interviewer: ". . . how true and applicable are many of Shakespeare's characterizations, and how well some of them fit some of our public men today."[14]

He also confessed to great admiration for Swift and Emerson. From Emerson he absorbed an element of stoicism that never left him. We can surmise what went on behind closed study doors those many evenings Borah spent at home from what he had to say about Emerson:

. . . nobody knows the amount of inspiration and comfort that I have received from his essays. Many a night, after a terribly trying day in the Senate, when everything has seemed to go wrong, when I have doubted even my own convictions, I have gone home and after dinner taken up a copy of Emerson, and turned to his essay on "Self Reliance." It has put new life into me, made me look at things in a different way and often when I have been on the point of giving up, that work has kept me sticking to my guns.[15]

When the interviewer pointed out the resemblance between Borah's and Swift's outlook on life, Borah remarked: ". . . other people have felt the same as you, but I am flattered at the comparison. After all, even if he was somewhat of a cynic, whatever weaknesses . . . he saw in human nature and in governments he tried to cure rather than increase."[16]

Passages from certain writers so impressed Borah that he copied them into a series of notebooks which he entitled "By the Light of

My Study Lamp." The quotations are arranged alphabetically according to authors. The notes on economics, government, and politics were evidently kept to be incorporated into speeches. Others were copied for self-instruction and rereading or out of sheer appreciation for the felicity of phrasing and the thought content. In these quotations we can detect fragments of the Borah philosophy. Said Benjamin Harrison: "There is a great sense of loneliness in the discharge of high public duties. The moment of decision is one of isolation." Oliver Goldsmith declared: "Great minds are bravely eccentric; they scorn the beaten track." Emerson wrote: "Nothing is at last sacred but the integrity of your own mind." He also wrote: "It is easy in the world to live after the world's opinion; it is easy in solitude to live after your own; but the great man is he who in the midst of the crowd keeps with perfect sweetness the independence of solitude."

From Plutarch he quotes: "There was in the whole city but one street in which Pericles was ever seen, the street which led to the market place and the council house. He declined all invitations to banquets and gay assemblies and company. During the whole period of his administration he never dined at the table of a friend." Balzac impressed him with this passage: "Believe me, a life of love is an exception to the laws of this earth; all flowers fade, great joys and emotions have a morrow of evil—if a morrow at all. Real life is a life of anguish; its image is in that nettle growing there at the foot of the wall—no sun can reach it and it keeps green." Another passage from the French genius amused him: "It is the privilege of the women whom we love more than they love us to make the men who love them ignore the ordinary rules of common sense." The range of these passages is very wide; their authors crowd the pages of twenty centuries. Some excerpts are well-known and descriptive, as from *Hamlet:* "It is a nipping and an eager air"; others are more obscure and profound, as from Humboldt: "Government, religion, property, books, are nothing but the scaffolding to build a man. Earth holds up to her master no fruit but the finished man."[17]

This lover of books was not altogether lacking in sociability. His very exclusiveness made him a much coveted guest or companion. A favored pastime was sitting in the small park near his apartment between Connecticut and Kalorama avenues, where he loved to watch little children at play or chat with them. Sometimes he gave them fruit or candy from his bulging pockets. On warm evenings his company might have been Maxim Litvinov from the nearby Russian Embassy, or it might have been a perfect stranger who later learned his name. Borah and his wife made occasional jaunts to the nearby zoo to watch the animals or ducks in the pond. For long stretches at a time in Rock Creek cemetery he pondered the St. Gaudens masterpiece, "Grief," sculptured in stone to commemorate the death of Henry Adams' wife. Aside from horseback rides and these diversions, there is little of light incident in his life for the biographer to record.

At one time during his career he contemplated writing a book. As projected, the work was to be a biography of James Otis. Borah told a friend that if he had the time and ability he would like to include the lives of Samuel Adams and Wendell Phillips, treating all three under the general heading, "The Agitators." He made some small preparation for this book but was always handicapped by lack of time and soon reached the conclusion that he was unfitted for the task. By 1938 he had abandoned all serious writing plans except for the numerous articles which he continued to contribute to leading magazines and newspapers.[18] Of these articles Bruce Bliven once wrote him: "When a statesman can turn journalist on short notice with happy results, it makes me wonder whether we who spend our whole lives in it have any right to call ourselves experts at all."[19]

When Henry Pringle's article on Borah appeared in 1928, C. P. Connolly congratulated him on his effort to increase public understanding of Borah: ". . . all the more for the reason that so many have misunderstood him, and that he is not the kind . . . given to personal explanation. He may not be perfect, but he certainly is a Matterhorn in the midst of the sagebrush."

Publishers had long besought the Idahoan to write his memoirs, but to all such requests he turned a deaf ear. The pressure of public affairs and lack of time were his standard excuses. Contemplating no publication during his lifetime, he had in mind following the example of John Adams, who directed that his papers be restricted from any use until twenty-five years after his death. To those who approached him for biographical material he was modestly firm. He did not think there was sufficient justification yet for such an outrage on the community. He told one woman who requested material: "I assume this is for publication and I feel that I should discourage you in this undertaking. It would not be a paying proposition, I am sure." To William Allen White, who was interceding for a friend, he wrote: ". . . without any assumed modesty, it is of course a joke . . . you can write my life in an afternoon on your way to catch a train and nobody would read it . . . I will protect you against such a task." Borah seemed to take a certain pride in the enigma created in the public mind by his steadfast refusal to reveal himself biographically. Requesting an interview, George Viereck wrote Borah that he was interested primarily in his soul, in his real self, not in the political aspect. Borah replied: "You say you are interested in my soul, my real self. Well, I have never yet succeeded apparently, at least I hope I have not succeeded considering the results, in making myself known to any interpreter."[20]

One might expect that the Borah collection of manuscripts, which is one of the largest on deposit in the Library of Congress, would contribute much to a clarification of the Borah enigma or at least reveal some aspects of the inner man. However, a great part of the seven hundred boxes deals with routine matters—letters to and from constituents, admirers, state executive officers, legislators, newspaper editors, businessmen, and citizens generally, to say nothing of the thousands of requests for copies of speeches or a statement of his views on all kinds of issues, momentous or petty. The great bales of letters reveal his lively interest in matters of concern to Idaho and its citizens, touching every subject from lumber, mining, beet sugar, wheat, public buildings for Idaho's cities and towns, agricultural experiment stations, potato conventions, the markings on potato sacks, hog cholera, oil conservation, and the depletion allowance in the income tax law, to a Payette family's personal grief over the loss of a son. The poignant letter reads: "Feeling as I do that you are a close friend of ours, I enclose a clipping, advicing [*sic*] You of Our great sorrow. We are All so sorrow, so sorrow. We can't see Our dear boy no more."

There were crank letters. One gentleman inquired why October 12 should be made a legal holiday when Columbus was never in North America. A war veteran sent him his purple heart and a diagram of his wounds: "Now if you can get me any compensation or pension from it will you please be kind enough to return it and I will put it in the hands of a party here and give him part of what he gets out of it." Aside from the usual requests for government publications, seeds, information, and the like, there are also requests for positions, loans, two prairie chickens, backing for inventions, a remedy for hay fever, release from sanatoriums, and magazine subscriptions, one of the latter coming from a shut-in who needed $80 to repair his wheel chair which was falling apart.[21] In these letters the reader comes upon almost every aspect of the human comedy (or tragedy). Borah never hesitated to make clear his position on local or national issues, but of self-revelation there is very little. There are letters to the humble and the prominent, but many of them are perfunctory replies; very few are personal. After one has read thousands of letters, the man's personality assumes shadowy substance but the enigma is still there.

At the turn of the century the reputation of the upper chamber of Congress was deplorable. One of the last bastions of conservatism, it was called the American House of Lords, Millionaires' Club, and "the eager, resourceful, indefatigable agent of interests as hostile to the American people as any invading army could be, and vastly more dangerous . . ."[22] A list of senators whose wealth was estimated at $300,000 or more included thirty men, i.e., Aldrich and Wetmore of Rhode Island, Depew and Platt of New York, Elkins of West Virginia, Lodge of Massachusetts, Newlands of Nevada, Hanna of Ohio, and Smoot of Utah.[23] Borah was clearly outclassed by them. His Boise practice netted him perhaps $30,000 a year, from which he had managed to save about $100,000. Now he was limited to an income of $7,500 a year while his expenses increased. Even in 1907 the cost of living was high in Washington.

A conservative cabal dominated the Senate Borah entered, and Nelson Aldrich, representing eastern manufacturing interests, was its leader. Theodore Roosevelt was at first forced to work through this cabal. They were an intelligent, resourceful group of men, firmly entrenched in their powerful positions. They were able; the trouble lay with their point of view. Eventually the hand of fate intervened in behalf of the Progressives. A few years later, either because of death or refusal to stand for re-election, Quay of Pennsylvania, Platt of Connecticut, Spooner of Wisconsin, and Aldrich of Rhode Island no longer held Senate seats. They were succeeded by forward-looking young men such as Jonathan Dolliver of Iowa, Albert B. Cummins of Iowa, Moses Clapp of Minnesota, Albert J. Beveridge of Indiana, Robert M. La Follette of Wisconsin, and Borah of Idaho whom Roosevelt wanted to become Republican whip in the Senate.[24] Their parliamentary power was out of proportion to their numbers because of their acknowledged ability and versatility; they possessed most of the brains and brilliance to be found in that body. Were their aim to be described in a phrase, it would be, to quote Borah: "an instinctive sympathy for the underdog." With an unparalleled *esprit de corps* they dared to smash political totems and traditions in the nonpartisan support they gave each other inside and outside the Senate.

With few exceptions the Progressives were small-town lawyers, teachers, businessmen, editors, and plainsmen with a narrow, nationalistic outlook who claimed they were acting in the spirit of the Roosevelt tradition. For most of them life had been full of toil and trouble; there had been little opportunity for social or financial advancement. The majority had graduated from their own state universities; not one of them had been educated in an eastern university. They remained provincial most of their lives. All came from states normally Republican and primarily agricultural. These newcomers to the Senate had behind them a long history of rebellion; many had won their way to office over the opposition of the official party organization in their own states. In the atmosphere which they created in the Senate the leadership of an Aldrich could not long endure. Men like Borah took orders from nobody.[25]

Like their spokesman, William Allen White, they were attracted by the Progressive promise to right the balance between industry and agriculture and to save the farmer from further encroachments by capitalism. For White and Borah the countryside—the great stronghold of the middle class—was the chief source of virtue. Urban life and industrialism, White implied, killed the great human virtue of neighborly relationships. In his estimation the Progressive revolt was basically a protest of the small-town middle class against the excesses of a money-mad plutocracy. Borah, the latter-day Jeffersonian, called attention to the hegira of the last thirty years from the farm to the city, which was beginning to "have its effect upon the whole economic life of this nation." He predicted that "things will only be better when the face of the American citizen turns from the crowded and congested conditions of the city to a more extensive life on the farm." He seems to have had little grasp of the implications of the agricultural revolution, which would increase rather than halt urbanization and would also enlarge the farm surplus, a problem he failed or refused to recognize. Furthermore, this "back to the farm" evangelizing came with peculiar irony from one who as an impatient youth left behind a dusty trail riding out of rural Fairfield.

The twenty-four western states sent half of all the senators to Washington. There they continued to vote their middle-class liberalism, just as men from the South and East voted their regional interests. Their liberalism operated as easily in one party as in another; it was destined to become the strongest political force in the United States and could, if desired, secure control of the Senate. Fundamentally, the Progressives were fighting for a method of control as well as for concrete propositions of legislation. For each member of Congress they wished to obtain absolute freedom of action. Theirs was not a compromising spirit; this refusal to compromise has often been regarded as their cardinal fault and weakness, although at other times it has proved to be their strength. Despite their lack of patronage and a political machine to safeguard their position, in addition to their unending feuds with Republican presidents, their states remained stubbornly loyal to them. We may conclude that, right or wrong, they spoke with the authentic voice of the West.[26]

Life for a western senator had its difficulties. There devolved on him all the duties of other senators and many demands unknown east of the Missouri River, growing out of public land policies, homestead entries, delayed patents, deserted land entries, surveys, reclamation projects, irrigation, mining rights, timber stands on the public domain, forest reserves, Indian legislation, reservations, oil, gas, and power leases on public lands, water power development, and so on.

The old guard in the Senate at first regarded Borah as a stalwart reinforcement in the holy work of resisting the new movement of reform. For an index they used his background as a corporation lawyer representing the big mining and timber interests in Idaho.

They misinterpreted the role he played prosecuting labor agitators in his state. Borah believed in agitation but not in conflagration. Finally, Aldrich completely overlooked the fact that in 1906 Borah had carried two of the strongest labor counties in the state. His only political enemies in Idaho were the reactionary politicians who resented his enthusiasm for Theodore Roosevelt's ideas. Ignoring this, Aldrich assigned Borah to the Committee on Education and Labor. In a letter from the chairman of the Committee on Claims, Borah was informed:

> You will have seen before now the committee assignments you received. They are the best accorded any new Senator. I was in hopes that we might secure you a place on the public lands committee as you desired, but Senator Heyburn, being older in service, was entitled to it . . . Of course, two from the same State could not be placed on the Committee. I retired from the Committee on Irrigation with the distinct understanding that you should be given my place and that was done. I also have you placed on my Committee on Claims. I think, as stated, that you have faired [*sic*] exceptionally well for a new member and am glad of it.[27]

At a White House meeting Aldrich's colleagues raised questions about Borah and expressed their alarm at putting an untried man in such a key position. Aldrich reassured them: "Oh, he's all right. I have had him looked up. He is the attorney for seven different corporations." This time, however, Aldrich had miscalculated. Senator Hale later remarked: ". . . we traded with Borah and got cheated."[28] Almost immediately after his arrival the newcomer resorted to disconcerting and, in the view of the old guard, traitorous practices. Soon his committee was reporting measures reducing the hours of labor on railroads, providing workmen's compensation for railroad employees, providing for employers' liability, and calling for an investigation of the twelve-hour day and seven-day week in the iron and steel industry. It was during his first term that Borah achieved whatever reputation he had for being a radical. When Aldrich tried to apply pressure by communicating with Borah's clients in Idaho, he found to his dismay that there were no clients. One day Borah stopped Aldrich in the Senate corridor and questioned him:

"Aldrich, why didn't you come to me direct . . . instead of first wiring to New York, having New York wire to Idaho, and Idaho wire to me?"

"I thought my plan was the better way," he replied.

"To save you the trouble hereafter," Borah said, "I will tell you that I severed all relations with corporation law practice when I was elected to the Senate."

"That was a pity," commented Aldrich.[29]

Shortly after that Borah was summoned to the White House. The President wanted him to perform a special service. He wanted a speech made in the Senate on the Brownsville incident by a new senator so that it would receive wide publicity. The 25th Regiment of U. S. Infantry was involved. Negro soldiers were charged with having "shot up" a Texas town one night in 1906 while absent from their barracks without leave, and the entire incident had been the subject of a congressional investigation. Three companies of the 25th Regiment were dishonorably discharged and disqualified for future military or civil service. Meanwhile, fiery Senator Foraker from Ohio had gathered evidence which convinced him that the Negroes had been unjustly treated, and he impetuously rushed to their defense with slashing attacks on the administration. He, in turn, was accused of waving the "bloody shirt."

The old unwritten Senate rule was that newcomers should look wise but say nothing for at least a year after they take their seats. However, Borah delivered his first Senate speech on April 20, 1906, in defense of the administration's role in this affair. The speech lasted an hour and a half. Instead of retiring from the chamber as they usually did for a maiden speech, nearly all the senators stayed and listened to him. At the outset he made it clear that his remarks were not meant as an answer to Senator Foraker. Borah compared the Brownsville fray with the murder of Steunenberg in Idaho. Actually there was no real similarity between the two events. His main thesis, however, was his concern for the preservation of law and order. He presented a long, careful analysis of the evidence in the Brownsville case as though he were making an argument before a jury. He concluded that it unquestionably supported the administration's position. He considered this spirit of lawlessness in the American army shocking beyond words. Of the Negroes generally, he spoke in the most complimentary terms summarizing their numerous contributions to American society:

The negroes have helped to build up this country. Their labors in slavery and out . . . have helped to build it, and their valor has helped to preserve it. No man would take from the colored race of this country one iota of praise or honor for the heroic climb which it has made from slavery to its respectable position in the civilization of the world.

However, for Borah the evidence was conclusive that the soldiers had participated in the raid and were thus guilty of the charges. Their conduct was denounced as "morally aggravated treason." In conclusion he said: "I can not imagine a more cowardly act . . . upon the part of a great party than to undertake to connive at a crime so thoroughly proved as this because of anticipated political exigencies. It is our duty to say to the people of this country that the party which gave the colored man his freedom will also teach him that this Government can only be preserved by observing the law and . . . the rights of citizens in their homes."[30]

At the end of Borah's speech Senator Bacon, the Democratic leader, congratulated him and said: "I don't know whether you are a statesman or not, but you are a lawyer."[31] The Brownsville tempest died down, and events later showed that the Negro troops were more the victims of local prejudice than the administration was willing to admit.[32]

Roosevelt left office with an impressive record of legislation, but some areas needing consideration were left untouched. For every trust broken up, a new one had been formed; tariff schedules went unrevised; and other reforms, still on paper, had yet to be translated into law. Roosevelt, who was in a sufficiently powerful position to name his successor, at first preferred Elihu Root, his secretary of state; Borah also wanted him, but for compelling reasons T. R. chose William Howard Taft, former secretary of war and governor of the Philippines. Taft was not at all acceptable to the Progressives and not wholly acceptable to the conservatives in the Republican party, but many Progressives agreed that he was better than four more years of Roosevelt. Advised to choose one of the midwestern liberals as his running mate, Taft was reportedly inclined toward Borah, but the Idahoan did not want the post. He pleaded with Taft to select Senator Cummins of Iowa, whom he considered the strongest choice available.[33] Taft ignored his plea.

On May 28 Borah received this invitation from Taft: "I should like it very much if you would be one of those to second my nomination at the Chicago convention. I am particularly anxious to show my strength west of the Mississippi River in the nominating speeches as I hope it will appear in the votes."[34] Borah was glad to oblige.

Frank Hitchcock selected Borah in the spring of 1908 for executive and advisory duties on the Republican National Committee. Taft, meanwhile, was nominated for the presidency, and second place went to "Sunny Jim" Sherman, a conservative political hack distinguished mainly for his nickname.[35] Borah's job was to help conduct their campaign but from Chicago headquarters. He was chosen because of the favorable impression he had made presenting his ideas before the western committeemen attending the Hitchcock campaign school at the Antlers Hotel in Colorado Springs in July 1908. Gradually Borah was coming to be recognized as the leading figure in Republican circles west of the Mississippi. At first Hitchcock planned to make him head of the Western Speakers' Bureau, but so many requests came from national headquarters for his services on the stump that he was directed instead to campaign for Taft throughout New England and the Middle and Far West.

Borah delivered his first campaign address to a rally at Richford, Vermont, on August 25. At Augusta, Maine, he spoke to a larger gathering, and through September he addressed meetings at Fair Haven, Portland, Point of Pines, and numerous other cities in Maine, Massachusetts, and New Jersey. In October he spoke to students at Evanston, Illinois, and Madison, Wisconsin, on his way west. When he reached Idaho, he collapsed from exhaustion before a speech at Blackfoot and was taken to Boise to recuperate. On his way back to Washington he told a reporter: "Secretary Taft is very popular in Idaho and in the West generally. Out there . . . we believe that he is a big man in more ways than one."[36]

Taft's election was a foregone conclusion. In an apathetic campaign Bryan carried the solid South and a handful of western states, while the Republicans won the presidency and control of both houses in Congress. The stage was set for a battle between progressives and conservatives in both parties, with the genial Taft a frequent target for attack as the sentiment for reform mounted.

VII The Insurgents

Every modern man knows in his heart that he must be a liberal.

—Ortega y Gasset

Pennsylvania Avenue was festooned in the presidential colors of white and green for the inaugural procession on March 4, 1909. On both sides grandstands were ready for the crowds. Gilded eagles, evergreen boughs, and medallions of liberty ornamented the White House and government buildings for the parade which would extend the mile from the White House to the Capitol.[1] During the previous night a storm had swept in from the Atlantic which downed telegraph lines and tied up rail connections between Washington and New York. The wind was still blowing gusts of snow into the faces of those who ventured outside early that morning.

The telephone rang in Borah's apartment to advise him, as a member of the Committee on Arrangements, that the ceremony would take place in the Senate chamber rather than on the Capitol steps. He dressed hurriedly, fumbled in a closet for his galoshes, and rushed to the hill to attend to last minute details. At the reception which followed the ceremony he heard the jovial new President earnestly assure his friends: "I feel in all my bones and nerves the disposition to make good."[2]

As Taft's term began with an extra session, the relations between President and Congress became increasingly uneasy. Borah, who had the enviable knack of disagreeing without being disagreeable, labored to preserve the harmony. He occasionally went to the White House as a luncheon guest, even while battling against administration measures like the Payne-Aldrich Tariff. At a G. A. R. banquet in May 1909, where Taft and he were the principal speakers, he condemned critics of the administration and blamed Congress rather than the chief executive for the failure to keep party pledges. He received vigorous applause when he pictured the perplexities of the President confronted by the reactionary who wanted to go backward, the standpatter, the progressive who wanted to move up a little, and the insurgent who wanted to "go like hell." As for himself, he explained, he didn't know whether he was a reactionary or an insurgent! He added that while he did not always agree with Taft, he thought the President was doing his duty steadfastly as he saw it.[3] However, all harmony was soon lost.

Taft, who was by instinct conservative and appeared even more conservative than he really was, was forced to watch with helpless dismay the breakup of his following into factions. Large though he was, he could not hope to straddle two horses galloping in opposite directions. The insurgents, as the assailants of monopoly and special privilege were called, were not at first against Taft's administration. Borah tried to point this out. For the most part they favored his legislative program; however, they associated Republican leaders like Speaker Joseph G. Cannon in the House and Nelson Aldrich in the Senate with plutocratic and predatory interests, refused to work with them, and openly contested their leadership inside the Republican party. Taft felt compelled to recognize the existing congressional leadership, and the old guard soon convinced him that the radical new men were treacherous to him and to his party. Eventually the people began to confuse Taft with old guard leadership, and although the President agreed in theory with much of the insurgent program, he was never willing to antagonize the conservatives upon whom he relied increasingly for counsel and support. The people misunderstood Taft, and perhaps he failed to understand them. He certainly failed to make his position clear, and with each blunder the revolt grew, the progressive cause gained, and the breach widened.

The principal wedge which divided the party was the tariff. Roosevelt had adeptly avoided tariff revision in his administration. However, demands from the Midwest had induced the Republicans to write into their platform of 1908, which Borah helped draft, a plank for tariff revision, retaining such duties as would equal the difference between the costs of production at home and abroad with a reasonable profit to American industry.

Weldon Heyburn, senior senator from Idaho, defined the position of the conservative Republicans when he said that no revision downward was ever intended or promised. He condemned the platform committee for including the revision plank.[4] Borah declared that he understood the pledge to be one of honest revision downward. Most high tariff advocates hid behind the ambiguity of the President's brief message to Congress. When it was too late, Taft was virtually forced into the more courageous position of affirming his party's pledge for revision downward; however, he always remained open to suggestions from the old guard.

The bill reported out of the House Ways and Means Committee was a sincere attempt at downward revision, which pleased even Senator Cummins of Iowa. However, the bill reported from the Senate Finance Committee under Aldrich increased many customs rates and made the free list a joke. The Payne-Aldrich Tariff was immediately subjected to a well-planned attack by a group of progressive Republicans including La Follette, Beveridge, Cummins, Clapp, and at times Borah, whose reluctance to go along with the low-tariff men was largely explained by pressure from Idaho to restore ore, hides, and lumber to protection. In principle, he conceded some merits to protection, but he wanted it to be accompanied by income taxes. He told the Senate: "The tariff tax . . . reaches at last most heavily the man of limited means. It is passed from the importer to the general merchant . . . from him to the retail merchant . . . to the customer. When you are taxing personal property, every cow, every horse, every animal, every piece of property that the man of limited means has is found, but the undiscovered millions locked in safe-deposit boxes never pay their proportion of taxes. I favor a system that will get them coming and going, if you can, for that is the only way you can get them at all."[5]

When the Payne bill came from the House, an inheritance-tax provision was attached to it which the Senate voted down. The reasoning in the House was that with tariff rates lowered, less revenue would be forthcoming and new sources would have to be found. Borah favored an inheritance tax but believed it should be reserved to the states, thirty-five or thirty-six of which had already adopted such a levy. A federal income tax, however, he thought long overdue. He told an Idaho reporter: ". . . We are the only civilized government on earth today boasting as we do of our equality of rights and freedom, which has not . . . the practical legal power to tax wealth for the support of the national government."[6]

In the midst of the tariff debate Borah and Joe Bailey, a Democrat from Texas, drafted an income-tax resolution which Bailey introduced as a substitute for the abandoned inheritance tax. Their proposal, calling for a flat 2 per cent tax on all incomes above $5,000, attracted strong support from progressive Republicans and Democrats. The Wilson tariff of 1894 had contained a provision for an income tax which the Supreme Court declared unconstitutional in the Pollock case a year later.[7] However, Borah was no more willing to let the Pollock decision stand than Lincoln had been to let the Dred Scott decision prevail indefinitely. To show that the court had erred in ruling that an income tax on real property or rents was a direct tax and therefore prohibited by the Constitution, he assembled American and British authorities covering two hundred years. If that decision were final, he argued, there was no means by which our government could find financial resources to meet a war or other emergency. He pointed out that the intent of the framers of the Constitution had not been presented to the court in 1895. One of the controlling factors in the income-tax decisions had since been rejected by the court. Borah felt that a law could be drawn in such terms that the court would approve it.

Alarmed by the mounting government expenditures, he said extravagance, which had destroyed every other republic on earth, had become almost a national disease. Only consumption, not wealth, was taxed; as long as this older system continued, men of wealth would make no effort to curb private and public extravagance. He thought it the duty of every citizen to share in his government's maintenance, but he believed the man of limited means paid more than his share. To the charge that the income-tax resolution was an assault on wealth, Borah replied in a magazine article:

> No sane man would take from industry its just reward or rob frugality of a fair and honest return. I believe in protection to wealth legitimately acquired and the absolute guarantee to property and property rights. These things are essential to the welfare of those who do not possess property as well as those who do . . . But equality of burden and equal opportunity . . . are also essential to any successful . . . plan for the protection of wealth and property . . . There is nothing in this world so blind, so incapable of appreciating the forces which in the end will destroy it as wealth . . . the man who walked down Fifth Avenue a few nights ago, hungry and haunted by the cries of his children, and threw a rock at the feasters in a palatial hotel, can no more be ignored in considering policies than the greatest of magnates who wearies with the burdens of his wealth.[8]

Senator Aldrich and his associates resorted to extraordinary measures to defeat the income tax. The old guard in both parties was not only opposed to it on principle, but feared it would produce so much revenue as to necessitate a revision of the tariff downward.[9] Borah and Bailey, determined to bring the proposal to a vote, threatened to filibuster against the tariff if their efforts were blocked. Two days before the amendment came up for a vote, Taft sent a special message to Congress (probably inspired if not written by Aldrich) advocating a corporation tax and recommending an amendment to the Constitution empowering Congress to levy an income tax. On the heels of this compromise came Senators Aldrich and Lodge with a proposed 2 per cent tax on corporation profits which they introduced as an amendment to the tariff bill. Aldrich openly admitted: "I am opposed to an income tax . . . except in times of stress or emergency when it is not possible to raise revenue from the ordinary sources."[10]

Outraged, Borah told the Senate he would support the corporation tax as a temporary measure if he were sure that it would reach the inactive wealth which paid practically no tax, but he perceived quickly that such a tax would only be passed on to the consumer in the form of higher prices. He advocated the income tax as a long-term policy. We are at the crossroads, he warned, and the question is the momentous one of changing our whole system of taxation. If we continue quibbling, the wrath of the people will awaken us to the fact that the disparity between wealth and poverty is caused not so much by the trusts as by our own unfair system of taxation. The French Revolution was not caused by Robespierre but by the fact that 85 per cent of the country's taxes were collected from the peasantry, forcing men from their homes and farms into "the sinks and dives of Paris, where the revolution was born." He feared that the small corporations could not afford to pay the tax Aldrich proposed without cutting wages.[11]

Although they condemned the tactics employed, progressives in both parties believed in the principle of the corporation tax and voted for it, insuring its adoption. Before the final vote for the resolution on the income-tax amendment Borah and Bailey made an unsuccessful attempt to provide for its ratification by state conventions rather than by the legislatures, but the conservatives rejected the proposal. The Senate approved the amendment 77 to 0.

Meanwhile debate on the tariff bill continued. Borah joined the "range senators" representing the Northwest who gave most of their votes to Aldrich in return for a 15 per cent duty on hides and a rate of $1.50 per thousand board feet on lumber. The President wanted lumber and hides on the free list. A compromise resulted, with the range senators accepting $1.25 on lumber. Hides went on the free list again, but with corresponding reductions in the duty on manufactured leather. The final bill, as it emerged from the Conference Committee, had a few reductions here and there, but the average rate on dutiable goods was 1 per cent higher than the Dingley tariff of 1897. President Taft signed the Payne-Aldrich bill and in a speech at Winona, Minnesota, described it as the best tariff the country ever had. In so doing, he alienated more progressive support.

To the surprise of conservatives and progressives alike, the income-tax amendment was ratified by one state legislature after another and became the Sixteenth Amendment to the Constitution on February 25, 1913. Of all the innovations during the reform era the graduated income tax was destined to have the most positive and enduring effect upon the American economy. When it was first attached to the Underwood Tariff of 1913, the rates were very low (incomes of less than $3,000 for unmarried persons were exempted); but by 1920 the tax was contributing ten times as much revenue as the customs, and that was only the beginning of its rise to predominance in financing a hugely expanded government. The growing tax burden was at least in part shifted to men of wealth, thus serving the purpose Borah and the agrarian liberals intended.

Borah's experience with the Idaho legislature in 1902 helps explain his untiring efforts to secure an amendment for the direct election of senators. In Idaho there was wide support for the new reform. By 1909 Idaho had a direct primary law, largely through Borah's efforts. By 1912 some thirty states had passed preferential primary laws and were, in fact if not in theory, choosing their senators by direct election. Men thus chosen became supporters of a constitutional amendment for direct election, and the Senate's resistance to the change weakened year by year.[12]

Final impetus to reform came from revelations of corruption in the Illinois legislature attendant upon the election of William Lorimer to the Senate in 1909. A state investigation, followed by a Senate inquiry, established that a fund of $100,000 had been raised by businessmen to elect Lorimer. The Chicago *Tribune* exposed details of bribery, and in July 1912 the Senate declared Lorimer's election invalid. Borah upheld the principle of the purity of elections but did his best to secure a modification of the resolution of condemnation, keeping it within constitutional limits.

Borah presented the Judiciary Committee report favoring an amendment for the direct election of senators on January 11, 1911. When he sought unanimous consent, he met immediate objection; delay and obstruction were employed from the outset by the old guard. Yet he pressed for the resolution at every turn, demonstrating that with the aid of Progressives and Democrats he had the votes.

This evidently prompted George Sutherland of Utah, a member of the opposition, to submit a substitute amendment giving Congress the authority to make or alter regulations as to the time and manner of holding elections for senators in place of the clause in Borah's resolution which transferred these powers to the states.[13] Sutherland made a direct bid for southern opposition to the Borah resolution. Borah argued that the states should possess the full power to regulate their elections since they managed them better than the federal government anyway.[14] However, whenever he tried to get a vote, Senator Penrose interposed an objection. Senators scheduled to make speeches on the resolution declared they were unprepared, and when it was Senator Heyburn's turn, he "didn't feel up to it." Filibustering, amendments, and senatorial courtesy were invoked to prevent action.

Borah, speaking on February 16, the day set for final action, asserted that Congress did not decide who should vote; it merely provided protection for those who had the right. He cited the decision in *Minor* v. *Hapersett* (1875), which drew from Senator Carter the comment that he was "an encyclopedia of authorities." He retorted: "I may not be an encyclopedia but I am capable of reading the decisions of the Supreme Court."[15] Senator Heyburn said he regarded the integrity of the state legislatures more highly than the representatives of "election booths along the wharves and rivers and in the heated centers of big cities . . ." He added: "The

Idaho legislature sent my colleague here; they elected him the first day and hour it was possible to elect a Senator under the law . . . They were competent . . ." Borah leaped to his feet to interrupt: "I appreciate the suggestion of the Senator, but the legislature elected [me] under direct instructions of a popular vote, which I felt the necessity of getting in order that I might be sure to get the other."[16]

Finally Borah succeeded in making his resolution "unfinished business," and the wearying discussion dragged on. The Sutherland amendment was passed 50 to 37, and on March 2 the Borah-Bailey resolution was lost 54 to 33, four votes short of the required two thirds. Among those voting against it was William Lorimer. Without the injection of the race issue it probably would have passed by a narrow margin. Disappointed but encouraged by the close vote, Borah announced that the resolution would again be introduced at the first session of the next Congress. "The friends of the measure may rest assured that the matter will not be permitted to be forgotten."[17]

In the special session the following spring Borah lost no time. Thirty minutes after the organization of the Committee on the Judiciary, of which he was chairman, he reported the Senate joint resolution for direct election. The House joint resolution 39 came to the Senate simultaneously and was referred to the Committee on Elections. Borah then had it transferred to his committee which reported it back to the Senate favorably by May 1. Borah's position was now strengthened by the fusillade of public criticism which had followed the defeat of his earlier resolution. Progressive newspapers excoriated Lodge as a "political Ichabod" and characterized Root as a man who looked eternally toward the past. The Kansas City *Star* predicted that most Americans would soon see the wisdom in the idea lately advanced to abolish the upper house.[18]

By the end of May 1913 the necessary thirty-six states ratified the proposal, which became the Seventeenth Amendment to the Constitution. Borah thus secured for himself a life option on a seat in the Senate. He had pressed this measure with resolution, courage, ingenuity, and skill against an entrenched opposition until he achieved success. It was an excellent public service, but few know or remember Borah's part in it. The fight had been long, cutting across party lines and pitting conservatives against progressives. Borah found this groping of the electorate toward a truer and more efficient democracy most heartening. He was particularly pleased by the transformation of the tiresome Senate.

As time progressed, the question whether direct election improved the character of the Senate aroused much difference of opinion.

In an article written in 1934 Borah found the record wholly favorable to the change. The feeble and corrupt, he wrote, will always be found in personal government, but in a true democracy neither incompetence nor dishonesty will long remain unexposed. "What judgment is so swift, so sure and so remorseless as the judgment of the American people?"[19]

In his annual message to Congress in January 1910 Taft recommended reciprocal tariff agreements with Canada, hoping to strengthen international amity, reduce the cost of food, and open Canadian markets to our manufacturers. The first response was favorable, but before long insurgents were able to argue that reciprocity was a good bargain for the trusts, which would gain a new market and free raw materials at the farmer's expense. Wheat, grain, paper, and wood pulp were to come in free. When the President called a special session in April 1911 to consider reciprocity, he found that Progressives as well as stalwarts from both parties were opposed to it, especially in New England and the Northwest.

On June 27-28 Borah made a speech for which he used the text: "The western farmer's instinct is wiser than Mr. Gladstone's philosophy." He maintained that the home market belongs to the American farmer as long as he is able to supply it. The farmer knows that as his home market is narrowed, his prices fall. Borah wanted more acres under production, more products on the market, and more taxes in the treasury. "What benefit does this agreement give us?" he asked.

> Wherein has Canada traded us any reciprocal thing for that which we have given to Canada? . . . Give us one definite, concrete proposition. Do not lead me away into sophomoric effusions about one language, one blood, and the brotherhood of man, but in this cold business deal, which Canada drove home with so much . . . selfishness, tell me what we got

out of it. What we got, sir, was a deal between the Canadian farmer and our eastern manufacturer, to give the eastern manufacturer cheaper raw material—a clear, cold-blooded discrimination against the American farmer.[20]

Despite agrarian protests the measure passed both houses and was submitted for Canadian approval. Meanwhile Champ Clark, the Democratic speaker, made some spread-eagle remarks about hoping to see the day when the American flag would float over every square foot of British North America. President Taft, with equal ineptitude, remarked: ". . . the tie that binds Canada to the Mother country is light and almost imperceptible." The patriotism of Canadians was aroused. The issue forced a dissolution of the Canadian Parliament, and in the general election which followed the Liberal government and reciprocity were defeated. Borah commented that Americans owed Canada a great debt of gratitude.

In the closing hours of the special session Senator La Follette and the Progressives jammed through the Senate the so-called "pop gun tariffs," which included a farmers' free list bill and a woolens and cottons bill which placed many new items on the free list and made large reductions in duties on cottons and woolens. President Taft, however, vetoed all these measures on the ground that they were hastily drawn, "unscientific," and political in purpose. One Progressive remarked that Taft had thus driven the last nail into his political coffin.[21] Division and defeat faced the party in the fall of 1909. In spite of the stormy atmosphere Borah continued to enjoy the confidence of the President. In January 1910 Taft invited him to the White House to discuss the proposed National Incorporation Act. Borah favored strengthening the Sherman Act and facilitating suits for damage by private parties against monopolies. He said the awards for damages should be made more attractive, for far too few suits were litigated because of the prohibitive expense.

At this meeting Borah brought up his plan for the issuance of thirty million dollars' worth of government bonds, bearing 3 per cent interest, the proceeds to be used in the completion of reclamation projects in arid and semiarid states. The sale of reclaimed land and the money collected for the use of irrigation facilities, he said, would pay off the bonds. Settlers were already on these lands and awaiting water. The President shared Borah's concern for these people but opposed the new bond issues, preferring to substitute certificates of indebtedness against the individual projects. Borah felt that the certificates would be more difficult to market than bonds. In his special message to Congress on conservation Taft outlined Borah's recommendations, and at the subsequent session Congress voted to set up a $20,000,000 reclamation fund as the senator proposed. Borah succeeded in securing $7,000,000 from the fund for his own state.[22]

One of the strongest stands Borah took during his first term in the Senate was in opposition to the federal administration of the public lands. He was at odds with federal policy not because he was opposed to conservation but because he saw inequalities in the laws as administered by the government. In debate with Smoot and Newlands he remarked: "Nothing I have said has been intended to be a criticism of the character of the work of Mr. Pinchot [Chief Forester], but I do say that the rules and regulations in reference to the manner in which these reserves are to be used are an impediment to the development of a large part of our State . . . the law making power of this Government rests with us, and there should never be given to any Department the power to make rules . . . absolutely conclusive against a citizen."[23]

Borah directed a fierce attack on the theory, which had originated in the days of Benjamin Harrison, that the President had the authority to withdraw public lands from sale or lease. He found the executive, under the Constitution, without such authority. Entire jurisdiction over the public lands belonged to Congress alone. Yet thousands of acres had been withdrawn, many of them for federal forest reserves; those in Idaho contained one third of the state's timber resources. According to Borah the land and its resources belonged to the states. He charged that the government placed all manner of obstacles in the path of the settler, depriving him without reason of the lands rightfully his.

In contrast, he pointed to the more liberal Canadian land laws and the increasing migration by Americans (500,000 in five years) to Canada. He wanted every acre of government land developed to prevent this. He lamented that some of Idaho's agricultural land was taken out of the settlers' reach and included in federal forest reserves where the timber was permitted to ripen, fall, rot, and burn. Underbrush in some of Idaho's inaccessible regions had gotten out of control, causing destructive forest fires that could be prevented only by permitting settlement on the fringes of these timbered lands. When government timber was occasionally placed on the market, Borah found its price almost twice that of commercial timber. He could see no point in bottling up such vast reserves as the national forests of Idaho, into one of which, he boasted, the great state of New York could be set!

The fault, he asserted, rested with a conservation policy framed by those who had never seen it in operation. Like R. A. Ballinger, newly appointed secretary of the interior, Borah wanted less so-called conservation of forests and more real benefit to the settler. "What does the government have these lands for?" he asked. "Jack-rabbits and coyotes, or for men?"[24] He offered several proposals. One, which passed the Senate without a dissenting vote, was his Three Year Homestead bill, introduced for the purpose of shortening the period of five years set by the law of 1862 and giving title to the homesteader whether he was located on a reclamation project or the public domain. He was also author of a bill bringing Idaho under the enlarged homestead law and a proviso allowing the homesteader to determine whether he would prove up under the old or the new law.

In February 1910 Borah and a group of insurgents in Congress forced Taft to drop the civil government bill for Alaska. Through John Hays Hammond, a mining expert and golfing partner, the President had been persuaded to permit the transfer of the control of government-owned Alaska mines from Washington to Alaska. Having secured new government machinery for the territory, the Guggenheim interests, which had an eye on Alaskan coal fields, could name their own mining commissioner. Borah was quick to attack the alleged scheme.

Taft, who was by then rather peevish, sent for Borah, who told him: "Mr. President, this bill is the sum of legislative iniquity." Senator Dolliver was also called in, and his comment was briefer. He stated: "This bill is rotten." The President dropped the bill, but he was hardly grateful to Borah.[25]

Dismayed by the trend of the times and baffled by his unpopularity, the unhappy Taft confided to his former chief: "The fight to comply with our party promises has been a hard one . . . La

Follette, Cummins, Dolliver, Bristow, Clapp and Beveridge, and I must add Borah, have done all in their power to defeat us. They have probably furnished ammunition enough to the press and the public to make a Democratic House. Whether they will bring a Democratic administration in three years remains to be seen."[26]

Borah campaigned in Wisconsin that summer for the re-election of La Follette. Within a single week Progressives delivered 189 speeches in various cities for "Fighting Bob" and other Progressive candidates, making important gains for their faction in the fall elections of 1910. The House went Democratic as Taft had feared; the Republican majority in the Senate was reduced to ten. By uniting with the Democrats the Progressives were now in a position to control the Senate, and their power was shown several times throughout the next session.[27]

Borah was a friend and admirer of Secretary of State Philander C. Knox, whom he regarded as an eminent constitutional lawyer. Knox found himself clearly overshadowed in Taft's cabinet by Attorney General Wickersham and was therefore determined to resign. Borah had a long talk with Knox but failed to dissuade him. Thereupon Borah took the newspaperman O. K. Davis into his confidence, and a few days later the full story of Knox's plan appeared in the New York *Times*. As Davis predicted, a complete denial of the facts in his story came from every Washington source from the White House down, including Knox—but the secretary stayed.[28]

When the bill regulating immigration was under discussion, Borah said he had no prejudice against foreigners but opposed the admission of immigrants who had neither an expectation of remaining permanently nor the qualifications for good citizenship should they wish to stay. He favored stringent tests of the intentions of the immigrant. If the alien's motive were simply to compete for a time in our labor market and then return to his homeland, Borah would deny him admittance. He concluded that good government and a high quality electorate go hand in hand. He would simply say that here is a home for all who truly intend to make it a home.[29]

On the whole, Borah was successful with the measures he introduced during his first term. He drew up the bill which separated the Department of Labor from the Commerce Department and gave its chairman cabinet rank. He was author of the bill which gave an eight-hour day to government employees, and he instituted an inquiry into conditions in the steel industry which helped bring about elimination of the industry's twelve-hour day in 1923. His bill creating the Children's Bureau, a government agency to gather and publish facts which would induce the states to abolish child labor, went through without serious opposition. Senator Bailey interrupted the debate to say: "I assume that the bill of the Senator from Idaho is somewhat similar to that provision in the agricultural appropriation bill which makes some sort of a similiar arrangement for calves and pigs."

"Exactly," replied Borah. "My bill seeks to have the government do for children what it has already done for calves and pigs."[30]

A senator of long experience once remarked: "Senator Borah is the most successful man in charge of a bill in the Senate since I have been a member of that body." He explained that "Borah always advocated just, necessary legislation; he refused to waste his time on anything which was not absolutely essential; he diverged sharply from the common run of legislators who, like government, have legislation on the brain and think that the primary business of Congress is to legislate, whereas in fact it is to look after the administration of existing laws so well that no new laws or very few are necessary."[31]

When he introduced a bill, it nearly always came as a complete surprise because he rarely consulted anyone about it. Wise enough never to press two important bills at the same time, he backed each of his measures with powerful arguments. He personally pursued his bills in the House after they passed the Senate, attempting to overcome opposition there as well as in government bureaus and departments. For example, he went to Speaker Clark and asked for help in passing the Three Year Homestead bill. Sometimes Borah performed stunning legislative feats, as in gaining passage of the Industrial Coal Commission bill in eight minutes. However, he felt the deepest pride in his Three Year Homestead law and the bill giving early patents to homesteaders on government reclamation projects. Despite his solicitude for Idaho's needs, he never regarded legislating for his home state as his primary function. He cared little who held the offices in Idaho so long as the incumbents were honest men; patronage was the least of his worries.

He advised few if any of his colleagues on legislative matters, nor did he seek their advice. His associates never knew how he would vote on their measures. Even if some senator believed he had persuaded Borah to vote for his bill, the Idahoan was likely to think it over carefully, grow suspicious, and vote the other way. He had no Senate following. His influence in that body was intellectual, not personal. If a group succeeded in bringing him into a conference, they found it impossible to keep him there. Almost instantly he became restless. First he would make the familiar pyramids with his fingers; five minutes later he would be fidgeting with his hat; and after ten minutes he would be gone. In all this observers perceived the man of thought, the philosopher in politics, not the man of action who knows the necessity of working with and through other men. Although Borah rarely appeared at party caucuses, there was hardly a movement in the progressive era of which he was not near the spiritual leadership. Usually, however, he was content to appeal to men's minds and work alone. In this he was more like Wilson than Theodore Roosevelt.[32]

Borah's best role was that of advocate. His talents were decidedly on the apostolic side. For him to espouse a cause was half the battle. Others may have stirred the Senate more, but he managed to move both the Senate and its masters who sat around hearth and kitchen stove and the cracker barrel. As Lincoln said, "Whoever can change public opinion can change the government." A score of lesser men in the Senate possessed the qualities needed to steer a bill through to enactment, but there was only one Borah to arouse public opinion to such an extent that the wheels of legislation ground into action.

Progressive colleagues recognized that Borah was a spirit apart. Sometimes they interpreted his aloofness as apathy. Although they admired him and achieved their triumphs more easily when his oratory served as a barrage for their arguments, they never trusted him as they did other insurgents. After a time Borah was rarely invited to their parleys, and they sometimes embarrassed him by staging a battle without him. In most Senate battles, however, insurgents found in him a strong rallying point, and when the smoke cleared away, Borah's black plume was seen waving on enemy ramparts.[33]

VIII The Eve of Waterloo: 1912

My hat is in the ring, the fight is on and I am stripped to the buff.

—Theodore Roosevelt

In March 1912 the Taft Club of Idaho sent Borah a wire demanding to know whether he would support Roosevelt or Taft for the presidential nomination. His answer came back, swift and unequivocal: "I am for Roosevelt and I want to see him win."[1]

In April Borah and Roosevelt talked over the approaching campaign at Oyster Bay. Borah, then national committeeman from his state, gave assurances that he would render any service he could in securing Roosevelt's nomination. The senator later reported that the question of a third party arose. In his talk with Roosevelt he expressed a strong hope that the party split would not lead to a third ticket, saying: "I am very much opposed to any such movement. A third party would get nowhere. We have got to fight it out in the convention and abide by the rules." He reported that Colonel Roosevelt used in substance the following language: "Our friends should not think or talk about a third party. Any such talk would weaken us in the fight and we want no third party. That would only result in the election of a Democrat."[2]

Borah worked feverishly to have Roosevelt delegates chosen to the state convention in Idaho. The Republican organization favored the re-election of Taft and also of Borah. In a meeting with Taft, which Borah did not attend, Calvin Cobb, the owner and editor of the Idaho *Statesman,* promised to deliver the Idaho delegates at the national convention. When Borah learned of this, he voiced his resentment so tartly that the editor broke with him; he could no longer count on the most powerful newspaper in his state for support in his own campaign. At the convention in Lewiston that May, Roosevelt delegates were selected to the national convention. Borah, elated over the result, wrote the Colonel: "I see the opposition are placing in their list four of the delegates from Idaho. I drop you a line only to say that I have no doubt that there are eight from Idaho solid for your nomination."[3]

The approach of the national convention in 1912 found the Republican party even more bitterly divided between the supporters of Taft and Roosevelt, and Borah increasingly determined to battle for the nomination of the Roughrider. Winding up business, the senator left Washington on June 4 for the preconvention meetings of the National Committee in Chicago. He was to serve on the Credentials Committee. Arriving in Chicago, he engaged rooms at the Blackstone Hotel and rested one day—the only really peaceful day he was to know there.

The Taft and Roosevelt headquarters were both at the Congress Hotel. In the thirteen states where presidential primaries were held, Roosevelt had secured 281 delegates while Taft trailed with 71 and La Follette had 36. In the remaining states, however, the delegations were almost solidly pledged to Taft, who would go into the convention, according to polls, with about 550 votes, enough to nominate him, while Roosevelt had about one hundred less. The National Committee was convening twelve days before the convention to decide upon 254 contested seats. The Roosevelt supporters hoped to win enough of these cases–many of them trumped up for this purpose—to swing the majority of delegates from Taft to Roosevelt. Borah's task was to lead the Roosevelt forces in the National Committee meetings, where they were in a distinct minority. So preoccupied was he with his strategy that he occasionally wandered around the hotel lobby deep in thought. One evening Mrs. Borah was chatting with friends and nodded to him as he walked by engrossed in conversation with a group of senators.

"Good evening, Senator Borah," she chirped.

"Good evening, Madam," he replied vaguely, failing to recognize his own wife.

Early Friday morning Borah made his way to the coliseum annex where the committee was to meet. Into its deliberations Roosevelt sent some of his most skillful fighters: Governor Stubbs of Kansas, Francis H. Heney of California, Borah, and Frank B. Kellogg of Minnesota. Taft sent men equally resolute: Murray Crane of Massachusetts, Congressman William B. McKinley of Illinois, and Chairman Victor Rosewater of Nebraska, who called the meeting to order. Scarcely an hour later Borah was on his feet presenting a motion to amend the rules. He unsuccessfully proposed that eight members of the commitee rather than the customary twenty be sufficient to demand a roll call.

On the following day Borah renewed his motion. Dennis Flynn, a Taft man, moved to lay it on the table, but Borah wished to debate it. Chairman Rosewater declared it undebatable and said: "This committee will conduct its proceedings under the usual parliamentary rules." Borah retorted: "But you shall not adopt any rule or gag by laying a motion on the table this early in the campaign." He stormily announced that they would not steamroller *him;* nevertheless, the steamroller passed over him while he was still shouting in stentorian tones, "Mr. Chairman . . . Mr. Chairman!" Flynn's motion was adopted by a viva-voce vote. Given ten minutes to state his case, Borah shouted: "I am perfectly willing that the steamroller should operate, but I want to say here and now that it does operate, how it operates, who is operating it. Men who have not the moral courage to record their vote before the people of the country are not worthy to represent the great Republican organization of these United States." Here the chairman interrupted: "The Gentleman from Idaho is out of order." And a committeeman added: "There is nothing before the house." Borah thundered: "*I* am before the house."[4]

The committee hearings, dragging into their third day, included important contests from Arkansas, Alabama, and Florida. Ormsby McHarg had been sent to the South by Roosevelt, and a good many delegates had been selected in spurious fashion. Borah made an apparently shrewd move when he demanded a roll call on the delegates-at-large from Alabama, but the showing of the Roosevelt supporters was so poor that no one voted to seat his delegates. It soon became clear that little real evidence supported the claims of Roosevelt contestants in the South. When a Negro from Florida arrived to claim a convention seat, presenting a rather threadbare appearance, Senator Dick asked him who had supplied the necessary funds to come to Chicago.

"De Lawd be praised," replied the Negro. "De folks done raise de jackpot in de church."

After that Borah left the committee room, freely expressing his disgust at wasting time in such farcical proceedings. That night he told the press: "The ninth Alabama and fifth Arkansas were the only contests heard thus far, which, in my opinion, had any merit. I do not believe contests should be presented which are not based on merit."

Said the editorial: "If such rock-bound warriors vote for Taft delegates it is because the Roosevelt claims are too preposterous for consideration by anybody outside an insane asylum."[5] In the Texas and Washington contests Borah stood for what he believed was right—the seating of the Roosevelt delegates; however, he could not stomach the claims of some other delegates and therefore voted with the Taft men.[6]

It was soon apparent that the committee, dominated by the old guard, was less interested in justice than in seating enough Taft delegates to secure his nomination. It gave credentials to Taft supporters even in states like Texas where Roosevelt had a clear majority. Borah appealed to the committee to go to the convention "with a clean record" and not have the nominee "tainted with fraud."[7] However, the steamroller continued to operate. He told a group in the lobby of the Congress Hotel: "I would cut off my right arm before I would vote for a man who was not rightfully and legally elected." However, he predicted that if all the delegates for the candidate he represented were seated, he would be nominated.[8]

Alarmed by reports over a direct wire to Oyster Bay, Roosevelt telephoned his manager, Senator Dixon, upbraided Borah and Kellogg for their stand on the contests, and announced he was sending Pittsburgh's smoothest boss, William B. Flinn, to take charge of his forces. Borah expected the Colonel himself to reach Chicago around June 15.

Of the 254 contested seats 235 were awarded to Taft and only 19 to Roosevelt, who undoubtedly had a right to 30 or more. Some thought T. R. should have received about fifty more, approximately the figure later arrived at by Borah and Herbert Hadley.[9] Thirty additional votes would not have given Roosevelt a majority in the convention, but their loss would have been a serious blow to Taft, permitting T. R. to dictate the organization of the convention, block Taft's victory on the first ballot, and procure either his own nomination or that of a compromise candidate.[10]

Tumult punctuated the closing sessions of the National Committee. On the Kentucky decisions Roosevelt leaders charged "outright robbery." Senator Dixon called the Taft committeemen a bunch of crooks joy riding on their steamroller, and Francis Heney observed that no one could gain recognition but a hand-picked, machine-made crook. At the daily Roosevelt revival meeting Borah said the National Committee believed "this is going to be another Titanic wreck, and that they will get away, while we go down with the sinking ship. The situation is in the keeping of the convention. I do not believe that when an appeal is made to the . . . delegates they will follow any ruling which binds them to commit fraud."[11]

Chicago was transformed by the convention. Roosevelt's supporters had rented the lavish Florentine room at the Congress Hotel, adding a large picture of the Colonel to cover one wall of its ornate interior. On Wabash Avenue the huge Romanesque coliseum was prepared to receive the 1803 delegates and 10,000 spectators. To add a final touch, the Colonel himself arrived June 15. Though it was hot and sticky, he shook many hands at the station and made a balcony appearance to greet the eager crowd. Sending at once for Borah, he declared that some means must be found to give the senator a seat on the floor of the convention. Roosevelt wanted him for one of his floor leaders. Had Idaho placed him on its delegation, he might have played the role filled by Herbert Hadley of Missouri. The best that could be done was to arrange for him to sit with other members of the National Committee.

On the eve of the convention thousands of Roosevelt enthusiasts jammed the Chicago auditorium for a mass meeting, while a large crowd waited outside. Flags were distributed, patriotic songs were sung, and the audience chanted "We want Teddy." Borah opened the meeting with a well-delivered arraignment of the Republican National Committee and standpat Republicanism in general. Colonel Roosevelt was expected to arrive at eight-fifteen, but he was twenty minutes late. Meanwhile the glee club sang until the crowd began to yell for Borah. When he saw no sign of the Colonel, Borah obliged with more remarks: "You people constitute the court of last resort . . ." He was in the middle of a sentence when Roosevelt plunged through a rear door and made his dramatic appearance. In a vigorous address T. R. condemned the members of the National Committee individually and collectively. Words like theft, crime, stolen, shame, treason, and robbery were interwoven with the names of senators, bosses, leaders, and "sure thing" men. He demanded that the 72 delegates whose seats were contested before the Credentials Committee stand aside and allow their cases to be decided by the thousand uncontested delegates.[12]

However, Roosevelt's managers vacillated. Their early hopes had been pinned on the action of the National Committee; their next move was never definitely decided. Some advised winning the temporary chairmanship for a Roosevelt man. Others were intent on the passage of a motion substituting 72 Roosevelt delegates for the 72 Taft delegates whose seats were in question. This motion was declared out of order, and the Taft delegates were allowed to occupy their seats while the convention voted for a permanent chairman. Not until midnight of June 17 did the Roosevelt forces decide to support Borah for the temporary chairmanship. At this stage, however, T. R. suddenly shifted to Governor Francis E. McGovern of Wisconsin, a choice calculated to win him some La Follette delegates.

Then in all the confusion the Taft forces succeeded in placing Elihu Root in the chair by a vote of 552 to 502. This meant the old guard would control the convention machinery. At the opening session on the morning of June 18, when Root thanked the convention for honoring him, the crowd laughed and jeered. From the gallery came the squeaking toot-toot of hundreds of toy whistles. Sheets of sandpaper were rubbed together imitating a steamroller. The crowd yelled in unison: "Roll her over on the sand tracks, Watson [James Watson, Senator from Indiana]. She's slipping again." Others hooted: "All aboard!" Looking on, William Jennings Bryan observed: "If you didn't know where you were you might think you were in a Democratic convention."[13]

The gavel had hardly descended after Root's keynote speech when Herbert Hadley was on his feet calling for the substitution of Roosevelt delegates. The Hadley motion was lost, 569 to 499. Following good legal precedent, Root permitted the seated Taft delegates to vote on their own cases amid angry cries of "theft," "fraud," and "steamroller." On each test ballot Roosevelt lacked more of the 540 votes necessary to nominate. Talk of a bolt was no longer merely whispered in small groups. Borah tried to stop it: "Personally I do not believe there is any chance of a third party or a bolt. History shows conclusively that no successful party was ever born under such auspices. It would be created only half formed and would go into the fight with the likelihood of the parent weighing it down."[14]

On the second day of the convention an even noisier crowd packed the coliseum and laughed at everything said or done for seven hours. They watched Borah, William Barnes, Boies Penrose, Herbert Hadley, and Hiram Johnson file into the hall with the cheerfulness of pallbearers. The leaders' names were called, but they declined to gaze upward and permit the crowd to see the worried expressions on their faces.

On June 19 a premature bolt occurred from the Credentials Committee meeting. Called back by Roosevelt, his men left again that evening declaring that they were out for good. They had bolted because the committee refused a full hearing on all the contested cases. The following morning after a conference with his delegates Roosevelt openly endorsed a bolt, advising them to act no longer with a "fraudulent majority." After caucuses held on June 20 delegates from Idaho and other states notified Taft headquarters that if forced to choose between the Colonel and their party, they would choose the party.

That same day, conceding that Roosevelt was beaten, Borah put his best efforts into an effort to obtain a compromise. He told Roosevelt that he could not be nominated and offered the Colonel a proposal which he said came from Taft leaders able to deliver the goods: "The roll will be purged of the 72 delegates we claim are tainted, a progressive platform acceptable to us will be adopted, Taft and Roosevelt will withdraw from the race, and we will name Hadley by acclamation." Roosevelt was seated at a table under a glass chandelier. He sprang to his feet, raised his fist, and smashed the chandelier; then, bringing his fist down on the table with a whack, he exclaimed: "By God, I will never do it. Let them purge the roll and then come to me and I'll tell them what I will do." There was a silence. Then Borah, white-faced, broke it: "Well Colonel, in the future you and your friends can do as you please, but you can't make a jackass out of me any longer." Then he left the room. Shortly after that Roosevelt issued a statement: "I can only serve the progressive cause by bearing the brunt of the fight myself."[15]

Hadley, who enjoyed great popularity with the crowd, had been approached several times to head a compromise ticket. So had

Borah. Three times William Barnes of New York sought interviews with Borah to urge him to allow the use of his name coupled with Hughes, and each time Borah refused to see or talk with him.[16] One morning the Idaho delegation marched into the coliseum wearing "Borah for President" hatbands, which they were quietly asked to remove. Borah would not even consider second place on the ticket. He had always said he would rather be Borah than vice-president. Neither the Taft leaders nor Hughes took the talk of a compromise candidate seriously, and, of course, Roosevelt would hear of no other candidate but himself.[17]

The convention had opened on June 18, 1912, the hundredth anniversary of the battle of Waterloo. Just opposite the elevator near the Roosevelt headquarters hung a painting of Napoleon's retreat from Moscow. Some of the Roosevelt leaders eyed it ruefully Friday evening before the balloting began. A few of them even suggested having it taken down, but such action could have been easily misconstrued so it was left hanging there.

On June 21 Taft was nominated on the first ballot: 581 votes were cast for him, 107 for Roosevelt, 41 for La Follette, and 2 for Hughes, while 344 Roosevelt delegates refused to cast their vote. Once again Taft's running mate would be "Sunny Jim" Sherman of New York.

In one sense, Taft received the nomination by manipulation. In another, he defeated Roosevelt by making use of the practices by which most presidents are made, including those used by Roosevelt himself in 1908 to nominate Taft. Events might not have proceeded in strict accordance with the rule of ethics, but they went according to the rule of politics.

The following day arrangements were made for the informal meeting of the defeated faction at Orchestra Hall, where Roosevelt was to announce plans for the organization of a new party. The Colonel was having a late dinner at the hotel when Borah arrived. "Well, Colonel," he said, "I have come to tell you goodbye. I guess I have done all I can. The thing is over."

Roosevelt stood up and took his hand. "I am glad you came in. I had a man out hunting for you. Borah, I do not know how you feel about it by this time, but if you feel that you can, I should like to have you take charge of this meeting at the theatre tonight."

"Well, Colonel," Borah replied, "I am sorry, but I have gone as far as I can go. I have always been opposed to a third party movement. I think it is a great mistake. I not only cannot go, but I would not like to see your friends go over there and commit you, practically nominate you, on a third party ticket."

Irritated, Roosevelt began: "Well, what would you have me do? Those men are in earnest. If they do not nominate me they will nominate La Follette. The movement cannot be stopped."

Borah tried persuasion. "Colonel, these men will do just as you tell them to do. Call in some of the leaders and tell them that you do not want any such action, and they will not take any such action." He asked Roosevelt to go home and think it over. If the demand persisted, he advised organizing from the ground up. Borah felt that had the matter been allowed to rest for a few days, the Progressive party might never have been born.

Roosevelt became more and more irritated as Borah continued. He boasted that he would break the solid South. At this moment a crowd of Roosevelt's followers burst into the room with a bundle of telegrams, shouting: "The country will not stand for it; the country is afire. You must lead us!" Borah slowly edged away and quietly slipped out of the room. Returning to his hotel, he packed his bags. Sunday morning he and Mrs. Borah left for Washington without a word of explanation to anyone.[18]

The trains out of Chicago were crowded. It must have embarrassed Borah and Alice Roosevelt Longworth to meet in a Washington-bound dining car. There was an argument, and Alice tried to talk the senator out of his Republican label. Borah was adamant, and for the duration of the campaign they remained political enemies. In the few speeches he made before going west, however, Borah continued to denounce the "theft" in Chicago.

Desertions followed the meeting in Orchestra Hall. Hadley wrote his regrets; six of the seven "little Governors" who had written the now-famous letter requesting his candidacy parted political company with Roosevelt, as did William Ward, Ormsby McHarg, Randolph Bourne, Senators Cummins, Kenyon, and Gronna, and others who evidently thought that a family quarrel was one thing, a divorce another. Roosevelt remarked: "What a miserable showing some of the so-called Progressive leaders have made. They represent nothing but mere sound and fury. A year or two ago, when it was merely a question of loud words, they were claiming to be much further advanced than I was, but they have not the heart for a fight, and the minute they were up against deeds instead of words, they quit forthwith."[19]

The nation did not know, of course, about the private talks Borah had with T. R. before and during the convention, and on the face of the situation many concluded the senator was a deserter. Later Borah declared: "I did not desert Roosevelt. I might just as well say that Roosevelt deserted me. We had both announced that we would stay within the Republican Party. Roosevelt left it. I stayed. But I supported Roosevelt to the limit in the convention until he bolted. All this is a matter of history and can be verified."[20]

Back home in Idaho Borah was faced with a complicated situation. Never had he been more popular in his own state. Not only did he have the support of Republicans, but thousands of Democrats were anxious to keep him in the Senate because of his record and the prestige his name had given the state. He received heavy support from women throughout Idaho (who had been given the franchise in 1896) and later attributed his success to them.[21] Nevertheless, powerful opposition from the old guard remained a threat. Calvin Cobb's conservative Idaho *Statesman* hinted that a regular Republican rival would be pitted against him and would receive the support of the paper. This was an empty menace, as time proved, for Borah's popularity was so great and his arguments were so convincing that no opposition candidate would have stood a chance. Chairman Hilles of the Republican National Committee demanded the dismissal of all members not supporting the party's candidate. According to him, any Republican unable to accept the final judgment of the party's representatives should get out. Politically, Hilles thought Borah was useless and lacking in moral courage.[22]

Borah opened his campaign in the Methodist Church at Meridian, a small farming town about ten miles west of Boise. His fighting speech sounded the keynote of his entire campaign. Declaring that he was a Republican who wished to make his fight within the party, he nevertheless declined to commit himself to either Roosevelt or Taft. He said:

> In one day this week I received communications from two candidates for the legislature, both on the Republican ticket. One . . . informed me that if I was not a Taft man he would not vote for me. The other said

he was a Roosevelt man and if I was not for Roosevelt he would not support me . . . I answer them now . . . publicly. These men seem to be hunting for an intellectual slave . . . They do not ask me whether I am a Republican or a third party man . . . They do not say 'Your record . . . has not been to the credit of your state, and therefore I must oppose you' . . . I reject their standards . . . If you ask me if I am a Republican, I answer 'Yes,' as I understand Republican doctrines . . . I am a Progressive, but I want to fight inside the old party. But inside or outside I propose to urge the progressive measures for which I, with others, have stood.

Borah challenged the state Republican organization to meet and declare that he was not a Republican. He would then get off their ticket, choose some other way to reach the people, and thus find out who constituted the Republican party in Idaho. He also invited the Republican legislators, morally obligated to vote for the Republican candidate nominated at the primary, to state clearly their intentions to the people. Borah knew nearly all the legislators personally and was confident that they would do the right thing. He was trying to give everyone the freedom of action which he claimed for himself. Whatever came, he would not change his views or cease to advocate them. Above all, he wanted the matter settled by the people, "the court of last resort," for Republicanism is what the countless thousands who constitute the rank and file declare it to be. He challenged the audience to name one issue in Congress or the campaign on which he had failed to take a positive stand. "It is because I am positive on all these questions that the opposition is coming from certain sources to my reelection . . ." he said. "If I were more uncertain they would be far more certain as to their support of me." He concluded: "A man who will not stand for what he thinks is right at home . . . will not stand [for it] . . . at Washington, and God pity the miserable creature sailing upon the turbulent political sea without convictions for a compass. I have seen them and there is nothing more despicable . . . I am for measures, not men . . ."[23]

Throughout September Borah stumped the state, hammering at the old guard and challenging its leaders to oust him from the Republican party, which undoubtedly they would have done but for the fact that they knew he would run on an independent ticket and win. The name Borah was already becoming magical in the state. He accomplished the phenomenal feat of establishing camp in the political no man's land between Taft and Roosevelt, remaining a friend of both but a supporter of neither one. Meanwhile T. R. was also stumping the West.

The whistle of Roosevelt's special train sounded in Idaho as it tore through the mountain states. It entered Montana from North Dakota, left it, and went on to the Pacific coast. Borah breathed a sigh of relief. The Idaho situation was a bit too ticklish for an embarrassing clash with the Colonel. He read newspaper accounts of Roosevelt's barnstorming through Washington and Oregon. Then came the thunderbolt.

Instead of continuing south down the Pacific coast, Roosevelt's train made an unexpected turn eastward, heading straight for Idaho. The news spread that Roosevelt was going to speak in Boise. As state leader and a candidate for the Senate seat who needed Bull Moose votes, Borah would preside at the meeting. How could he introduce Roosevelt?

Borah rose to the occasion. When the train crossed into Idaho, he boarded it and rode with T. R. to Boise. However, he wore a worried look as the two alighted at the station. Later they faced each other on the speakers' platform in a hall packed to the rafters. In a dexterous speech Borah introduced the former President and concluded by saying that if Roosevelt had received the Republican nomination at Chicago, the party would have swept the country. Then he waved Roosevelt to the rostrum with a low bow.

The Colonel stepped forward, quoted Borah's last sentence, and thanked him warmly for his remarks. "So I will explain," he went on with careful distinctness, "just why it was that I was *not* nominated and," he added with a merry grin, "I will ask Senator Borah to corroborate me." Borah tried to smile but not knowing what to expect, he stopped in the middle of it. The crowd howled.

The issue Roosevelt made in every western speech was that the nomination had been stolen from him. He now took up each state in turn, showing how it had elected delegates favorable to him and how their places had been stolen and given to others who would vote right. As he concluded each recital, he turned to the dismayed chairman and said with eager politeness, "Isn't that so, Senator Borah?" And the unhappy Borah was forced, each time, to nod his head and smile. He could neither refuse his nod nor qualify what T. R. said. He was obliged to listen while the Colonel made him the involuntary party to a speech arraigning the Republican organization as a band of thieves. After securing Borah's endorsement of every charge he made, Roosevelt concluded with an air of bland innocence, as if he were laying down a general axiom of no special application to anybody: "Anyone who is acquainted with the facts and does not condemn them is blinded to the light and has a seared moral sense."[24]

In Idaho, as in many other states where the Republican party was hopelessly split into factions, Wilson defeated Taft by a slim margin of popular votes. The Republican, John Haines, was chosen governor, and in the legislature the election gave the Republicans the largest majority they had ever had. When the next session opened on January 14, 1913, Borah was elected on the first ballot. He issued a statement thanking the people of Idaho for their approval of his effort to serve them. He pledged his time, energies, and whatever ability he possessed to the people of Idaho and the nation.[25]

For Borah there were thousands of third party and Democratic votes as well as the usual Republican majority in Idaho. However, for the Republican party as a whole the election of 1912 was Waterloo, as Charles Taft put it in his editorial.[26] Congress was now dominated in both houses by a Democratic majority. The election of Wilson was perhaps less important than the fact that it smothered progressivism in the Republican organization. Gradually the Grand Old Party became convinced that progressivism, like pioneering, did not pay, and it retired upon its conservative wing to maintain uncompromising hostility to liberal principles.

IX Wilson, Reform, and War

. . . it would be the irony of fate if my administration had to deal chiefly with foreign affairs.
—Woodrow Wilson

Fresh winds blew over Capitol Hill on the March morning Wilson was inaugurated. His inaugural address, calling for justice and only justice,[1] struck a high note of idealism. When Congress was called into special session for tariff revision, it found Progressives divided on this first issue. La Follette and other Midwesterners supported the Underwood-Simmons bill to lower duties, but Borah, Norris of Nebraska, Kenyon of Iowa, and other Progressives took the traditional position of most farmers, favoring moderately high duties on agricultural products. Borah continued to press for equality for the farmer in a tariff system which put him at a disadvantage. He considered this tariff measure unwise in many features and harsh to agricultural interests.

While the tariff debate was still in progress, Wilson presented Congress with a program for banking and currency reform; Borah took particular interest in the Federal Reserve bill. The senator was familiar with the central banking systems of Britain, France, and Germany, which controlled the issuance of currency, making it legal tender. To his way of thinking there could be no sound objection to government control of management and directorship. He pointed out that if bankers were allowed to expand and contract the currency, the state would be depriving itself of a sovereign right. "Not satisfied with giving over to private interest . . . monopoly of currency and credits," he said of the bill, "it gives them the astounding privilege to say how much [currency] we shall have or . . . shall not have."[2] Borah's position was similar to that of Bryan and the western farm leaders.

Wilson, who could not afford to ignore this western feeling, sought the advice among others of Louis Brandeis, a great legal mind thoroughly grounded in modern business and finance. In the end he yielded to some western demands: no banker had membership on the Federal Reserve Board, and all notes of issue became government obligations. Borah was dissatisfied with these concessions. He asked: "What is the benefit going to be to the large business interests of the country, to the farming and agricultural interests . . . of putting more money in the hands of banks to enable them to speculate it at an exorbitant rate of interest? Must we put it out to the banks at three percent and see the people pay eight or nine percent? Who are we legislating for—the money lender or the money user?"[3] Despite his objections the Federal Reserve Act passed the Senate on December 19, 1913, by a vote of 54 to 34.

Monopoly, thought Borah, is ten thousand times worse than black slavery; it is the father of class domination, the molder of chains both for the body and soul. Whereas T. R. wanted the regulation of "good" monopolies, and Brandeis and Wilson wanted to destroy all private monopolies, Borah demanded the destruction of *all* monopolies—public and private. "A Republic is strong enough to destroy, but never could be strong enough to regulate monopoly," he said. Borah felt that the Sherman Act would have been an effective statute from 1890 on if four or five men had been put in jail. "Most of the fellows," he lamented, "who should have been jailed turned reformers, and went into politics."[4]

He opposed Wilson's Federal Trade Commission, which he regarded as a device under which monopolies could make a supreme effort, with every prospect of success, to regulate their regulators. The Sherman Act, thought Borah, had been based upon the right principle—the destruction of trusts and monopolies. That and not regulation was what he wanted; he would be satisfied with nothing less. The FTC was a step toward bureaucracy and made a distinction between the large and small employer. He said: "Let us . . . see what kind of a strait-jacket are we undertaking to put the business of this country in by leaving the Sherman law as it is . . . and . . . enacting a law which says that unfair competition is unlawful without advising the business world . . . what does constitute unfair competition. And this strait-jacket will be far more embarrassing to small competitive firms . . . than it will be to great combinations . . ."[5] After the commission was established, Borah remained hostile; he was convinced it would be used by conservatives to further the process of consolidation. "I would not vote to put anybody on the

Federal Trade Commission. I would be glad to vote to repeal the law."[6]

His objections to the Clayton Act were even more decided, for he looked upon it as ". . . purely a political makeshift to mislead the people into the belief that something tremendous has been done on the trust question." Opposing the exemption of labor from the provisions of the Sherman Act as in the interest neither of the country nor of labor itself, he asserted that he was trying to see both sides of the labor question.[7] When constituents wrote objecting to the antitrust legislation, his stock reply was that the Republicans had nothing to do with it, Congress had nothing to do with it, and all legislation was by Democratic caucus under the control of the President.

At a banquet of Progressives and Republicans at Columbus, Ohio, on February 26, 1914, Borah was the principal speaker. He stated that the only hope of rejuvenating the Republican party lay in fighting monopoly. Even if the Republican party were at an end, he said:

> I could not join the third party so long as it stands as it now stands . . . on the question of monopoly . . . The President of one of these great trusts says he would like to be managed and regulated a little, but not dismembered in any way. Mr. Perkins, the most . . . powerful voice . . . of the third party, says that it is the thing to do, that these monopolies are the proper thing, and that all they need is a little regulation. I cannot imagine a more harmonious affair than my friend Beveridge as Attorney General and Mr. Perkins as head of a board engaged in the regulation of monopolies.[8]

The following day George W. Perkins, former partner of J. P. Morgan and chairman of the Progressive National Committee, sent Borah an irate letter. Referring to Borah's speech, he wrote:

> According to the newspapers . . . you made the statement that the Progressive party is in favor of regulating monopoly. Either you do not know what you are talking about or else you made this statement with the deliberate intention of . . . deceiving the voters of this country, for there is absolutely no truth whatever in any such statement . . . What is

your authority . . . for making such a charge? . . . If you have no authority . . . you owe it to the voters of this country to retract this statement.[9]

Perkins pointed out that the International Harvester Company was no monopoly; indeed, it was expanding rather than restraining trade and treating labor, consumers, and competitors fairly.

Borah sent Perkins a lengthy reply, stating it had not been his purpose to misrepresent him nor had he supposed he had done so. "I do not deny at all the efficacy of that philosophy which permits men to practice one thing all their lives and after gathering all the fruits that such a practice may bring—repent. But I had always believed that restitution ought to be . . . an accompaniment of these death bed repentances . . . Immediately after denying that you believe in monopoly, you enter upon a vigorous defense of one of the most unconscionable and shameless monopolies we have ever had in this country—the Harvester trust."[10] After making other grave charges, Borah handed his letter to the newspapers. Perkins at once replied, and Borah also received angry letters from Cyrus McCormick, president of International Harvester, and T. Coleman Dupont.[11] The joust with Perkins probably did the Idahoan more political good than harm. It made clearer his reasons for remaining in the Republican party in 1912. Henceforth Roosevelt frequently invited Borah to Oyster Bay, but the senator always complained of being "too pressed for time" or reluctant to miss "even one session of Congress."

As the 1914 elections approached, the political situation in Idaho looked ominous for the Republicans. The Bull Moose party was reorganizing all over the state, again threatening to split the Republican vote and throw the election to the Democrats. Borah urged the choice of a forceful, progressive ticket, but he suggested no names and made no endorsements. He was content, like the Israelites of old, "to stand still and see the salvation of the Lord."[12]

The returns in 1914 must have given Borah reason to feel that his stand in 1912 had been justified. Heading state tickets were Albert J. Beveridge, Amos Pinchot, Raymond Robins, Henry Allen, Francis H. Heney, Bainbridge Colby, Victor Murdock, and Hiram Johnson; all but Johnson were defeated in an even greater debacle than 1912. Of those who had left the party and sided with George W. Perkins, some few returned; others were never heard from again. Moreover, the old guard sent back to Congress such veterans who were defeated in 1912 as "Uncle Joe" Cannon, William B. McKinley, and Nicholas Longworth to join Henry Cabot Lodge, James Gallinger, and Reed Smoot in blocking progressive legislation. In Idaho winners were James H. Brady and the two Republican candidates for the House, Addison T. Smith and Robert M. McCracken, but John Haines, Republican candidate for governor, lost as a result of scandals in the office of state treasurer. Borah and Albert B. Cummins of Iowa deserved part of the credit for Republican successes after Waterloo two years earlier.

Early in December 1915 the Republican National Committee met in Washington to reorganize the machinery of the party. This meeting changed the basis of representation at national conventions, reduced the number of southern delegates, and gave full recognition to the direct primary in the election of delegates to national conventions. Triumphantly Borah wrote to Arthur Vandenberg: "The machinery of the party is now in the hands of the voters. They can write the platform and nominate the candidate. Hence my belief that in 1916 we will write a progressive platform, nominate a progressive candidate, and win . . ."[13]

The possibility that Borah might run for president in 1916 had been discussed intermittently since 1912, especially by hopeful Idaho friends. His consistent reply was that he had no money with which to wage a campaign and that he was interested primarily in good legislation. "I haven't a particle of desire to stay in Washington any longer if something is not to be done."[14] However, as a prominent Progressive and a leader in the movement to reorganize the Republican party, he was still considered by some a logical choice for the nomination. Before retiring as publisher of the *North American Review* and *Harper's Weekly*, George Harvey predicted that the next Republican candidate would be Borah. The fact that he had made a similar prediction about Wilson in 1911 gave authority to his words. The editor of *Current Opinion* wrote: "If the promoters of harmony fail with Senator Borah as their stalking horse, they may as well give up, for he is the strongest selection that could be made, and shows that the conservatives are ready to go the limit in concessions." At a dinner of the American Manufacturers' Association in Baltimore, Champ Clark also predicted Borah's nomination. Borah's good-humored reply was: "I am not accepting after-dinner nominations for the presidency today."[15]

As the convention drew nearer, Harvey reiterated his confidence that in the next campaign Republicans would cross the Mississippi to find the party candidate.[16] He wrote Borah that he was actively laboring to effect this object:

> . . . I have had several talks with Senator Murray Crane here and at his home in Massachusetts. He has always manifested a friendly feeling toward you but went much further last night when I told him I should like to send you a message from him. He promptly authorized me to say that he was as friendly as you could possibly desire and that nothing could please him better than to serve you in any way. He also said . . . that he had found a decided sentiment for you all through New England . . . I have not seen T. R. yet but hope to . . .[17]

In his Jackson day address at Indianapolis on January 8, 1915, Wilson attacked the Republican party and its leaders. Borah was chosen to reply. Senator John Sharp Williams furnished an opportunity on January 13 that he was quick to grasp. For an hour and twenty minutes he arraigned the Administration and especially its Mexican policy before a crowded Senate. Beginning with the Interstate Commerce Act, he traced the Republican record to the time of Roosevelt and found it impossible to point to any like period since the days of Pericles filled with so much progressive legislation. He objected to the fact that although the cost of living was higher than at any previous time, the emergency war tax would exact another hundred million from the people. He predicted that the cry in 1916 would not be for new ideas but for bread. Borah quoted a prominent Mexican as having told an American in Chihuahua: "We have murdered your men, we have ravished your women; we have insulted and spat upon your flag; tell us what we can do to make you Yankees fight and we will do it." He reached a climax when he said that the "flag which will not protect its protectors is a dirty rag that contaminates the air in which it floats."[18]

This speech had a strong impact on the Senate. Lodge and Root were prompt to offer their congratulations. Others crowded around

Borah's desk. Townsend of Michigan, coming out of the chamber, exclaimed: ". . . the reunited Republicans have found a leader! Borah is the natural voice of the party."[19]

The Republican convention opened in Chicago on June 7, 1916, amid great public anxieties. The war in Europe, about to enter its third year, seemed to be drawing closer to our shores. Large forces were massed on the Mexican border, and a note had been sent to Germany threatening the severance of diplomatic relations unless she abandoned unrestricted submarine warfare.

A chilling rain fell over the crowd milling around the entrance to the huge coliseum, where some 11,000 delegates and spectators were assembled. Outside thousands of woman suffragists, undaunted by the weather, paraded for an hour. When they reached the coliseum, Carrie Chapman Catt as their leader presented Borah, a member of the Resolutions Committee, with their proposed suffrage plank. He promised to do what he could to incorporate it in the platform. A bitter fight over the plank lasted all night. Against it were Senators Lodge and Wadsworth; among those favoring woman suffrage, if granted by state action, were Senators Madden, Sutherland, and Borah. On the following day Lodge read the committee report. When he came to the words, "The Republican party, reaffirming its faith in government of the people, by the people and for the people, favors the extension of the suffrage to women . . .," screams of exultation from the gallery set off the first spontaneous cheering of the day. Lodge waited until he could make himself heard and shouted, ". . . *but* we recognize the right of each state to settle this question for itself." The cheers died. Only Mrs. Catt stood unmoved, for she had been warned of the states' rights rider, the work of Borah, and was deeply disappointed.[20]

At the Chicago auditorium the Progressive convention was simultaneously in session. There was hope that the parties would agree on a candidate, and George Perkins said: "It will not necessarily have to be the Colonel." Little by little, the Bull Moose was shedding his progressive antlers. Roosevelt was not in Chicago, but a private wire between Oyster Bay and both conventions kept him in constant touch. Borah talked with him on convention eve, reporting his faith that in the end harmony would reign. Although he had previously supported Albert B. Cummins's candidacy, these conversations found him moving toward Charles Evans Hughes. He announced that he was going to release the Idaho and Wyoming delegations from their support of his own candidacy, which would mean additional support for Hughes.[21]

"Peace Committees," representing both conventions, were set up for the purpose of holding joint conferences and selecting a candidate whom all could support. The conferees included Murray Crane, Reed Smoot, Borah, Nicholas Murray Butler, and A. R. Johnson on the Republican side, and Hiram Johnson, Horace Wilkinson, George W. Perkins, C. J. Bonaparte, and Governor Parker of Louisiana for the Progressives. From the beginning Borah had little faith in these conferences and said so. It was evident that unity on any single candidate was impossible. The Progressives wanted Roosevelt and had no second choice. The Republicans would not accept Roosevelt under any circumstances and refused to suggest a name in advance of the balloting. Achieving nothing, the first meeting adjourned. Borah announced that he favored suspending further negotiations with the Progressives: "What we must do now is to proceed just as we would have done had there never been a third party . . . Harmony is to be desired but we cannot be expected to descend to bartering our dignity and independence."[22]

The platforms adopted by the conventions were similar. The Republican plank, which Borah helped frame, minced no words on foreign policy. Emphasizing Mexico rather than Germany, he faced threats from both areas squarely and "burned his German bridges behind him." He could never expect national hyphenate support again. On the convention floor he glared at the delegates from Chicago, Milwaukee, and Minneapolis and shouted: "Make our position strong for America first, for the protection of American rights here and abroad, and those who love America above all will be with us; the rest we do not want." The German-American delegates looked at him glumly as he continued: ". . . and a nation which declares itself too proud to fight will soon be regarded by the nations of the earth as too cowardly to live."[23]

Balloting began Friday, June 9. At noon on Saturday the Republicans nominated Hughes on the third ballot. Of the scattered votes on that ballot Borah received one each from the Alabama and Texas delegations. Charles Fairbanks was nominated for the vice-presidency, and the convention adjourned that same day.

The conference committee met Friday night, but failed again to reach an agreement and adjourned early Saturday morning. With no preliminary announcement Borah walked over to the auditorium hall Friday afternoon while the Progressive convention was in session and sat in the press box. Raymond Robins spotted him and half dragged, half coaxed him to the stage. The crowd shouted: "Welcome home, Bill," and "Borah is all right." Announcing that he had come unofficially, Chairman Robins introduced him. Borah said: ". . . Frankly, the chief explanation for my appearance here is that I wanted inspiration." As he introduced the magic word Roosevelt into his speech, cries of "We want Teddy" resounded through the hall. He waited until the chanting ceased. "It is well known the deep-seated affection I have for your leader . . . There is no doubt you want Teddy . . ."

"We want Borah, too," shouted the delegates, and Borah smiled as he swung into the main part of his speech. He reminded them that he was present as a member of a committee of another convention. He added: ". . . let us bear in mind that what these two conventions do here will perhaps decide the welfare of the United States for the next quarter of a century. We can only insure ourselves by working in close cooperation . . . it is essential that before we leave this great city it should be definitely determined that we will march and fight together . . . but if the two conventions agree upon your great leader, you will find no more enthusiastic supporter than myself."[24]

Even Roosevelt must have known by then that he had no hope of getting the endorsement of both conventions, for he sent his stupefying recommendation that the Progressives nominate Henry Cabot Lodge, "a man whose frosty breath had been blown against every important progressive measure for two decades." The Progressives scorned this suggestion and finally insisted on nominating T.R. who declined their nomination in a letter made public too late for the convention to name another candidate. "It was a dour and terrible hour," wrote heartbroken William Allen White, "the ebb tide for our cause."[25] Later, the Progressives endorsed Hughes.

Borah came out of the whole affair a more powerful figure. He induced members of the compromise committee, and especially

Crane and Smoot, to understand that they would be responsible for a Republican disaster if they refused to negotiate in an amicable spirit with the Progressives. Hughes would have been chosen without the assistance of the committee, but all agreed that its work brought levelheaded Progressives into line for the nominee.[26]

The Democrats, of course, renominated Wilson, who continued to urge strict neutrality and conduct a high-minded battle, although every political trick was used to discredit him.

Borah began his speaking tour through the Middle West in August when the thermometer reached 110°. As Wilson's strength grew, the senator's invitation to Progressives took on a new fervor. In Idaho he made a strenuous effort to bring the Republican party back to progressive ideals and to bring Progressives back to the Republican fold. He was ready to discuss any subject of public interest with his audiences. During September and October he stumped the West for Hughes, but his tour came to an end when he collapsed in exhaustion on the speaker's platform in Fond du Lac, Wisconsin. Returning to Washington, he spent the next few weeks recuperating. Idaho gave her vote in 1916 to Wilson, who won the election with a minority of the popular vote. Almost the entire Democratic state ticket was swept into office with Wilson, and Moses Alexander was one of the first Democrats in years to capture the governorship in Idaho.

By the time of Wilson's second inauguration world affairs were at a desperate stage. Across the Atlantic the war was entering its third year with no promise of a truce. Indeed, the Allies were coming to depend more and more upon American intervention, an eventuality which almost everyone in the United States contemplated with dismay. When the British passenger liner "Lusitania" was torpedoed by a German submarine in May 1915, Borah commented: ". . . to my mind the sinking of the steamship of a foe upon which happened to be found American citizens is by no means to be compared with the act of hunting out, robbing, assaulting and murdering American citizens in a neighboring country [Mexico]." He did not agree with what he called the administration's "peace at any price" policy south of the border. The republic should face a world in arms, he asserted, rather than have it said that American women may be attacked and American citizens murdered on its very doorstep. Wherever an established American right was challenged, whether on the sea or in Mexico, whether the nation responsible was large or small, he would meet the challenge without compromise. He stated: "I am not afraid of war if it is necessary to maintain the Republic. We cannot hope to play a part in the great affairs of the world if we are not brave enough to make a sacrifice for our rights."[27]

He urged accelerating the preparedness program and supported the Naval Appropriations bill of 1916 for the construction of new battleships and cruisers. A strong navy appealed to him as an assurance of peace, for "weakness is a source of war." He did not think a large standing army was essential. Limited in size, it should be backed by an enlarged militia such as that of Switzerland. Borah also favored extending military training to the schools and colleges. He coined the phrase: "America first, let it cost what it may."

Borah maintained that the rights of belligerents on the sea begin where the rights of neutrals end. He was one of fourteen senators supporting the Gore Resolution denying Americans the right to travel on the armed ships of belligerents. However, had he been permitted to do so, he said he would have voted for any intelligent measure embodying the principle that an American citizen could properly travel on a neutral merchant ship armed for defensive purposes. He said: ". . . It is a right which has been established under international law for these five hundred years, and in my judgment this is not the time for the great American Republic to begin to temporize and compromise . . ." He would prefer that our battleships be sunk a thousand times than to have the independence of the Senate compromised on this issue.[28]

Early in 1917 President Wilson delivered his "peace without victory" speech, in which he formulated the conditions upon which the United States might co-operate in maintaining world peace. Meanwhile German Generals von Hindenburg and Ludendorff convinced the Kaiser in December 1916 that a renewal of unrestricted submarine warfare would break the British blockade and destroy British morale, though the Germans fully understood the risk of involving the United States in the conflict. New assaults on our shipping followed.

On February 3 Wilson announced that diplomatic relations with Germany had been severed. Borah voted for the Senate resolution approving the President's action. While the nation prepared for war, he hoped it could remain neutral, declaring that a severance of diplomatic relations with Germany should not mean that we were on the side of the Allies. When the President asked for authority to arm merchant ships, Borah signed the round robin supporting the Armed Ships bill. However, he thought that the manner in which this bill was presented was unfair to the Senate: "The President should have acted . . . immediately after severing . . . diplomatic relations with Germany. But he procrastinated and side-stepped until a few hours before adjournment. It was all I could do to bring myself away from my resentful feelings but I voted to support the resolution because I thought it was the right thing to do and was not willing to waive my view as to what ought to be done in order to show my resentment as to the manner of its being done."[29]

In his message of April 2 Wilson asked Congress to declare a state of war with Germany.[30] The joint resolution meeting the President's recommendations was reported out of the Foreign Relations Committee favorably, and the debate began for its adoption the next day. Senators Harding, McCumber, Swanson, Lodge, Williams, Ashurst, Colt, Cummins, Pittman, Myers, and Borah were among those who spoke for it. Borah's remarks were brief:

> . . . I do not find it possible on my part to vote against it . . . The resolution does not commit this country to a war of aggression but . . . [the war] is being fought in the defense and for the protection of the rights of the American people . . . I join no crusade; I seek or accept no alliance; I obligate this Government to no other power. I make war alone for my countrymen and their rights, for my country and its honor . . . All factions . . . sectionalism . . . difference of opinion . . . partisanship will have been burned and purged away, and will have established once and for all as a security for our children and our children's children that there comes a time when even the American people, with all their love of peace, will take up the gauntlet of war.[31]

Senator La Follette spoke against the resolution in a four-hour flight of oratory, which Senator John Sharp Williams called a "verbal eternity." The resolution was adopted in the Senate 82 to 6 and in the House 373 to 50. Of all the votes he cast in the Senate, this was one which Borah stated he would like to have changed. If he could have foreseen in 1917 the price that had to be paid in blood and treasure for the crusade "to make the world safe for democracy," he would have voted against war.

A few months later during the debate on the Rivers and Harbors bill Borah made a speech warning Americans that they were too complacent about their part in the war. It was no time, he said, for parleying over how much money should go into Fish Creek. There was also no point in talking until Germany had been vanquished, and this would not come about until we threw our whole force into the conflict. "I believe," he said, "that a republic which exists . . . only in the affection of its citizens could not long survive the day when it refused to defend the right . . . of its citizens, and for that reason and for no other under the sun I voted for war, and from that hour, in my judgment, it became an American war."[32]

Once America entered the conflict, Borah became a war-party lieutenant with peace-party instincts. He insisted first upon a definite statement of war aims. He wanted taxation made the main basis of our revenue, bond drives and loans a secondary source. He fought war-revenue measures, under which men who did no fighting reaped the profits of war, and demanded a tax of 80 per cent on all war profits. He set himself against high wartime prices and introduced measures to punish profiteering, characterizing the men who raised their prices as "infinitely lower than a foreign spy."

Borah used his influence in the Senate to nourish what little liberalism survived during war days. For the moment La Follette was in eclipse. Kenyon, Walsh, and Norris had neither Borah's influence nor interest. Borah carried the fight for liberalism from one issue to another through 1917 and 1918. He denounced the Espionage Act as the product of a drumhead government and was one of six senators to vote against it. It flew in the face of the First Amendment liberties insisted upon by Hamilton and Jefferson. War measures, Borah warned his colleagues, do not suspend other provisions of the Constitution. He fought the wholesale raids of the Department of Justice, branding them as infamous. Though he lost more battles than he won, he gained greater prestige than ever. Events on more than one occasion proved his judgment was correct.[33]

He wanted the government to take over all the meat-packing houses in the Midwest and distribute food on a more equitable basis. He opposed the floating of bond issues. "Bonds" he said, "bring about inflation, increase prices and aggravate . . . the distress . . . of a great body of people. After the war, those bonds and their interest charges will be paid almost entirely by taxes on consumption. War profits will be gone, the burden falling upon those who now suffer particularly from high prices. The bond system has a strong tendency to make the same class who fight the war pay for the war. The amount of bonds issued . . . should be kept down to the lowest possible figure."[34]

Similarly he opposed the principle behind conscription, which he called the basis of militarism. Borah believed that had the President on April 5 called for 500,000 volunteers, 1,000,000 would have responded. Let us quit talking of "slackerism," he said; "it puts the brand of pharisaism on ourselves." He thought conscription had the tendency to eliminate that ". . . soul, that enthusiasm of free men . . . just as essential to a . . . fighting force as discipline itself." Moreover, he saw nothing equitable or just in calling young men between the ages of nineteen and twenty-five. He wanted the age limit raised to forty-five so that the student would not have to be torn away from his studies.[35]

The conflict brought Borah to the forefront in American politics and in the Senate so unmistakably that no subsequent failures of his party, not even those during the Harding administration, could take away the prestige he commanded. He supported the war as loyally as any Democrat, but he never hesitated to speak out against measures he regarded as unjust.

In April 1917 Borah made this quiet announcement from Washington: "It has for some time been my desire and it is now my purpose to quit official life at the close of my term March 5, 1919 . . . I feel it should . . . be made known in a public way to the people of my state . . . My public service will not end . . . I am not going to discuss my reasons for retirement . . . These . . . will appear and be better understood as my plans and purposes are developed . . ."[36]

Borah was then a man of fifty-two and was in his physical and mental prime. Thus far political fortune had favored him. His announcement came as a shock, especially to the people of Idaho. When the New York *Times* published his statement, it said that financial reasons had forced Borah to resume the practice of law.[37]

Borah gave the impression he was finding it increasingly difficult to make ends meet. He and his wife lived modestly in their Wyoming Avenue apartment. His personal habits still bordered on the frugality practiced during college days. The only luxuries he permitted himself were his horse and the books added to his growing library. However, Mrs. Borah's tastes were fine and expensive. In Idaho Borah's income had enabled him to cater to her whims, but in Washington he found this was becoming more difficult. During 1917-18 he called in several loans and mortgages, because, as he told Boise friends, he needed the cash. For a time, as rents continued to climb in wartime Washington, he talked about buying a house. They continued, however, to make their home in apartment houses. He tried to interest publishers in a collection of his speeches, but not until later was he successful. It seemed clear that if he retired from the Senate, he could earn a far higher salary. He was said to have considered an offer from a New York law firm for $100,000 a year with the opportunity of continuing his political activities on a less formal level. Advisers reminded him that if he entertained any presidential ambitions, the Senate was not a good point of departure; in fact, it had proved a political graveyard for men like Webster and Clay.

The best explanation for his desire to leave the Senate is to be found in a confidential letter to a friend in which he wrote that he was prompted neither by a desire to make more money nor by dissatisfaction with conditions in Idaho, but the situation in Washington was such that he simply felt he had to stand aloof. "Now I voted for a declaration of war," he wrote. "I did so because I felt that regardless of what had brought us . . . we had arrived at the point where action was . . . essential to protect the rights and honor of our country." However, he found many of the war measures adopted at variance with the views and convictions of a lifetime—views which he could not change. "I am unwilling," he said, "to Prussianize this country in order to de-Prussianize Germany. I do not think it necessary."[38] To another Idaho friend disturbed over the prospect of his resignation, Borah replied: " . . . I would rather quit and shovel dirt the rest of my life. I may often betray my country through ignorance, but I will never do it knowingly."[39]

No sooner had Borah's announcement appeared but from every corner of Idaho and from many other states came expressions ranging from sincere regret to open opposition. An informal campaign was launched to induce him to reverse his decision.

Some New York papers were loud in their praise. Said the *American:* "There is a resonant manliness about him . . . which commends him to this period of uncertainty and peril, a certain fearless honesty . . . a spirit of catholic patriotism and devotion to the Constitution and its ideals which are needed in Washington now and will be needed more especially when this war is done."[40] The often critical New York *Times* stated: "He is needed in the Senate. Can't he be induced to change his determination to retire . . . There ought to be a right of eminent domain by which such a man could be commandeered to hold office."[41] A most telling appeal was made by *Leslie's Illustrated Weekly Journal:* "It is hoped that the state which has been so highly honored by his faithful service will be able to dissuade him from his purpose. The nation needs Mr. Borah . . . now more than ever. An appeal to him on patriotic ground would, we feel sure, be made not in vain."[42]

In response to these appeals Borah consented to accept a renewal of his senatorial commission. Two Idaho seats would be vacated that year, one for the six-year term to succeed Borah and one for the remainder of the late Senator Brady's term. After Borah announced his candidacy to succeed himself, John F. Nugent, who had temporarily been appointed to Brady's seat, made his bid for the short term on the Democratic ticket. Former Governor Frank Gooding was the Republican candidate for the short term.

The Nonpartisan League was an organization of northwestern farmers which had spread from Minnesota and North Dakota through Montana to the western boundary of Idaho. The league's purpose was to gain for the farmer a larger share in the national prosperity which came with the war in Europe. After the United States entered the war, the league opposed conscription and the espionage laws and favored high taxes on war profits. By 1918 its program included state ownership (and distribution) of water power, railroads, warehouses, packing plants, grain elevators, and rural credit banks, and a high tax rate on idle real estate. The organization became an object of suspicion. Nevertheless, in North Dakota it controlled the Republican party, while in Montana and Idaho it dominated the Democratic party.

In July 1918 at its state convention in Boise the Idaho league deplored the quality of the state's delegation in Congress but noted "one splendid exception to this regrettable situation," and that was "the record and attitude of Idaho's senior Senator . . ." The league tendered him an "unsolicited and frank expression of appreciation." The endorsement Borah accepted was eagerly sought by other candidates; conservative Republican leaders in the state urged him to reject it, but he refused. He was in agreement with nine-tenths of the league's program and had only contempt for the "sheer political cowardice and . . . dishonesty" which charged farmers of his state with disloyalty. He stood ready to join in prosecuting any individual in the state against whom evidence of disloyalty could be furnished, but he regarded it as unjust and unwise to denounce indiscriminately thousands of men because they joined an organization when there was evidence only against certain individuals. "Their economic policies may be very wise or very unwise," he said, but "the best way to test false economic propositions is to submit them in the open arena of debate to the crucial test of public opinion . . ."[43]

In the congressional elections of 1918 Wilson privately urged the re-election of Borah. When ex-Senator Dubois of Idaho questioned the President on his attitude toward Borah, Wilson sent the following reply:

> I am free to say that the return of Senator Borah . . . would be entirely satisfactory to me, for I have appreciated very much Borah's friendly and helpful attitude and know that his support can be counted on, but I think you and he will both appreciate my scruple about saying anything for publication. The truth is that I hesitated upon grounds of principle to seem to be electing U.S. Senators, either directly or indirectly, or to seem to be exercising a direct guidance over the electors, who, I am sure will make their own proper assessment of men and measures . . . I feel constrained to express these views to you only in a private way . . . the interests of the country are paramount just now, and I feel confident that the Idaho situation can be worked out in the real interests of the country as a whole.[44]

If Wilson anticipated a fuller measure of co-operation from the Idaho senator in peacemaking than he had given in prosecuting the war, he was in for a severe disappointment. The outcome, on November 5, was the election of a Republican House and Senate. The entire Republican slate was elected in Idaho, for many of the Democrats, including a majority of the state committee, refused to support the candidates of the Nonpartisan League. Of the 46,000 Republican votes cast, Borah received 43,000; it is estimated that 6,000 of the 36,000 Democratic votes cast also went to Borah, along with 14,000 Nonpartisan votes. He carried most of the northern counties, some of them two to one. The state's direct primary law of 1909, never satisfactory, was discredited in this campaign by the Nonpartisan League's successful invasion of the Democratic primary ticket. Despite Borah's objections the legislature repealed the primary law the following year and enacted a new one providing only for the nomination of local officers.[45]

The election made possible the reorganization of the Senate by the Republicans. A conference of progressives was held in Borah's office to determine who would be supported for committee and Senate posts in the party caucus. Borah nominated Albert Cummins of Iowa, who was later chosen president pro tempore, while Senator Charles Curtis was again named party whip. Boies Penrose and Francis E. Warren were proposed by regular Republicans for the chairmanship of the Finance and Appropriations committees respectively, but Borah announced that he would not support Penrose. A ticklish situation developed because the Republicans had a bare majority of two in the Senate and any desertion of the organization would mean Democratic control.[46] By the end of the meeting Lodge had assurances from all the Progressives except Borah that they would support the caucus program.

Republican leaders tried to win the defiant Borah over with every means at hand, even giving assurances that Penrose would vote against the peace treaty and the League of Nations. Borah refused to compromise and insisted that Penrose must go. Senator La Follette strenuously opposed a fight over "poor old Penrose." If he were bypassed, the seniority rule would have to be set aside and the equally reactionary Porter McCumber would accede to the post. The Wisconsin leader told Borah he would go "the whole sled length" in a fight on principle opposing reactionary chairmen of *all* important committees, but he refused to single out Penrose for slaughter.[47]

Penrose, determined not to be displaced, sat silent in his office receiving hourly reports on Borah's state of mind. The day before the caucus meeting it was whispered that Borah intended to make charges against him that would provide a sensation. When the report was brought to Penrose, instead of trembling, he sent word to Borah that he might say what he pleased concerning his political career but if he made any personal charges, he would regret them to his dying day. Now it is very unlikely that Borah had any notions of dragging personalities into the squabble. In any case he did not attend the caucus, which selected Penrose, who was later accepted by a strict party vote in the Senate. Borah joined the other forty-seven Republicans in supporting him.[48]

It was later charged that Borah agreed to abandon his fight against Penrose in return for assurances from Lodge that the Foreign Relations Committee would be packed with a majority opposed to the President's peace program. Former President Taft, in an address reprinted in the *Congressional Record* (June 20, 1919), admitted that efforts were made to pack the committee in 1918-19. Senator Frank Kellogg should have been chosen over Senator Moses, who had been in the Senate only four months; however, Kellogg would give no assurances of voting the way Lodge wanted, and he had made a pro-League speech even before the League Covenant was included in the treaty. Yet Lodge asserted that the treaty was not a party issue![49]

Every indication pointed to a grim struggle when the reorganized Senate would convene to consider the peace treaty which President Wilson was to bring home from Paris.

X The Original Irreconcilable

Entertain no . . . compromise; . . . Have none of it.
—Abraham Lincoln

The "Great War," as contemporaries called it, was the only world conflict Borah lived through. Totally absorbed in domestic problems and affairs, he had shown little previous interest in the affairs of other countries until the United States went to war. World War I marked an important milestone in his career, for it was destined to change his outlook. He approached each problem in foreign policy in terms of its relation to domestic policy, as a general rule seeking to apply to it principles successfully employed at home. Such ideals as the rule of law rather than of force, open diplomacy, and the right of all countries to deal independently with foreign problems as they develop were American ideals Borah sought to project onto the international scene.[1]

While the war was in progress, it was rumored that Borah wanted to join the expeditionary force which T. R. importuned Wilson to permit him to raise; but when the President scotched the plan, Borah, who was then fifty-two and well over even his own prescribed fighting age of forty-five, confined his energies to the home front. In January 1917 he approved Wilson's peace note to the Allied and Central Powers only insofar as it requested terms on which the belligerents would discuss peace. He was one of the senators who forced the embodiment of this interpretation in Hitchcock's substitute resolution, thus indicating before America ever entered the war outright opposition to the President's suggestions for a League or for postwar co-operation among nations. Borah was the original irreconcilable. Even before the League Covenant was formulated, he announced his determined resistance to any plan involving international co-operation in the political sphere. Discussion of the Hitchcock resolution thus began a debate that was to last three years and would be recognized as one of the most portentous in the nation's history.

At an anniversary celebration of the Free Synagogue in New York in 1911 Henry Morgenthau, Sr., observed that Borah and

Wilson, the guests of honor seated side by side, were instantly antagonistic. "The air was electric," he reports, "with the clash of their dissimilar temperaments."[2] If Morgenthau's observations were accurate, even at this date the lines were being drawn for the struggle between Wilson and the Senate irreconcilables. When the armistice was signed, Borah stated: "The war is over . . . Germany cannot renew the fight . . . The task of reconstruction is at hand and presents questions far more complex and stupendous . . . than did the war itself. Where tyranny reigned yesterday chaos and hysteria and hunger rule today. We must help to rebuild . . . There will be no room for party politics, no place for holding back now, for permanent peace depends on how well we do the work of reconstruction."[3]

As a legalist, Borah was sensitive to precedent and wished above all else to preserve traditional American policies in foreign affairs. In a Senate speech he explained that he would maintain his position against the League not because he relied on his own judgment in the matter, but because he felt compelled to remain in the company of Washington, Jefferson, Madison, Monroe, Jackson, Lincoln, Grant, McKinley, and Roosevelt—men whose policies had been so conclusively justified by the severest of all tests, experience. "Their company," he asserted, "is safe enough for me." To the objection that Washington's policies were framed under wholly different conditions, Borah answered that historically conditions were "almost exactly the same" in the 1790's as those at the close of the Great War.[4]

In contrast to Borah, the traditionalist, Wilson had his eyes on the future and pushed forward toward his goal with a liberal's impatience. He thought America, both for humanity's sake and because its own interests were linked with Europe's, could not stand by idly while Europe moved headlong down the path of destruction. Borah's faith in the judicial process prompted him to seek stability through the formulation and application of international law. Wilson thought in terms of an international organization with broad authority to draw upon military might to compel obedience and defend the territorial integrity of every member state. Borah argued that Wilson's proposal to commit American armed forces to the protection of every little country would plunge this nation into the storm center of European politics. Both men had their roots in identical moral soil; both possessed the evangelical conscience. Wilson and Borah differed only slightly on broad aims and principles; on methods they differed widely.[5]

Wilson outlined his plan for a League in his "peace without victory" speech before Congress on January 22, 1917. Its broad humanitarian principles went unappreciated by Senate leaders. Though it was approved by the Allies and even by Austrian and German liberals, Henry Cabot Lodge, chairman of the Senate Foreign Relations Committee and a former supporter of the League to Enforce Peace, warned that such an organization might compel America to accept Oriental immigration and plunge us into another war. After hearing the President's speech, Borah introduced a resolution reaffirming faith in the Monroe Doctrine and in the policies of noninterference in Europe advocated by Jefferson and Monroe. "Internationalism absolutely defeats the national spirit and patriotic fervor," he stated. It would mean the subordination of the Constitution to a pact with foreign powers. It would mean the betrayal of the American Republic. He thanked God that the United States had such a rocklike national spirit and that its people would never submit questions affecting the country's honor to arbitration.[6]

When Wilson called on the electorate in 1918 to return a Democratic Congress, Republicans accused the President of casting a slur on their patriotism and rejoiced when they won a majority in both houses. There was more criticism when it was announced that the President would head the peace delegation in Paris.[7] Borah questioned the wisdom of Wilson's personal attendance at the conference, but once it was settled that he would go, the senator wished him eminent success. Scarcely a month after Wilson's departure Theodore Roosevelt fell gravely ill at Oyster Bay. In his last days he spoke in confidence to Lodge, and it was supposed that out of these conversations grew the strategy Lodge later employed to defeat the peace treaty in the Senate. Borah mourned the death of his friend on January 6, 1919.

On the League issue the Senate was divided into four groups: those who supported strong reservations, those who supported mild reservations, die-hard Wilsonians whipped into line by minority leader Gilbert M. Hitchcock, and the irreconcilables who wanted no treaty and no League. In the latter group Borah took the most intransigent stand. It was not a question of confidence in the

President, he said. "The President . . . is in favor of a League of Nations. If the Savior of mankind would revisit the earth and declare for a League . . . I would be opposed to it. That is my position and it is not a question of personality. It is a question of policy for my government and that I will decide regardless of individuals." This widely publicized statement identified Borah, at the very beginning of the struggle, as utterly uncompromising.[8]

In vain did Wilson cable from Paris urging senators to withhold comment on the treaty until it was presented to them. On February 19 Miles Poindexter made the opening anti-League statement in the Senate, and two days later Borah launched his expected attack in an address on "Americanism" lasting an hour and a half. Repeating Washington's admonitions and quoting his question, "Why quit our own to stand upon foreign ground?," he told packed galleries the League was not only a departure from Washington's policies but a negation of the Monroe Doctrine as well. If, under Article X, we interfered in Europe's affairs, we might expect Europe's interference in our own affairs. According to Article X, every League member would be obligated to preserve the territorial integrity of the British colonies. Branding the Covenant England's greatest diplomatic triumph, he said the British empire had thus obtained a guarantee of all its possessions without surrendering control of the seas. Moreover, each of the British dominions would have a vote. Glaring across the aisle, he thundered: "I ask you who are in favor of this League, are you willing to give to any nation five votes against our one?" Clearly the issue had aroused Borah's old distrust of British diplomacy.[9]

Wilson returned from Paris briefly for the adjournment of Congress, and just before his arrival he cabled the members of the Foreign Relations Committees of both houses inviting them to the White House to present their views on the first draft of the treaty he would bring with him, including the League. Borah refused to attend this meeting of February 26. He wrote Joseph Tumulty, Wilson's secretary: "I am sure no suggestion of mine would modify in the slightest the views of the President, and nothing could induce me to support the League . . . or anything like it . . . it would not be fair to accept information which I could not feel perfectly free to transmit to my colleagues or use in public debate . . . I mean no personal disrespect to . . . the President . . ."[10] Thirty-four senators and congressmen attended the conference; Borah and Albert Fall of New Mexico were the only absentees.

The *Nation* held that the form of his declination was unfortunate but the principle of refusing to be bound by the confidences of a social occasion was sound. A few anti-League papers praised Borah's conduct as fearless and straightforward, but critics accused him of bad manners. An invitation to the White House was regarded as a command. His truculence evoked a scathing editorial from the Indianapolis *Times-Star.* In his biography of Borah, Claudius Johnson states that most attacks did not disturb him at all, that "he probably enjoyed them." Borah assuredly did not enjoy this one! He sent an angry protest to ex-Senator Beveridge of Indiana, who replied: ". . . leadership in this great movement is now justly accorded to you. You must therefore expect attacks . . . those who stand with you . . . will not be moved, except to resentment by anything that anybody may say or do in an attempt to break the force of your blows." Beveridge agreed to expostulate with the *Times-Star,* but he informed Borah: "This will be the first time in my life that I wrote such a letter." In replying to Beveridge, the editor, Ernest Bross, promised to make no further attacks on Borah, but added: "I have no confidence whatever in his intellectual integrity. He is ranting around on this thing [the League] as a candidate for the presidency . . ."[11]

After Wilson returned to Paris, Borah continued to attack the League. He posed the question, "How are the armies of the League to be raised?" The answer, "by conscription in peace time," forced men to recall that he had opposed conscription even in wartime! Such a plan would require the largest navy in the world, at the expense of the American taxpayer, and would inevitably lead to war.[12]

Seriously disturbed when public opinion failed to respond warmly to anti-League arguments, Borah resolved to tour the country. Republican leaders were not enthusiastic, but he went ahead. He spoke first in New York, where he urged a popular referendum on the League.[13] A mammoth meeting followed at Tremont Temple in Boston two nights later, where five thousand people stood outside in the cold and drizzle unable to gain admittance to the crowded hall. Borah denounced Wilson's "league of diplomats" with its executive council in which Asiatic and European members could outvote Americans on purely American issues. Cheers greeted his declaration that Wilson's plan made no provision for the freedom of Ireland. He was at his oratorical best and even found enough voice to address the overflow crowd outside. Beveridge wrote: "Borah outdid himself."[14]

The tour continued through Troy, Albany, and Rochester, from which he returned to fill another New York engagement in Brooklyn; there he attacked the constitution of the League and described conditions in Europe as "not greatly different from those in Washington's time." He said, "America has arisen to a position where she is respected and admired by the entire world . . . She did it by minding her own business . . . the European and American systems do not agree."[15]

There were other meetings in Colorado and the Midwest. At Fort Wayne, Indiana, he declared the League would make it necessary for America to give back to George V what it had taken from George III. He was forced to admit that he had no substitute to offer for the League. "You cannot prevent wars," he told the audience. "You can only minimize them." On this tour he covered more than two thousand miles and made ten major addresses.[16] When he returned to Washington, he assailed his own party for its pusillanimous attitude on the League: "I am getting tired of this creeping, crawling, smelling attitude of the Republican party upon an issue which involves the independence of this Republic . . . If the Republican party has no creed on this matter there will be a party that has . . . The white-livered cowards who are standing around while the diplomats of Europe are undermining our whole system . . . will have no hearing when the American people come to know the facts."[17]

When Henry White, a member of the American delegation, cabled from Paris asking what amendments would satisfy two thirds of the Senate on the League, Henry Cabot Lodge replied that the only way to find out was to call the Senate into session. In this Lodge showed his most serious failing throughout the struggle. While always admitting that some kind of a league was desirable, he was unwilling to devote himself to positive action on a workable arrangement.[18]

This was a time of crisis at the Peace Conference. All through

April Wilson toiled manfully in Paris to secure some of the amendments suggested by Root, Hughes, Taft, and Lowell; at the same time he tried to compose the quarrels over French security, naval limitation, reparations, Shantung, and Fiume. Meanwhile Borah left Washington on April 1 for another speaking tour. Mildly enthusiastic audiences heard him at Huntington, Columbus, Chicago, Wichita, Topeka, and Tulsa. By the time he returned, some of the most frequently suggested reservations to the League Covenant had been incorporated in a revised draft completed on April 28, which included modifications acknowledging the Monroe Doctrine, reserving to every nation the right to determine such domestic questions as immigration, tariffs, and the right of withdrawal after ten years, and safeguarding congressional power to declare war. Although this draft had the unanimous consent of the conference, in Borah's opinion nothing had been done.[19] Article X, which provided for co-operative action to maintain peace, was left unchanged. Borah regarded it as the fundamental objection and nothing less than an allied pledge to maintain the *status quo* in Europe by force. However, he saved his bitterest invective for the secrecy in which the treaty was formulated. It was offensive to him that the terms of the document were withheld from the Senate until that body was called upon to debate it. These secret chamber proceedings represented "the most cowardly admission of the weakness of the whole program that could be made."[20]

Borah would not listen to any such proposals of compromise as the reservationists in the Senate favored. He scorned their efforts and insisted stubbornly that there was no way to amend treason. Republican leaders like Root and Lodge did not share his conviction that the League should be openly opposed on the clear-cut issue of acceptance or rejection. Lodge could perceive no political profit in such an extreme course of action, which would fail to win the support of all Republicans, especially mild reservationists. The Republican majority in the Senate was slight, and public opinion seemed favorable to the Democratic plan. Will Hays, Republican National Committee chairman, also favored a middle-of-the-road approach. He sought to convince Borah that the League was a nonpartisan issue, "an American issue." Borah was unimpressed. He said that all issues are American issues; the question was to determine on which side of this "American issue" the Republican party ranged itself.[21] His attitude on the League was embarrassing in high Republican circles.

In April Borah arranged another speaking tour of the Pacific coast. Before leaving Washington, he called at 1765 Massachusetts Avenue, Senator Lodge's residence. There the majority leader tried to convince him that outright rejection of the League was impossible. The average man, Lodge said, had not even read the treaty; the public merely assumed that since the principle was good, the plan must be good also. He therefore proposed a program of education in order to reverse the pro-League trend in public opinion. He also proposed delaying action by prolonged committee hearings and debate, giving League enthusiasm time to cool. Finally, he proposed urging all Republicans and some Democrats to unite behind amendments or reservations designed to protect what he called American interests, and thus improve the instrument.[22] In supporting this plan, Lodge assured him, the irreconcilables would still be free to vote against the treaty without reservations. Republican efforts to amend the document would have the effect of shifting the responsibility for killing the treaty from its opponents to its friends. Throughout their conversation Borah seemed skeptical. It took all Lodge's powers of persuasion and cold logic to convince the adamantine westerner. Only with the clear understanding that his group reserved the right to vote against the treaty, amended or not, did Borah finally agree to co-operate in Lodge's strategy.

As May advanced, the League promised to become the biggest political issue since the Civil War. Figures of every degree of magnitude were ranged for or against it. A few, like La Follette, reserved judgment until after they had seen the official text. By June 21, when Root set the party policy, the issue was one of amendment or rejection.

Because the parliamentary maneuvering in the Senate consumed most of Lodge's time, the task of mobilizing public opinion throughout the country in support of rejection fell to Borah, the leader of "the Battalion of Death." This band of senators included Johnson, Reed, Brandegee, Moses, McCormick, Knox, La Follette, Poindexter, and Thomas. Like Borah, they equated compromise with treason. The Idahoan not only led them but attempted to co-ordinate the anti-League forces in the country. His unique position in politics made him precisely the right man for the undertaking. He had the confidence of the liberals, who respected his position on domestic issues. Conservatives respected his knowledge of and devotion to the Constitution. He had his finger on the pulse of his native Midwest, where geographic, ethnic, and economic considerations, coupled with antagonism to many war measures, had stimulated the isolationist sentiment.

Few other senators had such wide hyphenate connections as Borah; yet the whole country knew his patriotism was unassailable. The alienation of disaffected hyphenates and immigrants from the Democratic party, which came as a result of the war, the harsh terms of the peace, and the Paris compromises on self-determination were exploited by the Republicans for their political value. Borah's rapport with German-Americans, Irish-Americans, and other groups can be readily explained by the consistency with which he had championed nationalism, self-determination, and democratic rights. The fact that the League fight coincided with the climax of the movement for Irish freedom helped weaken the League partisans' argument. Of all the hyphenate groups the Irish were the oldest, most numerous, most prosperous, and best organized. Their leader was Tammany Judge Daniel F. Cohalan, who had already earned Wilson's enmity. When Wilson rebuffed the Irish-Americans at Versailles, their leaders denounced the treaty and their delegates came home to drum up opposition against it.[23] All over the country the sons of Ireland sprang to battle.

Borah served as linchpin between this hyphenate group and the irreconcilables. A man of lesser stamina would have cracked under the strain, for he insisted on personally answering letters from all friends and foes. Cohalan was in almost daily touch. With the Irish victory fund in his hands, the judge converted the Friends of Irish Freedom into crusaders against the League, and Borah urged them on. He also drew attention to the claims for self-determination made by Egypt, India, and China. The strength of the Irish pressure group is best demonstrated by the fifteenth reservation affirming the Irish cause, which Borah supported. When the Hibernian hundred percenters escorted Eamon de Valera to Washington, they passed over four Irish-American senators and took the future Irish president directly to Borah, whose mother, at least, was Irish.

Borah enlisted the aid of several magazines and newspapers; his most influential ally was Frank A. Munsey, whose New York *Sun* attempted to offset the influence of important pro-League papers in the East. Borah told Munsey that if people got the truth about the League, an avalanche of hostile public opinion would smother it. Munsey did his best to serve the crusade and was supplied with plenty of material from Borah's office. The senator's indefatigable energy and wide connections wove together the various strands of noninterventionist thinking.[24]

In an interview in May Borah stated his opinion that nearly all Republican senators would insist upon amending the League Covenant, especially with reference to Article X. Unless it was changed appreciably, he predicted the treaty would not pass the Senate, despite Wilson's repeated insistence that Article X was "the heart of the Covenant." A month later Borah stated his willingness to vote for a drastic qualifying resolution that would put under reservation any points in the League Covenant to which its opponents objected, but he still preferred a fight on the issue—League or no League. That was how he wanted it presented to the American people. Borah would have accepted Wilson's challenge to adopt the Covenant as it stood or reject the treaty. He still believed that if this course were adopted, the treaty would be defeated. He demanded that if a qualifying resolution were insisted upon, it be drawn so as to virtually amend the Covenant. He asserted: "I will not vote for an innocuous qualifying resolution. I would support one that would keep the United States out of Europe, and keep Europe out of the United States."[25]

When the special session of Congress convened, Senator Johnson introduced a resolution calling on the secretary of state to transmit the full text of the Versailles Treaty to the Senate. During the debate Borah charged that copies of the treaty had been circulated in Europe and were then in the hands of certain "interests" in New York City. "The trail of the treaty of peace runs from Paris to Wall Street," claimed Borah, "and the thread will be taken up by financial interests in Washington and so on to the Senate. It is an amazing spectacle." In a confidential phone call from a New York lawyer he learned that Wall Street financial houses had copies of the treaty and were using them to advance their projects abroad. Before the Foreign Relations Committee Borah refused to disclose his source of information but offered to give the committee the results of his private probe. He said: "I will do all possible . . . to frustrate such a treacherous scheme to betray the American people. If that be treason, make the most of it."[26] On June 9 Borah brought in a copy of the treaty secured from Frazier Hunt, the Paris correspondent for the Chicago *Tribune.* He asked for unanimous consent to have it printed as a Senate document. When this was refused, he asked that the full text be printed in the *Record.* In the turbulent debate that followed the Democrats tried desperately to prevent the publication of a treaty not yet signed or submitted to the Senate by the President, but the vote was 47 to 24 to have the treaty published. Meanwhile Borah began to read the 80,000 word text to the Senate; after thirty-five minutes senators were rescued from boredom by the vote. Borah's accusation about a "leak" to special interests in New York now seems nonsensical. Wilson had nothing to conceal and delayed publishing the treaty to oblige Lloyd George.[27]

The treaty was signed June 28. A day later Wilson sailed home on the "George Washington," reaching the White House on July 8. His return tended to bring issues into focus. On July 10 he appeared before the Senate to report on the conference and was escorted by Lodge, Hitchcock, Williams, McCumber, and Borah. When the senators filed out to meet the President, there was a ripple of laughter as the Idahoan, who usually wore gray but was dressed in black, joined them. Most of the laughter came from the Democratic side; even Borah himself smiled.

The treaty was presented to the Senate on July 14, but hearings were not begun until July 31 as part of the tactics of delay. The document had hardly started on its way to the Foreign Relations Committee when Lodge's strategy went into operation. A familiar sight thereafter in the Senate cloakroom was a huddle of Lodge, Fall, Brandegee, Borah, and one or two others. The hearings began in July and lasted two months. Wilson himself appeared before the committee, but most of the testimony heard was from witnesses unfriendly to the League.[28] As the committee struggled with amendments, Borah showed less inclination to support them and leaned toward an open fight for ratification or rejection. Just when Lodge's scheme was working out to perfection, Borah seemed about to abandon the reservationists. A feeling of optimism was sweeping through the ranks of the irreconcilables, and Borah was convinced that they were strong enough to defeat the treaty in an open fight.

A break almost came when Key Pittman of Nevada urged an outright vote on acceptance or rejection. Borah, leaping to his feet, took up the challenge, declaring that the real issue was whether or not it was fundamentally right to enter the League. Lodge was horrified. He quickly drew Borah into the cloakroom and explained all over again that the Senate majority wanted the League, so it had to be defeated indirectly and the only way this could be done was by demanding revision. Borah shook his head in doubt, protesting that he could shout the thing down if given enough time. Lodge smiled, but persuaded him that time was of the essence. Finally Borah agreed to stay in line; however, as they strode out on the Senate floor together, he was heard to mutter grimly: "If my country's going to be sold, I'm not interested in the bill of sale."[29]

Seventeen members of Congress were present at a White House conference on August 19, this time including Borah and Fall. They attended only on condition that every word would be taken down by stenographers. The scene was unique. The great iron gates of the White House, locked during the war, were opened to admit the guests. Some of them, like Lodge and Johnson, arrived in limousines; John Sharp Williams came in a small electric car; Swanson and Hitchcock motored up to the east portico talking earnestly; Borah walked, carrying a bulky copy of the treaty under his arm, looking like a boy on the way to school.[30]

Borah and Johnson questioned the President closely on the withdrawal clause and the secret treaties. Wilson asserted that he had no knowledge of those treaties prior to his arrival in Paris. This testimony was incredible to the senators and amazing to the public, who attributed his remarks to an awkward lapse of memory. Wilson's mood was not uncompromising; he seemed anxious to reach an agreement, but the debate brought out the fact that lawyers could not agree on what the treaty meant because language does not mean the same thing to two sets of minds, especially when one is Republican and the other is Democratic.[31]

The President thereafter considered it useless to discuss the matter with the Senate. He decided on an appeal to the country, which he had contemplated for months. His tour took him through the Middle and Far West, which furnished most of the opposition to the League. Simultaneously, at a Washington luncheon given by Senator Knox it was decided that Johnson would go to the Pacific coast, Borah would stārt in the Twin Cities and work west, and others would follow. They planned to trail Wilson and counteract the influence of his speeches. Before leaving, Borah wrote a friend: "They [Democrats] all seem to think that because the President is away those who are trying to save their country's honor and integrity should be quiet out of personal consideration . . . I am not pleased with the situation here . . . It is possible the thing is getting on my nerves a little."[32]

At the Chicago coliseum on September 10 Medill McCormick presided over an anti-League meeting at which Johnson and Borah spoke. Banners waving in the audience read: "WELCOME TO THE MEN WHO ARE BRINGING OUR BOYS BACK FROM SIBERIA." As Borah spoke, he strode up and down the stage, his thumbs locked in his armpits, hurling loaded questions at the audience:

> No two men who wrote that treaty can agree now as to what it means. We in the Senate want to construe that treaty if possible. I don't want to go into a league at all, personally, but I didn't make the issue. Now I am particularly anxious to find a way to get out of it if we must go in. Do you want to go into a league that you can't get out of?

"No, no," shouted the crowd.

"Is there an American who wants a foreign nation to say when and where the Monroe Doctrine should apply?" Borah asked.

The audience gave the same negative response.

"England has suggested (all England has to do now is to suggest) that we send 100,000 men to Constantinople," he told them.

"Don't let 'em go," they yelled.

"Yes, they will go," Borah said, "but . . . without the consent of the American people." He proclaimed that Wilson had betrayed the Fourteen Points. "Who quit?" Borah demanded.

"Wilson," roared the crowd. "Impeach him! Impeach him!"[33]

Borah's tour included major addresses at Des Moines, St. Louis, Fort Dodge, and Omaha. Wilson's trip continued into Kansas and Colorado, where it ended in tragedy. He collapsed at Pueblo and later suffered a paralytic stroke which made him a helpless invalid for months. All through his illness he continued to cling to the notion that the treaty had to be approved as written or not at all.

His broken health was an important factor in the events which followed.[34]

The Foreign Relations Committee completed its hearings, and on September 10 the majority made its first report proposing four reservations to the Covenant and forty-five amendments to other articles. Borah then set out on another tour of the Midwest, returning to Washington on September 29. He was encouraged by the strong nationalistic sentiment growing in the West. The Chicago *Tribune* was convincing tens of thousands that the League would lead us into another war, and George S. Viereck was conducting a vigorous campaign designed to convince German-Americans that the League would betray both this country and the fatherland.

The action of the committee was too drastic for the Republicans, about twelve of whom joined the Democrats in voting down the amendments on October 29. The idea of amending was given up; on November 6 Lodge proposed a resolution of advice and consent to ratification subject to fourteen reservations, of which twelve were accepted by the Senate. Borah, of course, disagreed with the whole procedure. He conceded that the "Lodge reservations" were a step in the right direction in that they reduced the responsibilities of the United States, but he suspected that the major aim of the reservations was to promote the political interests of their sponsors.[35]

In the closing debate on these reservations, which Borah thought would be adopted with the treaty, he made the greatest speech of his career to packed galleries alerted for the occasion. In his best Websterian manner he spoke against the treaty for almost two hours. He was convinced that the reservations would be wholly ineffective in protecting the interests of the United States; they were the dire resort of those who regarded it as dangerous to enter the League and impolitic to stay out. The chief reason why he was prepared to record his vote against the treaty was because it imperiled the first principle of the republic, the right of the people to govern themselves, free from all restraint, moral or legal, of foreign powers. Borah could not exchange the doctrine of Washington for the doctrine of Frederick the Great translated into mendacious phrases of peace. He predicted: ". . . we shall be a party to the rule of force . . . the maxim of liberty will soon give way to the rule of blood and iron." Even if the treaty meant peace, Borah would not pay the price—part of our independence. "But your treaty does not mean peace," he told the Democrats, "far, very far from it . . . it means war." To the taunts of those who called the irreconcilables "little Americans," he responded: "Leave us the word American, keep that in your presumptuous impeachment, and no taunt can disturb us . . . leave us the consolation and the pride which the term American . . . still imparts."[36]

The response to Borah's tour de force was favorable. Lodge confessed: "When I find myself in tears, I know I am listening to a great speech." Vice-President Marshall sent Borah a note: "May a mummy say that you almost galvanized him to life." From the press gallery came another message: "The Battalion of Death of the press gallery salutes the Mirabeau of the new freedom." Beveridge wrote: "Nobody can answer it—nobody will try."[37] That same day the Senate voted 39 for and 55 against the treaty with the Lodge reservations. The final vote on the treaty without reservations was 38 for and 53 against. The Senate refused to reconsider it; thus they repudiated Wilson's Covenant and the League of Nations. Borah regarded it as "the greatest victory since Appomattox."

The first battle was over. Borah had contributed to the inspirational side of the controversy; the hard drudgery of lining up votes and keeping them was done by others. In the struggle personal feelings, parochial considerations, senatorial rebelliousness, sincere patriotic convictions, concern for our basic national interests, and partisanship were all combined.[38]

Borah received an ample share of the credit or blame for defeating the treaty. Beveridge wrote: ". . . nobody deserves more credit than you do for the victory. Indeed, it could not have been won but for the magnificent fight you made and everybody concedes this to be true . . . it was you who . . . first ran the flag to the top of the mast; and . . . you stood by your guns without fear or faltering through the long hard fight."[39] It is true that he displayed some special qualities in this parliamentary struggle. For resoluteness of purpose and adroitness in what appeared at first a hopeless task, Borah had no equal, not even in the intrepid Lodge. Borah's devotion to his country and world peace was as great as Wilson's. His immense, if specialized, knowledge of affairs enabled him to expose the defects in the Versailles system. Without dealing in personalities, he was able to equal the vindictiveness of Lodge and the vituperation of Reed in the savagery of his onslaught. At times he painted a lurid picture of the consequences proceeding from our entry into the League. At times he appealed to the emotions of his audiences to drum up resentment, especially against Great Britain. As a result, he emerged from the great debate a dedicated but unlovable figure.

It is difficult to withhold a certain admiration for Borah's sincerity in the League fight. Of partisanship, jealousy, or personal hostility there is no trace. He stated: "My opposition . . . is based on sincere views as to the peace of the world and the preservation of American institutions." To substantiate this statement he inserted in the *Congressional Record* a speech which he made before Wilson revealed his views on the League of Nations. Borah opposed the principle of the League before it became a Democratic issue. He later added that his opposition had not resulted from any personal dislike of the President: "I am opposed to any form of amendments, reservations or interpretations. I don't want to be placed in any position where I will lose a chance to vote against the treaty straight or have no vote at all."[40] Even the sick man in the White House was convinced of Borah's sincerity; otherwise he would not have been invited to the Wilson Foundation dinner in 1922.

Thus, if the motives of other antagonists are unclear, Borah's motives in opposing the League are uncomplicated. A League maintained by force looked to him like treachery. The motives behind this treachery also seemed clear enough to him. Bankers, he thought, wanted the League in order to gather from it the fruits of investment and exploitation. Essentially old-fashioned in his Americanism, Borah at once created and reflected the American mood of those confident years when minds, given to absolute decisions, thought of alliances as the only avenue leading to foreign turmoil. He helped swing popular opinion back to the older concept that American self-interest demanded a return to insulation from Old World political intrigue. Some new plan to keep the peace would have to replace the old balance of power, but for him the League was not the answer. He used arguments strident in their nationalism because he was convinced of America's capacity to handle matters arising from Old World instability when and if they impinged on her own welfare.

The progressivism of many westerners on domestic issues in contrast to their conservatism on foreign affairs has puzzled many who have attempted to understand the sources of isolationism in this country. In his analysis William A. Williams complains that the term isolationist has been bandied about indiscriminately until it has become almost meaningless. The confusion and ambiguity in accounts of American foreign policy in the 1920's, he thinks, stem from concentration on the League of Nations issue. Those who wanted to join were labeled internationalists; those opposed were called isolationists. An examination of the subsequent action of most of the latter group belies this simple classification, just as the later policies of those who favored the League cast doubts on the assumption that they were willing to arbitrate questions of national interest. Far more pertinent to Williams are two questions: why did certain groups or individuals favor the League, and what programs did they later support?

At the core of the reaction in 1919, he submits, was the quandary between fidelity to ideals and the urge to power. Borah and his followers had few illusions about the importance of power either in human affairs or as it concerned the authority of the United States in international politics. Before the war he supported such vigorous expansionists as T. R., but the war jarred him into a closer examination of their assumptions. Borah was one of the few who had become firm antiexpansionists by 1919. He did not deny the power of the United States; he sought to extend it. He never sought to isolate this country from the mainstream of world commerce. Neither did he think the nation could ever become self-sufficient economically or impregnable in its strength. This is why he continued to urge a series of world economic conferences after 1922, and it also explains why he wanted the United States to stand with Russia to check Japanese and German expansion. The question with him was not withdrawal from world affairs, but when and where and how much to use the country's influence. Another generation of expansionists disclaimed political imperium but planned to build and maintain a similar pattern of control through the use of American economic might. Replying to them, Borah and others argued that if Washington's influence was to be effective, it would have to be used to support movements of reform and colonial nationalism rather than be deployed in an effort to dam up and dominate these forces.

For these very reasons he opposed the Versailles Treaty, because it committed us to guarantee the territorial integrity of all members and oppose such colonial movements for self-government as might develop in Egypt or India or Pakistan. It was unjust, he thought, and impossible to preserve the *status quo*. He saw little chance for peaceful change under such an arrangement. For these reasons he also opposed any reorganization of the international banking consortium; the Webb Pomerone Act, which repealed the antitrust laws for export associations; and the Edge Act, which authorized foreign banking corporations under the Federal Reserve Act. From the same perspective Borah fought to end intervention in Russia and the suppression of civil liberties at home. He hammered away against armed intervention in Latin America, played a key role in securing the appointment of Dwight Morrow as ambassador to Mexico, and sought to align the United States with instead of against the Chinese Revolution.[41]

One could hardly expect introspection from a homespun theorist like Borah. Though he regretted voting for World War I, he never regretted voting against the Versailles Treaty. In fact, he considered this opposition the highest achievement in his public service. As events in the postwar years unfolded, they served only to reinforce his belief that he had been right. He read John Maynard Keynes' books and stored up new arguments for future debates; the spate of war-guilt revelations ramified his skepticism; the worsening of German relations after 1924 and the League's ineffectiveness in coping with this and other problems were factors reaffirming his original conviction that Europe had a set of interests and problems peculiar to herself, in which we could play no rightful part—an idea not too far from the thought habits of the American people. He found much natural response from plain men and women who shared his beliefs as traditional and sound. Viewed at a distance, a definite philosophy (some might regard it as more a triumph of instinct than of intellect) guided Borah. There was even a certain consistency in his approach to foreign affairs. His views were significant, for Borah sought, and to a degree succeeded in fashioning and following, a foreign policy which mirrored the "aspirations and hopes" of many Americans.[42]

When the treaty was brought before the Senate a second time, Borah predicted for it an even more overwhelming defeat. He was as determined as Wilson to fight in the approaching campaign on the League issue and was against any "pussyfooting." Even if his party, through defeat, could save American traditions, it would render a service second only to that of Lincoln. If, on the other hand, his party was in favor of the League proposition, he defied it to say so and "let those who abhor such hideous cowardice fumigate themselves and get out."[43]

In an effort to save the treaty a series of bipartisan conferences, in which the irreconcilables were not represented, was arranged to work out a compromise agreement on the Lodge reservations. Borah never liked the idea and told Frank Munsey: ". . . I think in all the history of politics there has never been such a pitiable exhibition of political cowardice or what is worse, subserviency to sinister influences . . ."[44]

When Lodge was reported in these conferences to be yielding on modifications to Article X and other points in conflict, he was dragged from a conference with Senator Simmons and other Democrats to account for himself at a protest meeting on January 23 (a Friday afternoon) in Johnson's office, attended by Knox, Brandegee, Moses, McCormick, Borah, and others. Borah did the talking, demanding to know what was going on behind closed doors. When Lodge refused any explanation, Borah shouted: "You won't be majority leader a day longer . . ." Lodge replied he would resign. Borah countered: "You won't be given a chance to resign. We will make it a public exhibition . . ." Lodge, who later complained that a man of his years should not have been subjected to such rough treatment, was warned to stand firm or be driven from his post. There were no further reports of progress from the bipartisan committee, which quietly disbanded.[45] The treaty was resubmitted on March 20 with the same reservations, and the vote was 49 for and 35 against. Last-ditch Wilsonians and irreconcilables composed the opposition.

Borah's New Year's resolution for 1920 was to force Frank Lowden and other prospective candidates for the Republican nomination to declare where they stood on the League. Shortly thereafter Senator Johnson and the New York *World* criticized Leonard Wood for his heavy campaign expenditures. Borah fired more lead into Wood's camp when he charged bribery; he threw suspicion, as well, on the sources of Lowden's campaign funds. Wood's managers made a vehement denial: "Senator Borah is assuming too much in making himself a censor of Republican politics. He has no legal authority to demand a statement from any candidate." Lowden's friends answered for him. "Impertinent political blackmail," replied Clarence M. Woolley of New York in a telegram. "Take Proverbs 25:5 for your guide," the editor of the Jersey County (Illinois) *Democrat* advised Lowden, "and tell Borah to go to hell, and that you are a better American than he is." Lowden himself issued a reply to Borah on the League question in the Chicago *Tribune* on January 6, 1920. Borah carried the hue and cry against excessive campaign expenditures to the floor of the Senate in March 1920 when he introduced a resolution forbidding a candidate for the presidential nomination to disburse more than $10,000 in any one state and obliging him to file a list of all contributions with the attorney general. The resolution was approved by both houses and the President.[46]

Borah favored Hiram Johnson for the nomination in 1920 because he was the only candidate who came out unequivocally against the League. Johnson enjoyed little support outside of California. In the Republican convention, which opened at the Chicago coliseum on June 9, Wood, Lowden, and Johnson were heading into a deadlock which threatened to destroy them all. As experts cautioned, it was only one step from a deadlock to a stampede. Senator Watson, heading the Resolutions Committee, appointed a subcommittee including Borah, Smoot, Lodge, Lenroot, and Wadsworth. On the day of their first session Murray Crane called a "steering group" to his Blackstone Hotel room to discuss the platform. He demanded a clear endorsement of the League with the Lodge reservations. Borah pounced on Crane accusing him of catering to bankers. Drawing attention to his connection with the House of Morgan, he charged him with favoring the League to reap a financial harvest. Borah declared: "If there is any pledge of ratification of the treaty with or without reservations, you can count me out. I reserve the right to denounce the Republican platform in every state of the United States."[47] In the midst of this heated discussion Ogden Mills pulled out the draft of Root's ambiguous plank praising *a* league but not *the* League. It was accepted at once by the Blackstone group.

Borah threatened a bolt on the League plank, and at the same time he continued to attack Lowden and Wood for "their perfectly brutal and shameless use of money." He issued another ultimatum: the party's nominee must not be a candidate who used improper means in the preconvention campaign. He sent men with megaphones into the hotel lobby announcing a meeting "to prevent the sale of the United States to someone without clean hands." He told the delegates he had been a Republican all his life; he had even voted for Taft in 1912, which was "going some," and was willing to support any man who was clean. "I have the right to demand of you the nomination of a clean man." He then made a last appeal for Johnson. Borah was scheduled to put the Californian's name in nomination, but Johnson was so worried that Borah's eloquence would result in a stampede for the Idahoan that he chose instead Charles S. Wheeler to make the nominating speech.[48]

William Hard once reported that one of the greatest journalistic difficulties about Senator Borah as a politician was that he did not smoke! For this and other reasons most Washington correspondents doubted that he was an insider in Republican presidential politics, and they were probably correct. Whatever the influence certain senators wielded in that smoke-filled room on that fateful Saturday night in Chicago, Borah was conspicuous only by his absence. It was just as well, for at the next session of the convention Warren G. Harding of Ohio was finally nominated on the tenth ballot. Calvin Coolidge of Massachusetts was nominated by a tired convention for the vice-presidency. As Borah was leaving Chicago, a reporter queried: "Are you happy?" "No, I'm not," was his reply. "But then, it's because I'm ill. Too much heat, too much work, not enough sleep, I guess."[49]

The Idaho senator was greatly disappointed by the failure of the Johnson campaign and withheld his support from Harding until late in September because of Harding's fluid stand on the League. After his Des Moines speech, however, in which the candidate stated, "It is not interpretation but rejection I seek," Borah came out strongly for the Chicago ticket, which was elected in a Republican landslide. Borah later said that if the Democrats had won, he would have left the Senate. However, there was little danger of a Democratic victory in 1920. As a contemporary viewed it: ". . . it is unfair to say Cox was beaten, for he was not in the fight; and it is incorrect to say that Harding won. If the convention had adjourned without nominating anybody, the people, in the mood they were in then, would have voted Republican presidential electors just the same and let them pick their own candidates."[50]

XI The Republican Restoration

Weak was the Old World,
Wearily war-fenced,
Out of its ashes,
Strong as the morning,
Springeth the New.

The Republican party returned to power after eight years with no one to fill the place vacated by Wilson. Had a commanding figure like Theodore Roosevelt been alive in 1920, the party leadership might easily have been his once again. As it was, the man who was to be president for the next two years expressed his bankrupt philosophy at Boston a few weeks before the convention when he said: "America's present need is not heroics but healing; not nostrums but normalcy; not revolution but restoration; . . . not surgery but serenity."

Harding had been in the Senate with Borah since 1914. Together they served on the Foreign Relations Committee, and the Ohio senator had been impressed at its meetings by Borah's arguments against the League. He had even confessed his inability to swing his home state around to an anti-League position and had unabashedly asked Borah to speak in Ohio for him. Now that he was President, he would have to speak for himself on at least some issues of foreign policy. The results were marvels of obfuscation.

Nor was Borah's fight against the League a finished chapter. During the campaign he had persisted in the task of keeping Harding in opposition to it, and now he would have to maintain the same vigilance against Harding's vague proposals for an association of nations. To Borah one was as bad as the other; in fact, he declared the association more dangerous than the League, which was at least definite in its commitments, whereas the association would place all responsibility for positive action in the hands of the President.

While Wilson was president, hostility to his proposals had assured unity among his opponents. Now that he was retired, Borah, Brandegee, Johnson, and Lodge, who had joined hands as leaders during the League fight, resumed their trenchant individualism.[1] Some of them had assisted in the selection of Harding in Chicago. Ordinarily the power of presidents does not rise much above its source. Moreover, the time had come for a swing back to legislative leadership as a normal reaction against executive dominance during eight trying years. Initiative passed to Congress and would remain there until some new turn of events brought back a strong executive. With this shift of power the Idaho senator provided a natural focal point for any movement which would give new force to the Senate. Mark Sullivan believed that leadership in the Senate had in fact already passed to Borah. So far as there was any Republican opposition to the President, he inspired it.[2] He was often joined by La Follette, other Progressives, and some bitter-enders. Borah sounded a rallying cry when he declared on the Senate floor that he would neither change his judgment to suit the administration nor be a party to any action which waited upon the nod of Harding.[3]

Harding shortly sent for Borah and asked him to become administration leader. The Idahoan refused, saying: "Mr. President, you can get along without me, but I cannot get along without my views."[4]

The President was advised to appoint a strong cabinet, but when the names of Charles E. Hughes and Herbert Hoover were submitted to the Senate, the bitter-enders and Progressives bristled. Borah and Johnson led the opposition, interpreting the appointments as an indication of pro-League sentiment in the administration. In the end, however, the Senate confirmed both men. Penrose summed up the situation when he said: "It makes no difference who is Secretary of State; the Senate will make the foreign policy."[5]

The Harding administration was as dull as Borah was colorful. His personality as much as his policy accounted for his increased popularity during the twenties. Will Rogers commented that if he were to leave Washington, "they might as well make stove-wood of the seats in the Senate gallery." He had definite convictions on every issue of the day, and his views were nearly always interesting. In a conversation with Clinton Gilbert he observed: "The administration has no definite policies."[6] This made more difficult the settlement of such important questions before the Foreign Relations Committee as the peace treaty with Germany, the Colombia treaty, the Yap treaty, disarmament, and the League.

Borah favored expediting a peace treaty with Germany to assist in the resumption of trade relations. On July 2, 1921, Congress passed Senator Knox's resolution establishing a technical state of peace with the Weimar Republic. The actual treaty took shape under Secretary Hughes, who set up a claims commission by executive order and included other appropriate provisions. When his treaty was ready, he called Borah for an interview, spoke of his abhorrence for confiscation of enemy property, and declared that the instrument he had framed offered a sound program. The senator asked for some explanations; when Hughes gave them, he said he would raise no objections.[7]

In the Foreign Relations Committee, however, Borah did present strong objections and threatened to engage in "guerilla warfare" unless they were met. He wanted the treaty to make no mention of the Versailles Treaty. He opposed the appointment of American representatives to sit on the Reparations Commission created at Versailles. He insisted that the treaty would enmesh the United States in Europe's affairs, obligating us to enforce German reparations, disarm Germany, station troops for a continued occupation, and execute other pledges of the Versailles settlement. The next step would be sending delegates to Geneva, bringing us into the League through the back door.[8] His colleagues were a little startled, and Lodge reported his action to Hughes. Despite his opposition the Senate ratified the separate treaty with Germany by a vote of 66 to 20 in October 1921.

Yap Island was of special interest to Secretary Hughes, who wanted it internationalized because of its importance as a cable station. His object was also to prevent Japan from fortifying islands in the Pacific received as mandates from Germany. Under a separate agreement of February 11, 1922, the United States secured free access to Yap Island as well as equality with Japan in establishing cable stations there. Borah was ready to support a quitclaim, but he called this arrangement "a dangerous entangling alliance" in the ownership of one fifth of a former German possession. He felt that when we took the Philippines, we had repealed the Constitution, and that now we were repudiating the teachings of

Washington. The mandate system, he told the Senate, was invented to avoid the stigma placed upon the secret treaties consummated during the war.[9]

When the treaty to pay Colombia for the seizure of the Canal Zone was debated, Borah declared he had opposed its principle in 1917 and was still opposed. He could find no evidence that the United States had abetted the Panama revolution. "Theodore Roosevelt was not a common adventurer and John Hay was not a liar," said Borah, adding that if the Senate ratified the treaty, it would permit the world to say that it had at last confirmed the charge that Roosevelt stole Panama. He offered an amendment declaring that ". . . neither said payment [to Colombia] nor anything contained in the treaty shall be . . . regarded as an admission that the secession of Panama . . . was in any way aided . . . by the United States . . ." The Senate rejected his amendment 49 to 39. He wrote a friend: ". . . can't we beat the Colombia treaty? What a smearing, smirching, humiliating thing it would be to pass that."[10] However, the Senate in April 1921 ratified the treaty 69 to 19.

Borah was one of eight Republicans to bolt on the wool schedules in the tariff bill, one of four to vote against repeal of the excess profits tax, one of two opposing the treaty with Germany, and the only one to vote against the Fordney-McCumber Tariff. As the months passed, several Progressives left the Senate. William S. Kenyon, for example, was made a federal judge. There were hints of other such appointments. When Carter Glass encountered Borah at the Capitol one day, he said with a twinkle in his eye: "Good morning, Judge."

"Not yet," was Borah's reply. Glass nodded and smiled.[11]

Peace not only failed to bring about a new era of international reform; it produced a harvest of social and political unrest, an armaments race, and a general revival of international tension. Americans had been led to look upon their part in the recent conflict as a crusade to end all wars.[12] Borah shared in the postwar disillusionment, one clear indication of this being his oft-repeated statement of regret for his vote in support of the war resolution in 1917. This disillusionment reinforced his utopian belief that war could best be abolished by eliminating the competition for power. In harmony with this assumption his search for peace in the two decades between wars was characterized by attempts to deprive nations of the instruments of coercion and to exorcise war by declarations of principles.[13]

Americans with few exception have held the belief that heavy armaments lead inevitably to war. Armament itself was frequently cited as one of the factors in causing World War I. Two years after the armistice the political rivalry of Japan, Great Britain, and the United States had engendered a costly and dangerous three-cornered race in naval construction. Borah, beholding "a spectacle of competitive armaments in a world at peace," began earnestly to plead for disarmament and pacific agreements. He avoided any reference to the designs of Japanese expansionists on China or to the complex factors that bring nations into collision, but he warned that ". . . war with Japan could easily come within the next quarter of a century should we get into a great naval competition accompanied with threats and denunciations; that is all indeed the path of war." Japan's statement of her willingness to co-operate with the League Disarmament Commission encouraged Borah to frame a proposal for naval treaties limited to Japan, Britain, and the United States. He termed the international arms race "nothing less than a crime against humanity."[14]

Borah's assumption of leadership in the disarmament movement represented an important shift in emphasis. In 1916 he had taken his place with the big navy men by voting for the three-year building program. His speeches during that debate had supported the theory that battleships were the "great grey guardians of the peace." However, he never considered himself bound by any action previously taken; besides, the war was over and won. What foreign menace now required building a navy second to none? No purpose but continental defense could justify naval expansion, and there was no conceivable threat to the American continent. As far as Borah was concerned, the preservation of America's status in world politics depended on nothing more than its own independent will and moral strength.

Prior to 1920 Borah's approach to foreign affairs had been essentially negative. He was an ardent nationalist and therefore advocated exemption of American coastwise vessels from paying Panama Canal tolls; he also wanted a forceful policy in defending American rights in Mexico; he was an anti-imperialist and therefore looked askance on American acquisition of territory in the Pacific, even for purposes of defense; and finally he was a traditionalist opposed to participation in any league, association, court, committee, alliance, or agreement which would depart from the policy of non-entanglement. In Idaho Borah had never had a law partner. For much the same reasons he never wanted his country to surrender any part of her independence to any partner in war or peace.

In a thoughtful analysis J. Chalmers Vinson examines Borah's motives for shifting to a positive position after 1920. It went without saying that Borah loathed war and placed the cause of world peace above all other considerations. His opposition to the League was based on principle, but prior to 1920 the League was the only agency which provided any means for regulating the competition in arms. There was a rising public demand for something more than mere denunciation of the League, and to meet this demand Senator Thomas J. Walsh presented a resolution proposing that the United States accept the League invitation to confer with it on disarmament.[15] Borah's position thus became increasingly uncomfortable. The irreconcilables were being held accountable for the failure to join the League and the breakdown of efforts to halt the ruinously expensive naval program. Borah had often inveighed against the high cost of military preparedness as reflected in taxes. Now petitions calling for American leadership in a world program of disarmament began flooding the Senate.

For these reasons and perhaps others, without consulting the incoming President, Borah on December 14, 1920, introduced a resolution authorizing the President "to advise the governments of Great Britain and Japan to send representatives to a conference with the view of coming to an understanding by which the naval building programs of each of said governments [and the United States] . . . shall be substantially reduced annually during the next five years fifty percent of the present estimates . . ."[16]

The resolution had the virtue of simplicity and gained immediate public favor. It served to salvage Borah's position without sacrificing any of his ideals. An American plan, it would not infringe on

American sovereignty. There were no commitments to action in unforeseen contingencies. It was destined to be the nucleus of the popular movement for limitation of armaments.[17]

The agitation for arms limitation was by this time a full-fledged movement. Two weeks after Borah introduced his resolution, the movement was assured support from all elements in the population: reformers, women's organizations, churches, the press, labor unions, and even military groups represented by Generals Tasker H. Bliss and Pershing. The Newark *News* marveled at Borah's readiness to trust Britain and Japan in a disarmament agreement when he would not trust them in a League. The Memphis *Commercial Appeal,* calling the resolution "a trap to relieve an accusing conscience," asserted that Borah could not escape a certain amount of blame for the revival of militarism. Only President Harding, his advisers, the Hearst papers, and the big navy majority in the Senate Naval Committee, aided by Senator Lodge, hesitated over arms reduction. The tide of public sentiment proved strong enough, however, to overcome this opposition, and it spurred on Borah's drive. As he later admitted, "public sentiment was the real author of the move for disarmament."[18]

In the midst of the debate on the disarmament conference proposal on January 25 Borah abandoned his first resolution and submitted another (S.R. 433) to suspend our naval building program for six months pending an investigation of "what constitutes a modern fighting navy" and the value of the battleship.[19]

This second resolution was supported by Senators King, Walsh, Thomas, Reed, and La Follette, all of whom were opposed to naval increases. However, Harding opposed the plan, at least until after he should take office. He warned Congress to cease its efforts to "force the hand of the executive."[20] Some administration leaders and the Senate Committee on Naval Affairs also opposed suspension. Hearings proceeded, during which Secretary of the Navy Daniels told the Foreign Relations Committee that it would be a fatal mistake if the United States stopped work on the six battle cruisers then under construction.[21]

When a special session began after the inauguration, Senators Frederick Hale and Miles Poindexter served as the administration's lieutenants in an effort to defeat Borah's former resolution calling for a disarmament conference. Borah countered with a successful appeal to public opinion. When the administration realized that the tide of public sentiment driving forward the Borah proposal could no longer be denied, a last-ditch effort was made to introduce a weak and hastily drawn substitute for the Borah resolution. However, the President refused to declare publicly his opposition to the Borah proposal, and Harding's forces in Congress accordingly refused to continue the fight without his open support. Suddenly Senator Poindexter emerged from a White House meeting and announced that there would be no further opposition to the Borah resolution. The administration was in full retreat. On May 25 the Senate adopted his resolution by the overwhelming vote of 74 to 0. Hiram Johnson called this "the greatest personal triumph" won by a senator during his time. On June 2 a sharply reduced Naval bill passed 54 to 17, and by the end of June the Borah resolution had the overwhelming approval of both chambers.[22]

This ended one of the greatest debates since Bailey and Spooner crossed swords on the Senate floor during the Roosevelt administration. Secretary Hughes took the initiative in sending out invitations on July 10, 1921. Thus was born the Washington Disarmament Conference, designed to give humanity a breathing spell of hope and new, if not lasting, security. Editorials hailed it as "a step toward sanity" and the "greatest crusade of the ages."[23] Borah expressed great personal satisfaction, but he was soon displeased to learn that all nine allied and associated powers had been included in the invitations, for he had wished to confine the conference to the three leading naval powers. France and Italy, he believed, would not seriously consider arms reductions. It was intimated that land as well as naval armaments would be discussed, as Harding was now eager to go a step beyond mere naval limitation. Finally, the agenda included Far Eastern problems, a total rejection of Borah's original demand that they be excluded. All these changes evoked sharp criticism from the man most responsible for the conference. In time, even the credit for calling it went to Harding and Hughes.[24]

Though skeptical, Borah hoped something could be salvaged from the meeting and devoted his energies to a battle for open diplomacy in the conference sessions. He sponsored a Senate resolution to give newspapermen access to the meetings and to exempt their reports from censorship. After much debate a resolution introduced by Senator Pat Harrison incorporating Borah's ideas was adopted. In August Borah told the President the meetings should be highly publicized. At Asbury Park, New Jersey, he reiterated his plea for open sessions, charging that "the war spirit is at Washington; it is not in the breasts of our young men." He told a Schenectady audience that we would never rid ourselves of war until we got rid of that practice of leaving the determination of our destinies to a few men.[25]

The Washington Conference opened November 12, 1921, with a detailed proposal by Hughes for a ten-year halt on the construction of capital ships and the scuttling of other battleships so that Japan, Britain, and the United States would be left with the ratio of 5-5-3. So closely did his statement conform to Borah's ideas that he is said to have moved his presentation to the opening day for fear that Senator Borah would "steal his thunder" by prior presentation of a similar proposal in the Senate. As the conference proceeded, Borah's resentment mounted. He was dismayed, for example, by the unwillingness of the powers at Washington to limit the building of auxiliary vessels such as submarines; he soon found still greater reasons for taking offense.

Unlike the expendable League, Far Eastern problems were at the heart of disarmament, and Hughes knew these problems could not be dismissed. Secret negotiations had been under way since June for the abrogation of the Anglo-Japanese alliance, and meetings continued in the Hughes home into late November. The result of all this work was the Four Power Treaty presented to the Washington Conference on December 10. It provided for the cancellation of the Anglo-Japanese alliance, a general pledge on the part of the signatories to respect each other's Pacific island possessions, and consultation to defend these interests. The crucial political implications of this agreement were not lost to the irreconcilables, especially in Article II, which provided that if a signatory's rights were threatened by the aggressive action of an outside power, all signatories would "communicate with one another . . . in order to arrive at . . . the most efficient measures to be taken . . . to meet the exigencies of the particular situation . . ."

After Lodge offered the Four Power Treaty, Borah locked himself in his room for three hours of intense study. When he emerged, his opinion was firmly negative: the treaty was an alliance and he was against it. Thus, the Four Power Treaty became the subject of a major parliamentary battle consuming over two hundred pages in the *Congressional Record.*[26] The bitterest attack was led by the League irreconcilables—Borah, Johnson, and Reed—who once again sprang to the defense of nationalism. They charged that the Washington Conference had been turned aside from the limitation of naval armaments to the execution of a new alliance, an insidious "quadruple alliance," Borah called it, which, like the League of Nations, would entangle the United States in the toils of an alien balance of power in order to serve the selfish designs of predatory nations and secret financial interests. Borah, who had been the prime mover in calling the conference and who had condemned just that kind of secret diplomacy which had produced this treaty, looked upon the Four Power pact as "transferring to the Pacific the old system of political groupings which had tormented and tortured Europe for three hundred years." The race in armaments was merely shifted to another track. With alarm he pointed to the similarity between Article II of the Four Power Treaty and Article X of the League Covenant, and he suggested that the provision for consultation concealed a secret agreement between the United States and Great Britain. Would Japan give up her alliance with England merely for a promise to consult? He based this charge on a stenographic report of Paul Cravath's statement before the Council on Foreign Relations, which merely said that the Washington Conference had resulted in a closer understanding between England and the United States. The New York *Times* accused him of behaving like "a police court petti-fogger."[27]

Supporters of the Four Power Treaty, particularly Lodge, vigorously denied the charges that the treaty was an alliance, repeatedly emphasized the absence of any obligation to enforce its provisions, and warned that its rejection would result in the failure of naval limitation and other projects of the conference. These were hard words to live down, but the unwavering Borah was convinced that the treaty *was* an alliance; it *would* call forth counteralliances from the powers excluded from the agreement; it *would* result in the domination of the Far East by Japan; the United States *would* be restrained from exerting any influence there; the rights and ambitions of China *had* been disregarded; and ultimately the treaty would lead not to peace but to war. Even the League of Nations, he argued, was a safer proposition than this, for at least it included so many nations that rival alliances would not be a consequence.

In the end, Borah's arguments went unheeded. The Four Power Treaty surmounted its opposition because the irreconcilables were not numerous enough and because those who thought it a poor substitute for the League preferred to have some sort of an agreement on armaments limitation rather than none at all. The Senate approved the treaty by a vote of 67 to 27, but only after attaching a reservation asserting that there was "no commitment to armed force, no alliance, no obligation to join in any defense." Borah was one of the four Republicans who voted against the treaty.

The Washington Conference ended in a burst of publicity which hailed it as "a brilliant achievement in American diplomacy." There were substantial gains, and if there were losses, notably in a decline of American power in the coastal waters off Japan and China, this was the fault of Congress and public opinion, not the diplomats at Washington. Conspicuous among the gains were the naval reductions—a first step toward disarmament, "the rainbow hope of nations." As for lasting results, wishful thinking was the unsubstantial basis for the wave of enthusiasm and hope that flowed across the world. The cold realities of international politics were to reveal a decade later that the real sources of war are not exorcised by depriving nations of the instruments of coercion.[28]

After the Washington Conference the Harding administration leaned back to survey the scene. Albert B. Fall took advantage of the lull to lease Teapot Dome and do a little naval pioneering of his own. The lease delivering the oil fields in Wyoming to Sinclair was signed April 7, 1922. When Senator La Follette demanded an investigation and report on April 29, Borah was one of the five senators who manifested any interest. Senator Knute Nelson of Minnesota wanted to know what was the use of having another report on Teapot Dome when Fall himself had written one! It would be another twenty months before the public interest would be aroused.

Ten years before Hitler began raging against it in Germany, Borah emerged as the arch critic of the Versailles Treaty. He made numerous speeches after the war predicting that peace and recovery would never come to Europe as long as the treaty went unchanged. Writing to the manager of the Minneapolis *Tribune,* he declared: "... When the facts are finally known such congresses as that of Vienna will appear very respectable compared with the one at Versailles. In the imperialistic disposition of peoples, in the trading about in an unconscionable way of the rights and privileges of whole nations and in the trampling upon the first principles of self government, nothing has ever exceeded the peace conference at Versailles."[29]

In a Senate speech on September 26, 1921, Borah excoriated the treaty. Three years had passed since the war, affording an opportunity to view the treaty's effects on peace. "We know now," he said, "the cruel punishment it has visited upon friend and foe alike; it has given in exchange for promises of independence and freedom, dependence and spoliation, but that is not the worst." He continued:

> 'If it were done when it is done,' we could turn our backs upon the past and hope to find exculpation in doing better things in the future. But we know this treaty has in it the seeds of many wars. It hangs like a storm cloud upon the horizon. It is the incarnation of force. It recognizes neither mercy nor repentance, and discriminates not at all between the guilty and the innocent . . . Its one-time defenders now are frank to admit it. It will bring sorrow to the world again. Its basic principle is cruel, unconscionable, and remorseless imperialism . . . economic breakdown . . . awaits its execution; and . . . millions of men, women and children, those now living and those yet unborn, are to be shackled, enslaved and hungered if it remains the law of Europe . . .

Borah admitted that America had to do her part, but she could not serve the cause of reconstruction by encouraging "this vast scheme of repression and destruction." He was especially determined to prevent American representatives from sitting with the Reparations Commission:

> . . . Neither can we long retain our self-respect, nor the respect of others, by having our ambassadors and agents sitting about the councils and commissions of Europe like human hawks to prey with others upon the

oil wealth of Mosul or of Mesopotamia, or perchance gather some moiety of trade from plundered peoples and then take wing in case the victim stirs. This Republic . . . can not afford to pursue such a course . . .[30]

In the perspective of a war-wise generation sobered by an unsuccessful effort at settling a second world conflict and hardened by its cold and hot wars, the Versailles Treaty appears less iniquitous than it seemed to the disillusioned liberals and idealists of its time. Nowadays Versailles arouses nostalgia. It was at least a settlement, and one that in the best moments of the 1920's seemed a basis for slow improvement in international relations. Scholars now point out how admirable and skillful Wilson's role was in drafting the treaty, considering the obstacles confronting him in that cockpit of international rivalries. Some of these obstacles were beyond his control, or for that matter beyond the control of any of the much-maligned statesmen and politicians at the conference table. While demanding immediate revision of the treaty, Borah made complimentary references to Wilson, who he said had been contravened in his principles at the peace conference. He realized that there were wide differences of opinion between the United States delegates and others. When invited to the New York dinner in the former President's honor sponsored by the Wilson Foundation in 1922, Borah sent his regrets; however, the telegram also stated that the differences in their views did not blind him to the "great policies and principles" Wilson stood for. He hoped his cause could succeed.[31]

Though Borah appreciated the sincerity in Wilson's efforts, it was as Edmund Burke said of the plans of the British government for the American colonies: "However pure the intention of their authors—we all know the event has been unfortunate." The Treaty of Versailles was the case in point. Next to disarmament, Borah thought the rewriting of the treaty was most essential to the restoration of peace and economic sanity.[32]

Borah's sympathy for Wilson's ideals did not extend to other European statesmen who sat at the conference table. He charged that M. Clemenceau was the man responsible for "the present misery of Europe" because he stood in the way of the American attempt "to mollify" the peace treaty and was now asking the

United States to help enforce this "inhuman" document. The senator kept alive a transatlantic debate by statements that the French were a great people but had spent too much time in contemplating that part of the Lord's Prayer which read "forgive us our debts." His animosity for France continued and was most strikingly shown when Clemenceau visited this country in November 1922. Borah refused to serve on the committee to greet him and arraigned French policy in the Senate, charging militarism at home and "obnoxious and indefensible" imperialism abroad [Syria]. In his analysis of the visitor's speech Borah found no message except that of "punishment, of vengeance, of anticipated war."

> We are invited back to the Old Europe with its secret treaties, its secret diplomacy, its militarism, its imperialism, and it is that policy the American people are asked to furnish their money, their means, and their men to enforce.

The Idahoan ventured to declare that the American people would reject his message. "They will separate the policy from the man, and while giving the man a royal welcome they will with magnificent unanimity reject the policy."[33]

In another mood Borah concluded that there was not much to be gained by analyzing past events or by inquiring into the intent or motives of men who stood in places of responsibility at a particular juncture of human affairs. What matters generally, he said, is the question: has the plan stood the test? Has it worked for good or evil? Then he went on to show that the Versailles Treaty had worked no more disastrously for those against whom it was directed than for those who dictated it. The whole world was paying the penalty. To Borah and other liberals of his time, including the eminent economist John M. Keynes, it seemed an unsound, revengeful peace, above all disastrous in its unrealistic reparations policy. Some historians agree that Wilson's most serious failure at Paris was his consent to the reparations clauses of the treaty. They brought little benefit to the victors, while in Germany they created a feeling of grave injustice, especially when viewed in connection with the "war guilt" clause and other economic provisions of the treaty.[34]

When Borah made predictions about the economic breakdown of

Europe under the Versailles Treaty, it was to reparations payments that he referred. He emphasized that Germany could not pay the sum imposed on her. Europe was trembling, he believed, in fear of Germany's economic might. France was not justified in trying to pull Germany down, for once this was done, he warned, Europe itself would be ruined.[35]

Borah's cry for "instant revision" of the Versailles Treaty so that "Europe can live" was regarded by critics as unworthy of his reputation as a serious student of public affairs. He was accused of taking out his hatred for the defeated League on the unfortunate treaty. Actually he believed the League, though unwise, was founded upon an idealistic principle, whereas through every page, paragraph, provision, and covert phrase of the treaty "vengeance crawls and writhes and hisses." The New York *Times* accounted for his belief that Europe was on the road to economic ruin by the fact that he had "more than once shown himself somewhat credulous in the matter of stories coming from Europe." To his objections that the treaty did not conform to the economic life in Europe, critics offered the solution of sending American representatives to the Reparations Commission in order to adjust the payments and perhaps relieve some of the heavy pressure of the first few years, but Borah objected to this as well. Finally, critics lost patience with him because he seemed to believe that the Versailles Treaty would be easy to rewrite; ". . . he cannot really believe this," commented a New York editorial. "Why, then, should a public man talk about it in a way that gives him the air of a child grasping at moonbeams?"[36]

In fairness to Borah it must be stated that the reparations bill *did* exceed Germany's capacity to pay. Downward adjustments were made from time to time until the reparations debt was liquidated at Lausanne in 1932. Furthermore, it helped engender a sense of grievance that became a powerful weapon in Hitler's propaganda in the thirties. In any event, no peace is achieved with the signing of a treaty. The preservation of peace is a continuous and arduous task. Wilson recognized the treaty's imperfections, but he hoped that they would be eliminated through League machinery. Borah made his position indefensible by helping to destroy the League and thus leaving no means for the treaty's improvement.[37]

President McCracken of Vassar College wrote Borah from Basel on August 23, 1922, describing the galloping inflation, gloom, and crisis in Germany and France, and asked: "Is there no chance of leadership from America? Will you not speak out?" Borah responded:

> . . . Europe would have none of certain great policies and principles Wilson carried to Europe . . . She built the treaty on principles of vengeance, military dictatorship and therefore the treaty is a menace to the world's peace. No league, no cooperation from us will save Europe so long as she clings to that instrument of . . . destruction. What Europe needs now . . . is not coddling, not sentimental sympathy, but she needs to be told the actual truth that she is persisting in her own suicide. Unfortunately, our foreign policy is conniving at the program.[38]

Anticipating Germany's failure to continue reparations payments late in 1922, France's armies invaded the Ruhr Valley. Borah condemned this action as ruthless militarism, a violation of the armistice, the treaty, and an offense against humanity. He predicted inestimably evil consequences were certain to follow. Criticizing the State Department, he said: ". . . it ought not to be permitted for the world to look upon us as conniving at this program by our silence . . . We should declare our attitude and make our protest; this is the very least we can do, and we should do very much more."[39] The Harding administration took the attitude that nothing it might do could change the state of affairs; indeed, such a protest as Borah favored was considered "impractical and hurtful . . ."[40]

Despite his critics, Borah was seeking within his limits a positive approach to the problems of peace. He devoted much time to the study of foreign affairs in 1922-23. He wanted reparations reduced to a point where Germany could afford to pay, and to this end he outlined a program for Europe. We should be willing to cancel our war debts if Europe would change its principles of militarism and adjust its economic conditions so that American producers could count on European markets at least for the next twenty years. Europe should stand ready to revise the Versailles Treaty, reduce arms, ratify the Washington treaties, expose secret military conventions, recognize Russia, and waive France's right to take possession of the Ruhr. He wanted all these matters settled at an international economic conference. "Then," he submitted, "there will be something upon which to work out a plan of salvation."

When lecturing Europe through the American press, Borah's favorite method was to wrap his advice around a brick and hurl it at Europe's head. Playing the pharisee, again he served notice that Europe could expect nothing from us until it recovered from "its war madness." In its staggering totality his plan was impractical, but there was one noteworthy exception. He stood alone in advocating an international economic conference in which he seemed ready to modify his narrow nationalism. At least he saw the necessity of winding up the tragic bookkeeping of the war, but his offer to cancel war debts was contingent upon the settlement of numerous other questions. Using the debts as a bargaining weapon only further complicated a complex situation. There was no sense in making the settlement of one problem contingent on settling all the others. While waiting for such a great and wonderful achievement as Borah hoped for, all the problems would remain and nothing would be done.[41]

Borah feared all the advantages gained at the Disarmament Conference would be lost unless America was willing to help break the reparations deadlock which threatened to provoke another war. Accordingly he proposed a resolution calling for "an international conference to consider the economic problems now obtaining throughout the world" on December 21, 1922, but it was subverted when Senator Watson, speaking for the administration, informed the Senate that the President had already sent out "feelers." When Borah inquired if this meant negotiations had been opened, Watson adhered to the term "feelers" while Lodge interjected "conversations" as a substitute. Borah said: "Well then let it be conversations across the seas. If I am assured . . . that the President has instituted such conversations, I certainly do not wish to embarrass him. I will withdraw my resolution."[42]

Subsequently the administration made no more than a timid suggestion to France, which was laughed at. Borah vowed he would never consult the President or State Department again when he planned to offer a bill. He reintroduced his resolution for a world economic conference as a rider to the Naval Appropriations bill of 1923. By this time he was anxious to advance the idea of outlawing war and thought the conference would provide an opportunity for its promotion. However, as in the case of the first resolution for an economic conference, he did not follow his proposal with sustained action, leaving the burden with the administration while giving the impression that he was anxious to remedy the international situation even if no one else in government was. Couched in generalities, his resolution had in it the spirit of the League and the World Court, but in every way it tried to disassociate itself from both. He was compared with the characterization of Hallam, "his mouth filled with cabbages and contradictions."

During these much-publicized debates in which Borah outlined his position on world affairs, he surprised many by denying that he was an isolationist. Isolation had never been a Republican policy, he asserted. It had consistently favored participation in foreign negotiations affecting American interests, had always favored the peaceful settlement of disputes, and had done much to develop arbitration as a means to that end. However, the Senate irreconcilables cried apostasy when Borah devoted his time to the logical outgrowth of the thesis that the problems of Europe are the problems of the United States. Hiram Johnson denounced him for such a view, charging rank inconsistency. Irvine Lenroot told the Senate Borah's statement indicated the most outstanding "conversion" since that of Saul of Tarsus. Borah replied that Saul was saved by his conversion. Carter Glass added that by his conversion Saul saved the world as well!

The press generally praised Borah for advocating a larger role for America in world affairs. The Springfield *Republican* noted with satisfaction that "the old Borah . . . warning his countrymen against entanglement in transatlantic affairs is no more . . . in this crisis Mr. Borah becomes splendidly inconsistent." Mark Sullivan thought he had such a grasp on the public imagination that he qualified as the successor to Wilson. One editor suggested sarcastically that soon he would be offering a resolution to ratify the Versailles Treaty!

If Borah did gradually abandon the intransigent stand he took in 1919, there is also evidence that he was prompted by domestic economic conditions. At this time he was receiving hundreds of letters from farm organizations and farmers complaining of a two-horned dilemma: the high costs of land transportation, and the lack of foreign markets for American produce. They stated that 25 per cent of American wheat and 50 per cent of American cotton had to be marketed abroad, and economic distress in Europe was reducing that market drastically. Borah had always recognized a certain degree of economic interdependence. In distressed conditions he was willing to recognize more. There would clearly be no farm recovery here until European economic recovery became a reality. The problem was more complex than the American farmer or Borah realized, but a revival of international trade was a spoke in the wheel of progress. It was undoubtedly a motive behind the resolutions for an economic conference.[43]

There were many reasons for Borah's implacable hostility to the Fordney bill, better known as the Soldier's Bonus bill, which passed the House but was buried in the Senate Finance Committee in 1921. It was fated to become one of the most controversial issues of the twenties. President Harding came before the Senate to urge the recommitting of the Soldier's Bonus bill and was promptly attacked by Borah and La Follette for invading the prerogative of the legislature, setting "a dangerous precedent." Borah called the motion to send the bill back to the Finance Committee "moral cowardice." Basically he was opposed to a cash proposition of any character, maintaining that it did not perform the obligation which existed, if any did exist. A trifling four or six hundred dollars could hardly be called compensation for the sacrifices made in the Great War; such service defies compensation. He regarded a cash bonus degrading to the soldier and incompatible with the reduction of taxes. It would add five millions to an already crushing tax burden at a time when investigations were revealing neglect by the government toward those veterans broken in health, mangled in body, or shattered in mind. Nor could he foresee the government's ability to pay such a bonus for the next few years, which explains why the bill as framed stated no payment would be made until after 1922. He proposed having the future Congress, which would be obliged to appropriate the money, decide on the merits of the bill.[44]

Senator Fordney reintroduced the measure in March 1922. The plan of payment was altered somewhat, and largely through the efforts of the American Legion it passed both houses. Harding vetoed it. The House overrode his veto, but the Senate sustained it 44 to 26. Though Borah was opposed to "adjusted compensation," he said he would vote for a land-settlement bill. He wanted more generous sacrifices for the permanently disabled veterans and thought Congress should draft another bill saying flatly that the government was unable to sustain cash payments at that time. Borah's continuous opposition throughout the debate made him unpopular with veterans in Idaho. In a telegram Pocatello Post No. 4 of the American Legion notified him: ". . . you opposed the war . . . foreign loans . . . sending troops . . . the espionage law. You are apparently opposed to everything but Borah. We can hire an obstructionist for less money. The nation needs constructive work and fewer speeches." Borah replied that nothing but a "slimy creature" would buy his office out of the public treasury.[45]

On June 6 Borah wrote the President urging amnesty for political prisoners convicted during the war for violations of the sedition and espionage laws. Calling attention to the example set by England and other countries on this matter and charging that the spirit and letter of the First Amendment were disregarded in many of these cases, he asked Harding to give the situation his personal consideration. Borah wrote many letters and made numerous speeches in conjunction with the Civil Liberties Union when he could spare the time. Opening the campaign for general amnesty in Chicago, he contended that the men jailed, most of whom were members of the I.W.W., were thus deprived of their constitutional rights. It is a dangerous thing, he said, to set aside the Constitution during wartime. "Instead of persecuting men with ideas to express, we should hire halls for them. Their patriotism would prevent trouble."[46]

Commenting editorially on Borah's "wandering into the eccentricities of professional radicals and wrong-headed sentimentalists," the New York *Times* pointed out that free speech was not absolute, at least when designed to overthrow the government or endanger it. While not condoning sedition, Borah believed that if a man thought the war was unjust, he had an absolute right to say so and that the men in question should have been given their freedom when the war acts were repealed. An independent investigation conducted by Senator George W. Pepper of Pennsylvania found no ground for the conviction of some of the men in prison. As a result of their efforts, amnesty was finally proclaimed in 1923 by another president.[47]

Borah sided with the Democrats in opposing the Fordney-McCumber Tariff. During the debate he urged the Senate not to rush passage of the bill and opposed invoking the closure rule.

Talk in the Senate could be halted, he warned, but not throughout the country. Reviewing Republican proposals to take money from the Treasury (e.g., the bonus, ship subsidies, increased taxes, and the increased national debt), he accused the administration of failing to fulfill its pledge to lessen the tax burden. He could not point to one single measure reducing the taxes of the people. There could come a time, he warned, when our reserves, economic and financial, would be called upon, and the government should be preparing for that time. Though he wanted to get what tariff advantages he could for the farmers, stockmen, and beet-sugar growers, he regarded this bill as an emergency tariff which did not follow Republican principles of protection faithfully. Associates were amazed when he voted against tariff increases on such typical Idaho products as sugar, lumber, and wool. He wrote:

> . . . We are not supposed to build a wall around the United States which gives to the producer . . . a monopoly of the American market, which enables him to charge all which conscience or the lack of it will permit. It has always been my understanding that we keep alive competition, but that we favor the American manufacturer or producer to the extent of starting him off even, as it were . . . But this bill is prohibitory of all foreign importations as to many . . . articles which the people of this country must have in order to live.[48]

In August 1922 the bill passed the Senate 48 to 25. Borah had opposed 95 per cent of its provisions and was the only Republican to vote against its final passage. Along with Edmund Burke, he held that he owed his time and energies to his constituents, but he owed his judgment only to himself. He favored protection but not a tariff dictated by special interests. His position was regarded as representing "the public judgment of the work of this Congress."[49]

Foes of pork-barrel legislating faced a Senate defeat in February 1923 when in spite of their opposition the $56,000,000 harbors item passed. Borah introduced a measure to cut the appropriation to $27,000,000, charging that some of the streams scheduled for improvement were not deep enough during some months for ducks! He stated that the budget was rarely given attention, but this represented the most pronounced assault on it. Similarly he opposed Mellon's program for reducing the high taxes imposed on incomes and excess profits during the war. The Mellon bill provided for the reduction of the highest surtaxes from 65 per cent to 25 per cent. Through the influence of opponents like Borah the surtax levy on the highest incomes was lowered to 50 per cent and not to half that rate as proposed by Mellon.[50]

The Ship Subsidy bill introduced during the spring session of 1922 failed, according to Borah, because it threatened to jeopardize Republican chances in the fall elections. He thought the party would "commit suicide" a second time by reintroducing the bill and advised postponing action, for it was not the appropriate time to introduce "something that would relieve a certain class from taxation." High operating costs made it unprofitable for American ships to compete with foreign vessels; yet it was considered vital to defense to preserve an American merchant marine. Like many other Americans, economy-minded Borah found it difficult to choose between the only possible alternatives: government operation at a loss, or private ownership with subsidies. He regarded this bill as a drain on the Treasury, establishing a vicious system of tax exemption for one group, and predicted it would not grant relief but would burden the future as much as voting a bond issue. The methods used by the U.S. Shipping Board also aroused prolonged controversy. Under the Merchant Marine Act of 1920, the board had been authorized to transfer government-owned ships to private American owners on easy terms. Loans were also made available to companies willing to operate new routes. In July 1922 Borah framed a measure to reduce the Shipping Board from seven to three members.[51] He maintained that seven members at $12,000 a year represented a waste of public funds and a burden on the taxpayers. If we are to get rid of some ships, he said, why not get rid of some commissioners!

In the fall of 1922 the Borahs returned to Boise after an absence of three years. In a rented office on Main Street the senator held conferences or just talked with old friends and answered his mail. Once more he found himself at odds with state leaders who were opposed to the direct primary. The state's direct primary law of 1909, never satisfactory, was discredited in 1918 by the Nonpartisan League's successful invasion of the Democratic primary ticket. In 1919 the legislature repealed the law and enacted a new one providing only for the nomination of local officers. From that time forward Borah insisted that the Republican party pledge itself to enact a new state-wide primary law, and he devoted his energies to that end in the campaign of 1922. The Republican state convention, held at Wallace in August, was dominated by politicians who were hostile to popular government and refused to recommend such a law. In Borah's estimation their platform was "a colorless, unconstructive, painted glass affair."

He stumped the state, defying the Republican machine, condemning the constabulary, splitting his party wide open, and "not giving a damn." In Spokane he predicted that a third party would sweep the country in 1924 unless the Republican party did something about the unrest abroad in the land. He compared the current "people's movement" to Theodore Roosevelt's Bull Moose campaign of 1912 and the political revolution which took place in the Republican party between 1852 and 1860.[52] The fall elections came as no surprise to him. Republicans in Idaho and nationally made a poor showing. Charles C. Moore managed to win a majority of nearly ten thousand votes, but it was held that his majority would have been greater if Borah had not given indirect aid to the party's enemies. Borah failed in his 1922 fight for a direct primary, but there were enough Republicans in the legislature in 1923 to enact a new primary law, which Governor Moore promptly vetoed. There the matter stood until the new primary law of 1931 was enacted.[53]

Originally Borah had intended to confine his speeches to the international situation in the approaching campaign and to criticize the administration's weak foreign policy, but he then decided to include such other issues as extravagance in government expenditures and the administration's failure to call a world economic conference, recognize Russia, or outlaw war. All this would, of course, be interpreted by the newspapers as an attack on Harding with Borah's own political motives just beneath the surface, but the senator disclaimed "playing any game" in the coming two years with the sole view of getting back into office. He could see no reason why his speeches should have any effect on the presidential situation, but experts guessed they would. In a speech on "Reorganization of the Republican party" at Akron in March 1923 he assured his audience he had not come to the President's home state to attack him. In order to win, however, the party would have to put behind it the vengeance and intolerance of the war and stop Treasury tapping, wasting public funds, and operating on such low standards. He urged stronger leadership, a return to states' rights, and the dismissal of federal agents and spies. He made no bid for any third party and declared he was no candidate for the presidency, but some doubts persisted. "So Caesar once refused a crown," a skeptical editor commented. Borah's Senate term would expire in 1924.[54]

David Lawrence regarded this Akron speech as the big opening gun in Borah's personal campaign for renomination. Attorney General Daugherty accused him of injecting an anti-Harding flavor into his remarks, and Harding's followers were disturbed because they did not expect his renomination. By then La Follette had already declared against him. Despite these ripples on the political surface, Borah and Harding remained on good personal terms and had long talks before the President left on his ill-fated western vacation. Borah continued to disagree with the administration's foreign policy and believed the party would suffer unless some changes were made. Administration sources entertained hopes that he would come around to their way of thinking on the World Court because it would be awkward to have Borah opposing one of the big issues in the 1924 campaign.[55]

Finishing up committee work and correspondence, Borah left for Idaho and arrived in Boise on June 16, 1923. En route he held a press conference in Chicago and visited with his sister, Sue Lasley, and her family. He planned to spend most of the summer at home resting, visiting with friends, and trout fishing. Despite these intentions, he was soon swept into a whirl of engagements. Almost everyone wanted to hear him speak, consult him on farm problems, or just shake his hand.

Borah, the campaigner, was a treat for the listener; he was straightforward, forceful, and well-informed. He usually traveled throughout Idaho in a second-hand car driven by Ray McKaig or Jim Young, his secretary. Out in the fields on farms there was little strain in campaigning because he was among friends who thought nothing of the dusty boots, rumpled shirt, and old bent straw hat he wore to shield him from the hot sun. From one campaign year to another the Republican National Committee sent him $2,500 to cover expenses, and year after year he wrote out checks in two installments and returned the money. He told the chairman that his campaign expenses rarely exceeded two hundred dollars, which he preferred to pay out of his own pocket so that he could campaign independently.

At Rigby that summer he joined in the Pioneer Day celebration and addressed a crowd of ten thousand. At Kellogg he shared the annual picnic meal with the miners and smelters, later to speak at another meeting in Grangeville. The busy summer went by like this. Harding was greeted warmly by Borah when he came through Idaho en route to Alaska. The Idaho senator announced that he was happy about the President's "masterly retreat" on the World Court in his St. Louis speech and that there were no longer any serious differences between them. Borah stood ready to support Harding in 1924 if he would discard the advice of Root and Hughes and insist that the International Court of Justice disavow its League parentage. He predicted Congress would do nothing with the World Court when it came up again for discussion.

On August 3 Borah was informed of the sudden death of President Harding after a short illness in San Francisco. Speaking at Spokane a few days later, he characterized the late President as "a sincere, high-minded, patriotic public servant." He asserted gravely, "Fate and circumstances have made Calvin Coolidge president," and he called on the public "to give him a chance to make good." He believed Coolidge was the logical choice for the presidential nomination in 1924.[56]

XII The Conscience of the Republican Party

The only guide to a man is his conscience; the only shield to his memory is the rectitude and sincerity of his actions.

—Winston Churchill

Coolidge was on good personal terms with Borah before 1923. He had often sat in the Senate listening to him, admired his intellect, and liked him, despite the fact that on several important issues they disagreed. Like Taft, Coolidge felt the need of a friendly enemy whose advice, no matter how disagreeable, was certain to be honest. Borah was to assail Coolidge's policies more vigorously than Taft's; yet he was to be rewarded by an even greater confidence. He had easier access to the White House than Curtis, the official Republican party leader. A shrewd judge of character, Coolidge recognized Borah as a fearless fighter, cantankerous and obstinate at times but with a passion for realities and a zest for righteousness.[1]

As time passed, Coolidge's courtship of Borah became an absorbing puzzle. Few things in Washington politics were so much discussed. Borah was frequently summoned to the White House for dinner or a conference, or asked for a weekend on the "Mayflower." It was considered effective flattery to be invited on the presidential yacht. The list of guests was usually given to the newspapers, and good political use was made of the old boat; however, there was probably no one in Washington on whom these attentions had less effect than Borah. He continued to hammer away at his pet projects regardless of whether the White House approved or not; he went along with the administration when it pleased him, which was seldom.[2]

In a series of speeches in December 1924 Coolidge framed a program which included support for the World Court, the Mellon Plan, the debt settlements with Italy and Belgium, the protective tariff, and repudiation of the farm bloc. He urged caution toward Soviet

Russia, economy in government, and the defeat of the soldier's bonus. Borah accepted the last two points in the President's program and did his best to wreck *all* the others.

In their White House talks he offered evidence that the World Court was a creation of the League. In reply the President stared out the window. Borah tried to prove that trade with Soviet Russia would be profitable. Coolidge listened and then gazed at the setting sun across the Potomac. Borah insisted that the State Department could not refuse a visa to the Russian Count Karolyi. Coolidge watched the clock and counted the rubber bands on his desk.[3] Borah denounced as "a betrayal of the public trust" the administration's failure to press Congress for farm legislation. He also declared that he despised many of the officeholders still under Coolidge. The President probably thought that by conferring with the Idahoan and staying friendly, he was holding his insurgency to a minimum. If Coolidge didn't try to tame Borah, there was no telling how wild he might become. On such hot political issues as the defeat of the soldier's bonus Borah led the fight for the administration, while old guard Republicans scurried to their political dugouts.

Borah was not averse to the reputation of privy councilor to the President. When he became chairman of the Foreign Relations Committee, it was natural for the two men to confer on the Turkish treaties, Tacna-Arica, and extraterritorial rights in China, but this does not explain why Borah and Coolidge should have been discussing aviation, Muscle Shoals, coal unions, surplus crops, railway consolidations, and co-operative marketing.[4] Another explanation offered for their strange affinity was the familiar theory that opposites attract. Coolidge was extremely cautious, cryptic, self-effacing, and silent, while Borah was at times incautious, ostentatious, and voluble.

The farm bloc, a loose association of senators representing western agricultural states, was well established by the spring of 1921 and was determined to act as a lever upon the two major parties in securing legislation for the farmer, hard hit by the postwar depression. The grievances of western agriculture were well publicized by eloquent spokesmen representing the section in both houses, but acceptable proposals for reform were lacking. Four attempts were made between 1924-28 to solve some of the farmer's problems. To raise prices either the surplus had to be reduced or exports sold at the world market price had to be subsidized in some manner. When a plan for subsidization, in which the costs were to be defrayed by an equalization fee imposed on farmers, was introduced in the McNary-Haugen bills, Borah said he would vote for it if the compulsory payment of the fee was eliminated. According to Borah the McNary bill did not do enough for the farmer. With taxes consuming nearly 16 per cent of total farm income, he demanded: "How can we ask the farmer to pay for remedial legislation never imposed on any other industry in the United States?" In a letter to a constituent he wrote: "It does not seem to me the solution is for the farmer to take the money out of one of his pockets and put it in the other, especially when neither pocket has any money to take out. But as I understand it, some of these measures propose that the farmer shall assess a fee upon himself to make up for low prices. For the life of me I cannot see how that is going to relieve the farmer."[5]

Borah told a Trenton, Missouri, audience that the problem not only concerned the farmers but was a distinctly national issue, involving the interest and welfare of the whole people. There can be no such thing as permanent national prosperity with agriculture in distress. A sound protective principle, such as Hamilton advocated, applied with a just regard for all interests, was vital to the farmer because it would build up the home market. In Borah's judgment the solution of the farm problem depended on enlarging the home market and devising methods by which the farmer could reach the market without the waste, loss, and exactions forced upon him.[6] He also wished to provide machinery enabling the farmers to hold surpluses for domestic needs in lean years.

The McNary bill passed, despite Borah's objections, with the equalization fee. Coolidge gave it a strong veto, and there the matter stood until the Republican convention of 1928. Borah had conferred with the President two months before his veto message of February 1927 on farm relief legislation, and they found themselves in general agreement. Divisions within the bipartisan farm bloc prevented unity except on broad general principles. Meanwhile Borah offered little in the way of a substitute program.[7] His idea of farm relief was to build up a great governmental marketing institution for all agricultural products. If such a system were thoroughly organized and established, and if the farmer could get one half of what the consumer pays for his products, the farm problem would be solved; moreover, Borah thought the farmer could get that one half under any system of intelligent marketing.[8]

He argued that as labor and all lines of business had organized themselves, farmers had to do likewise. If the United States Steel Corporation dumped its products on the market without any intelligent study, it would be bankrupt by the end of a single fiscal year. He cited the California berry growers as one successful cooperative marketing association and noted that others were organized for marketing almonds, raisins, prunes, and apples. He said that with more exertion wheat growers could do the same, but no comparable success would be forthcoming from the organization of production.

Alarming reports revealed the degree of demoralization in American farm life. The farmer did not hold an equal place in the economy either regarding taxation or transportation. While he was entitled to aid in marketing his surplus, Borah asserted, he should not be called on to surrender his initiative and economic independence to an autocratic bureau at Washington. As an example he used the Russian peasant who refused to allow the Marxian bureaucracy to market his products for him. ". . . Today," said Borah, "he is an independent agricultural unit, as independent as lives under God's shining sun."[9]

Neither his proposals nor his analogies got to the crux of the matter. He failed to explain how the government was to sponsor a vast marketing institution for all agricultural products and still leave the farmer his initiative and economic independence. Nor did he consider what was to become of the ever-increasing agricultural surplus, which even scientific marketing could not eliminate. His vagueness on the subject prompted Chester Davis to conclude that he had no sounder understanding of the farm problem than Andrew J. Mellon![10] Borah continued merely to advocate a high protective tariff on farm products, a proper marketing system, the abolition of freight rate discrimination, public ownership and development of water power, and the development of waterways. He voted for the $500,000,000 appropriation for the Federal Farm Loan Board and carried his crusade for the farmer into the campaign of 1928.

Borah thought that the most important domestic problem in 1923 was tax reduction, and he found Coolidge's proposals both "drastic and courageous."[11] In a Senate speech he painted a dismal picture of the tax burden destroying industry and producing moral retrogression. It was not only an economic problem but a moral one as well; families suffered, young people were deprived of opportunity, and children did not receive proper educations. He pointed to the Veterans' Bureau as an example of incompetency, waste, and graft.[12] He favored doing away with tax-exempt securities, a part of the administration's program, but he thought a constitutional amendment unnecessary. "We can do away with them if we just have the nerve and courage to do it."[13]

The worst problem confronting Coolidge arose out of the scandals of the Harding administration, the major facts of which were not revealed until after Harding's death. The fact that Coolidge kept Harding's cabinet gives at least some indication that he knew little about what had taken place. He retained Fall, Daugherty, and others in office until congressional pressure and public opinion forced their removal. Coolidge's limpness may have been prompted by a belief that the charges against them were primarily political in origin, brought by the opposition to weaken his party. He hesitated to push the cases until the evidence was so strong that failure to approve the investigations would have weakened his party's chances in 1924.[14]

During one of their White House conferences Coolidge told Borah to make any suggestions he wished. Borah replied: "Get rid of Daugherty." This was before the oil scandals became public knowledge, and Coolidge was astounded. Borah went on to explain that trouble was ahead for the administration and that Daugherty would be a millstone around the President's neck. Coolidge seemed impressed, but he declared that the removal of Daugherty would be regarded as a repudiation of the Harding administration and would be resented by large numbers of citizens. Borah disagreed.[15]

A month later hearings were opened on the oil leases after Senator Thomas Walsh of Montana, in charge of the investigation, had been gathering evidence for a year and a half. Secretary Denby was cleared, but his stupidity and lack of responsibility aroused an uproar that forced his resignation.[16] When Fall's misconduct was brought to light, Coolidge announced late in January 1924 that every law would be enforced and every right of the people would be protected. On January 29 Senator Wheeler introduced his resolution calling for an inquiry into the Department of Justice and the resignation of Attorney General Daugherty for his failure to prosecute corruption in high places. This brought matters to a crisis. As Frank Kent declared, ". . . the smugness and serenity of the Coolidge counselors . . . vanished over night." A day or two later Coolidge sent for Borah, who asked if the matter were ordinary business or urgent. He was told that it was urgent, so he hurried to the White House.

When Borah was received in the President's study that Sunday evening, he was asked to state frankly his views on Daugherty. He did, and about fifteen minutes later Daugherty entered the room and joined the conference. "Now Senator," said Coolidge, who had slyly brought the two antagonists together at this private meeting, "I wish you would state your position again." Borah was flabbergasted and hesitated to say anything. Daugherty thereupon interrupted sarcastically and said: "Well, don't let my presence embarrass you." Recovering his poise, Borah replied: "I think I should be the least embarrassed person here." Then he proceeded to tell Daugherty why he should resign. The people no longer trusted him; no such man should remain at the head of a department on which the public depends for justice.

A hot discussion followed. Daugherty resented Borah's attitude, declaring that the matter was one for the cabinet to discuss and not for the Senate or any senator. He is reported as having finally said: "I don't know why you want me to resign. I have never had to turn you down. You never asked me for anything." Meanwhile the President sat silently twirling his horn-rimmed glasses in his hand and letting Borah and Daugherty talk it out. This was his way of dodging responsibility.[17]

The next day the President talked with Senators Fess and Willis. They advised him that the removal of Daugherty would be very unwise; it would split Ohio and give it to the Democrats in the next election. Coolidge replied: "I reckon you are right." Daugherty remained attorney general.[18]

Then Borah redoubled his efforts to get rid of Daugherty. In a Senate speech he warned that the full responsibility for his remaining or leaving rested with the President, but said he was ready to join with anyone in impeachment proceedings against him if the

President failed to act. He admitted Daugherty should be given a fair trial, but he was not concerned with individual derelictions of duty, only with the question of public service.[19] Meanwhile Wheeler, who had been holding off his inquiry on the understanding that Daugherty would quit, began his investigation.[20] It unearthed evidence that the Department of Justice was collaborating with certain big business interests, and Daugherty was accused of conspiracy to defraud the government. When Daugherty refused to answer the committee's questions on grounds of self-incrimination and also refused to give the committee access to certain files, the President finally felt compelled to demand his resignation in March 1924.

It is enlightening to consider Daugherty's own account of all these proceedings. He tells us that Borah for some unaccountable reason played into the hands of the radicals in the labor unions by favoring the recognition of Russia. Secretary Hughes saw the danger in this unexpected attack on the policy of the American government and thereupon asked for the Harding administration records in the Department of Justice on Soviet activities in the United States. "We gave them to him," Daugherty tells us, "when he locked horns with Borah." Daugherty tries to impress his readers with the belief that the information given out by his department concerning Russian propaganda helped defeat Borah's pending resolution in the Senate for recognition of the Russian government. This made Borah furious, says Daugherty. Though friends for many years, he thus hopelessly alienated a man whose ability and integrity he had never questioned. "I noted Senator Borah's position with uneasiness," he reports. Finally, Borah's assault "dealt him a vicious blow." He found it unforgivable that Borah should use his power as a senator "to even a personal score." He relates:

> Hearing that Borah had gone to see the President I went to the White House on Sunday afternoon and talked with Coolidge, and asked him to send for the Senator. This he did. I went back to my apartment and returned about eight o'clock that evening. I wanted the President and Borah who arrived in the meantime to discuss the matter before I got there.

A two-hour discussion followed during which Daugherty invited Borah "to lay his cards on the table." Against Borah's insistence that he resign, Daugherty protested that he would not do so unless asked by the President. It was *his* cabinet, not the Senate's. Borah told him that the country, the press, and the Senate were against him. Daugherty replied that they were deceived by liars. Borah finally stated it made no difference; the whole thing had been planned on Capitol Hill. Daugherty had to go. Through all this Coolidge said very little and appeared much distressed. Borah left. Some time later, as Daugherty walked to the door of the study, the President slipped his arm around him, looked into his eyes, and through a mist said: "I'll never strike you a blow."

Some months later, on March 28, after many other "scenes and acts," Daugherty received the President's letter requesting his resignation on the ground that an accused official cannot perform the duties of office and at the same time defend himself. In the end Coolidge discharged Daugherty after as one-sided an investigation as possible, but one which did establish that there had been corruption in the Department of Justice. The whole episode exhibited Coolidge's weakest side.[21]

John James Ingalls once said that the purification of politics is an iridescent dream. For years Borah had been fulminating against corruption in high places and was only laughed at. As the sordid facts surrounding the Teapot Dome oil lease were unfolded, he was vindicated. No Democrat was more critical of the Republican party in this affair. He hoped that the scandals would be given pitiless publicity and that the revelations would lead to a general house cleaning. Appalled by the fact that the most venal persons implicated in the scandals got off with little or no punishment, he lamented: "The flag covered those grafters long enough to let them escape." However, there was the prospect that public property would be recovered, and "other crooks" were warned. There would be cleaner government at least until the people lost interest again. Borah wanted the investigations finished up; ". . . it is time," he said, "to get back to our own business of legislation."[22]

This attitude forestalled all plans for making him chairman of the Republican National Convention in 1924; all hopes for a ringing keynote speech by Borah went out the window with his criticism of the party and its leaders. He seems to have deliberately discouraged the attempt to make him the voice of the Coolidge campaign. He was reminded of the aphorism, "if you lie down with dogs you get up with fleas." The Baltimore *Sun* commented: "As a roaring lion seeking whomsoever he may devour, the gentleman from Idaho is a national asset. As a domesticated animal wearing a Coolidge collar and a [C. Bascom] Slemp license tag, he would be a total loss."[23]

Investigations showed that Harry F. Sinclair, oil magnate, had contributed more than $200,000 to the Republican National Committee in 1920; Borah insisted that it was the obligation of the party to return this money "tainted with oil." Accordingly, he wrote Chairman William Butler:

> . . . This money was not given as an ordinary campaign contribution. The whole transaction . . . had in view an ulterior and sinister purpose . . . No political party is responsible . . . for the wrongful transactions of individual members . . . but when the transactions become known to the party it must necessarily become responsible if it fails to repudiate the transaction and return the fruits thereof . . . I feel that this money should be returned to the source from which it came. We can not in self respect . . . keep it. To do so is to say that political parties are above the law and exempt from the ordinary precepts of morality. I venture the opinion that there are plenty of Republicans who will be glad to contribute from one dollar up to any reasonable sum to clear their party of this humiliating stigma . . . all you have to do is to indicate that course.[24]

Borah received an insolent reply from Butler, which was not made public. The chairman said he had no authority to return Sinclair's money. It would be necessary for the entire committee to act. "Whatever the transactions were," he wrote, "they were . . . completed long before my election as Chairman . . . As I see it, the obligation, if any, for restitution, is upon those who conducted the transactions."[25] Borah considered this reply "unsatisfactory," decided to act without Butler, and thus made a direct appeal to ordinary Republicans. He felt that his party could not escape responsibility simply because there had been a change in committee chairmen since the campaign of 1920. His conscience bothered him and he assumed other Republicans were equally disturbed; as a result, he launched a one-man campaign to raise the money by individual contributions. The burden fell on his office staff to collect the incoming donations. The Cleveland *Plain Dealer* called it "an unprecedented undertaking." It was, in fact, the most idealistic scheme Borah ever conceived.

In March he deposited the first $1,490 in the bank. A month later the total was far short of $260,000. "We will raise it," he promised; "We must raise it before the next campaign." By the end of April the fund was lagging around $7,000. Donations ranged from one cent to one thousand dollars; Senator Cutting of New Mexico made the largest single contribution of $1,000. A number of crank letters accompanied the donations. One writer suggested that Borah add the "oil quiz" to his questionnaire for party candidates in 1928. Disappointed but reluctant to give up, Borah said he would, if necessary, continue his fund drive at the Republican National Convention. Finally, however, he had to admit defeat. The total never reached ten thousand dollars, and it then became his obligation to return all the contributions to those morally indignant Republicans (and a few Democrats) who sent them.

Senator Nye called the campaign "the most foolish step that Senator Borah ever took." Nye was right. As usual his motives in initiating the campaign were above reproach, but it was senseless to tax people who couldn't afford it in order to make a donation to Sinclair! There was a growing realization that the sole beneficiary would be Mr. Sinclair, who stood to get back his $260,000. The rank and file of Republicans reasoned it was far better to suffer a little from the proddings of an accusing conscience than to give anything back to the former lessee of Teapot Dome, and the Democrats wanted to hear even less about Borah's scheme because Doheny of Elk Hills notoriety had given them $75,000 in 1920!

The prospects of the Republican party in 1924 were not Borah's only concern that spring. After Congress adjourned, there would be his own campaign for re-election. He wrote a friend that if Republicans in Idaho adopted the platform suggested, they would be badly beaten in November, and he along with them. He complained:

> The situation here is very deplorable and very demoralizing. I have felt for the last few weeks more keenly and more firmly than ever that I would like to get out. I can't see anything much ahead . . . except dreary hard work and not very much in the way of results. Perhaps a man ought not to feel that way; it may be his duty in such situations to all the

more firmly resolve to stay through. But I have never been so discouraged . . . by a situation as I am now. The whole thing seems rotten to the core.[26]

Borah only entertained these ideas for a short time; as in 1918, the force of public opinion induced him to stand for re-election. He proved receptive to friendly persuasion.

Not only was he assured of his seat in the Senate, but he was also flattered by a boom which originated in Idaho and spread to California. The BORAH FOR PRESIDENT movement circulated throwaways and chain postcards calling on Americans "to get into step and declare as with one voice: William E. Borah for President, 1924." The "Borah-chain" postcards stated:

Link by link and vote by vote, it will carry him into the White House. Wm. E. Borah stands in the van of the progressive movements of this country and has a record of public service of the highest order . . .

Recipients of these cards were asked to pass them along and "not break the chain."[27]

At a Senate luncheon Borah was joined by James Couzens, the wealthy Republican senator from Michigan, and Charles McNary of Oregon. They talked about the approaching campaign. Out of the conversation came a serious offer from Couzens to finance a "Borah for president" movement. The Idahoan was asked merely to draw up a budget and plan of campaign.[28] There was little doubt in some minds that if Borah rose from his Senate seat and announced that he had cut loose from the Republican party, he would be acclaimed a new Moses; even if he remained in his own party, it would matter little whether his platform were liberal, radical, or slightly progressive. Most liberal movements had found him their champion: he supported recognition of Russia, amnesty for political prisoners, withdrawal from Haiti, disarmament, and collective bargaining. Borah was a leader around whom a liberal or progressive party could rally; the causes he furthered provided a ready-made platform.[29] His lack of sympathy for Harding's foreign policy, his arraignment of the Republican party, and his statements that a third party was more than a mere possibility led to the assumption that he might be induced to take up the banner.

However, he refused to encourage the movement. Borah was above all a sound, practical politician. His instinct for self-preservation taught him to be wary of third parties. He had not put off the Republican label in 1912; he was less likely to do so in 1924.

Three reasons have been offered for Borah's failure to join La Follette and the Progressives in 1924; one was the proposal made by "Battle Bob" that the Supreme Court be denied the power to declare an act of Congress unconstitutional. Although he deplored its five to four decisions, Borah was unwilling to go this far. The second was his faith in Coolidge's personal integrity. Although Borah did not like all the men in the administration, he trusted the President. Finally, he was convinced that the third party movement was futile.[30] Borah had great respect and admiration for the seventy-year-old Wisconsinite. Though Borah asked for and received from La Follette a letter of endorsement for his own candidacy, and on many premises agreed wholeheartedly with him, he refused to speak for him. Borah's coolness to La Follette was no indication of any great warmth for Coolidge, for when asked if he would attend the Cleveland convention and make the nominating speech for the President, Borah sent a swift reply to Colonel Harvey: ". . . I think you had better communicate with the President and ask him to make other arrangements in regard to that." Referring to the chairmanship, he wrote: "As I now view the situation, I could not, under any circumstances, accept it if tendered."[31]

Allegedly Coolidge approached Borah about taking second place on the 1924 ticket. The Idaho senator's differences with the party did not seem vital to the President. Borah, however, apparently declined the offer because he would have been forced to support party policies on the national ticket which he opposed in the Senate. As the delegates prepared to assemble, Secretary Mellon was urged to persuade Borah to accept the offer.[32]

The Republican convention opened on June 10 at Cleveland. There was one noticeable difference between this gathering and the one four years earlier. The senatorial clique so prominent at Chicago exercised very little influence at Cleveland. Senator Lodge, who had three times been permanent chairman of previous conventions, was ignored on committee appointments and remained throughout very much in the background.[33] Borah didn't even go to Cleveland to mingle with what some reporters termed "the nonentities of 1924."

Coolidge would most certainly be nominated. He had even planned it that way. Shortly after assuming office, he had started the machinery moving. By Thanksgiving 1923 he had secured the support of most of the conservative Republican wheel horses. He then turned to the business interests; with the competent assistance of William M. Butler, a textile industrialist and chairman of the Republican National Committee, he received their backing. However, the candidacy of La Follette threatened to drain off much of the western and midwestern support Coolidge needed to be sure of winning the election. This seems to explain why he was so interested in Borah for his running mate.

In conversations Coolidge said Borah could make his own platform in his acceptance speech. He would stand by and give the speech his approval. The making of the campaign would be largely his, for duties would keep the President in Washington. Borah at first demurred, but found it increasingly difficult to say no to such an urgent request. Coolidge evidently did not think he had a "no" from the senator. Borah may have intimated that if the vice-presidential nomination came to him without the exertion of influence at the convention by the President or anyone else, he might be induced to accept it. Flimsy though it seems, this is the only explanation which approaches a clarification of the strange events which followed.

At the Hotel Cleveland, Secretary of War John W. Weeks, Nicholas Murray Butler, Senators Watson, Curtis, New, and Gillette, Secretary Mellon, Charles Hilles, and Nick Longworth conferred on the choice of a running mate for Coolidge. They discussed many names all day and night. Someone had objections to every name proposed. As fast as the group in Week's suite on the sixth floor settled on a man, word would come from Chairman Butler on the fourth floor that he would not do. Finally, by four in the morning Harry New arose and solemnly announced: "I am going off to bed. The kind of man you are looking for as vice-president was crucified nineteen hundred years ago." At midnight the following evening they agreed to offer the nomination to Charles Curtis of Kansas. Hilles went to Butler and informed him of their decision. Of course, this was all done under the pious pretense of leaving the selection of the President's running mate to the delegates themselves.[34]

Sometime between midnight and two the next morning (June 11)

Butler talked with Coolidge over the telephone; he was told that Coolidge wanted Borah, who would take the nomination. Whether Butler heard wrong and misunderstood what the President had said, or whether Coolidge misunderstood Borah, which is more likely, the slip was made. Perhaps the wish was father to the thought, or perhaps Butler wanted to kill the Curtis candidacy and interpreted what Coolidge said to suit himself.

Anyway, that same morning at two o'clock Butler went up to Weeks's suite escorted by Hilles. Weeks related the group's deliberations enthusiastically. Butler looked at Weeks with an impassive face and said: "I have just been talking by telephone to the White House. We must nominate Borah for Vice-President." His statement was received with a silence which could have been cut with a knife. After a few seconds Chairman Butler said to Weeks: "Mr. Secretary, what do you think of Borah?" Weeks, coming forward to the front of his chair, replied with a stream of expletives which would not look well in print. There was more silence. Then Chairman Butler turned to Secretary Mellon and said to him: "Mr. Secretary, what do you think of Borah?" The secretary, gazing dreamily into the distance, took his characteristic little cigar from his mouth and said placidly: "I never think of him unless somebody mentions his name." Chairman Butler then withdrew. Soon after he left, the Curtis boom was dropped and the word went out for Borah. It came as a surprise to everyone at Cleveland, especially as Borah had been industriously informing his friends and supporters for weeks that under no circumstances would he take the nomination.

More surprised than anyone was Borah when he was called out of his bed at three that morning. Albert Beveridge informed him of what had been given out in Cleveland. Borah told Beveridge emphatically that no one had any authority to make any statement regarding his attitude. To say he would accept was a stupid misrepresentation, and he would do nothing of the kind. The Cleveland *Plain Dealer* also aroused Borah that night only to be told that he would decline the nomination if it were forced on him by the convention. He then wired Frank Mondell, the permanent chairman: "I am informed it is reported I will accept the Vice Presidency. This information is incorrect. I will not accept the Vice Presidency." Similar wires were sent to Weeks, Wadsworth, and John Hart, chairman of the Idaho delegation.

The next morning Coolidge sent for Borah. He couldn't be found at home, but everyone knew he was horseback riding. Ted Clark, the President's secretary, was sent in search of him in an automobile and instructed to bring him to the White House. After winding through the roads of Rock Creek Park, Clark finally spied the lone rider and they drove back to the executive mansion.

Coolidge said he was pleased with the reports that Borah had accepted the nomination and merely wanted to confirm the press dispatches and telephone conversations with Cleveland. Was it true that Borah was willing to accept a place on the ticket? Borah was supposed to have made the now famous reply, "Which place, Mr. President?" Under other circumstances Coolidge might have appreciated the joke. Borah then stated simply that he was not a candidate and would not be one even to please the President. Even if he had ever seriously considered the place, which is doubtful, he was now determined against it since Coolidge had broken his promise to keep hands off the convention. His reason for refusing the offer was that he could render better service in the Senate. He suggested Judge Kenyon of Iowa as an alternative. Coolidge was noncommittal.

William Butler had little to say from that time forward. He had pulled a political boner by giving the Republican leaders what proved to be the "wrong dope." Unwittingly, he had torn aside the curtain which revealed the White House pretense of keeping hands off. Observers thought his slip—announcing at Cleveland that Borah was selected—was a fatal blunder, for it had given Borah the opportunity to refuse the nomination before it had been made. Under different circumstances they calculated that he might have accepted. While the convention might have taken Borah, they would not have Judge Kenyon. Second place was offered to Lowden, largely as a sign of revolt against the dictatorship of Butler. Lowden refused, and the nomination finally settled upon Charles G. Dawes, director of the budget.[35]

The Senate committee to investigate campaign expenditures established its headquarters in Chicago; Borah, its chairman, stopped en route to Boise and told the press that he wanted reports from the campaign managers sent to the committee every ten days, covering the amount of money spent, the means of getting it, estimates of the amount to be spent, and any limitation on the amount that could be spent by individual campaigners.[36]

There was the usual large crowd at Boise depot to welcome Borah home. Settled in the comfortable Baird home at 804 North 17th Street, he told reporters that he would gladly accept the support of the Progressives in Idaho for his senatorial campaign. Not having any other candidate for the seat, the Progressives planned to put Borah's name on their ticket, headed, of course, by La Follette. He spent his time writing letters and campaigning through the newspapers. An editorial in the Democratic New York *World,* urging the people of Idaho to re-elect Borah, was widely circulated. The columns of the Boise *Capital News* were opened to his use, and he enjoyed similar support from the Pocatello *Tribune,* the Wallace *Miner,* the Lewiston *Tribune,* and other papers throughout the state. As usual he had no assistance from the Republican state organization in 1924, nor did he attend the state convention in August. He gave as an excuse that his presence there would mean a fight over the platform. The administration had at least called off conservative Republican opposition to Borah in Idaho, as in Michigan against Couzens. The Progressives, successors of the Nonpartisan League of 1918, nominated Borah, who went into the campaign with two endorsements as in 1918. He also had the support of labor, the Anti-Saloon League, and a host of newspapers. This explains why he could delay so long in making an active campaign.[37]

Opening his own campaign at the Colonial Theatre in Idaho Falls, Borah charged that the Republican party was on the defensive because it supported Lorimerism and Newberryism, piled taxes on the people, created offices for slavish henchmen, and tolerated in the departments of the government the miserable spawn of broken-down political machines. "I despise them all," he said, "and politically, I would dynamite them all if I could." He thanked the La Follette-Wheeler organization for endorsing him. "They knew at the time they endorsed me that I was a Republican and expected to remain such."

For the Republican machine in his state he had these words: "I am not unmindful of the fact that there are those . . . who think I am not a good party man . . . there have been times that I have voted . . . out of harmony with what appeared to be the policies of the party. It would be insincere on my part to apologize for the past and I would be misleading and deceiving you if I were to say that you might expect anything different in the future."[38] Of Coolidge Borah merely said he was "a clean man" and praised him for vetoing the bonus bill, a measure not consonant with a program of economy. Bryan had said about the same thing in Boise a few weeks earlier. This speech was a declaration of Borah's political independence within the party.[39] In that sense it was a disappointment to La Follette and the Republicans; both expected Borah to throw his weight on their side. When La Follette charged that huge slush funds were being used in the campaign, Borah canceled all his engagements to speak for Coolidge in the northwest and said that his work on the committee would require all his time until election day. Progressive leaders were glad that Borah was out of the campaign.[40]

The outcome of the election was no surprise. Coolidge won a thumping victory. The electoral college gave him 382 votes to 136 for John Davis, his Democratic opponent. La Follette won Wisconsin's 13 votes and made a good showing in twelve other western states, indicating that progressivism was still alive. Considering the extent of Borah's campaigning in Idaho, which amounted to little more than a personal canvass of the state, his majority was smashing. He defeated his Democratic opponent, Frank Martin, by a plurality of 74,647 votes.[41] Elated, Borah wired Frank Wyman in Boise: "Very happy. Very proud of all my friends. Tell them all."[42]

Borah's campaign cost $992.47. In early September Salmon O. Levinson, a wealthy Chicago lawyer, had sent Borah's secretary a check for $1000 to be used for the campaign which he considered vital to advancing the cause of outlawry of war. He wrote: ". . . whether the money is spent directly for outlawry or directly for the election, the viewpoint is identically the same."[43] Miss Rubin sent him a reply, thanking him for the contribution which came at an opportune moment when the total in his campaign fund was $100. Borah also received $2500 from the Republican National Committee to cover campaign expenses. Late in November he wrote Senator Moses: "Enclosed please find my check for $1500. You were kind enough to send me a campaign contribution of $2500; $1000 of it I have already returned, and the balance is covered by the check. My expenses in the campaign fortunately turned out to be very inconsequential, and there is no reason therefore why I should draw upon the Committee for anything."[44] Moses replied to Borah and acknowledged receipt of the money: "It is good to know that any Senator was elected with 'inconsequential' expenses, and it is particularly gratifying to know that this good fortune fell to you."[45]

Commenting on the Republican victory, Borah noted that nearly one fifth of all who voted registered their conviction that neither of the old parties was fit to administer the affairs of government. The primary task of Republicans now was to rid the government of malfeasance and corruption. The country had passed through a period of disregard for the simplest and most fundamental principles of public service. He found nothing like it in history since the days of Walpole, when the paymaster stood near the gangway of the House of Commons and settled in cash with the "political Judases." The issue of economy in government had won more votes than all other issues combined. Borah had not the slightest doubt, after investigations and talks with people, that five billions of the national debt represented waste, extravagance, and profiteering at a time when the farmer was being taxed to death.[46]

In December of 1924 Borah received two unusual Christmas presents. One was the chairmanship of the Senate Foreign Relations Committee; the other was the editorial, "Our Bill," penned by his one-time friend and supporter, Calvin Cobb:

MERRY CHRISTMAS, Mr. Borah. You have six more years during which you will be "answerable only to God." You may, if you choose, enjoy that "splendid isolation" the New York Democratic editors have been trying to wish on you.

You will probably go far afield during these years, perhaps to seek the inspiration of anarchy at the fountainhead, perhaps stand bareheaded before the scarlet bier of the man who played a ghastly joke on civilization, perhaps meet on friendly terms the active members of the gang which has the blood of twenty millions of innocent people on its hands. You may find much in that country, Russia but you will not find Christ. He is prohibited in Russia. If you take the Lord's Supper with you there, you will be a bootlegger.

You will doubtless walk in many political paths and advocate many policies. How strong you are when defending the country from dangerous tendencies; how weak you are when favoring the election of those who advocate dangerous tendencies!

You have wonderful gifts, Mr. Borah. You should go far along the road called straight. You are personally most likeable and a loyal friend, but politically you have not even been your own friend.

After all your wanderings you will come back to your people. Then you will be sixty five years old and doubtless have a full appreciation for the G.O.P. which gave you opportunity. Idaho will then be a rich and powerful state made so by the party which kept you in the Senate for 24 years and which you never helped to the control that directed Idaho's progress to prosperity and gave it statehood.

The hand that writes this will not be writing of you then. It is a hand that rocked your political cradle, too, and now, at the zenith of your power, a hand that pens the wish that you will go forward with the best that is in you to power and glory.

MANY, MANY HAPPY NEW YEARS TO YOU, BILL.[47]

Early in 1925 Congress voted 64 to 18 to raise the salaries of members of the House and Senate from $7,500 to $10,000. Borah was absent when the Senate voted. The next day he moved for reconsideration, but nobody supported him. He charged that the measure had been discussed in a haphazard way. It was not right, he said, for members of Congress to raise their own salaries and disregard the claims of other officials for a raise. He had voted consistently against the bonus bill, the postal pay increase, and now this. To a friend Borah explained his position: "The million and a half extra burden is by no means the most important feature of it. It means, in my judgment, the beginning of the end of our economy fight. I do not see how we can ask the people to economize when we are unwilling to do so with ourselves nor can we keep down other people's salaries when we are raising our own."[48] To another friend he wrote: . . . "Those who are in office and not satisfied with their salaries always have the privilege to retire and I doubt not their places will be filled with people quite as capable to fill them and willing to work for the same salaries."[49]

In February Borah filed an amendment to the Deficiency bill repealing the salary increase, but in spite of his efforts the salary increase became effective in March. Borah then sent a letter to Charles Pace, financial clerk of the Senate, who automatically deposited his monthly salary ($625) in the Riggs National Bank with these instructions: "Will you kindly, in depositing my salary hereafter, deposit the same amount in the future that you have in the past. Please treat this as merely personal . . . and not for the public."[50] Until he was re-elected in 1930, Borah refused to accept the salary increase since he had been elected at the salary of $7500 and felt obligated to await the electorate's mandate for $10,000. For two years he secretly turned back part of his salary. Even when Senator Heflin of Alabama taunted him for accepting the increase to which he had objected, Borah guarded his secret, which was disclosed by a Treasury official two years later.

Domestic affairs absorbed attention in the Coolidge administration, but in foreign affairs, a field deserving fuller attention than it received, Borah was soon to play a conspicuous role.

XIII Sagebrush Diplomacy

> There is no more useful form of patriotism than that which expresses itself in efforts to cultivate and preserve friendly relations between one's native country and foreign nations.
>
> —Henry W. Taft

In November 1924 Senator Lodge, chairman of the Foreign Relations Committee, was stricken by a cerebral hemorrhage and died. The death of Senator Brandegee of the Judiciary Committee made vacant that chairmanship as well, and left Borah with a choice. He took what was conceded to be the most important of all committee posts and became the new head of the Foreign Relations Committee. The *Nation,* which advocated a foreign policy similar to Borah's, commented: "The fact that Senator Borah has replaced Senator Lodge . . . is one of the best New Year's gifts which the world could have."[1]

Borah and Lodge provide an interesting contrast in character, background, education, and outlook. Lodge, the "scholar in politics," was a Boston Brahmin, gifted and well educated, an aristocrat of wide knowledge and experience. Borah was a son of the prairie who had risen from the grass roots with none of the opportunities Lodge enjoyed. However, even if Borah was not the finished scholar Lodge was, he had devoted all his leisure since college to reading. He was equally fixed in his opinions, many of which were further removed from the administration's than those of the Sage of Nahant. Borah's speeches compared favorably with those of Lodge. His mind was as exact as Lodge's and more alert.

Borah looked upon the ancient prerogatives of the Senate as an essential element in the practice of diplomacy. If the senators were consulted, Lodge was satisfied; he merely insisted that the President recognize the Senate. However, Borah demanded that the Senate play a more vigorous part in the conduct of foreign affairs. In this he was inspired by a faith that meant little to Lodge,[2] a faith in the ultimate righteousness of an appeal to the people. Believing it the duty of Congress to force the President to consult the whole electorate, he was far more determined than Lodge to make the Senate a major partner in diplomatic affairs.

The history of secret diplomacy in Europe made a deep impression on Borah. He believed that the wars and miseries of mankind were attributable chiefly to the irresponsible intrigues of diplomats, while legislatures and popular majorities were by nature pacific and just. The essence of his philosophy was that bad deeds are done in the dark and that light brings righteousness. He never seemed to consider the possibility that popular sentiment might impose its will upon statesmen who wished to deal rationally with such issues as debts and reparations.

Once, when arguing that treaties should be discussed publicly in the Senate, Borah was told by Senator Brandegee that too much plain talk might give offense to foreign countries. Borah asked: "What are these delicate questions which may offend foreign powers? These . . . questions are too often questions of dubious righteousness." Only a man who had risen by appealing to audiences rather than by making executive decisions would have said that,[3] and at that moment the country lacked a powerful executive. Coolidge was a man of repressed characted and limited abilities. Borah, with a personality of signal force and with decided abilities, was equipped for leadership as a result of study, moral earnestness, and a passion for equity. Like Hildebrand, he meant to "love justice and hate iniquity."[4]

Feelings were mixed regarding Borah's accession to the chairmanship. They ranged from the elation of the *Nation* to the consternation of critics, who called him a hothead, an opportunist, an actor, and even a bolshevik. Seniority, the critics asserted, was his only conspicuous qualification. They marshaled alleged mistakes in judgment to prove their case and declared that his views were marked by prejudices and animosities which incapacitated him for constructive thinking. For refinement, scholarship, dignity, and poise they placed Lodge in higher esteem; Borah by comparison seemed uncouth.[5] However, those who were anxious lest he prove too impetuous in international affairs could remember that the next ranking Republican on the committee was Hiram Johnson. Borah sought to justify his chairmanship by working hard at foreign relations and spent many more hours a day in his office than most public men would consider compatible with their health.[6]

Observers found it remarkable that from the remote, ill-populated, and then utterly insular state of Idaho Borah held such commanding power over the foreign affairs of the United States. The secretary of state then counted for little. Whether Borah's power was wisely exercised was another question, but the point is that it was a senatorial power based merely on the suffrage of "a handful . . . whose total assets would hardly have made a noticeable entry in the daily deposits of a single New York bank." Borah's voters would have been lost in any one of New York City's five boroughs. He was not important because of Idaho, but because of the Senate's mode of doing business, which made him more influential in his day than all the senators from New York, New Jersey, Pennsylvania, Ohio, and Illinois put together. The foreign office of the United States was often in his hat, and the secretary of state, as Dexter Perkins has said, was often eating out of his hand. Only defeat or death could take this power from him. His mandate from the committee of which he was chairman lasted almost ten years, and thereafter the influence he continued to wield as a ranking minority member was interrupted only by death.[7]

Apart from his importance as a leader, Borah was a symbol of the change through which the American mind passed after 1920. As firm as ever in his opposition to political alliances, he had a sound realization of the economic interdependence of Europe and the United States. He was far ahead of the administration in urging conferences on disarmament, war debts, reparations, recognition of Russia, and the hopeful though illusory scheme of outlawing war. Most significant of all, Borah, unlike Lodge, was an anti-imperialist. In relation to Latin America this difference in spirit was likely to be important. In the long run, it was no particular plan of his which counted, but rather the stirring and educative effect of his speeches and personality.[8] To the extent that the Senate and administration accepted his guidance, a new chapter in international relations began with his chairmanship.

Borah will probably rank as the most vocal of all the chairmen of foreign affairs. He set forth his position on practically every diplomatic issue that arose, usually in brief statements from his office. Though he spoke for himself only, he came to be regarded as a sort of senatorial minister of foreign affairs. It apparently never occurred to him that he might not enjoy the same freedom in this new position which he enjoyed in the Senate. He continued to comment on all acts of foreign powers, their statesmen, their national habits, their ambitions, and their negotiations, however delicate relations with them might be. Secretary Kellogg shared State Department secrets with Borah, even though subordinates in the department warned him that revealing confidential data to Borah was like giving it to the press.[9] Borah boasted that no diplomatic restrictions curbed his utterances.

He corresponded with such European statesmen as Lord Lothian, Lord Derby, Ramsay MacDonald, Lord Robert Cecil, M. Poincaré, and Maxim Litvinov. A steady stream of information from European capitals flowed into his office and kept him supplied with facts for his speeches and press statements. Of course, the authenticity of this information was sometimes questionable, but Borah made only occasional efforts to verify it.

Latin-American affairs came to absorb so much of his time that he attempted to learn Spanish. He had gained only a smattering of Latin and German in college. At the age of sixty-one he studied like a high school boy so that he would not be handicapped in his study of Mexican, Haitian, and Nicaraguan problems. In time, as a result of wide reading, correspondence, and a steady stream of Latin-American visitors, he became well informed on affairs to the south, but he never gave any evidence of fluency in Spanish.

To interviewers Borah expressed himself with restraint. He was extremely considerate of other people and receptive to ideas. However, once he made up his mind, he was firm. He often seemed plodding rather than brilliant, for he went through frequent mental struggles with himself. He admonished his contemporaries: "Don't pray for wisdom; we know what is right. Pray for courage. We are often afraid to do what is right."[10]

A perplexing question then as now is why this chairman of the Foreign Relations Committee consistently refused to travel to Europe. The explanation is not simple. Borah himself once remarked: "I should add little to my knowledge by infrequent brief trips to Europe. It is often wiser to stand off and obtain a clear picture. One might become merely confused by first-hand information." Subconsciously Borah wished to travel through Europe as an observer of economic and political conditions, talking with people in all walks of life as he did with the folks back home. Three times he made tentative plans, but on every occasion he canceled the trip, offering the excuse that pressing duties prevented him from leaving Washington or Idaho.

Senator Elbert Thomas once said that the only reason why Borah refused to go abroad was because a fortuneteller predicted that he would be drowned at sea.[11] Another unsubstantiated story relates that as a boy he almost drowned in the Wabash River near his home in Fairfield. Borah disliked the water, avoided boats, and never swam on his vacations in Maine and Idaho. More plausible is the explanation that he feared a visit to Europe would involve him in a variety of state functions, social obligations, and official visits such as he studiously avoided at home, and that they would prevent him from learning the facts about foreign problems. He often lamented that foreign travel was a luxury he could not afford. He made no objection to Mrs. Borah's trip to France, but before her departure he warned her to make no comments and to avoid speaking to reporters.

Borah observed that while Kellogg was our ambassador to the Court of St. James's, he, like many predecessors, became thoroughly inoculated with British ideas. He noted how successful the British were in captivating those Americans whom they chose to cultivate, and he feared that in visiting England he would be exposed to the same danger.

Nevertheless, Britons like Ramsay MacDonald and Lord Lothian continued to invite him to visit their island. In the British mind Borah was ranged with Lindbergh and Mark Twain. Lord Derby approached him through the American ambassador and invited him to come to Knowsley to tour the mills and industrial cities of Lancashire, so he could see for himself that the British were not "ogres." At first Borah encouraged Derby but finally replied:

> . . . I do not need to be shown that the English are not ogres. I have never said anything of that kind . . . I should like to know upon what Lord Derby bases his desire to enlighten me . . . I appreciate his missionary spirit but really I do not feel in need of his gospel of enlightenment. I would really like to visit England and hope I may find an opportunity to do so. My mission, however, will not be that of hunting wild game such as ogres, but to see and to know better a people whose highest encomium is that of always having been loyal to their own flag . . .[11a]

Another Briton, George Bernard Shaw, once wrote George S. Viereck on an open postcard: "He [Borah] is the only American whose brains seem properly baked; the others are all either crumbs or gruel. Perhaps that is because he is the only genuine one hundred per center."[12] Borah well realized that Shaw was in greater demand in America because he had vowed he would never cross the Atlantic.

The Foreign Relations Committee usually met on Wednesdays. All treaties and germane bills, resolutions, and nominations were referred to it before being considered by the Senate. It was left to the chairman to determine what would be placed on the committee agenda; he could thus smother a bill himself by refusing to bring it up before the committee. Items on the agenda were customarily delegated to a subcommittee, which would investigate them and hold hearings if necessary. After the subcommittee reported, the matter was taken up by the committee and then, if adopted, went to the Senate. The reports were usually submitted by the chairman, but if the committee disagreed, he generally designated another member for this purpose.[13]

Rarely did the President meet with the entire committee. Unfortunately the Senate had a strong dislike for such meetings. This was illustrated by Borah's refusal, as a member of the committee, to attend Wilson's White House dinner to discuss the Versailles Treaty. On a later occasion he created a sensational disturbance at a meeting which he attended in order to discuss neutrality legislation with President Franklin Roosevelt. Information obtained at the State Department on several occasions did not satisfy Borah, who then dealt directly with the foreign governments in question. Furthermore, State Department requests to keep confidential certain information imparted to him always aroused his resentment.

Shortly after Borah became chairman of the Foreign Relations Committee, Secretary Hughes retired from the cabinet. He and Hughes had never gotten on well. Borah's accession to the chairmanship was unquestionably disappointing to Hughes, and when the secretary resigned, it was widely rumored that Borah's enhanced power was the cause. Hughes steadfastly denied this, pointing out that it was a matter of principle with him not to let personal feelings disturb public business.[14] When Hughes met Borah on Inauguration Day, his greeting was cordial. "I am amazed by your success," he said. "Treaty matters have never before been disposed of with such celerity in the Senate."[15]

A sensitive problem marred Borah's relations with the new secretary, Frank B. Kellogg, who took office in March 1925. Borah never was willing to admit that his power was limited to vetoing and amending the result of a long and complicated negotiation or to offering public and private advice at intervals. At times it almost seemed that two foreign offices vied with each other at either end of Pennsylvania Avenue. This was, of course, an old controversy with two sides. However, it seems clear that the policy of the secretary of state should prevail, for he has agents abroad to inform him and he alone conducts negotiations which are the heart of diplomacy.[16]

En route to Washington from Idaho in the autumn of 1925 Borah stopped off at Chicago where he stated that the Locarno Pact was "one of the greatest contributions to the cause of peace of all time." He noted with satisfaction that the signatory powers did not recognize the World Court, but created their own arbitration commission. The great accomplishment was for England and France to sit down at the conference table and agree upon an amicable settlement.[17] However, after more careful study of the Locarno Pact Borah ceased to share the optimism of enthusiasts.[18]

On his return to Washington he was invited to outline a series of recommendations for Coolidge's annual message to Congress. Coolidge wanted to know them, even if he had no intention of acting upon them. Borah spoke against the World Court and for the recognition of Russia. He condemned the policy of Secretary Work upon reclamation projects as calculated to bring financial ruin to thousands of settlers unable to make their payments. He and Coolidge were in accord on the question of foreign debts, but he thought the government was too lenient with Belgium.[19] During the congressional adjournment in December 1925 Coolidge wanted Borah to go to Europe as a delegate to the Geneva Disarmament Conference. Coolidge believed the opportunity for inquiry and observation would be helpful to him in his position as chairman.[20] However, after consideration Borah rejected this proposal. This was unfortunate, as he might have learned firsthand how difficult it is to reach an agreement in the maze of rival problems of powers.[21]

Harding and Coolidge had hoped to associate the United States with the Permanent Court of International Justice. Membership was open to all nations, whether they belonged to the League or not. At Hughes's suggestion Harding had proposed our adherence to the World Court protocol in February 1923, but Lodge had kept the project shelved. Coolidge took up the issue in his first message to Congress. Public opinion was strongly in favor of adherence, and both parties incorporated World Court planks in their 1924 platforms. When the Foreign Relations Committee came under Borah, who considered the World Court "a League Court," he lent the weight of his official position to its defeat. Tactics of delay were again adopted. Hearings were postponed, and schemes were advanced for divorcing the Court from the League. Most influential groups in the country were for it, but the Foreign Relations Committee continued to defy the general will.

Borah considered this a momentous opportunity for public education by discussion. He asserted that the League and World Court were vestiges of "Old World imperialism"; both institutions were joined by shackles of binding adamant that could not be broken. Although he favored a world court, he was opposed to the one set up by the League. The basis of his opposition was not that the Court was an agent of the League, but that the League was expected to enforce the Court's decrees. Friends of the Court should insist, he said, that decrees rest on intrinsic moral and legal weight and not on material force; otherwise the United States would be put in the position of accepting the League without joining it. He charged that one of the reasons for trying to get the United States into the Court was so that we would help pay League expenses.[22] He predicted that the World Court would be impotent because it could not enforce its own decisions and would be subject to the manipulative tactics of European politics.[23]

In a speech at Chicago Borah announced that if the Court were separated from the League, debate in the Senate would last only an hour. He desired world peace based upon international amity and understanding rather than on "armed force." He did not see the question as a court or no court; the question was whether the world was going to have an independent judicial tribunal governed by international law or a dependent tribunal governed by international politics.[24] His prerequisites for an effective international tribunal were two: first, full international respect for treaties and the rights of others; second, a properly codified body of international law under which a court could operate. He said: " . . . if you are going to have a real Court, you must first have a body of law under which that Court will operate; not the broken pieces of statutes and customs and habits, and the opinions of scholars found in books, but a code agreed upon and accepted by the nations of the world."[25]

Another of his objections to the Court was the League's right to call upon it for advisory opinions. He maintained that the League treated the Court as its "Department of Justice." He did not believe it wise to join a court whose most important function, as he saw it, was to render these opinions on quasi-political matters.[26] In a speech to Boise laborers Borah called the court an "ambitious and presumptuous effort to establish judicial despotism" because its judges could not be elected or recalled. If he were forced to make a choice between resigning from the Senate and voting for this Court, he would resign. The people were not hearing the truth about it. He was quoted as saying: "I am utterly opposed to the use of force or of economic sanctions in the enforcement of the decrees of an international court."[27] He wanted a tribunal like the American Supreme Court, which, he said, relied upon peaceful acquiescence in its decisions. Public opinion, he said, should execute the judgments of the Court.[28] Borah absolutely denied that decisions of the Supreme Court are backed by a force that is latent. The first to advocate orderly government at home, he refused to establish the necessary power on which the success of an international organization must ultimately rest.

Borah was criticized as a "doughty defender of dogma" for his attitude on the Court. His opponents said that he seemed to be unfamiliar with its work. His charge that the Court was the League's "Department of Justice" was unfounded, for the Court had kept itself free from political influence.[29] Former Attorney General Wickersham said it was utter nonsense to hold, as Borah did, that the Court would have no principles on which to work until the codification of international law was completed. No matter who set for himself the comprehensive task of codifying law, he added, Borah would be the first to find fault with it and demand that it be done over again.[30]

When Walter Lippmann asked if Borah was prepared to entrust

the creation of a code of international law to men like Curzon, Kato, Hughes, and Poincaré, the senator replied that if public opinion were organized in the right direction, we would not have to do this; however, he would rather assign these men to the task than allow them under the scheme of the League of Nations to govern the world without any code at all.[31] Not until December 1925 did the matter reach the Senate floor where the old "Battalion of Death," under Borah's leadership, put up a bitter fight. It was understood that more than the necessary two-thirds would support the World Court if given the opportunity to vote. The opposition was shrinking; Borah was practically its sole remaining source of strength. A month before the Senate debate thirty-eight notables wrote Borah warning him that an attempt to defeat the Court proposal by indirection would amount to plain opposition to the will of the American people: "We appeal to your fairness and respect for the American people to put no obstructions in the way of that opportunity."[32] Observing that the thirty-eight notables were all devoted advocates of the League, Borah sent a long reply, advising that he had been twice elected by his constituents on a pledge to keep this country out of the League.[33]

In the Foreign Relations Committee crippling reservations were formulated. The Idaho senator had learned a valuable lesson from Lodge. An examination of the five reservations proposed and adopted shows Borah's firm hand. They could only have the effect of prolonging the controversy; a new protocol would have to be drawn embodying the consent of the member nations and meeting the five reservations.[34] The Swanson resolution of United States' adherence to the World Court, along with these five reservations, was placed before the Senate on January 27, 1926. The vote was 76 to 17 to join the Court, if the reservations were accepted as written.[35] However, following the passage of the resolution Borah and Reed of Missouri announced that they had just begun to fight. They intended to stump the country on three propositions: to get out of the Court, to keep out of the League, and to defeat those senators who had voted for the Court.[36]

Washington's birthday was a great day for "Big Bill" Thompson, the mayor of Chicago, who had invited Borah there to speak. Bands were playing and flags waving as three thousand automobiles formed a thirty-five-mile parade through the city. That afternoon the Chicago coliseum, which Ruth Hanna McCormick hired for Borah, sheltered a meeting attended by twelve thousand. Borah's speech, which was broadcast coast to coast, was a huge political success. He told the crowd that they had lost their first fight in the effort to save the policies of Washington. The next fight, he said, was being organized to take the United States into the League of Nations. He was incensed by the fact that American requests for codified law, the right of appeal for small nations, and discontinuance of advisory opinions had so far been rejected by the Court. "What a mess we are in!" he said.[37]

Borah made similar speeches in Wisconsin, where he and Reed attacked Senators Lenroot (Wisconsin) and McKinley (Illinois) for their position on the World Court. Senator McKinley rushed to Washington and demanded help in the approaching April primaries. The White House remained aloof. The *Times* commented: ". . . there is as much discretion as valor in the invasion of Illinois and Wisconsin by the senatorial scalp-hunting expedition of Borah and Reed." Their strategy was not very glorious, for they were busy slaying senators who were already slain.[38] Friends of the Court later denied that Lenroot and McKinley were defeated because of their stand on the World Court. The circumstances which brought about their defeat were not connected in any way with the Court issue.

At a conference in Geneva in December 1926 the League Council accepted four reservations but rejected the fifth. The council would not guarantee the United States an absolute veto, a privilege not even enjoyed by League members. President Coolidge, rarely one to put up a fight for an idea, refused to ask the Senate to modify its position. Borah was exultant, and there the matter stood for two more years.[39]

Public opinion forced the reopening of negotiations for American adherence to the World Court during the Hoover administration in 1929. Officers of the League drew up two protocols revising the statutes of the Court to meet the fifth reservation proposed by the Senate. A committee of the League Council agreed on Elihu Root's formula for American adherence to the Court. All requests for advisory opinions were to be submitted to the United States; American objections were to have the same weight as those of members; if not sustained, the United States was to have the right of withdrawal from the Court. Before the Senate got the Root formula, the Wall Street panic struck. Hoover delayed submission until December 1930 when he went before the Senate and asked for speedy approval of the two protocols which had been signed by Secretary Stimson and ratified by nearly all the members of the Court.[40]

The Foreign Relations Committee voted to postpone consideration until December 1931. Thereafter another Battalion of Death was formed strong enough to prevent a vote during the remainder of Hoover's term. The fifth reservation was readopted as if the Root formula had never existed. The other reservations were also resurrected along with some new ones. The Hearst press, the Chicago *Tribune,* Huey Long, and Father Coughlin intensified their attacks on the Court.

Hysterical and often dishonest appeals to narrow nationalism were made. Thousands of telegrams poured in upon wavering senators. Forty thousand letters of protest were sent to Washington against entry into the Court. Despite an urgent appeal by Franklin Roosevelt, the final vote of January 28, 1933, defeated the World Court protocol 52 for and 36 against, seven votes short of the necessary two-thirds.

So ended twelve years of effort. The rift between Borah and Johnson was closed by their final victory over the Court. After the vote they left the Senate chamber arm in arm, laughing and slapping each other on the back. Borah was heard to say: "Johnson, it's a great victory. It will be many a decade before this thing comes up again. It's the most important development since the World War."[41] Time was to demonstrate the utter bankruptcy of the narrow nationalistic policy which the irreconcilables decreed and to which the Harding, Coolidge, and Hoover administrations submitted with such disastrous results.

It was hard to make much of Borah's Latin-American policy up to 1916. He gave an equivocal impression. His attack on Bryan's "drumhead diplomacy" in Nicaragua represented his policy of playing no favorites as between this country and its smaller neighbors. On the other hand, his championship of Panama Canal tolls exemption for United States' coastal shipping represented a policy more nationalistic than that of Lodge or Theodore Roosevelt. Borah had not agreed with Wilson's policy of "watchful waiting" in Mexico in 1915. Instead he demanded that United States forces be used to protect our citizens. Weakness, said Borah, is a source of war.

During the 1920's he saw Caribbean "imperialism" in as harsh a light as any European. In an article on the Monroe Doctrine Borah insisted we had no right to interfere with an American government. No stepmother's creed, the doctrine was called into being because we needed security. Criticism of our policy, he said, was due to a false construction of the doctrine. Elihu Root, as secretary of state, placed the proper construction on it: no victories, no territory, no sovereignty but our own.[42]

As secretary of state, Hughes had no intention of limiting our commitments in Latin America. What he tried to do, however, was to convince these republics—along the lines initiated by Root—that the United States had no ulterior motives with respect to their freedom and no intention of employing superior power to their disadvantage.[43] When Hughes resigned and was succeeded by Frank B. Kellogg, there appeared to be a retreat for a time from the more beneficent Latin American policy Hughes had tried to implement. Coolidge's insistence on the right of the United States to protect the person and property of its citizens, wherever they might be, opened the way to renewed intervention in the internal affairs of Latin American countries.[44]

The most important instance of such interference occurred in Nicaragua. The United States landed five thousand troops there in 1927 to maintain order and protect American interests. Borah expressed hope that the troops would be taken out of Nicaragua as soon as assurance could be given to Americans there of their safety. In January Borah attended a White House conference with Kellogg, after which he attacked the administration's policy, criticized the landing of marines, and demanded new elections in Nicaragua.[45]

In February he introduced a Senate resolution empowering the Foreign Relations Committee to travel in Nicaragua and Mexico (which continued to uphold the rival regime in Nicaragua) to take testimony there and study relations with the United States. Borah held that much of the agitation over conditions was exaggerated, and he intended to ascertain the facts independent of the State

Department. The trip was to span the recess from March 4 to December. There was immediate objection from the State Department, which suspected that Borah wanted to tie the hands of the administration during the long recess. There would be some obligation to act on the suggestions in the committee's report. Serious questions were raised about the effectiveness of their proposed work in gathering testimony, for they could hardly expect American business interests to testify against themselves and government officials were known to have been extremely reluctant. There was no opposition to private travel, and Latin American countries would prefer unofficial visits to the kind of inquisition Borah proposed. Senators Edge, Lenroot, and Moses blocked Borah's resolution in committee. Adjournment left Kellogg with a free hand in Central America. One newspaper wryly suggested that if Borah wanted a trip to Nicaragua at the government's expense, he could join the marines![46]

President Coolidge finally sent Henry Stimson to work out an agreement between Nicaragua's opposing factions, and this Stimson succeeded in doing. New elections held in 1928 under American supervision brought at least relative stability there and also improved our relations. A national guard trained by Americans was established; when this force was competent to police the country, our marines were withdrawn, putting an end to the dirty business.[47]

A quarrel with Mexico, growing out of the nationalization policy of President Calles, also threatened trouble for a time. Business interests insistently called for intervention to safeguard American property rights, but this time the Coolidge administration was determined to avoid hostilities. Emphasizing the cleavage between the administration and one senator, Borah again wanted some specialized information and directly addressed President Calles on the oil controversy, inquiring:

> If agreeable, may I be advised as to the exact facts relative to oil companies accepting the new petroleum law. How many have accepted and how many have not . . . I would like also to be advised of the names of important companies which have accepted.[48]

Calles replied promptly that three hundred eighty companies had accepted the law, among them Standard of Indiana. "I am pleased at the interest which you are taking in this matter and God grant that the data submitted to you may be of use."[49]

Borah was severely criticized for his letter. In unofficial quarters he was charged with violating the Logan Act.[50] He scorned "this hypocritical cry" to prevent him from obtaining the information he needed. Defying a heckler during an address delivered in New Haven on March 20, 1927, he shouted: "As Chairman of the Foreign Relations Committee, I have a right to get my information from any source I wish. This I propose to do, and I know of no power that can stop me. We have not yet got Mussolini in the United States." The charge against Borah was, of course, absurd. If he was violating either the letter or spirit of the Logan Act, then every newspaper with foreign correspondents was violating it. He concluded that there was no connection, as the administration charged, between the Russian government and the recent radical land reforms in Mexico. He demanded arbitration for all: "not one kind for small nations and . . . another for large and still another for very large . . ." Slanderous statements about Mexico would bring no good to the American people nor protect American interests in Mexico. "There is a higher and better . . . more peaceful and lawful method by which to protect our interests. God has made us neighbors—let justice make us friends."[51]

The issues in the dispute with Mexico were finally resolved through the skillful diplomacy of Ambassador Dwight Morrow, in whose appointment Borah was influential; before Coolidge left office, substantial progress had been made in placing relations with Mexico on a better footing than they had been for many years.[52] Meanwhile, however, pressure on Mexico was supplemented by threats of force and other types of intimidation, which continued for almost three years. Our relations were further complicated when, just before the opening session of the Seventieth Congress in December 1927, the Hearst newspapers announced the forthcoming publication of documents "proving" that President Calles of Mexico was the center of a Communist plot to overthrow the government of the United States. The papers also charged that certain highly respected persons had accepted bribes to influence the policy of the United States toward Mexico. On December 9, 1927, readers of the Washington *Herald* were astonished by the sensational headlines:

$1,215,000 ORDERED PAID TO FOUR SENATORS BY MEXICO

The story unfolded a plot revolving around an allegedly secret order of the president of Mexico to pay certain senators huge sums for pro-Mexican propaganda. Facsimiles of documents reproduced to accompany the story had the names of the senators blacked out. The Senate immediately ordered a special investigation of these allegations. The committee included David Reed of Pennsylvania, Hiram Johnson of California, Joseph Robinson of Arkansas, William Bruce of Maryland, and Wesley Jones of Washington. Their first witness was William Randolph Hearst.

Under oath Hearst testified that he had paid approximately fifteen thousand dollars for these documents to an agent, Miguel Avila, who, according to his story, had "received them from government employees in Mexico City." Of Avila, an American engineer of long experience in Mexico told the committee: "This traffic in documents is a business in Mexico City. You can get any kind of document you want. Avila is one of the purveyors of these documents . . . He is notorious for that . . ."

The four senators alluded to in the newspapers and named by the committee were Borah, Heflin, Norris, and La Follette. Hearst blandly admitted that he had not for a moment believed that the Mexican government had ever paid such a sum to the four senators. Yet he had printed evidence to show that such bribery had been attempted because he believed in this way a congressional investigation would be forced. The senators' names did not appear in print, for he had considered the penalties of libel. None of the four had been interviewed before publication of the charges. Hearst said his chief reason for accepting the documents was the opinion of American Ambassador Sheffield, to whom they were shown, that they "looked" authentic. Handwriting experts representing both Hearst and the committee were unanimous in their agreement that the documents were a shabby forgery. They could never have been part of the Mexican government files. Added to this, the committee had flat denials of the whole fantastic tale from the Mexican government.

In the committee room each of the four senators had to take the stand and deny the charges. When Borah's name was called off with a fifty thousand dollar annex, by far the largest single sum allocated for bribery purposes, Borah smiled and the spectators in the crowded room roared with laughter.

Riots broke out in Shanghai and Canton in 1925 which endangered the property of foreigners and threatened to bring outside intervention. America was generally sympathetic to the Chinese. Since 1917 Borah had been urging that America should seek a community of interest with China. On June 10 he issued a statement advising all foreigners to keep out of China and attacked interventionist demands. He began a sturdy campaign for the abolition of treaty ports and the long-standing extraterritorial rights of appeal to foreign courts of law. The senator burned with a sense that the Chinese people were being humiliated and victimized. He asserted that foreign exploiters, including Americans, had carried on a wicked drug traffic, had deprived China of the right to collect tariff revenues which she greatly needed, and had enjoyed an improper immunity from Chinese justice. "There is no place where the blood of helpless children is so coined into dollars and cents as in China," he said.[53] The country was racked by civil strife; however, if outside nations would help the Chinese people rather than hinder them, permanent peace might come within sight.

The "old China hands" and others experienced in dealing with China's problems rallied indignantly against Borah. He was meddling ignorantly with questions which he did not understand, they protested. The New York *Times* commented that his crusade against extraterritorial rights was a gesture noble in spirit but ill-timed, and that he offered "a melancholy case of great natural ability and a deep moral sense habitually misapplied."[54] Thomas Millard, adviser to the Chinese Foreign Office, tried to discourage him from pursuing his battle against extraterritorial rights, arguing that Chinese justice was not yet sufficiently advanced to be trusted. The American Chamber of Commerce in Hankow protested that Borah was doing great harm and playing into the hands of Russian intrigue, which it declared was rampant in the Far East. Borah retorted that the chamber was "part and parcel of the imperialistic combine that would oppress and exploit the Chinese people."

Unquestionably Borah's bold stand encouraged Chinese liberals who were struggling to rid their country of the fetters placed on the control of its customs and its system of justice. Chungting T. Wang, the director-general of Sino-Russian negotiations, praised "the voice of a great statesman of a great country, advocating international justice and humane principles." Harry Hussey, a prominent Peking architect, wrote Borah in the summer of 1925: "Your remarks did more than anything else to restrain the Chinese when things looked very dangerous here in China. Until you spoke, the Chinese were desperate . . . Your speech showed them that they had a friend in America and this fact was so used by the conservative element that they were able to control the others."[55]

The American government in 1928 met in part the demands of the Kuomintang leaders. It restored China's tariff autonomy, so far as Americans were concerned; however, it did nothing to surrender extraterritorial rights, which remained a heavy grievance with all Chinese patriots. Borah attributed the antiforeign movement which persisted in China solely to the unequal treaties and thought the entire situation could be remedied by sweeping concessions to the Chinese Nationalists. Back in Idaho again for the summer in 1927, he told reporters: ". . . the nations are marking time until the strength of the Nationalist Party in China can be determined. The Communist wing will never control the Nationalists . . . they are like Lindbergh, who started with an idea and himself. They borrowed everybody they could to start their party but they will never permit control of the party by Communists."[56]

The Borahs vacationed in Boise that summer. Mary Borah went west earlier than the senator to visit her Portland and Moscow relatives; she set up house in Boise for his arrival, which was delayed while he underwent a tonsil operation.

En route to Idaho, Borah stopped at Denver to address a convention of international advertising men, using his voice for the first time since the operation. He told them he wanted federal funds invested in such projects as a seaway connecting the Great Lakes and the Atlantic, flood control of the Mississippi, and conservation and power projects on the Colorado River in preference to delusive efforts to aid Europe. He did not seem to understand that keeping investments at home, putting all surplus capital into work projects here, would only increase the farm surplus which European markets could only afford to buy with money earned from American trade.

Leaving Denver, he continued to Boise where his wife and friends were on hand to welcome him at the depot. When he appeared, the famous straw hat was perched uncompromisingly on top of his dark thatch of hair, now beginning to show a touch of gray. He wore a gaily colored waffle-patterned bow tie and looked rested as he stepped from the train. They rented the Stewart apartment at 420 Bannock Street. On the spacious, cool porch he told reporters about his plans for the summer, which included several trips into the northern part of the state and speeches at Burley and Kellogg. "I haven't anything that's burning to be said," he told them. "I've come to Idaho for a rest. Having arrived earlier than usual, I hope to be able to visit more of the state . . . Oh, not to talk, but just to see how things are going."

After the Sacco-Vanzetti trial Borah received a wire from Jane Addams soliciting his help in pointing out to Governor Fuller of Massachusetts the serious consequences to our international relations should the two Italian anarchists, convicted by a Massachusetts court, be executed.[57] Borah replied:

> The fight for Sacco and Vanzetti can properly be based on innocence or unfair trial and that alone. In the testing of that question I would gladly help insofar as I could. But it would be a national humiliation, a shameless, cowardly compromise of national courage to pay the slightest attention to foreign protests or mob protests at home. We all know your fine devotion to humanity but neither humanity nor peace can be served by deferring to foreign criticism or mob violence in the execution of our criminal laws. This foreign interference is an impudent and willful challenge to our sense of decency and dignity and ought to be dealt with accordingly.[58]

The Citizens' National Committee then wired Borah asking if he would consider acting as counsel for Sacco and Vanzetti in connection with the pending application for appeal to the United States Supreme Court. Pertinent evidence in the files of the Department of Justice, they told Borah, should be released to the defense counsel to determine the innocence or guilt of the two men.[59]

Borah replied that he would be glad to go over the case with the defense counsel and if he found he could be of service, he would volunteer his time. He also telegraphed the Department of Justice requesting the privilege of seeing their files relative to the Sacco-Vanzetti case.[60] Wiring the President at his summer retreat in Rapid City, South Dakota, Borah went one step further:

> I know you have thought the matter all over but I cannot help saying I feel deeply that the files of the Department of Justice ought to be made public before the execution of Sacco and Vanzetti. I have hesitated to wire you but in view of the charges made and the widespread interest in this phase of the case, I thought it proper to do so.[61]

However, the high hopes engendered by Borah's intervention were soon crushed when it became clear that the authorities refused to co-operate. From George Farnum, acting attorney general, Borah received a wire: "No evidence in Department files tending to prove either innocence or guilt of Sacco and Vanzetti. Files will be made immediately available to Governor and Attorney General of Massachusetts."[62] This was, of course, side-stepping Borah's original request. Governor Fuller refused to order a stay of execution, and eventually the sentence was carried out. As for Borah's role in the latter history of the famous court case, John Haynes Holmes had this to say: "The action was wholly characteristic of your great mind and heart, and I shall never cease to regret that it proved unavailing."[63]

Writing Jane Addams at a later date, Borah said there could never be a time when the nation could permit foreign interference in the judgment of our courts. "If our courts are incompetent or corrupt," he said, "it is for us to deal with them. Besides, those people who were denouncing us from abroad knew no more about the facts than I did and I know practically nothing." Borah believed that foreigners were not proceeding on the theory that the men were innocent, as shown by the record, but that they had to be rescued, innocent or guilty. This, he said, is mob violence.[64]

President Coolidge was learning how persistent Borah could be. He was now preparing to introduce a proposal to outlaw war, an idea which seemed to have caught the public fancy.[65]

XIV In Search of a Peace Plan

What all men are really after is some form, or perhaps only some formula, of peace.

—Joseph Conrad

Even though he had denied the efficacy of Wilson's instrument in the search for a comprehensive peace plan, Borah recognized the necessity for positive action. He felt a strong responsibility for formulating some effective program which would replace the defunct League, and as a first step in this direction he had championed a disarmament conference. During 1922 and 1923 he began considering another plan for peace, the outlawry of war. The plan was associated with Salmon O. Levinson, a wealthy Chicago lawyer who had made his fortune reorganizing decrepit business ventures. Already by 1918 he had evolved his plan to make all wars illegal. In 1919 he had gone to Washington to throw his support to the League of Nations, but while there he became convinced that the League was a negative agency while his outlawry proposal was a positive approach to the problem of permanent peace. He had his program circulated in a pamphlet, "A Plan to Outlaw War," and sent eleven hundred copies to the Washington Disarmament Conference.

Borah and Levinson first met in December 1919. The intrepid philanthropist had first tried to enlist Senator Philander C. Knox in the outlawry cause; when Knox failed to follow through, Levinson, impressed by Borah's fight against the League, sought to interest him in the plan to outlaw war. Borah thought Levinson's plan "masterly," or at least so he said. However, despite all efforts, the senator refused to be distracted from his concentrated efforts against the League. Levinson soon learned that Borah was difficult, capricious, and anything but pliable, "a law unto himself." Nevertheless, with unparalleled vigor he continued to emphasize the value of his plan, its strong appeal to the voter, and the necessity for a positive approach. He sought to win the Idahoan's approval by booming him for vice-president in 1920, seeking a place for him in Harding's cabinet, preparing briefs for him on disarmament, and attempting to have him selected as a delegate to the Washington Conference. In countless ways, but especially in long letters, Levinson sought to influence Borah to become the champion of outlawry of war in the Senate. However, Borah was so unresponsive at times, so downright unco-operative and apathetic, that Levinson must have been near despair. Nevertheless, Borah continued to study the project during the hectic months of the Washington Conference and had the pamphlet on outlawry printed in the *Congressional Record* and sent out to thousands of readers under his frank. At a dinner party in Chicago on December 9, 1921, the American Committee for the Outlawry of War was organized, and thereafter Levinson spent himself untiringly in its work. The lawyer was prepared to spend upwards of $15,000 a year for his cause,[1] whose name, "outlawry of war," was first used by the chairman of the committee in a magazine article.[2]

Levinson kept his idea alive during the ensuing months by busily writing letters, making speeches, and trying to enlist prominent people. He succeeded in winning over John Dewey, the well-known philosopher; Reverend John Haynes Holmes of New York's Community Church; Nicholas Murray Butler, president of Columbia University; Dr. Charles C. Morrison, editor of *Christian Century*, whose columns soon became a sounding board for the movement; Colonel Raymond Robins, an earnest reformer and Red Cross worker; and the "wavering convert," Senator Borah.

At times Borah delayed action because he was not satisfied with some features of the plan. At other times the pressure of other duties forced it aside. The basic dilemma rose out of the plan's vital weakness—the question of enforcement. Originally Levinson believed force necessary to implement his scheme and offered no real objections to the employment of sanctions, as provided in the League's machinery. Borah refused to support any peace plan which rested ultimately on force. "With that provision in there, nothing stirring," snapped Borah. He told Levinson, "You'll have to figure out some way to eliminate it," challenged him to develop a nonmilitary sanction for the outlawry of war, and stubbornly refused to present a resolution until the issue was settled to his satisfaction. After much wavering, Levinson finally became convinced that military force was not needed, but Borah felt that some substitute was necessary; he could not accept the suggestion made by

Knox and Levinson that the plan might be enforced by some modified form of the League. The framing of a Senate resolution which Levinson was prodding Borah to complete hung on the solution of this problem. Borah delayed because he thought the opportune moment had not come. This was during the summer of 1922 when there was little possibility of gaining much publicity. Moreover, Borah was still worried about the method by which the judgments of an international court, a part of the outlawry plan, were to be executed. When he did introduce a resolution in the Senate in December 1922, to the disappointment of Levinson and Robins it called for an economic conference; this would promote the outlawry movement, explained Borah.

Levinson continued to court Borah because he thought the senator indispensable to the outlawry movement. With the campaign of 1924 approaching and the administration showing signs of seeking membership in the World Court, Borah finally went into action. He introduced his first resolution (S.R. 441) in the Senate on February 13, 1923:

> Resolved . . . that war between nations should be outlawed as an institution or means for the settlement of international controversies by making it a public crime under the law of nations, and that every nation should be encouraged by solemn agreement or treaty to bind itself to indict and punish its own international war breeders or instigators and war profiteers under powers similar to those conferred upon our Congress under Article I, section 8, of our Federal Constitution, which clothes the Congress with the power to define and punish offenses against the law of nations.[3]

At first reading the whole idea seemed too simple, like a resolution to end snowstorms in March. Yet the plan was carefully thought out and backed by practical men like John Dewey. For the support and public interest it aroused, the proposal compelled consideration.[4]

The first feature of the plan outlined in Borah's resolution was a universal treaty making war a public crime under the law of nations and binding every nation to punish its own war criminals and war profiteers. The basis of the whole structure was to be a comprehensive code of international law. Borah observed that civilization had discovered two methods of compelling the settlement of human disputes, law and war. He proposed bringing all international affairs under a reign of law. Under existing law, war had never been declared a crime. Wars must be made illegal before their underlying causes, such as commercial rivalry, could be eliminated. The third feature of the Levinson-Borah plan called for a judicial substitute for war, or the creation of an independent world court modeled upon the United States Supreme Court with compulsory jurisdiction and full power to decide all controversies involving a construction of international law or treaties. It was explained that this authority did not include the right to use force in executing decisions but rested on "the compelling power of enlightened public opinion." The first step for enforcing the code of international law, requiring the people of each nation to punish their own war criminals, was a feature of the plan which Borah believed to be his work, although Levinson proposed just such a feature in his correspondence with the senator. Anyway, it had the effect of meeting Borah's principal objections. Such a feature also protected the sovereignty of individual nations from encroachment by a world court.

The whole plan was to be sustained by well-directed public opinion. When we bring war or peace nearer the people, Borah reasoned, we advance the cause of peace. As Wilson had once said: "People do not make wars." It was far better to be governed by law, thought Borah, than by secret diplomatic intrigues, politics, and force.[5] There was no debate on the resolution and it received very little publicity, but Borah could be counted on to use it to rouse the conscience of America.

Lord Robert Cecil, the English pacifist who visited America in the spring of 1923, protested that we had not yet reached the stage where it was desirable to attempt the codification of international law. Borah wanted to know why. He reminded the Englishman that Americans believe in a government of law and not of men, a principle infinitely more important in international affairs involving war and peace than in domestic affairs.[6]

The World Court and the approaching presidential campaign were major issues to which Borah turned his attention in the early months of 1924. Levinson noted a growing indifference to foreign relations in general and outlawry in particular on Borah's part. While it is true that emphasis in these months shifted to domestic issues, such as the Harding scandals, Borah did not lose interest in foreign affairs. In his speeches he continued to advocate outlawry and his own version of an international court. The enterprising Levinson was quick to perceive the advantage to the outlawry movement in having Borah boomed for the nomination in 1924 on any ticket, even a third-party ticket. Certain of his utterances gave assurance that he would be an active candidate, but when it became clear that he would not desert the Republican party, Levinson tried to induce him to accept second place on a Coolidge ticket. This, we have seen, left Borah cold.

When Coolidge became president, he was a disappointment to the outlawry group, for he gave the movement no outright endorsement and gradually deserted it altogether by furthering the Harding-Hughes World Court plan. Borah's long-awaited Senate speech on outlawry never was made. He gave the excuse that he did not wish this issue to be used as a cover for corruption during the campaign for Daugherty's dismissal. Once Daugherty was out, Borah turned to advancing the unpopular cause of recognition of Russia. Levinson, though bewildered, convinced himself that Borah's hesitancy was the result of circumstances and not lack of sincerity. Throughout 1924 the senator continued to argue for outlawry in a series of articles which appeared in *Christian Century, Pacific Christian Advocate,* and *New Republic.* At the end of 1924, just as Raymond Robins was complaining of "the futilities Borah permitted himself to become immersed in," Borah became the new chairman of the Senate Foreign Relations Committee. The advocates of outlawry were beside themselves with joy.

As the hope of American participation in the World Court faded, a lull in the peace crusade ensued, during which the untiring Levinson prodded the reluctant Borah to action. Borah believed the tide was running in favor of outlawry, but the advocates should wait until it reached its peak. He was not in favor of haste. He wrote Robins: "We must clear away some underbrush and rubbish before we begin to build."[7] Nor did he approve of the use of the words "aggressive wars" in any treaty. He said: "There has scarcely been a war in three thousand years that the instigators did not claim to be attacked . . . That is one of the vicious features of the World Court Protocol. It undertakes to define aggressive war and then make aggression dependent upon the judgment of ten men rather than upon the merits or demerits of the controversy. All these things are but the traps of militarism."[8]

After much further prodding Borah reintroduced his resolution for outlawry in December 1926, but with no major Senate speech. Such was the extent of his advocacy until the issue was reopened by the premier of France in April 1927. James T. Shotwell of Columbia University furnished the necessary link between the outlawry forces and the French Foreign Office. Returning from Germany in 1927, he stopped in Paris for talks with Aristide Briand, the foreign minister whose liberalism and clarity of vision meant so much to France. Their discussion centered on how the United States could co-operate with the League in the interest of peace. Out of these talks came Briand's famous proposal of April 6, 1927, to renounce and outlaw all wars between France and the United States.[9]

Briand's message, addressed directly to the American people, reached the United States on the tenth anniversary of our entry into World War I. It was inspired and perhaps partly written by Shotwell, who was in general sympathy with the idea of renunciation of war.[10] Briand probably saw in the suggestion an opportunity to tie the United States in a passive way to the new system of alliances France was building. The scheme would at least insure the benevolent neutrality of Americans in the event of war.

An answer to the Briand note came not from the secretary of state but from the chairman of the Foreign Relations Committee. Borah, who was informed of Shotwell's activities in Europe,[11] was not yet sure "just how much politics and how much outlawry" there was in Briand's statement. He welcomed the Briand proposal, but in a speech in Cleveland on May 10 he urged a multilateral treaty rather than Briand's bilateral arrangement and suggested that all the world be invited to participate. This was the first important public pronouncement for the treaty in the form in which it was eventually written, and Borah himself evolved the multilateral formula. The French were not enthusiastic about it.[12]

Secretary Kellogg was cool to the idea of a treaty with France, for he feared being tricked into an alliance. Moreover, he strongly resented the interference of volunteer diplomatists and peace crusaders who were forcing the State Department into tortuous diplomatic maneuvers. In one of his many outbursts he referred to them collectively as "a set of ——fools."[13] Borah grew increasingly wary of Briand's original idea. "The more I study the Briand proposal," he wrote, "the more I think it a piece of dynamite for outlawry."[14] Nevertheless, he trusted that Briand would reduce his suggestions to a draft treaty so that the United States government could deal "intelligently" with the subject of outlawry.[15]

Months went by during which Briand's proposal remained unanswered until Kellogg was pushed further by public opinion. On June 20, 1927, Myron T. Herrick, American ambassador in Paris, was handed a treaty drafted by Briand which supplied the wording for the pact finally adopted. Another long delay ensued, during which President Coolidge found a constitutional argument against outlawry. In an unofficial statement he implied that the chief obstacle was the provision of the Constitution which reserves to Congress the power to declare war.[16] That same day Borah gave his opinion that the proposal took away no constitutional power of Congress to declare war, but created a condition where it would never be necessary to exercise that power. Borah fully realized that Briand's proposal did not contemplate outlawry "in any sense." "It is merely an agreement," he wrote. "Although the pistols are at your feet and the code of honor requires you to use them under certain circumstances, nevertheless you agree not to do so. But everyone knows that agreement is worthless when the exigency arises . . ."[17]

Borah planned to make an appeal for a multipower pact in a speech in New York. At the last moment Mrs. Borah fell ill and he had to cancel the address. He incorporated his appeal, however, in this message: "M. Briand has suggested the first step. Let us suggest the second and include Great Britain, Japan, Germany and Italy. That would furnish a real foundation for outlawing war sincerely."[18]

Kellogg had been busy, meanwhile, in conference with M. Claudel, the French ambassador who visited Washington to negotiate the Kellogg arbitration treaty of February 1928. During all the discussions of arbitration the proposed antiwar treaty remained uppermost in Borah's mind, but he did nothing to interfere. In fact, when Claudel's work was finished and he was about to sail home, he singled out Borah as the one who had done most to further these negotiations and sent his formal thanks.[19]

Secretary Kellogg testified before a closed hearing of the Senate

Foreign Relations Committee on December 22, 1927. The ostensible reason for his appearance was to explain the arbitration treaty, which included in its preamble a sentence "condemning" but not outlawing war. The reason for its insertion was obvious. The members of the committee showed no great interest either in Kellogg's explanation or his treaty. Chairman Borah said he assumed their silence meant consent.

"But, Mr. Secretary," he added, "all this does not dispose of the proposal to outlaw war." Kellogg shifted nervously and looked displeased. He replied that a treaty between France and the United States outlawing war meant nothing less than an alliance between the two countries.

"But, Mr. Secretary," persisted Borah, "the American counterproposal should be a pact to outlaw war between all nations of the world. We should point out that this is too important to confine only to this country and France." Borah then began to poll the leading members of the committee on his proposition.

"That's the best way to get rid of the damned thing," growled Senator Moses. "Put the baby on their [France's] doorstep. Extend it to all nations. France would never consent to outlaw war with Germany."

The other senators were either definitely affirmative or noncommittal. Borah concluded: "I think, Mr. Secretary, you may consider it the sense of this committee that you go ahead with the negotiation of a pact to include all countries."[20]

That same month Borah reintroduced his outlawry resolution in the Senate. Six days after the committee meeting Kellogg sent Briand a proposal for a multilateral treaty to outlaw war. The secretary of state had been jarred into action by Borah.

If Borah's resolution had been left as the final authoritative reply to France, the path of negotiations would indeed have been difficult, but Borah himself undertook to free the whole discussion from the doctrinaire element. He was not interested in splitting juristic hairs but in the earnest furtherance of international peace. He sought ways to harmonize the Levinson plan with one acceptable to other governments. In an article entitled "One Great Treaty to Outlaw All Wars," largely written by Levinson, Borah suggested to France a way to honor her continental alliances and sign a multipower antiwar pact at the same time. A breach of the proposed treaty, he argued, would automatically release the signatories from their obligations thereunder. Upon violation of the pact, say by Germany, France would be released from the antiwar treaty and might proceed to the aid of Belgium under the terms of the Franco-Belgian alliance.[21] Borah and the pro-League Shotwell never got on well, but even Shotwell was prompted to comment: "Senator Borah has cleared away much of the obstruction in the path of negotiations."[22]

While Briand grew reluctant to accept an arrangement so different from his original proposal, Kellogg became enthusiastic for a multipower treaty and pushed it with vigor. He had caught the popular infection and came to envision his counterproposal as a great contribution to world peace. His note of February 27, 1928, reminded France that if she could sign a bilateral treaty renouncing war, she could just as well sign a multilateral treaty.

Finally, Kellogg received an acceptance from France, whereupon he invited Britain, Germany, Italy, and Japan to join in the agreement. At an impressive ceremony in the Hall of Mirrors at Versailles, the Kellogg-Briand Pact was signed on August 27, 1928. Borah, then in Idaho for the summer, had hoped the ceremony would take place in Washington because he thought of the pact as distinctly an American contribution. The pact was the virtually unchanged text of the note of June 23 containing the American interpretation. The signatories agreed "to condemn war as an instrument of national policy" in their relations with one another. Eventually almost every nation in the world joined them. Borah regarded Kellogg's efforts as "an exhibition of the highest statesmanship." Kellogg replied: "It has been a long and troublesome negotiation and I think, if I had not had your backing, I should have long ago gotten discouraged."[23] Borah assumed the task of piloting the Pact of Paris through the Senate to final passage, and the Foreign Relations Committee reported it with no reservations. Borah would permit none.[24] However, the committee's report explained the Senate's position on the treaty and its relation to the Monroe Doctrine.

France made it clear that the pact did not refer to wars of self-defense or wars in pursuance of obligations under existing treaties, such as the League Covenant or the Locarno Pact. After the treaty was reported out, a Senate cabal of isolationists including Hiram Johnson and George Moses made repeated efforts to append reservations meeting their objections and to have the Senate vote on the committee's explanatory report. England stipulated that the right of self-defense included certain regions which constituted a vital interest for her peace and safety. The proponents of the treaty regarded these reservations and interpretative notes as completely inconsequential. Kellogg took pains to make clear that they were in no way a part of the pact. Borah sought first to prevent reservations and then to prevent the impression that they modified the agreement. Dismissing them as no more than expressions of a personal opinion, he wrote:

> . . . I may be extremely obtuse, but I am unable to understand how talks and suggestions on the side can have the slightest effect upon the terms of the treaty as it will be signed . . . I had a letter yesterday from Professor Borchard in which he seemed to think that these statements made by the British Government and by France would have the same effect upon the treaty as if they were reservations to the treaty. If there is any such doctrine or principle as that, the treaty would not be worth a damn.[25]

In a speech in Carnegie Hall on November 13 Borah promised to do all he could to hurry the Kellogg treaty through the Senate. At the same time he announced he would vote for the Naval Appropriation bill to add fifteen heavy cruisers to the fleet. Failure of the bill, he reasoned, would jeopardize passage of the antiwar treaty. However, critics logically could ask: if there will be no more wars, what will you do with your new warships? He was certain that the American navy would be used only as a defensive weapon and that the sole war admissible under the Kellogg treaty would come under the "higher law of self-defense," which can never be given or taken away from a nation by treaty.[26] Borah struck a severe blow at his own peace plan when he declared from the Senate floor that if England did not come to terms with us on the freedom of the seas, then we would simply build a navy greater than hers!

On New Year's Day, 1929, Secretary and Mrs. Kellogg were entertaining the diplomatic corps at a breakfast in the Pan American Union building.

"Why, where is Senator Borah?" Kellogg asked Mrs. Borah as she walked up the steps. She smiled and replied smartly: "He said that if you asked for him I should say he was at home working on your damned treaty." The Kelloggs had a good laugh. "That's all right. I want him to work on the treaty," the secretary replied as they went in to breakfast.[27]

When the Senate reconvened, the debate on the Kellogg treaty was resumed. The *Nation* thought that Borah's strategy showed none of his old aggressiveness and confidence. He failed to press for an early vote. Answering a question by Senator Reed of Missouri, he made one damaging admission by stating that our going to war with Spain in 1898 would not have been affected in any way by this treaty. Borah's construction of the situation was probably correct, but it tended to confuse people because it came after Coolidge's Wisconsin address of August 1928, in which he assured his large audience that had there been a Kellogg treaty in 1914, it would have delivered the world from all the misery inflicted by the Great War.[28]

By January 11 Borah was bored with his colleagues' long speeches and continuous sniping at the underlying meaning of the pact. He sought to limit debate to thirty minutes for each senator, but failed to obtain unanimous consent. Many senators wanted an interpretative declaration before they would vote on the pact. By January 15 events were moving to a climax. Shortly after Vice-President Dawes called the Senate to order, Borah asked him to step outside to the vice-president's office. There he proposed the adoption of an explanatory report of the Foreign Relations Committee (which stated specifically that it was no modification or reservation to the treaty). Dawes telephoned Coolidge, who agreed they had done all they could. Kellogg also acquiesced. Thus fortified, Borah went back to the Senate floor and asked for a vote that very day.[29]

Many senators regarded the treaty as a "noble gesture" but approved it with skepticism. Senator Reed called it an "international kiss." Before voting on the Pact of Paris, Senator Carter Glass of Virginia served notice that he was not simple enough to suppose that it was worth a postage stamp in the direction of accomplishing permanent peace. He predicted it would confuse the minds of many good and pious people, but he agreed to vote with the rest for the ratification of this worthless but harmless peace treaty.[30] Borah then read the report of the Foreign Relations Committee, and shortly afterwards the Senate voted 85 to 1 for the Pact of Paris. Senator Brookhart observed that at that moment Russia and the United States were the only two countries that had ratified the treaty. "I hope," said Brookhart, "these two great revolutionary countries will now proceed to outlaw war throughout the world."[31]

Public opinion was almost universally favorable to the Pact of Paris. Seasoned critics were more skeptical. Elmer Davis wrote the editor of the New York *Times:* "The various millennial proposals of Senator Borah and Lady Astor deserve a little study before we swallow them offhand." He found Borah's idea of outlawing war moderate. "If only he will add a clause providing that on and after January 1, sorrow and suffering shall be forever prohibited, I am with him."[32]

Although Edwin Borchard and David Hunter Miller were convinced that the Pact of Paris contained at least implications that international consultation would be required, Borah denied any such thing. In the debate on ratification of the pact he said: "If a nation violates the treaty, are we under any obligation, express or implied, to apply coercive or punitive measures? I answer emphatically, NO!" There was no provision in the treaty for enforcement, and Borah was proud of the fact that it carried no obligation to apply sanctions. Nationalist feeling kept from it any hint that it created an obligation to come to the aid of any power or do anything except abstain from war as an instrument of national policy. It was no more than a pious expression of hope, reflecting that strange misconception of international politics which dominated American thinking during the twenties.[33]

Borah himself admitted the possibility that some country could construe the treaty out of all reason, and nothing could restrain such a nation except the public opinion of the world. Public opinion, however, is not enough; it must be informed and find expression through organization. Few neutral men could discern much difference as between enforcing peace and outlawing war in the number of men and battleships which would be required, but Borah trusted implicitly in the power of moral suasion and the force of enlightened public opinion. Like a bad law, this treaty was written to be broken. It was destined to fall apart almost of its own weight the moment a strong national interest reared its head. Moreover, the moment was not far off when Japan, in fulfillment of what she felt was her national destiny, occupied Manchuria.[34]

Some of the difficulty was the result of Borah's imperfect understanding of the fundamental causes of war and the natural relation between politics and the conditions out of which wars proceed. The plan was ridiculed as lacking in intellectual seriousness and respectability, and was compared to the forlorn sign discovered at Gettysburg, still intact after the battle:

Shooting Forbidden on These Premises Under Penalty of Law.[35]

The most devastating criticism of Borah and his plan for peace came from Walter Lippmann, who found it a curious fact that this former irreconcilable, identified with active opposition to every established institution for the prevention of war, should take the lead in the campaign for outlawry. Lippmann attacked the whole plan as Borah first introduced it in Congress. He observed that Borah had subsequently made no effort to create the machinery which was an integral part of his original plan, i.e., the codification of international law and an international court. How much easier it is, said Lippmann, to arouse a large audience to a denunciation of war than to persuade them to agree on the principles of a code. Yet a code was essential and no single world conference could create it. Whether Borah liked it or not, his plan necessarily implied the establishment of a world legislature with authority over all major international disputes. He questioned Borah's sincerity in proposing a plan whose implementation was so contradictory to his known convictions.

Earlier Borah had generalized that only law and war existed as methods of compelling the settlement of human disputes. This was to ignore the countless other methods that have been used with effect: diplomacy, mediation, conciliation, conference, arbitration, compromise, and friendly intervention.

On the judicial substitute for war, which was central to the whole idea, outlawry foundered. The slow judicial procedures intended for use were not adaptable to the exigencies of international affairs. If such a court as Borah proposed were confronted with a question for which no rule of law existed, the court would have to invent law or, in the guise of law, make political deals. Such a court would inevitably become entangled in the politics of the world. As for modeling an international court on our Supreme Court, Lippmann declared: ". . . we shall as soon behold the sun stand still in the heavens as see the irreconcilable senator from Idaho argue that nine judges at The Hague should have the same power to annul a law passed by Parliament or Congress as our Supreme Court has to annul the acts of a State legislature."[36]

The Pact of Paris was a perfect expression of the utopian idealism which dominated American attempts to compose international conflicts and banish the threat of war in the interwar period. Borah, who always had an open mind for peace schemes which did not involve force or political entanglements, had given the movement the promise of a bright future once he was finally persuaded to become its champion. Like the Washington treaties, the Pact of Paris was the result of a strange interaction between popular sentiment and power politics. The senator, who was quick to catch up with the wave of favorable public opinion which he had helped to generate, considered the pact an "incalculable contribution" to the security of nations. However, the basis of all this popular enthusiasm and approbation was just as insubstantial and unrealistic as the basis on which the nation had embraced the Washington treaties. The American people were fooled and Borah with them. Only the argument of forthcoming events could have transformed the fundamental approach toward international relations that misinformed the nation's anxious search for peace without power.[37]

XV Sons of the Wild Jackass

> The public may not realize it, but these 'Sons of the Wild Jackass,' with rare reinforcements from the regulars on both sides of the aisle, have been riding the Senate bareback for a decade.
>
> —Ray Tucker

Anticipating another Coolidge victory in 1928, Republicans were rudely jolted by that terse announcement the President handed newspapermen at the summer White House in the Black Hills of South Dakota on August 2, 1927: "I do not choose to run for President in 1928." Almost immediately party factions began grooming their candidates. If ever Borah were to seek the presidential nomination, it would have to be in 1928; otherwise he would be too old. His partisans reminded Republicans that they had another Grover Cleveland knocking at their gate if they but knew it. The senator's qualifications included a long and varied experience in national affairs, insight into government, a wide knowledge of history, rare oratorical talent, mental, physical, and moral vigor, profound faith in the integrity and patriotism of the people, and aggressive devotion to the Constitution. As one writer said, "Borah is a Republican in the best Democratic sense."[1] Idaho led off with a warm endorsement of its favorite son, and other western states were reported to be rapidly swinging into line.

Meanwhile, during the summer of 1927 Borah rode serenely along the Yellow Pine trail or fished in the trout streams of the Elk Mountains in Idaho. On a trip with Mrs. Borah and their friends he climbed the Elk Creek summit and engaged in a snowball fight nine thousand feet above sea level. This made excellent news and pictures.[2]

The best key to Borah's own thought on the subject is an exchange of letters with James Hawley, a Democrat, lawyer, and close Idaho friend who hoped that he would receive the nomination for President—"in which event," he wrote, "I am afraid a whole lot of us life-long, hidebound Democrats would forget our partisan feelings and give you hearty support."[3] Borah replied:

. . . a letter of this kind from you is about as fine a thing as could happen in one's lifetime. I have had a great many things written to me and said to me within the last few months which perhaps justifies the belief that I have considerable popular support throughout the country. I have not permitted myself to become enthusiastic about it for I realize some single move here might dissipate it overnight. And of one thing I have thoroughly made up my mind, and that is that my action here in the Senate must be in accordance with my views and convictions whether it is political advancement or political retirement, and it may be the only thing I will have left after all these years of hard work will be the record in the Senate, and that I do not propose consciously to mar, although unconsciously I may often do so.

Even if Coolidge would not be a candidate, Borah saw no way he could win enough delegates at the convention. He related what a prominent New York businessman told him: "Senator, personally I would like to see you President, but the people with whom I associate and play the game think you are entirely too independent, and they do not know where an administration of yours might lead." They admitted he was loyal to the Constitution, but would not predict what he would do inside the document.[4]

The winter of 1927-28 brought a crystallization of sentiment. By spring the aspirations of all rivals were doomed by the irresistible tide that swept Hoover into prominence. Proof that Borah did not take seriously his own chances for the nomination came when he invited Hoover to Idaho for two or three speeches. He seemed ready to deliver Idaho's eight delegates to the secretary of commerce. Why did he thus turn so rapidly to Hoover in 1928? One possible reason was that Hoover agreed with Borah's Latin American policy, although not publicly. Another was that he was unpopular with many Republican leaders; so was Borah. Perhaps Borah admired the man for possessing real moral fiber and shared with him the distrust of party wheel horses. At any rate, Borah was contemptuous of the other candidates: Lowden because he was implicated in the Missouri scandals of 1920 which Borah helped to expose; Hughes because he had been attorney for the Standard Oil Company; and Dawes because of his connection with the Lorimer bank scandal. Hoover also appealed to Borah because he was known to favor a restriction upon foreign loans.

As events ran their course, Borah aspired to become not president but a western Warwick; he hoped not only to name the Republican candidate for president but dictate the platform of 1928 as well, and thus become a power behind the throne. In the preconvention period he forwarded questionnaires on prohibition to all the likely candidates in 1928. He was afraid both parties would ignore what he considered to be the central issue in the campaign. His insistence that prohibition was the issue, day by day, made it the issue. In a New York speech in November 1927 Borah said only the deaf and dumb would not be discussing prohibition in 1928, but accused the two major parties of planning to keep it out of their platform. He appealed to the women of America to rally to the Constitution and the home. Hoover's reply to Borah's questionnaire ran:

> . . . I feel that the discussion of public questions by reply to questionnaires is likely to be unsatisfactory and ofttimes leads to confusion rather than clarity. Reply to the scores of such inquiries on many questions is impossible.
>
> Out of my regard for your known sincerity and your interest in the essential questions, I will, however, say again that I do not favor the repeal of the Eighteenth Amendment. I stand, of course, for the efficient, vigorous and sincere enforcement of the laws. Whoever is chosen president has under his oath the solemn duty to pursue this course.[5]

In Senate debate Walter Edge, a wet from New Jersey, asked why the Eighteenth Amendment should be singled out for enforcement. What about the Fourteenth and Fifteenth amendments? Borah rejoined that he was ready to urge a Republican platform pledging enforcement of these amendments also. Some were surprised that he considered it necessary to answer a challenge that answered itself. He continued: "Under proper leadership the people of the United States will enforce any law which they are unwilling to repeal. Under proper leadership they will repeal any law which they are unwilling to enforce." He proposed a national referendum on prohibition, not only a great moral cause but preeminently a constitutional issue. Nullification of the amendment, he thought, would break down respect for all laws.[6]

Hoover and Borah were in daily conference during the week of June 8 preceding the convention, for the senator was scheduled to go to Kansas City early to serve on the Resolutions Committee. Borah wanted the party to assume full responsibility for the Harding scandals, demand full publicity for campaign expenditures, promise tariff increases on all agricultural products, and pledge rigid enforcement of the Volstead Act with no revision or modification. He wanted a hands-off policy in Central America, no compromise on the World Court, and approval of the bilateral treaties Kellogg was busy negotiating.

Upon arrival at Kansas City, he immediately went to work on the platform. He devised a compromise plan to aid farmers with increased agricultural tariffs and a federal farm board to build up co-operatives and decrease destructive competition. He personally drafted the driest plank ever adopted by any large national party: "The Republican party endorses the principle of the Eighteenth Amendment, pledges itself against its modification or repeal, and for its efficient and honest enforcement." It was accepted by the committee and the convention.

Other planks included an anti-League statement, one favoring the Pact of Paris, adherence to the World Court with reservations, a completely free educational system, approval of Coolidge's foreign policy, and publicity for campaign expenditures. Not all of them suited Borah, particularly the two concerning the World Court and foreign policy, but he dictated most of the others. At Kansas City he became a sort of godfather of the Hoover candidacy; never before had he played such an important role. Hoover's advisers were dismayed by what they regarded as his politically impossible proposals. They warned that enforcement of the Eighteenth Amendment would alienate the East and that the plank on campaign funds would dry up their sources of money. No one knew or cared what his foreign relations plank meant. In spite of the grumbling, Hoover accepted all of Borah's proposals and the convention voted for all the important ones.[7]

The Idahoan fired the convention by striding out on the stage and paying Coolidge a warm eulogy: "Sincerely, courageously, and often lonely, the President has struggled to lower taxes . . . The greatest boon to the independence of the American farmer ever conferred was when Coolidge vetoed the McNary-Haugen bill. The time will come when the farmer will appreciate the statesmanship and vision of the man who saved him from being a bureaucratic rat." When he finished, the convention rose in a burst of genuine enthusiasm. Called to the stage to close the debate on farm relief, he left his seat among the Idaho delegates and walked slowly up the steps. In the glare of the lights men could see that twenty-one years in the Senate had left its mark on him. His determined face with its short, tipped-up nose, wide mouth, and heavy, square chin was deeply lined. The sturdy figure drooped with weariness after two nights' work on the platform; in forty-eight hours he had had only five hours' sleep.

Crossing the lobby of the Muehlebach Hotel one morning after breakfast, Borah met Senator Smoot, who had sat in on all the meetings of party leaders. "Who's going to be nominated for Vice President?" asked Borah, showing only mild interest.

"Cox of Massachusetts," replied Smoot casually.

"What the hell is the matter with you, have you all gone crazy?" Borah exploded. He backed Smoot into a corner. "I don't know much about politics but evidently I know a thousand times more than Hoover. What do you want to do, crucify us all in November?"

"Why, what's the trouble?" gasped Smoot.

"Trouble?" exclaimed Borah. "None, excepting that nobody outside of Massachusetts has ever heard of Cox. This convention has got to nominate Curtis and is going to nominate him or I shall know the reason why. Let me warn you here and now, Senator, you can tell the Hoover crowd that Curtis has got to be nominated to keep the western states in line and if anybody else is put up I shall go before the convention and present his name myself and make a fight for it and I think I can put his name across."

"Oh, don't do that. Just hold off and I'll see about it." Smoot hurried away. In a short time word came from Washington that Curtis was acceptable. Borah himself put Curtis' name in nomination in a happy little speech with the air of a fully satisfied man. Curtis was nominated unanimously.[8]

After the convention Borah was asked if he could now be regarded as a regular, since he seemed in harmony for once with his party. Borah replied: "I am too old to change. Whoever the next president is, he'll get my support when I think he's right, and when I think he isn't, he'll get something else."[9]

When he returned to Washington, Borah announced that he was going into the corn belt to take off his coat for Hoover. A striking feature of the campaign was the battle he conducted for Hoover, who relied mainly on him to combat Al Smith, the Democratic candidate. Borah welcomed the battle with Smith over prohibition and farm relief. As for the religious issue, he said at the outset: "I despise intolerance and they need expect no speeches of intolerance from me. The religious question is a disgraceful thing to inject into a campaign and no word will be spoken by me having to do with Governor Smith's religious affiliations." His speeches in the South, where Hoover's popularity was already high, were credited with turning both bigots and more sensible people toward the Republican candidate. In April 1927, when Smith released his famous answer to inquiries by Charles C. Marshall on his religious obligations as a Roman Catholic, Borah commented: "The letter was most excellent." Henry Pringle noted that the Idahoan was always more of a man than a politician.[10]

Borah opened the campaign in Detroit's Orchestra Hall, praising Hoover as an "executive genius" with a broad view and firm grasp of the essential tenets of humanity. He reviewed his record and declared his creed "safe."[11] He followed Smith into doubtful southern, border, and western states to "wipe out Al's tracks." The Republican National Committee mapped out an itinerary which took him to Louisville and Bowling Green, Kentucky, Memphis, Tennessee, Richmond, Virginia, and then Texas, Missouri, South Dakota, and Nebraska, finally winding up with a major address at Minneapolis on October 1, where twenty-five thousand heard him in Convention Hall discuss three major issues: the St. Lawrence seaway, prohibition, and farm relief. Hoover wired: "Greatest speech of the campaign."

Chairman Work and other members of the committee who financed his tour had trouble inducing him to travel in a private car. He had never done it before. Austere in his personal habits, Borah bluntly expressed his preference for the day coaches. He finally yielded when the unwonted luxury was excused on the ground of conserving his health, allowing him to rest between speeches on a strenuous tour. The enthusiastic reception southern cities gave him alarmed Democratic leaders and led Borah to predict that Hoover would carry Tennessee, North Carolina, Kentucky, Virginia, and Florida (he carried all but Florida).

Hoover repeated his denunciation of farm subsidies in a New

York speech which was built around his fear of "state socialism." Borah, campaigning in the Middle West, hurried to Washington to tell Hoover that the grain growers interpreted his remarks as an attack on any kind of farm relief and were up in arms over his declaration. Hoover promptly reversed himself and allowed Borah to promise the calling of a special session of Congress to deal with farm problems.[12]

The liberal press was disgusted with Borah for the role he assumed in support of Hoover; the *Nation* called him the "sorriest figure" in the whole campaign. It was bad enough for a man of his ideals and standards to stoop to nominating Curtis, but for him to go about the country proclaiming Hoover a "miracle man" was decidedly too thick. For years Progressives like Borah had been shouting down the power trust and demanding an investigation by the Federal Trade Commission. Borah had on various occasions expressed his preference for nationalization of the nation's power sites, and now he threw his support to Hoover, who was violently opposed to their public ownership. Every newspaperman in Washington knew that there had been no severer critic of Hoover than Borah in 1918-19, and statements he made at that time were now thrown up to him.[13] He replied to his questioners by saying: "Mr. Hoover contended he was doing the best possible under the circumstances. I contended to the contrary but I never questioned his honesty or his patriotism."[14]

In a speech in Chicago Al Smith criticized Borah's sudden *rapprochement* with Hoover and his do-nothing policy on the farm problem:

> He [Borah] posed for altogether too many years as a great political advance agent of progress, a great progressive from the great wide open spaces of the West, talking for everything that is high and lofty. But the evidence today pretty clearly indicates that he is more interested in the success of his party than he is in the vindication of any principle that he ever espoused. He didn't always think so much of Mr. Hoover.

In relation to Hoover's work as relief director after World War I in Europe, Smith quoted Borah as having said: "No man who has such perverted views of decency ought to be entrusted with unlimited power to deal with $100,000,000." He continued: "Borah was either right in 1919 or he is right today . . . Will anyone pay attention to him?" He concluded that Hoover had traded a gold brick for an Idaho potato![15]

Though ignored by Coolidge and Mellon and viciously opposed at the outset by Wall Street and the farm bloc, Hoover won an overwhelming victory in November, polling 21,392,000 votes against 15,106,000 for Smith. In the electoral college he had 444 votes to 87 for Smith. Hoover thought the issues which defeated Smith were general prosperity, prohibition, farm tariffs, Tammany Hall, and what he called "a snuggling up of the Socialists."[16] When the returns came in, he gratefully telegraphed Borah:

> Now that I can more fully appreciate the enormous effect of your support by the reports all through the West, I wish to record this preliminary appreciation.[17]

Borah's services to Hoover at Kansas City and on the stump built up a political debt which experts believed would result either in a close friendship or in bitter enmity. No bargain had been made before the campaign. It is probable, however, that Hoover accepted Borah's platform planks anticipating his support. The conduct of "Herbert's godfather" was very different from that of 1920, when it was hard to tell whether his speeches were for Harding or not, and unlike that of 1924, when he refused to go on the hustings for Coolidge at all.

Some analysts saw two paths open to Borah now: he could become chief spokesman for the administration in the Senate, an embarrassing position for the foremost critic of former administrations; or he could enter the Supreme Court. This was the cloister where he could find happiness in studying the implications of the Constitution which he loved to interpret.[18] Keen observers, however, realized Borah would follow neither course. They devoted their time to speculating on whether President-elect Hoover, out of gratitude for his services in the campaign, ever offered Borah the secretaryship of state. No official bulletin was given out on this subject. In Russia, Germany, Hungary, and Czechoslovakia correspondents expressed hope that Borah would succeed Kellogg in the State Department. The Russians were especially favorable to the idea. However, the German press expressed grave doubts that

Borah would accept the post if it were offered. The Austrians believed that he favored an *Anschluss,* but opinion there was divided as to whether he could exercise a strong influence on German affairs.[19]

Early in November Borah wrote an Idaho friend: "I do not think . . . for a moment that the secretaryship of state is going to be tendered to me. I have reason to know that Mr. Hoover feels grateful to me for what I did in the campaign, but I do not anticipate anything in the nature of an offer to go into the cabinet."[20] Friends who were certain Borah would be thus rewarded strongly urged him to accept, while others who feared he would abdicate his independence warned him to refuse.

At a Washington dinner party shortly after Hoover's election some of the guests brought the conversation around to the President's cabinet choices. The host, a friend of Borah's, tried desperately to avert direct questions and might have succeeded but for the fact that Mrs. Borah, utterly unperturbed, joined the conversation at its most crucial point: "You must realize that I can't say very much about it right now, but since I feel perfectly sure that I'm in the hands of my friends, I'm going to tell you all . . ." The host tried to check her, but Mrs. Borah went on, ". . . that the secretaryship of state has been offered to the Senator . . . [gasps from the guests] by everyone except Mr. Hoover." Remarks like these won for Mary Borah the title, "the perfect wife for a public man."[21]

On January 18, 1929, Borah was Hoover's luncheon guest in the house on S Street. Rumors circulated that they were discussing candidates for the State Department. Emerging from the conference, Borah was asked by reporters who had been mentioned for the post. He replied: "No one but Mr. Hoover and myself knows. Therefore you will have to get it from Mr. Hoover."[22] No clarification was made at the time. Hoover has since stated that he never offered the post to Borah, who, he recalls, was in no rush to retire from the Senate.[23]

Borah, who scrupulously dictated a record of what occurred at White House conferences, related the substance of his conversation with Hoover after lunch at the executive mansion. Stating that he wished to discuss the State Department post confidentially, Hoover said: "Your name has been mentioned in connection with this office." As Borah started to reply, Hoover interrupted: "Let me state further before you reply. It is natural that the public should associate your name with this office and I should like to have you at the head of my cabinet." Then the President said something to the effect that the matter rested largely with Borah. What were his wishes? Before he could reply, Hoover added: "But while I feel, as I say, that I should like to have you in my cabinet, I must say that I would regard your going out of the Senate as a loss to the country. There you are the greatest moral force in the nation today. Now I have stated my views candidly."

Borah told the President he presumed his name had been associated with the post because of his activities in the campaign. He assured Hoover he had not gone into the campaign with that office in mind. Moreover, he told Hoover that he didn't have the financial means to be secretary of state. Both the financial and social obligations were beyond his reach. Finally, Borah said he did not feel he ought to give up his work in the Senate. If as secretary of state he found it impossible to agree with the administration on some matter of foreign policy, he would be forced either to surrender or get out, neither of which he would want to do, but the latter of which he would do if necessary. Borah probably foresaw that such an exigency would leave him with no real political future.

The two men discussed various individuals for the place. Borah expressed a preference for Dwight Morrow, but Hoover doubted that he could be recalled from the valuable work he was then doing in Mexico. The Idaho senator recalled that Hoover was favorable to Morrow, Stimson, Perkins, and Robinson in about this order.[24]

Borah interpreted Hoover's curious conduct as an expression of appreciation for his efforts in the campaign. He believed Hoover's offer of the secretaryship was entirely sincere, but Borah was equally clear in assuming that Hoover did not prefer him for the post. "In this," Borah confided to his memorandum, "his judgment was sound. I would never have felt the least disappointment had he never mentioned the subject to me at all. I could never adjust myself to a position where I might have to surrender my views in order to get along with the administration . . ." Thus the President-elect satisfied his sense of obligation by a halfhearted offer of a position which he felt Borah would not accept.

The Idahoan departed with no less respect and friendliness for

Mr. Hoover. Upon reaching his awaiting auto, he repeated his favorite lines from Emerson: " 'It is easy in the world to live after the world's opinion. It is easy in solitude to live after your own; but the great man is he, who in the midst of the crowd keeps with perfect sweetness the independence of solitude.' Let us at least imitate the great."[25]

At a dinner which Borah attended on February 21 the conversation was devoted entirely to a discussion of candidates for the attorney generalship. William J. Donovan was mentioned, but Borah opposed him because he favored repealing the Volstead Act and the Eighteenth Amendment. The senator supported a New York lawyer, William D. Mitchell, for the position. Hoover hesitated; it is said he had already offered the post to Donovan, an old friend. He feared there would be objection to his naming a Democrat, but Borah assured him that such criticism would amount to nothing. "A few people may grunt and groan about it," he said, "but not very loud, and it will not cause one vote against his confirmation."[26] In his account of talks with Hoover, Borah reported that the attorney generalship was never directly or indirectly offered to him. If Hoover ever had any such idea in mind, he never made it known to the Idaho senator. It is equally clear that Borah was more interested in public questions than appointments.[27]

Hoover had taken an unhappy step when he yielded to the importunities of Senator Borah and authorized him to announce that if elected he would call a special session to increase agricultural tariffs.[28] Republicans controlled the Seventy-First Congress when it convened on April 15, 1929, and the old guard tried to control the Republicans. George H. Moses was president pro tempore of the Senate, James Watson was floor leader, and Simeon Fess was whip. This trio typified the old guard, whose antagonism to Hoover went back to 1919. Able men like Joseph Robinson and Thomas Walsh directed the Democratic minority. Insurgent Republicans constituted a major threat to Hoover's leadership in the Senate. At no time during his term did the President have a united party behind him, and therein lies the principal cause for his much emphasized "political failure." A dozen insurgents could and did co-operate with Democrats to exercise effective control. The alliance of these rebels with Democrats, called "the coalition," varied in membership. Borah was its nominal leader, but George Norris and Robert

La Follette, Jr. supplied a driving energy and organizational ability which Borah demonstrated only fitfully. James M. Couzens, Michigan's multimillionaire senator, was liberal by fits and starts. Hiram Johnson, Smith Brookhart, and Peter Norbeck were other consistent Progressive champions, while T. H. Caraway of Arkansas and "Pat" Harrison of Mississippi were Democratic conservatives who served with the liberals. No wonder these "sons of the wild jackass," as Moses soon called them, annoyed the President![29]

Hoover asked Congress for increased tariff protection for agriculture and for the establishment of a farm board to promote orderly agricultural marketing. Protracted debate delayed the passage of the Hawley-Smoot Tariff until June 1930, but the Agricultural Marketing Act was pushed through and signed by mid-June 1929. This act created a Federal Farm Board along the lines Borah had proposed, with a revolving fund of $500,000,000 (the figure he had suggested) which the board could make available for loans to co-operative marketing associations owned and controlled by the farmers. The board was also authorized, under special conditions, to establish stabilization corporations to buy and take off the market a sufficient portion of the crop surplus to maintain prices.

Agrarian reformers were dubious about the measure and wanted to amend it with a provision for export debentures—a plan whereby the government would pay a subsidy on agricultural exports equivalent to one half the American tariff rate. Though Borah had opposed the equalization fee in the McNary-Haugen bill, he now went on record as favoring the debenture, which he regarded as "the saving clause" of the farm relief bill. The Idaho Grange also supported the debenture plan, as did numerous other farm organizations throughout the West. Hoover's mind was set against the export debenture scheme, which he believed would result in overproduction, increased taxation, and foreign retaliation and would yield no benefit to the farmer. Borah's work in the Senate for the export debenture, which was incorporated into the farm bill, aroused the old guard and served to warn Hoover that the Idaho senator was no man's lackey. Borah emerged as the leader of a revolt in his own party over farm relief within six weeks after the election. As one observer put it, "the honeymoon is over."

Hoover had said during the campaign that he opposed subsidizing the farmers. The bill, as he wanted it (and as it finally passed), was designed to give the farmers an initial advance of capital. In other words, he wanted to help the farmers to help themselves. However, it was charged that privately the President had led an influential group of senators (including Borah) to believe he would accept the export debenture plan. Then, after the Senate Agricultural Committee reported favorably on the measure, he publicly repudiated the proposal. A recent biographer of Hoover claims the charge is not true. In any case, impish Jack Garner offered to buy a new hat for anyone who could cite a ten-day period in which the White House had not contradicted itself, and a senator from Indiana asked: "How in hell can a man stand behind this President, unless he has St. Vitus' dance?"[30]

Senator Fess badgered Borah for inducing Hoover to call a special session and said it was now his duty to stand by the President and vote against the export debenture plan.[31] Borah, along with the coalition of progressive Republicans and Democrats, voted for it; the debenture was accepted by the Senate but was killed in the House. The other farm relief measure which the administration promised, an increase in the tariff rates on agricultural products, opened a Pandora's box. Hoover hoped for limited rate changes on industrial goods in exceptional cases to meet the difference between the cost of production at home and abroad. In the measure which came from the House, however, of the thousand tariff increases proposed, 75 were on farm products and 925 were on manufactures!

The House bill (the Hawley Tariff) was referred to the Senate Finance Committee. On June 13 Borah introduced a resolution to restrict tariff revision to agricultural schedules and directly related commodities. He openly attacked the whole principle of the House bill; however, his resolution was rejected by one vote, 38 to 39. The close result was heartening and spurred him on to make a resolute fight against the Hawley bill, which, as he put it, opened the door for the worst spectacle of lobbying and logrolling that Washington had seen since the days of the infamous Payne-Aldrich Tariff.[32]

Hoover refused to take a stand on the Borah resolution, but the day after its defeat the White House announced that the President was opposed to general tariff revision! Out of the administration's failure to seize upon Borah's effort to save the day for agriculture grew the insurgent-Democratic coalition, which accepted Borah's leadership and prepared to write into the bill amendments designed to strip industrialists of many tariff privileges. Had he followed Borah's advice, Hoover would not have been faced eventually with the choice of accepting a law which took away all his powers to change tariff rates or becoming the first Republican president to veto a tariff bill passed by a Congress of his own party.[33]

Hoover's principal aim was to keep the tariff bill free from farm-relief riders and to "expand" the flexibility of the measure by enlarging the powers of the Tariff Commission. The President was convinced that flexible tariff provisions were absolutely essential because they provided a prompt means to correct injustices and avoided the necessity for constant legislative revision. With this in mind, Hoover conferred with Borah to enlist his support.[34] Borah convinced himself that the flexible tariff deprived Congress of its constitutional authority, and he persuaded the "coalition" to oppose it as reactionary. Hoover writes: "I had him to dinner but was unable to overcome his opposition. He was looking for an opportunity to go into his traditional attitude of opposition to the current Administration. The Supreme Court subsequently ruled that the idea was entirely constitutional."[35]

On the floor of the Senate Borah bluntly warned Hoover that he could not seek to influence Congress with regard to the flexible tariff and then avoid responsibility for the rest of the measure. "Having put his hand to the plow," said the New York *World*, "the President cannot turn aside because of rough furrows." When Hoover argued that flexible provisions were necessary to afford adequate protection to the farmer, Borah wanted to know about the higher duties on pig iron, shoes, and cement, none of which were products of the farm or depressed industry. He said the bill was either an administration measure or not. As it was, it certainly did not square with campaign pledges. Borah demanded to know whether Hoover approved the industrial schedules.[36] He led a campaign to require that all recommendations of the Tariff Commission be approved by Congress. His coalition succeeded in amending the House (Hawley) bill to include the export debenture plan. More than anyone, he was responsible for the Senate defiance of the White House. Of his recalcitrance William C.

Murphy remarked: "When he reascends Olympus it might be appropriate to canonize him as the patron of political mischief makers, for Washington will be a far duller place without him."[37]

The special session ended when the House, under administration control, refused to accept most of the 1253 amendments to the tariff bill adopted by the Senate. The deadlock necessitated a conference committee through which the President succeeded in getting the debenture plan out of the bill and flexible provisions in, although the Senate had defeated the flexible tariff by a vote of 47 to 42. It was not until the following spring that the Hawley-Smoot Tariff bill was ready for the President's signature. The Senate vote was 44 to 42, Borah standing with thirty Democrats and eleven insurgents against the bill. It raised the general average of duties from 33 to 40 per cent and the rates on farm products from 20 to 35 per cent. Over one thousand leading economists thought the new rates were far too high and urged the President to veto the bill, but on June 15, 1930, it became law with Hoover's signature.

After the tariff fight Borah was rarely invited to White House conferences. Hoover sided with the conservatives and accused Borah's coalition of causing business uncertainty and impeding recovery after the stock market panic in the fall of 1929. Borah bitterly resented this imputation, which steadily widened the gulf between him and Hoover.

Once more Borah was becoming an outcast, the role he played so well and evidently preferred. He saw his party under Hoover being taken over by the Hustons, Binghams, and other "agents of reactionary interests." Explaining his concept of the role of the representative in relation to the executive, Borah made no apologies for his differences with Hoover, some of which he had mentioned in the middle of the campaign. "Nothing is at last sacred but the integrity of your own mind," he wrote. He pointed out how on one issue or another, such as the recall of judges, he had even differed with Theodore Roosevelt whom he dearly loved.[38]

Since the early twenties Americans had forgotten the familiar doctrine of thrift. In 1928-29 borrowing became very heavy in expectation that prices would continue higher and allow selling at a profit. Those who sold bought other stock with the proceeds. Very few had the good sense Borah had to invest in government bonds, liquidate all other assets, and play safe. Then with all the suddenness of "a far-flung avalanche" came a succession of breaks in the stock market, culminating in the great crash of October 1929 which swept thousands to ruin.

In December 1930 Borah expressed open disgust that members of Congress showed reluctance to act in the face of deepening distress following the stock market crash. "This talk about Congress disturbing business," he said, "is an effort to assign a patriotic excuse for going home or going to Europe. It is a strange thing to me to have men fighting to get into Congress and telling the people all the things they want to do, and then making every possible excuse to go home and do nothing. I suggest they turn their salaries over to the hungry until they get back." He pointed out that legislation was needed to help, not hurt, business. Only Congress can legislate, he said, although he observed of late that Congress showed an inclination to delegate that power too.[39]

When the Senate adjourned in June 1930, Borah was a sick man. He visited the Johns Hopkins Hospital in Baltimore, where he was advised to take a long rest. Examinations showed that while no organic trouble existed, he was in a weakened condition. In recent years he had never been away from work except for a few days. The summers in Idaho afforded him some rest and relaxation, but the work in 1930 had been very heavy. During the last twenty-two days of the session the temperature ranged from 100° to 108°, and the humidity was usually 85 per cent. Overwork and the sultry weather caused a breakdown. He left Washington in June for the Poland Springs House in southwest Maine, planning to campaign in Idaho for re-election in the fall. He also planned a speaking tour through the West on behalf of the farm relief program. He was still determined to see through the export debenture. It was announced, however, that this tour had to be canceled for reasons of health.

His condition was greatly improved when he arrived in Boise on September 7, tanned and smiling, following two months' rest in the Maine woods. "I'm feeling fine and I'm glad to be home," he told friends who met him at the station. Boise welcomed him home that year with a mammoth picnic in Julia Davis Park. He remained there for six weeks prior to the election and stayed at the home of his old friend and law associate, Charles Cavanah.

Mrs. Borah joined him after a visit with relatives in Portland. The state convention was held at Idaho Falls in August. Borah was renominated with only four dissenting votes from Franklin County, whose delegates would not support him because he failed to vote for higher tariff duties on sugar. The convention enthusiastically ranked him with Stresemann, MacDonald, Briand, Gladstone, Clay, Themistocles, Sennacherib, and other world figures![40]

His election was taken for granted even by the rural public accountant, Joseph Tyler, who was his opponent. Tyler tried to withdraw from the race several times but yielded finally to friends who persuaded him that even Achilles had a vulnerable heel; perhaps Borah would have a bad year, they said. Save for a single canvas sign, which read REPUBLICAN HEADQUARTERS, flapping lazily from a second story window on Main Street, nothing about the neat capital of Idaho indicated that its leading citizen was up for re-election. There were no posters, no billboards, no signs in store windows, no political ads in the newspapers, and no banners displayed on Republican state headquarters. Borah's headquarters consisted of two rooms over a corner drugstore where any morning at 8:30 one could find a secretary and a stenographer answering mail. Even the plain smoked glass on the door of his temporary third-floor office carried no more than the legend, WILLIAM E. BORAH–ENTRANCE, painted in packing-case ink by the unsteady hand of a janitor. Distant newspapers had good reason to predict "Idaho will not give up Borah for the sake of strengthening discipline in the Republican Party. He will stay in the Senate as long as he lives."[41]

The election returns in November gave Borah 94,938 votes and Tyler 36,162.[42] Arthur Krock regarded him as "the strongest personal leader in Congress, who sways more members . . . by the position he assumes than any other man . . ." He thought that Borah and a handful of other senators could force another extra session if they chose to try.[43]

En route from Chicago to Washington after casting his vote in the Idaho election, Borah heard reports of a progressive plot to force an extra session to compel action on the export debenture, Muscle Shoals, and the Lame Duck Amendment. The old guard, as a countermove, threatened to force reorganization of the Senate and surrender control to the Democrats. Borah said that he would never join a filibuster. More suntanned and a little heavier in weight, he declared it was "superlative impudence" to imply that Democrats and Progressives had less regard for accomplishment in a crisis than regulars. Important issues would come before Congress, and he did not wish to be hurried in dealing with them. As for the threat to reorganize the Senate, he said: "I wish I were as sure of the Kingdom of Heaven as I am that the Republicans will never give up their Senate Chairmanships while they have the votes to retain them."[44]

As the winter of 1931 wore on, the depression grew steadily worse. The Hoover administration was all but paralyzed by a crisis that soon became a disaster. Hoover clung tenaciously to the trusted shibboleths: a balanced budget, rugged individualism, and a desire to aid business and stimulate public works. What was urgently needed was relief for the needy and unemployed.

In February 1931 a $25,000,000 relief bill was up for passage. House leaders, echoing the administration, declared they would not pass it. Borah made a blistering speech in the Senate: "This talk about setting a precedent or establishing the dole system is rank intellectual dishonesty. Congress is merely being asked to do what it has done again and again in this country and in foreign countries—appropriate money for the relief of people who are suffering from what we are pleased to call 'an act of God.'" Borah served notice that no more appropriations of any kind would pass until provision was made for supplying food to the hungry. He read a letter from a Red Cross worker in Tennessee describing the pitiable plight of a mother with three small children she was trying to feed on a concoction of soured meal and rancid pork meat. "Yet we are told," he continued, "that for the Government to feed this woman and her sick children would destroy her self respect and make a bad citizen of her. Does *anyone* believe it? It is a cowardly imputation on the helpless. I resent it and I repudiate it."

When Borah finished this speech, senators and spectators leaped to their feet, cheering and applauding. Barkley, McKellar, and Robinson, all Democrats, rushed to grab his hand. His effort was a ringing challenge to the administration and its leaders.[45] Borah was a voice crying in the wilderness of a bankrupt economic philosophy, preparing the way for the direct action of the New Deal.

The German government appealed to the world in June 1931 to

reduce reparations as an alternative to a catastrophe which would engulf all of Europe. Borah reversed his former position on the war debts by issuing a statement that revision of German reparations was expedient economically and fundamentally just. He had always favored the reduction of allied war debts as a *quid pro quo* for the reduction of armaments. Now he asserted: "To grind the German working people into unspeakable misery would be a calamity the evil consequences of which, to say nothing of the inhumanity—no tongue can properly express."[46]

A few weeks later Hoover responded to the international banking crisis by announcing a moratorium postponing for one year all payment on intergovernmental debts, reparations, and relief payments. Congress was not in session, but the President secured the consent of twenty-one key senators and about eighteen representatives. Borah at first called it "a splendid step in the right direction." Europe must be ready to accept the proposal, he said, and follow it up with a program adjusting her own affairs; otherwise no good could come of it. "If Europe cannot conquer her suspicion, her antagonism, her hatred, how is it possible for our people to be of any service to them?" he asked. All during the summer Borah was in direct communication with the President. They went over the entire question of debts, and Hoover was convinced that it was unnecessary to call a special session of Congress or a conference of the European countries involved. Privately, however, Borah later wrote a friend: "I do not regard the moratorium of any great value in and of itself. It will prove valuable only in case we utilize the time given to do all the things . . . essential to recovery. Reparations must be drastically adjusted, armaments reduced, and the Versailles Treaty revised, before Europe can possibly recover. These things seem impossible but not so impossible as the recovery of Europe without them."[47]

By September Borah was still clamoring for government support for the victims of the depression. He stated:

If the wealth of the country does not voluntarily contribute to the end that we may take care of them, there is only one thing to do, and that is to feed these people from the treasury of the United States, and increase the Income Tax, particularly in the higher brackets, to enable us to do it . . . If the public dole system is established in this country,

> it will be forced by those who, having the means, refuse to do their part in feeding the hungry. If the great wealth . . . of the entire world were a bit more constructive in its selfishness, if it would but learn that unfertilized land cannot yield forever, our economic troubles would be as evanescent as rainbows.

Will Rogers, who admired Borah unqualifiedly, added: "It's all right to say the Government don't support the people, but who got the people in the shape they are if it wasn't the mismanagement of the Government? . . . Them's true words, Willie. No wonder they won't run you for President."[48]

During the second week in March 1931 insurgents in Congress arranged for a Progressive Conference, to be held at the Carlton Arms Hotel in Washington. Borah made the opening speech, concentrating on agriculture and declaring that a solution must be found for the problems confronting it. He spoke in favor of the export debenture plan and said that despite its promises, the administration had done nothing toward a permanent settlement of the farm problem. Even Borah with his limited grasp of the elements involved, recognized that the Agricultural Marketing Act did not fulfill campaign promises. However, when it came to the task of formulating an affirmative program, the conference floundered. The three outstanding Progressives (Borah, Norris, and the younger La Follette) were leaders, and their individualism superseded all else. Not one of them was able to suggest an economic program in definite and practical terms which could readily be converted into legislation.

After a long interval Borah was again invited to lunch with the President. This was regarded as an effort on Hoover's part to recapture the progressive support he had lost. Will Rogers commented: "You can't afford to be on the outs with Borah—that is, if you want to get anything done." They spent nearly two hours discussing Haiti and Nicaragua prior to Hoover's trip to the Virgin Islands.

The breakdown of Coolidge-Hoover prosperity was a bitter dose for the Republican party, which had persuaded the country not only that the prosperity was genuine but that the party had invented it. Early in 1931 there were faint signs of improvement and administration sources boasted prematurely that the country was on the road to recovery, but by March these uncertain tokens vanished and the depression worsened.

The new Senate of the Seventy-Second Congress, which convened in December 1931, comprised forty-eight Republicans, forty-seven Democrats, and one farmer-laborer, "But actually we had no more than 40 real Republicans," wrote Hoover, "as Senators Borah, Norris, Cutting and others of the left wing were against us."[49]

Borah thought that the depression was caused by the uneconomic, intolerant, and ruthless policies growing out of World War I, and carried on as if war were still in progress. Writing in the *Exchangite,* he quoted Mantagu Norman, head of the Bank of England, as saying that economic difficulties were so vast that he could not see through to the end. Borah maintained that the depression was foreseen by no less an authority than Mr. Norman himself. He said: "Let us snap out of this gloom, realize our awful condition, but realize it with courage to undo what brought it on. In the presence of the mistakes of the Versailles Treaty, reparations, debts, demonetization of silver in the Orient, of political interference with trade and commerce, we seem paralyzed with fear and doubt, whereas we ought to recognize the task and go to it."[50]

In an interview with Theodore Knappen, Borah said nothing in the world was more important to the well-being of our internal affairs than the economic stabilization of the world, particularly of Europe. "The death's head at every prosperity festival in this country today is hopeless Europe."[51] The central feature of Borah's proposed solution to the crisis was the need for a world economic conference. He planned to make this the dominant subject in the December session of Congress. His first call for the conference came in a radio speech at Minneapolis on July 23, 1932, in which he mapped out a four-point program: the restoration of world trade (which had for its basis the recognition of Soviet Russia), the reorganization of our monetary system (including the remonetization of silver to benefit Oriental peoples), the easing of the pressure of war debts, and the revision of the Versailles Treaty. Borah said: "We have been living in a fool's paradise talking about disarmament and better times . . . ever since the Versailles Treaty was signed, we have been drifting toward the rapids." Hoover showed some willingness to write off Allied debts by shipping surplus American farm products to Europe; but first, Borah insisted, the load of reparations and armaments costs had to be lifted from Europe's shoulders, and the only means of doing this was through a world economic conference.[52]

At a Berlin convention of the Steel Helmet War Veterans' Organization, Colonel Duesterburg said as a curtain raiser: "Every ex-serviceman in Germany stands behind the government's efforts to obtain equality in armaments with other nations and to bring about the revision of the Versailles Treaty." When Borah was asked to comment, he replied that Germany was justified in her demands for equality; however, it should be brought about by other nations reducing their armaments rather than a German build-up.[53] The situation was more serious since the nations engaged in the arms race had denounced war as an arbiter between nations. He said: ". . . our deeds impeach every syllable of that treaty."[54] He thought the marvel of all history was the patience with which men and women submitted to burdens unnecessarily laid upon them by their governments, especially in the instance of armaments.

While he saw the economic crisis of 1930-33 partly as a product of world conditions, unlike the administration which insisted that world economic dislocations alone were responsible, he found ample domestic causes for the most costly economic disaster in American history. He pressed for curbing loans to speculators and supported the Federal Reserve Board's program for curtailing broker's loans and the abolition of the daily settlement plan then in vogue on the American market. He wanted to substitute the weekly or fortnightly system used in Europe, wherein a loan could not be called for two weeks during which period the interest rate was definitely fixed. "Stock market speculation in this country is almost a sumptuary habit, like drinking," he commented. "Law will not easily curb it. To gamble with a view to getting rich quick is nowadays almost as human as to err in other directions. Perhaps salvation will never come for the sucker in Wall Street, as Mellon suggests, 'until gentlemen prefer bonds.'"[55]

The Progressives in the Senate were outspoken in their demand for more adequate legislation for unemployment relief. By 1932 there were thirteen million unemployed, and less than one fourth of them were receiving public aid. This prompted the introduction of the La Follette-Costigan bill for direct relief to the unemployed, debated in the Senate in February 1932, and the remarkable statement from Senator Fess of Ohio that the character of the American people would be impaired if they were given the dole. The federal government can not help the unemployed, he said, because they are poor business risks. Borah lashed back at the Ohio Republican: "He [Fess] says if we keep them from starving we will undermine their character. I denounce that as a libel of American citizenship. Ninety percent of our people would return to work tomorrow. They would scorn your charity. They would refuse your gifts if you would give them the opportunity to get to work . . . You may call this a dole but hungry people call it something to eat. A government which does not protect its people is flying a flag which is a dirty rag and contaminates the air."[56]

The economic breakdown was so serious that Borah was willing to take unusual steps. There was one thing more sacred to him than the Constitution, and that was the welfare of a depressed people. Men were driven to entertain measures which in ordinary times would have received no consideration. They were doing things for which there was no authority in the Constitution. "We are compelled to act. Self preservation still remains the supreme law." According to Borah, theory disappears when people are hungry.

The battle went on for three hours on the Senate floor. Visibly angry and at times breathless, Borah exchanged a flow of caustic remarks and sarcasm with Fess, who became so ardent in his assault on the federal relief measure that he split his knuckles rapping the top of his desk! For the next ten minutes he stood with the bleeding hand wrapped in a handkerchief and continued to speak. He was constantly interrupted by Borah, whom he ordered to sit down. When Borah finally got the floor, he said precedent had no more to do with the federal government's saving its citizens from starvation than social precedence on a sinking ship. He maneuvered Fess into admitting his willingness to support the creation of the Reconstruction Finance Corporation, though he opposed this relief measure for the unemployed. The La Follette-Costigan bill failed by a vote of 48 to 35. "Just think," commented Will Rogers, "if a hungry man had to stand outside and wait not until he gets relief but just 'till all the plans for his relief was read . . . If the hungry could eat paper it would solve the food problem for the whole winter."[57]

On one matter Borah seemed to agree with Hoover. He declared there would not be a dollar voted for the veterans as long as they remained in Washington. "I will not vote for the soldier's bonus," he stated emphatically, "and even if I had been for the passage of such a bill I would be against it now with these veterans in Washington seeking by their bodily presence . . . to compel Congress to pass this legislation. Nor will I vote a dollar for them for any purpose while they remain in the national capital."[58]

Borah thought "the boys" made a mistake going to Washington. The only reason they would not get the cash bonus, he told Paul Leach in an interview, was because the country was not in a position to pay it. There was no legal reason why they should not have been in Washington, but when Congress handled the matter in a dignified way, Borah thought they should have packed up and left. When Congress failed to accede to their demands, there was no reason, as far as he could see, for getting excited. After troops expelled the veterans from their shacks with tear gas, Borah commented: "I can't see any justification for their treatment last week." Whether such action was justified or not, the event served to drive home to observers the seriousness of the nation's economic condition.

Borah's reputation as an oracle on foreign affairs reached its zenith in October 1931 when Pierre Laval, the premier of France, visited Hoover in Washington to discuss economic problems and French security. It was not to the White House nor the State Department, but to the Idaho senator's office that the thirty French journalists accompanying Laval flocked for an interview arranged by Henry Stimson. The meeting had to be moved to the Foreign Relations Committee room because Borah's office was too small.

They were warned at the outset that he was expressing personal views, not those of the Senate. He was ready to agree to the cancellation of Allied war debts and reparations in their entirety. If they could not be canceled, then they must be cut back; the time was past for moratoriums. He put his foot down against any French security pact, rumored as the real purpose of Laval's visit. France would have to determine for herself whether she was in danger of attack; Borah would not quarrel with her judgment. Europe would have to consent to a peaceful revision of the peace treaties with Germany, Austria, and Hungary or there would be another war. Questioned more closely on this, he admitted he wanted the arrangements relating to the Polish Corridor, Danzig, and Upper Silesia changed "by arbitration"; he also wanted the restoration of Hungary's boundaries as they were before the Trianon Treaty, making possible Hungarian economic integration. The recognition of Russia was essential to the improvement of the European situation. He reiterated his hostility to any plan for collective security because it meant "making eternal the status quo."

Borah's remarks created a sensation. When they were recounted to Laval, he replied acidly (in rough translation): "I have not come . . . to engage in polemics with Senator Borah and to discuss the revision of the Versailles Treaty. Tell the . . . journalists not to be disturbed by the words of a senator which represent only his . . . opinion."[59]

After Laval's hot words reached the editorial desks on the Quai d'Orsay, the telegraph wires began to burn with pleas for a qualifying statement or retraction. None was forthcoming, for Laval feared it would be interpreted as yielding to Borah's demands. Borah himself was surprised and puzzled by Laval's reaction, and began to surmise that he was being made the culprit in a delicate situation where some excuse was needed for the almost inevitable failure of the Hoover-Laval talks. Although Borah's remarks to the French press yielded him a bumper crop of cheers and jeers from all the capitals of Europe and the United States, seasoned observers felt he had rendered a distinct service; he had spoken at the request of the French press, giving the kind of insight into significant American opinion which could have been conveyed in no other way. The French, who were realists, would find it useful in the months to come.[60]

At a stag dinner given by Stimson, Borah and Laval, through an interpreter, had an opportunity to exchange views under more pleasant circumstances. Borah asked about disarmament and revision of the Versailles Treaty. Laval told him there were no prospects for revision in the foreseeable future and disarmament in France would only be possible after she received security guarantees against future aggression. When Stimson and David Reed of Pennsylvania joined the conversation and questioned Laval about the French attitude toward Germany, Borah was struck by the candor of the cigar-smoking peasant from Auvergne in his reply: "If you people will quit loaning money to Germany and encouraging Germany, we can take care of Germany and we can bring about an adjustment, or settlement which ought to obtain." One of the first to leave Woodley, Borah told reporters before entering his waiting automobile: "We had a very pleasant visit . . . About all I can say is that we were not any closer together at the end than we were at the beginning."[61]

When Borah quit the capital for a much-needed rest in Idaho in the summer of 1931, it troubled Hoover's advisers to learn that he took with him for careful study a mass of correspondence from all over the country urging him to declare his candidacy in 1932. Arriving at the Owyhee Hotel in Boise, he enjoyed his first Idaho meal of mountain trout before confronting the reporters awaiting him in the lobby. They found him reticent on the forthcoming campaign. When informed that Progressives had launched a "Borah for President" boom, he said, "Let's talk of something more feasible."[62]

Signs of revolt against the conservative wing of the Republican party were more manifest than ever in 1932. Borah was considered by some a most likely figure to profit by this rebellion of western Republicans against Hoover. This was deemed the ideal time for him to break loose without risking his Senate seat. His term expired March 4, 1937. The Progressives formed the nucleus of an excellent campaign organization, and he had the prospect of financial support from Salmon O. Levinson. Borah was certain to ride along on the current wave of ultranationalism, then an important by-product of the depression. However, he remained skeptical, convinced that the character of the party in the South would assure Hoover of its delegations, while the reactionary sentiment of the East was with him as well. Despite the depression, Borah decided that this was an unbeatable combination.

He celebrated the Fourth of July with a speech at Parma and later was heard at Lewiston, Caldwell, and Nampa (Idaho), Spokane (Washington), and Big Bend (Oregon). He dedicated a monument to pioneer women at Cottonwood and ended his vacation at Moscow, home of the University of Idaho, where he took part in the ceremonies dedicating Levinson's William E. Borah Foundation for the Outlawry of War on September 24-25. As he traveled eastward, his admirers at Sioux City, Iowa, questioned him about his candidacy in 1932. "Show me how to get by the convention," was his retort. In Washington he told reporters: "It is politically axiomatic to say that a party is bound in its fundamental interest to renominate a president in office. Anything else would be suicide. Sometimes a party may be headed for the political graveyard anyway but to repudiate its own record by refusing an incumbent . . . the renomination would amount to asking to be sent to the cemetery."[63]

Ever since his experience with the labor disturbances in north Idaho during the 1890's Borah had been a strong advocate of enforced prohibition. Martial law had been proclaimed over that troubled area, and he had been permitted to observe firsthand the orderly, peaceful results following a ban on the sale of intoxicating drinks. Personally dry, in spite of his twinkling eye, comfortable jowl, and double chin, Borah never made a real "temperance speech," but it was true that his reform work was responsible for helping to remove drinking and gambling saloons from the main street of Boise, which soon came to resemble a respectable thoroughfare. Thereafter he became one of the most determined prohibitionists in American life. He would have accepted prohibition by local option, in keeping with his customary deference to states rights, but the liquor traffic, which he called a "curse to humanity," presented a unique problem in interstate commerce; he soon reached the conclusion that federal law presented the only solution to the problem of enforcement in a dry state which could not prevent a bordering state from shipping liquor across state lines.

Speaking at the Presbyterian General Assembly in Baltimore, the Idahoan announced his contempt for spirits with these words:

Whether sold in the open saloon or the brothel, its natural haunt, or secretly purveyed in defiance of law, the wicked stuff works its demoralization and ruin on individuals, communities and states. From the time it issues from the coiled and copper-colored worm in the distillery until it empties into the hell of crime, dishonor and death, misery and poverty and remorse mark its maledict course.[64]

In a memorable debate sponsored by the Roosevelt club of Boston in April 1927, Nicholas Murray Butler chose the affirmative position on the proposition: "Should the Republican National Platform of 1928 advocate the repeal of the 18th Amendment?" Borah took the negative. Six of the nine unofficial judges selected by the Boston *Herald* awarded the 6:3 decision to Borah. In his argument Borah stated that the American people would never consent to the repeal of the Eighteenth Amendment until it had a fair trial. He asked for a period of twenty-five years in which to test the dry law. Then it would be time enough for the Republican party to declare for repeal, after they had attempted and failed in enforcement. He wanted his party to fight the evil of liquor as it had fought slavery. He branded modification of the Volstead Act as a matter of sheer political expediency to enable candidates to get by the election without revealing their position. The proposal for repeal, he said, was born of confusion; it would rot the pillars of government inside half a century. Uncle Sam should not be put into the liquor business. Mr. Charles G. Staiger of New York City, who heard the Boston debate, told the author that after leaving Symphony Hall he headed for the first "bootleg joint" he could find and ordered a double Scotch. Borah's argument was so convincing that he feared otherwise he might never have touched liquor again.[65]

When the evidence poured in that enforcement was breaking down, Borah demanded a nationwide referendum on prohibition that would coincide with the election of 1928. He also announced his opposition to the proposed New York referendum which sought to modify the Volstead Act. Once the states secured the authority to decide what constitutes the content of intoxicating liquor, he said anarchy would result. New Yorkers in particular resented his slurs on the state's legislative proposal for modification. Congressman Fiorello La Guardia stated that the law never could be enforced and gibed at Borah that there was more drinking per capita in Idaho than there was in New York City. When the Wickersham Commission, appointed by Hoover to investigate the failure in law enforcement, issued its report, Borah showed little interest. He maintained it could not make any clearer the meaning of the law nor contribute any new facts. The trouble lay in no real determination to enforce the law. "The snoopers do not snoop sufficiently efficiently." He made the damaging assertion that there would be no enforcement until the existing personnel in the Treasury Department was replaced from top to bottom.[66]

On May 10, 1932, Senators Borah and Fess attended a luncheon conference at the White House with the President and James R. Garfield, Hoover's choice to head the platform committee at the approaching Chicago convention. Hoover claims that he told Borah at this meeting that the Eighteenth Amendment and the Volstead Act could not be enforced and that the whole question should be returned to the states. "To my great surprise," narrates Hoover, "Borah said that he agreed with me and would go along." Hoover pointed out that highly important witnesses to Borah's attitude included Secretary Wilbur, Secretary Mills, and Postmaster General Brown. Hoover's plan, as stated, appeared indefinite and ambiguous. If Borah really understood it and agreed to it, he soon changed his mind. Garfield left the meeting with three different proposals for a prohibition plank. One was Borah's, stating that the Eighteenth Amendment was written into the Constitution by the will of the people of thirty-six states and could be taken out in no other way.

Borah's views were disquieting to party leaders who were convinced that wet sentiment was in the ascendance. Borah and Hoover were at loggerheads on several other issues including the export debenture, the World Court, the recognition of Russia, and federal relief for the unemployed. The only interest they held in common had been their joint determination to enforce the Eighteenth Amendment; even that disappeared after Borah, paying one more visit to the White House, became convinced that Hoover, under pressure, would agree to a resubmission plan. He then told the President that political parties could not bind Congress to any set prohibition course, thus throwing the whole situation into new uncertainty. As Borah had predicted, no serious opposition developed to Hoover's renomination in June. Confronted by probable defeat, no one challenged him. After a sharp fight the so-called "wet-dry plank" was finally adopted, a vague formula proposing a constitutional amendment which would allow the states to deal with the liquor problem, subject always to the power of the federal government to protect those states where prohibition existed. Hoover was nominated on the first ballot. After Borah had called the plank "the queerest combination of hypocrisy and insincerity" he had ever seen, Hoover and his advisers held hurried conferences, recognizing the importance of the Idaho senator's influence in the campaign. They made every effort to win him over, but to no avail.[67] On June 30 the Idaho renegade precipitated a country-wide sensation by sinking an ax into the Republican platform. In a forty-minute speech he declared: "From a reading of the text nobody can tell where the Republican party stands on prohibition." He held that the majority of the convention delegates and their leaders were for what he termed "naked repeal." That, he explained, was repeal without any proposal for a substitute system. He served notice that he would carry the issue to the people.

In the campaign which followed, Borah won the title, "William the Silent." He felt no purpose could be served by supporting Hoover, since everyone knew that they differed on all important issues. During the campaign he never even mentioned Hoover's name. Interviewed in Chicago, he was asked if he would support the party ticket. "I haven't put in yet," was his tantalizing reply.[68] On August 9 he left for Idaho, where the campaign turned into a private affair between the ursine senator and his constituents. The Idaho voters learned all about issues and nothing about candidates from Borah.

This does not mean that he gave support to the Democrats. On four subjects he disagreed with their nominee, Franklin D. Roosevelt, even more than with Hoover: prohibition, farm relief, reparations, and the bonus. Although Borah did not wish for a Democratic victory, he did nothing substantial to prevent it; it was clear by November that he was resigned to the inevitable. When pressed, he explained he was not active in the campaign because both platforms failed in his estimation to meet the real issue for the American people, the economic crisis.[69] At Burley he demanded the scaling down of farm mortgages. When it came to spending, he said: "you can't tell a Republican from a Democrat." At Nampa he attacked Al Smith for his antiprohibition utterances. All public questions for Smith, he asserted, are reduced to one: "Give us beer." Asked by a reporter if these remarks meant he would vote for Hoover, he said yes but that he had no plans to support the Republican candidate.

When Borah returned to Washington after Roosevelt's election, his first announcement was that no modification of the Volstead Act would be allowed in the coming session. Observers were amazed at his supreme disregard for what had happened. He continued to assume that he had his old power of vetoing legislation as though the Republicans had won the election! "Hereafter," said the New York *Times*, "it would not do for him to set himself up as ruler of the Senate or expect the world to tremble when he made one of his pontifical utterances. Like Samson, the Lord is departed from him."[70]

Nevertheless, since there was no one to take his place, Borah continued to instruct Europe, admonish his countrymen, and criticize the party in power. While others were fumbling in their pockets for their train tickets and vanishing from Washington for years to come, perhaps for ever, Borah stayed on. After eight eventful years of service, with the ratification of some 168 treaties to his credit, the sixty-seven-year-old Idahoan turned over the chairmanship of the Foreign Relations Committee to a Democrat, Key Pittman of Nevada. However, the loss of this post was not expected to result in any great diminution of his influence, for he exercised whatever power he possessed quite independent of office. His earnestness, patriotism, eloquence, and energy made him the one senator who approached the position held by Clay and Webster before 1850. By nature he was far better fitted to work in a minority than a majority.

Few Americans have enjoyed the power which Borah exercised during the twenties. Holding a pivotal position in the Senate, he felt himself privileged to use the prestige of his office to promote the influence of his opinions. To liberals he represented the comforting thesis that the Republican party was no exclusive appanage of corporate greed and political reaction. To intellectuals he represented the voice of conscience in national politics. He was both the victim and beneficiary of a system by which a state with fewer inhabitants than Baltimore was permitted a great influence over national policy. He used his studious habit of mind, capacity for hard work, and genius for political utterance to commit his country to policies, not all of which have stood the test of time. During the long hours spent at his desk he studied the will of the people. Never once did he speak with indifference of the aspirations of the populace, and as a result his errors were of fact rather than of spirit. Though he was called everything from an opportunist to a bolshevik, no one ever seriously questioned his honesty or the quality of his mind. He could never be accused of cant or blind partisanship.

His policies could be embodied in a single concept—moral law. Ironically, he was a western copy of the Wilsonian model, the moralist in politics. Standing less for intellectual insight than moral courage, he thought American policy must reflect the moral conscience rather than the immediate mundane interests of the American people. Believing that the way to eradicate human evil was to forbid it by law, national or international, he applied this principle to prohibition, disarmament, and even war. He seemed to think that a declaration of justice was equal to its realization.[71]

One way in which to view Borah's chairmanship of the Foreign Relations Committee is as a continuous and somewhat effective educational influence on him. He needed the education badly, but the reasons for this have not been generally understood. In both foreign and domestic matters one easy explanation for his devious course was his passion for wreckage. He was naturally a dissenter, a destructive statesman. No one since Jerry Simpson had been so prompt in attacking other men's schemes and so weak in suggesting substitutes. He was accused of vanity in frequently taking the negative side in a period full of "yes" men. In all this there is a measure of truth. He was a strong personality surrounded largely by negative characters. He had the frontiersman's simple distrust of too much law and too complex a government. However, no easy formula of dissent explains Borah. The Washington Conference, the Kellogg Pact, his proposals for a World Court, and his attitude toward the debt settlement, along with his perennial plea for the recognition of Russia, were all based on arguments that were constructive. To talk of him as merely a wrecker is absurd.[72]

His course in domestic and foreign affairs is often explained as a natural expression of the western spirit. This idea contains a measure of truth, but if pushed very far it becomes fallacious. If he was ever progressive, it was not only because of his environment but also the result of his political experience, the nature of the Senate, its long term of six years, his success in putting through certain progressive measures, and the nature of his constituency. If he was ever an isolationist, other westerners like Porter McCumber, Knute Nelson, and Franklin K. Lane were vigorously opposed to isolationist views. Moreover, Borah had been for twenty-five years more a resident of the East than the West, for he was often to be found in Washington between sessions and he was certainly not guided by the dictates of his constituents. No senator acted with greater independence. He dared to defy the voters, as in voting against the constitutional amendment for women's suffrage after Idaho women had held the ballot for fifteen years.

The fundamental weakness in Borah's initial approach to foreign problems lay deeper than any of these surface explanations. It was rooted in a basic conflict between his mind and his emotions. In him there was combined a set of conservative traditions drawn from the distant past together with his own natural progressive tendencies, which he gave full play in his first term. His record was that of a man who wished to be a complete realist but was unable to escape certain romantic prepossessions, which led to wavering and inconsistency. No senator prided himself more on his devotion to principle and obedience to logic. He was the sworn enemy of sham. Nevertheless, as a matter of fact, he always clung desperately to a few unrealistic and illogical convictions which were implanted in his mind early in life and nurtured by his western environment. These emotions may be divided into three groups.

One was his opinion that Europe has a set of primary interests wholly different from ours, that the designs of European nations were wholly sinister, and that European displomacy was skilled in overreaching younger, more honest peoples. Much of his opposition to the League was based on this belief. He railed against England and painted for his listeners lurid pictures of India, wallowing in ignorance and burdened with taxes after more than a hundred years of despotic rule; Egypt, robbed of her birthright; and Ireland, carrying on a seven-century struggle for independence.

The next few years saw Britain freeing Egypt and Ireland and helping devise a new constitution for India, while the United States proved its self-governing capacity by the scandals of the Harding administration.

His beliefs remained unshakable because they were linked with another of his emotional convictions: that the fathers of the republic were a group whose wisdom has never been equaled in any country or era and whose admonitions to their own time must be followed by succeeding generations. The suggestion that not all eighteenth-century ideas fitted the twentieth was treason to Borah. He could never force his mind to give it honest scrutiny because his emotions stood in the way.

The third and most important of his prepossessions was that the United States needed a fierce national patriotism. He thought the League would sterilize nationalism. As a step in the direction of internationalism, it was a step in the wrong direction. More than one of his early speeches was devoted to the same militant gospel preached by Theodore Roosevelt. His question "Are we yielding our Americanism before the onrushing tide of revolutionary internationalism?" could have been asked by either of them. Roosevelt never had a more earnest admirer than Borah, even after they parted political company. With a certain whimsey Borah said: "Since Roosevelt left the White House there has been no leader of the Republican Party I could cooperate with."[73]

He was slow to realize how rapidly the modern world moves and how vast a change had overtaken the country in its development. His robust honesty constantly required him to face the facts of a world where a Wall Street crash shook Europe and where European poverty meant forty-cent wheat in the Mississippi Valley. His romantic prepossessions made him cling to Washington's idea of 1796 on America's place in the world.

In spite of this, Borah always wished to keep an open mind on complex problems, with the result that his service as head of the Foreign Relations Committee witnessed the weakening of his romantic notions and a steady extension of the field in which his logic governed. In the early thirties he showed some hopeful signs of a changing attitude. He no longer spoke of European democracies as a gang of criminals. Similarly, he took a less impatient tone regarding disarmament. After the depression began, his stand on reparations, war debts, and the economic problems of the world was steadily liberalized. He hailed the agreement at Lausanne to reduce German reparations to a trifle as "the hope of the world." Repeatedly he told audiences that the world's peace and happiness, including our own, depended on the rehabilitation of Europe. In his radio speech of July 23, 1932, he earnestly urged the calling of a world economic conference.[74]

That Borah's conception of world affairs, of the subleties and complexities in power politics, of the real nature of the causes of war, and of the interplay in national interests which underlie world tensions was imperfect, no one will deny. Assuredly there was an element of obstruction, impracticality, and starry-eyed idealism in some of the causes he championed or blocked. He never denied the charges of inconsistency hurled at his conduct; neither did he resent the criticism of his destructive tactics. He was proudest of the several causes, especially the League of Nations, which he helped to defeat. If he was incapable of creating effective policies of his own, he was a powerful force in preventing other men's policies from going into effect. He was against many things because he was so passionately in favor of a few others, notably the democratic system and what he called the democratic virtues. One consistency at least runs through all he said and did: he was unassailably American. In what he affirmed and denied, he could never be mistaken for the citizen of another country. Historians in future generations will continue to have a field day wrestling with his enigmatic personality and the almost unfathomable dimensions of his political philosophy, for he did not, as a public man, fit neatly into any category such as conservative, radical, reformer, administrator, or liberal. He shared Jefferson's and Lincoln's faith in the common man. He believed in an orderly, efficient, and powerful national government. He was a curious mixture of the conservatism of Hamilton and the liberalism of Jefferson, who championed the right of the states to order their internal affairs for themselves. Knowing that America enjoyed an effortless superiority, he would not bargain with her sovereignty to save the world.

In an assessment of his merits Borah deserves the same justice he championed in his lifetime. We cannot hold him responsible for his failure to formulate a workable peace plan. Perhaps his World Court plan was impractical, but so were some of the features of the Harding-Hughes plan, which proved ineffective in operation. Disarmament still plagues the heads of states. If Borah was an enigma, so was our interventionist policy in the Far East and our isolationist policy in Europe. His failure was that of the era he represented. For recovery and stability in Europe a more active role in European affairs was demanded of the United States, requiring for an indefinite future a formidable military power resting ultimately on a philosophy of force to maintain order, an idea distasteful to Borah and Anglo-Saxons generally.

XVI A Chapter in American-Soviet Relations

> I therefore contend, that as we never scrupled to treat with the princes of the House of Bourbon on account of their rapacity, . . . so we ought not to refuse to treat with their republican imitators.
>
> —Charles James Fox

As the year 1933 dawned, only one of the great powers still held out against renewing diplomatic relations with the Soviet Union, and this hostility of the United States was shared throughout the Western hemisphere. Latin America continued to adhere to the principles of the joint nonrecognition agreement of 1920.[1] Senator Borah never agreed with the policy; one of the most persistent efforts of his public career, stretching over sixteen years between World War I and the Roosevelt administration, was his campaign for the admission of Russia into the family of nations.

The key to his attitude on Russia was his sympathy for the underdog. While he did not agree with the principles underlying the Russian Revolution, he sympathized with the efforts of the lower classes to increase their power and better their condition. He had nothing to gain politically from this attitude; in fact he stood to lose from it because most of his Idaho constituency and the American people were conspicuously opposed to recognition. Labor was against it; so were business and the clergy.

Borah's views on Russia were colored by his study of the French Revolution, of which he knew more than anyone except special students, for that episode fascinated him as a moment in history when thought became action, when philosophy was translated into violence, and when men tried to transform ideals into reality. He made the inevitable comparison between the Russian and French revolutions. Our government had been quick to recognize the revolutionary French government; he thought we owed as much to Russia.

Borah's position on Russia offers the most serious challenge to interpretations which classify him as an uncompromising isolationist. Refusal to recognize a government because it did not meet American specifications was a policy inaugurated by Presidents Roosevelt and Wilson, and which was continued on a bipartisan basis after 1917. American policy was based on the assumption that what the United States disliked was wrong and doomed to failure. Washington did what it could, for example, in extending postwar famine relief to assure the Russian people of our friendship; at the same time it did all it could to weaken the government in Russia. Nonrecognition was more than an expression of disapproval; it indicated official hopes for the end of the Soviet Union.

The attitude of liberals toward Russia, for the most part, was one of fidelity to an illusion rather than loyalty to a conspiracy. The liberals offered convincing reasons for their support. Conservatives argued for recognition from the sound practical standpoint of increased trade. Borah combined this economic argument with several others. He found the revolutionary government no less tyrannical than the czarist government which preceded it. We owed recognition, he said, to the Russian people. He maintained it was a waste of time to separate the people from a government which, whatever its other failings, was improving their lives. More influence could be brought to bear on the development of the Russian Revolution by extending recognition than by maintaining a posture of antagonism. Official policy, he noted, was designed to strengthen Russia and Germany, driving them together. Alliances against them would endanger the peace of Europe. He finally announced that the United States could never expect to check Japan or Germany without the aid of the Russians, whom he believed could be trusted.

Because of his power in the Senate, Borah became the leader of those who criticized the practice of blaming Russia for all the troubles in the world. The United States, they submitted, should work with movements of nationalism and domestic reform everywhere. On the whole this group, and especially Borah, was more successful in modifying American policy toward Latin America and China than toward Russia. The depression did more to force American policy makers to re-examine their position with regard to checking Germany and Japan than did criticism from Borah.

William A. Williams agrees with Richard Leopold that in studying the twenties certain stereotypes have tended to mislead us. As if to contradict the thesis that the American public wanted nothing more than to withdraw from the turmoil of foreign affairs, there were actually more than one thousand organizations for the study of international relations in 1926. Foreign travel was constantly expanding. There were different concepts of the national interest and wide disagreement over means to be employed in extending American power. Williams insists that Borah sought to extend American power; he never sought to isolate the United States:

> . . . Senator Borah was anything but an isolationist in his concept of the power of economics and ideas. Borah not only favored the recognition of the Soviet Union in order to influence the development of the Bolshevik Revolution, and as a check against Japanese expansion in Asia, but also argued that American economic policies were intimately connected with foreign policy crises.[2]

Soon after our entry into World War I Borah made a speech in the Senate pleading for a clear-cut statement of war aims and for an unremitting effort to vanquish Germany, keeping Russia in the war. He said: "If there is any power to be exerted in prayer, the American people may well offer a prayer at this hour for the guidance and preservation and success of Kerensky [leader of the moderate revolutionary faction which set up a liberal provisional government in Russia]. If this gallant leader, standing at the head of his disorganized forces, meets either the assassin's bullet or failure, it means a leaven which will disorganize and demoralize the situation beyond any power that language could portray." Borah warned that with Russia out of the war, a million American soldiers would find European graves.[3]

In the October revolution the Kerensky government was overthrown and the Bolshevists, under Lenin's leadership, seized power. Early in 1918 they sued for peace with Germany. Borah was extremely suspicious. He thought it was the duty of the United States to exert its influence before a separate peace between Russia and Germany was signed. "We should send men powerful to deal with such a situation, not for a visit but to stay until order is brought out of chaos. We ought to determine to defeat Germany in this game; otherwise we shall have some difficulty in defeating her upon the field of battle. Unless we do something . . . it would be well to modify our pretensions as to making the world safe for democracy."

Borah thought that there could be no possible conflict of interests between Russia and the United States. He was under the impression that Russia needed and wanted American leadership, while a separate treaty would place her under the control of Germany, which could offer a steadying power. Accusing Germany of turning the revolution in Russia to her advantage, he urged the sending of a commission composed of men sympathetic toward Russia's aims, such as Raymond Robins and perhaps even Borah himself. In other words, he strongly favored the kind of unofficial support given to the American revolutionary cause by France, Poland, and Prussia. "What did Kosciusko know?" he asked. "The healing, uplifting power of heroic deeds often puts to shame the cold calculations and foresight of the most practical."[4]

After the treaty of Brest-Litovsk was signed in 1918, Borah continued to deplore the lack of a sane American policy toward Russia. He again compared the Russian uprising to the French Revolution and pointed out that behind a handful of traitors was a noble people struggling to be free. "Trotsky is an incident," he asserted. "Lenin is of no concern in the final adjustment of things. But the Russian people are of . . . concern and are entitled to the sympathy of . . . people . . . everywhere . . . Let us have faith in humanity and the cause of freedom . . . and go in every way possible to the aid of Russia."[5]

Most objectionable from the American standpoint was the Russian revolutionary government's repudiation of all the debts assumed under the czarist and Kerensky governments. Borah, writing Governor Stokes of New Jersey, was naïvely optimistic in judging that Russia would assume all her legitimate indebtedness. Moreover, he thought the conduct of the Allies was a crime "almost as stupendous in its consequences as the war itself."

I have never in all my reading run across anything so utterly unstatesmanlike . . . as Lloyd George's whirligig policy with reference to Russia. At the very time he was sending the peace delegates to Lenin and Trotsky he was furnishing arms to . . . White Russian or counter-revolutionary leaders. Such has been his duplicitous and . . . inconsistent attitude and we have trailed along with him . . .[6]

Some authorities maintain that the Bolshevist attitude toward the United States was exceptionally friendly. Louis Fischer points out that special treatment was accorded to American business interests, such as International Harvester, Singer Sewing Machine Company, and Westinghouse, some of whose properties were not confiscated in 1918-19 when other foreign firms suffered nationalization. He asserts that the exception was due largely to the influence of Raymond Robins, who frequently conferred with Lenin and insisted that the United States was best equipped to undertake the gigantic task of developing the resources of the Soviet Union. The Sinclair Oil Company concessions in North Sakhalin were confiscated, however, pending American recognition.

The Washington Conference of 1921, concerned mainly with Far Eastern problems, extended no invitation to Russia. Bainbridge Colby had previously addressed a note to the Italian ambassador in Washington which enunciated our policy for years to come.[7] All decisions of importance would be held in abeyance until Russia was no longer in the grip of a nonrepresentative government whose only sanction was brute force. The United States had no faith in the permanence of the Soviet regime. Despite Colby's note, Italy continued her negotiations with Moscow, while Great Britain began talks which were to end in the commercial treaty of March 16, 1921, although Winston Churchill looked upon the Russian experiment as so much "baboonery." At the same time a spirit of distrust grew in America and flourished in a climate of hostile public opinion, intensified by the intolerance of the twenties, best typified by the "Red scare."

On May 15, 1922, Borah offered his first resolution (S.R. 293) for the resumption of diplomatic relations with Russia, specifying recognition of the "Russian Soviet Republic" and *not* the U.S.S.R. It was allowed to lie on the table pending further consideration. The New York *Times* termed Borah's resolution "an impertinence." Even if it were passed unanimously by the Senate, it would be a wasted gesture, for it is an executive function to recognize new governments. It said: ". . . Foreign nations are bewildered and intelligent Americans disgusted by these corporate or individual pretensions, vagaries and meddlings."[8]

After introducing the resolution, Borah began a private campaign aimed at its ultimate acceptance. His advisers on Russian matters included, besides Robins, Alexander Grumberg (secretary of Amtorg, the Russian-American trading organization), Norman Thomas, Norman Hapgood, Felix Frankfurter, James C. MacDonald, John Haynes Holmes, Samuel Gompers, Sherwood Eddy, and Walter Duranty. His attitude was set forth in speeches and letters which emerged from his office in a steady stream, and in articles which he contributed to leading periodicals. In a Senate speech on May 31, 1922, he expressed disgust with the Genoa Conference because it had failed to discuss two pressing problems, German reparations and the recognition of Russia. It was about time, he said, that the United States had a foreign policy of its own, and the place to formulate it was at the State Department, not at some international conference. He aligned himself with Washington, whose best wishes "were irresistibly excited whenever in any country he saw an oppressed nation unfold the banners of freedom." Borah believed recognition of the *de facto* government of Russia would be in the interests of world peace, the economic rehabilitation of Europe, and the ultimate triumph of democracy.[9]

In a letter to a friend he argued that the ". . . recognition which Washington made was founded on the honest conviction that through the French revolution the people of France . . . would in the end come into their own." "That," he wrote, "is my deliberate judgment with reference to Russia. I do not expect the present form of government of Russia to obtain for any great length of time. But it is the only method in my judgment by which there will ultimately be established in Russia a sane democracy . . . In my opinion if we were standing at the table with Russia—even with her present leaders—our influence in still further modifying those views would simply be tremendous."[10]

He reasoned that no nation, through an act of recognition, was influenced to pattern its government on Bolshevism. The Russian government was a *de facto* regime which had existed for four years, and as such we should recognize it. We had done business with the czarist government for one hundred and fifty years. If we could tax our people and take twenty millions from them to feed the Russians, upon what theory could we withhold recognition? If Russia were an economic vacuum, Borah wished to know when it would improve under the treatment it was getting from the Allies. In his opinion the Western treatment of the country since the war had no parallel for shortsightedness, cruelty, and injustice in the whole history of international affairs. The Allies argued that Russia had nothing to exchange; Borah argued that recognition would help stabilize conditions in Russia so that her people could live and do business. Our course was only helping to spread Bolshevism, he charged. Whatever government finally becomes permanent in Russia, he predicted, will have developed step by step from the Bolshevik government.[11]

In a speech in Symphony Hall in Boston Borah declared that if Harding would extend recognition to Russia, he would lead the world to peace. We could not outlaw 140,000,000 people and expect peace in Europe. He believed the government represented 90 per cent of the people, who had suffered and sacrificed to produce it just as we had produced our own in 1789. He reminded his audience how at one time, in World War I, it was Russian soldiers who saved civilization. "The Russian people are a great people, they will be a powerful people, they will come in time to be a controlling people in the affairs of Europe," he said, "and it is infinitely better that they be our friends than that they be our enemies." Another large meeting in Madison Square Garden, under the auspices of the National Labor Alliance for Trade Relations with and Recognition of Russia, enlisted Borah as the principal speaker. He noted that the Soviet government was stable and was protecting lives and property, particularly foreign trade. If sixteen nations were then trading with Russia, he asked, why shouldn't the United States?[12]

The American government had at first refused to grant licenses for the importation of Russian goods; however, early in 1920 it permitted a thin trickle to come in and by midsummer of that year lifted its blockade.[13]

After 1921 hope revived for a change in the official attitude toward Russia. Raymond Robins became the driving force behind the campaign for recognition, and Borah was the public protagonist. Senators Pittman and Robinson favored a *rapprochement* with Russia, and men like William Allen White, Al Smith, Samuel Untermyer, and Gifford Pinchot agreed with Borah that it was the greatest undeveloped market in the world. The economic forces behind recognition were concerned with short-term gains or the creation of a steady return on investment. Borah and Robins, while confident that trade with Russia would exert a stabilizing influence on the American economy, were primarily concerned with the promotion of lasting peace. There was little co-ordination and never any exact community of interest between the Borah group and the economic forces. As early as December 1922 Robins made earnest but largely ineffective efforts to consolidate the forces for recognition.

By 1923 Harding, in an attempt to stave off persistent pressure, authorized Robins to make a confidential visit to Moscow. When he reached Berlin in August 1923, he learned of Harding's death and hastened back to Washington to talk with Coolidge. Borah also went to the White House to convince the new President that some step should be taken. They had great hopes for Coolidge's first message to Congress, but he merely said that he had no objections to commercial relations between American and Russian citizens. While he did not propose to make "merchandise of any American principles," and while the favor of the United States was not for sale, he would be willing to make large concessions to assist the Russian people.[14] Russia's Foreign Minister Tchitcherin interpreted this as an invitation to open negotiations and was quick to send a message to President Coolidge expressing his government's readiness to bring about the desired renewal of friendship with the United States.[15]

Then followed Secretary of State Hughes' blast at Russia contained in his reply to Tchitcherin dated December 18 and addressed to our consul at Reval. Hughes stated: "There would seem to be at this time no reason for negotiations." He went on to say that if Soviet authorities were ready to restore the confiscated property of Americans, make effective compensation, repeal their decrees repudiating Russian obligations, and discontinue their efforts to overthrow the institutions of this country, then our government would enter into negotiations. In a letter to Robins, Borah called Hughes' reply "exceedingly unfortunate."[16]

This reopened the whole subject for further discussion, with Borah demanding more light on the question of Soviet propaganda in America. He finally secured the assignment of a congressional committee to investigate the extent to which the Soviet government and the Third Internationale were related, and whether their propaganda activities were serious enough to bar recognition. Complaining of State Department obstruction, the senator wrote a Cleveland editor: "It is pretty hard to investigate a Department which rears back upon its dignity and says that it is incompatible with the public interests to go more than so far. But we shall do the best we can."[17]

Borah took a skeptical view of reports describing the wide extent of Russian propaganda. "No living man," he wrote, "nothing less than omniscience can separate the truth from falsehood, the genuine from the forged documents, in this mass of lying and crimination and recrimination which has been going on for five years." He reiterated Philip Gibbs' allegations that in Riga and Helsingfors factories of lies were busy with cables accusing the Soviet government. Moreover, he believed that the *émigrés* and their sympathizers held the world's record for the quantity, production, and marketing of untruth.[18]

Senator George W. Pepper of Pennsylvania, who was opposed to the investigation and to Russian recognition but who served on the subcommittee, reports that in the three days of hearings, witnesses for the State Department presented an admirably prepared and well-documented case, perhaps with the help of information Attorney General Daugherty ordered released to Hughes by the Department of Justice. The death of Lenin that same month clouded the whole subject with such uncertainty that hearings were suspended; it was declared unnecessary to take further testimony. Pepper was convinced that nothing would change the attitude of the United States government toward the Soviet Union. He observed that the shelving of Borah's proposal for recognition was accomplished with a decent regard for the Idaho senator's feelings.[19] Borah's offensive was beaten off by the skill of the State Department, and the issue remained dormant for years.

Nevertheless, Borah persisted in this unpopular cause because he believed recognition necessary to eliminate the threat involved in a permanent disagreement between the two great world powers. It would insure the reduction of armaments and hasten economic recovery. The restoration of foreign markets for American farmers depended on a Russian adjustment, for while our farmers could not sell directly to Russia, our businessmen and manufacturers could, and this would broaden the home market for farm products. When normal conditions were restored, Borah believed Russian-American trade would expand, e.g., in shoes and cotton, articles currently going to Russia through English and French factories.

In 1924 when the MacDonald government recognized the Soviet Union, Borah lauded the move as "statesmanlike and courageous." He said it pointed to a new moral and spiritual regime. At the same time influential Communists in Moscow, led by Litvinov, violently opposed accepting the League membership which was offered to Russia. It was expected that other European nations would follow Britain's lead, but the big question remained unanswered: would Russia enter the family of nations as an equal among equals or would she retain her hopes of world revolution, which would make her entry that of a conspirator rather than of a friend?[20]

Borah continued to hammer away at our official position. Wilson, Harding, Coolidge, Hughes, Colby, and subsequently Hoover, Stimson, and Kellogg, all opposed recognition under the existing conditions. Borah wrote to a friend:

> What irritates me about this whole business . . . is this humiliating lack of faith in the intelligence and patriotism of the American people. The more of that miserable fustian you feed them the more they will spew it up. Besides, no one outside the kingdom of heaven is able to tell when the errors of today will become the truths of tomorrow. I say let the discussion proceed.[21]

By virtue of his outspoken stand on Russian recognition Borah's name carried weight in Russian official circles. He was looked upon as the country's friend and champion. Litvinov developed a strong liking for the fearless, courageous Idahoan, and a letter from Senator Borah counted for more in Russia than credentials from the State Department. In May 1929 Borah averaged three such letters a day, which were issued only to acquaintances or persons vouched for by acquaintances who wished to travel in the Soviet Union.

Forces working against recognition outside the State Department included the Commerce Department under Hoover; the A.F. of L. and its conservative leaders who feared the rise of more radical labor groups; various religious organizations who viewed Russia as conducting a war against religion; and White Russians, who were violently anti-Bolshevist in sentiment and used their influence accordingly. These Whites did not hesitate to employ forged documents in influencing official American circles.[22]

At one time, when Standard Oil of New York made a large number of petroleum purchases from the Moscow Naptha Syndicate, Ivy Lee, Standard's adviser on public relations, commenced a campaign for Russian recognition. However, Sir Henry Deterding, magnate of the Royal Dutch-Shell Company and closely affiliated with Standard of New Jersey, which had failed to secure a monopoly of Russian oil, soon persuaded Standard Oil to desist. Deterding became a major figure in the background of antagonism to Russia.[23] Unscrupulous forces offered "documents" alleging that the chief American proponents of Russian recognition, Borah and Norris, were actually in the pay of the Soviet government. Some "evidence" of this nature had been supplied to a special Senate investigating committee, of which David A. Reed of Pennsylvania was chairman. Borah was aware that the Reed committee was inquiring into charges that he was in conspiracy with the Soviet government, but Norris evidently knew nothing about it until he was called before the committee to testify in January 1929.

During the Mexican forgeries investigation Reed had received eight photographs which purported to show that the two senators received large amounts of money to work for the Soviets. The alleged go-between again was Dudley Field Malone, as in the Mexican forgeries. Malone had written a letter of introduction for a friend, which evidently fell into the hands of some agent of a forgery ring selling diplomatic documents designed to discredit the Soviets. The original papers were offered to a member of Senator Reed's committee in Paris for $50,000. One of the photos reproduced a receipt in this form:

> March 7th 1926
> RECEIVED OF MR. DUDLEY F. MALONE THE SUM OF ONE HUNDRED THAUSEND AMERICAN DOLLARS
> (signed) Wm. E. Borah

If there was any doubt whether the receipts were forged, the German spelling of "thousand" ended it. Borah announced on January 10, 1929, that he had initiated steps to have the Russian government find the forgers. He felt the American government, as well as the Soviets, owed it to him to clear the matter up; furthermore, he was certain that if the State Department asked the Russian government to run the forgers down, they would. When another bogus letter from a Mr. Rakowisky was dragged out, he went directly to Boris Skvirsky, unofficial representative of the Soviet government in Washington, and lodged his complaint. The upshot was a telegram from Litvinov, then acting secretary of foreign affairs, assuring Borah that his government was "ready in every way possible to assist in the investigation of the whole matter."[24]

In the Senate the report of Reed's committee took precedence over the Kellogg treaty as a matter of the highest privilege. No efforts were spared to expose every link in the chain of forged evidence. Both Norris and Borah appeared before the committee in Washington and denied under oath that they had received money from the Soviet government. Some years later, in a letter to the editor of the Chicago *Tribune,* Borah wrote:

> After the Reed committee made its investigation, some of us whose names were used made a move to uncover this bunch of crooks who seemed to be plying their trade principally in Paris. I became satisfied after pretty thorough investigation that it was impossible to do anything unless I could have the vigorous initiative and cooperation of the French government. I could hardly hope for that. So . . . I have made no further effort in the matter and do not know of anything I can do. It would cost a fortune . . . to run them down even if I had the help of the French government. So I have concluded to let them go forward with their manufacturing business.[25]

While the Reed committee was still conducting its investigation in Italy, Senator Reed as well as Borah and the State Department were informed that the Berlin police had arrested two well-known counterrevolutionaries and international spies, Orlov and Sumarakov, on a charge of forging a new set of documents implicating Borah in taking bribes from the Soviet government. The Berlin police uncovered the fact that Orlov had at least seven Paris accomplices, and ascertained that he had probably been concerned in the fabrication of the earlier set of documents sent to Senator Reed's committee from Paris.[26]

It seems that Orlov attempted to sell this second set of forged documents to a Berlin correspondent of the New York *Post*, Hubert R. Knickerbocker. An intermediary, Felix Dassel, showed Knickerbocker some photostats, one of which the newspaperman bought. Using great ingenuity, he gathered a set of facts which he immediately reported to the police, enabling them to round up the forgers and place them under arrest. Orlov, Sumarakov, and one Pavlonovsky were arraigned and their trial was scheduled for June.

At the trial Orlov said that he had constructed the documents purporting to show that Borah had accepted bribes from the Soviet government from an original G.P.U. document formerly in his possession. The state's witnesses were Knickerbocker and one Sievert, a Russian *émigré*, who asserted that the accused had likewise sold him forged documents. The presiding judge restricted the testimony to the actual indictment charge, refusing to permit the defendant, Orlov, to enter into a discussion of the Soviet Intelligence Service. Since his testimony was constantly restricted by the judge, Sievert suffered a breakdown toward the end and the trial hinged mainly on the testimony of Knickerbocker.

He explained how Dassel came to him and offered to procure for him incriminating material against Senators Borah and Norris, which was in the possession of a former member of the G.P.U. (Pavlonovsky). Having read about the Reed committee's forged documents, Knickerbocker acted interested when Dassel came to him again and offered to arrange for an interview with Rasputin's daughter. The documents Pavlonovsky finally produced were proved to be forgeries; after his arrest the former employee at the Soviet Embassy in Berlin contended they must have been forged by Orlov, from whom he had obtained them in good faith. Orlov claimed that the G.P.U. had forged them in order to discredit him. Borah's name was included in one coded copy to arouse Knickerbocker's interest, the police asserted, and to induce him to buy. Orlov relied for his defense on the allegation that the letters he had forged gave a true reading of actual documents.

Orlov and Pavlonovsky were both sentenced to short prison terms. Pavlonovsky was expelled from Germany, but Orlov was allowed to retire to his country seat in Prussia. The sentences were described by *Vorwaerts,* chief organ of the largest government party, as "ridiculously lenient."[27]

Altogether, three separate efforts were made to discredit Borah by making it appear that he was an *agent provocateur* in the pay of the Soviet government. By far the most fantastic story was reported by Hamilton Fish, representative from New York's Hyde Park district, who served in 1930-31 as chairman of a House committee investigating communism in the United States. He relates that he received in the mail from an anonymous informant cancelled checks drawn on the Bank of France and made payable to William E. Borah. He states that the signature on the checks, amounting to approximately $250,000, was in Borah's hand, which Fish knew well. He was advised by Charles Evans Hughes, he said, to take the checks to the State Department. Undersecretary Castle, upon questioning, could recall nothing of this incident, although Fish alleges the checks were taken by Castle and filed away or misfiled in the archives of the State Department. It now seems doubtful that they ever reached the archives. Mr. Fish insisted that Borah went to his grave never having known any of this. Because he considered himself a close friend of Borah's and did not wish to do anything which might hamper the work of his own committee, Fish states he made no further effort to establish the validity or falsity of the documents he claims to have received. He could have done his friend a much greater service by exposing the documents.

However, Borah knew about the papers Fish possessed, for in 1932 he wrote Colonel R. R. McCormick: "There seems to be any number of these documents. You will remember the Reed Committee had some . . . not only purporting to involve myself but others. I have been informed that the Fish committee has some. I have also been advised that the State Department was offered some. I have not made inquiry as to the details of any of these documents."[28]

Little serious thought was given to these charges during Borah's lifetime, but after his death, when it became public knowledge that he left an estate estimated at over $250,000, the pieces in a seemingly sordid chain of evidence were linked together to make it appear that for his championship of the Soviet Union he was remunerated handsomely. This is a gross injustice to Borah, whose assets consisted largely of government bonds, some of which were purchased during the Liberty Loan drives with money earned in Idaho. An investigation of his finances, including bank accounts and bond purchases, reveals that nearly $100,000 in bonds was purchased prior to 1926, long before these alleged payments were supposed to have been made. Moreover, Borah's conduct throughout these episodes was open and forthright. Letters and papers relating to the charges, including the State Department communications, were filed with his correspondence under "miscellaneous" in such a casual manner as to denote that he never gave the subject a second thought.

From student days in Kansas Borah had practiced frugality, and though the estate left to his wife after his death showed he was a man of means, no one would have guessed it during his lifetime. He himself was responsible for perpetuating the popular image of a public servant whose expenses so outran his income that he never had one dollar to rub against another. He gave financial difficulties as a reason for threatening to leave the Senate in 1918 and again in 1924. He wrote an Idaho friend in 1925 that he was looking around for a house within his purchasing power because rents in Washington (the Wyoming Avenue apartment cost $160 a month) had become almost unbearable. "A man feels like he is being robbed once a month. So I am going to try to purchase a house," he wrote. Yet at the same time he would make some generous gesture like donating $50 worth of books to the general library every year in the University of Idaho, or sending his widowed sister $75 a month for her support until her death in the thirties, or turning over the copyright on his book of speeches, *American Issues,* for fear it would be thought he went into the publishing business to make money. He kept thousands of dollars deposited in a Boise checking account; when his thrifty secretary advised transferring it to a savings account, his reply was, "Leave it there." Borah was not a poor man, but he created the impression he was. The money in his "Go to hell fund," as he called it, was set aside to support him and his wife when old age or political defeat, or both, overtook him.

As the shadows of Japanese expansion lengthened over the Far East, Borah intensified his efforts in urging a Russo-American *rapprochement.* He believed that in spite of the Communist party line, which seemed inimical to the most elemental instincts of human nature (the family, religion, and private ownership) 80 per cent of the Russian people were home-loving, law-abiding, deeply religious, and industrious. He stated:

My view is that the present government of Russia will continue to modify its views and policies until there will be established in Russia a democracy, not such a democracy as we believe in, but such a democracy as will best fit into the lives of the Russian people . . . Russia is traveling over the road which will eventually lead to sound government . . . My faith is founded first upon the absolute faith in our own people and . . . institutions, and secondly, my faith in the Russian people.[29]

Neither Hoover nor his secretary of state, Henry L. Stimson, showed a more friendly disposition toward Russia than their predecessors.[30] Borah used whatever opportunities presented themselves to prod Stimson. During the summer of 1932 he wrote the Secretary from Boise and expressed alarm at the press statements of Baron Uchida relating to Japan's foreign policy. He apprised Stimson of information received from a friend in Tokyo to the effect that a treaty of great significance was then being negotiated between Japan and Russia. Borah felt more strongly than ever that our relationship with Russia ought to change. "I am satisfied," he wrote, "that by proper steps taken upon the part of our government any close relationship between Russia and Japan could be avoided."[31]

Stimson replied that he was giving the matter close attention. His conclusion was that the United States was making a world-wide fight for the integrity of international obligations. "If . . . in this emergency," he wrote, "we recognized Russia in disregard of her very bad reputation respecting international obligations . . . the whole world and particularly Japan would jump to the conclusion that our action had been dictated solely by political expedience and as a maneuver to bring forceful pressure upon Japan . . . I felt that this loss of moral standing would be so important that we could not afford to take the risk of it." Stimson trusted that negotiations such as Borah reported were of only a transitory nature. The rivalry between Japan and Russia in Manchuria was so keen that he thought it unlikely they would enter into any substantial permanent relations.[32]

Louis Fischer relates Borah's version of a conversation he had during the summer of 1932 with Stimson in a Washington park. Borah believed that Stimson was leaving office with a heavy heart because of tasks undone, one of them being the recognition of Russia. In Borah's opinion Stimson would have recognized Russia had it not been for Hoover. Borah believed that Hoover was hostile to Russia because the Bolshevists had confiscated some of his properties (the Urquhart holdings) and because he was "such a colossal individualist and conservative." On the other hand, Borah was reasonably certain that Franklin Roosevelt would recognize Russia soon after his inauguration despite the fact that Bernard Baruch was opposed to it. Owen D. Young and Cordell Hull both favored recognition. Raymond Moley, Hull's assistant, told Louis Fischer he also favored recognition.[33]

At the beginning of 1933 the United States was the only great power which still stood out against diplomatic relations with the Soviet Union. This hostility was shared throughout the Western hemisphere, for at the same time when the American position in the Far East was menaced by Japanese imperialism, Russian relations with Latin America deteriorated. There seems to be little doubt, despite Stimson's remarks to the contrary, that Japanese expansion was a determining factor persuading the United States to close the breach with Russia. The Manchurian crisis had re-emphasized the common interest of Russia and the United States in opposing Japan. This was at least one of the main currents in world affairs which was to combine in the course of the coming year to force a reversal of policy leading in November to the long-deferred step of recognition.

Although in Russia political considerations were uppermost, another current stressed here was economic advantage. In 1930 we had supplied Russia with a quarter of her imports; by 1932 we supplied only 5 per cent. Banks were by then hostile or insolvent, and Germany, who could offer credit, replaced us as Russia's chief supplier. Advocates of recognition, including Borah, now urged with more vehemence the establishment of normal relations, which would produce an increase in orders of American goods and ease the depression. By the end of 1932 this argument was finding support in influential political as well as business circles. Little attention was paid here, except by men like Borah, to the disturbed balance of power in the Pacific. Though still committed to nothing short of unconditional recognition, Russia, too, was more anxious than ever to come to an agreement with the United States.[34]

The initiative which led to recognition was taken by Maxim Litvinov, head of the Soviet delegation to the London Economic

Conference, where he proposed to Secretary Hull that the differences between their two countries be reconciled. In June 1933 William Bullitt called on Litvinov at the Soviet Embassy in London and a talk was arranged between the Russian secretary and Raymond Moley, then assistant secretary of state. During the following autumn Bullitt was again the intermediary for the Roosevelt-Kalinin letters, which paved the way for Litvinov's arrival in Washington on November 7, 1933. Their negotiations lasted until November 16, when notes were exchanged between Roosevelt and Litvinov, who promised that his government would refrain from promoting any propaganda in the United States. Americans in Russia were to enjoy freedom of conscience and worship. When diplomatic relations were restored, Litvinov promised that his government would negotiate on the issue of the debts contracted under preceding Russian regimes. As these statements of policy were satisfactory to President Roosevelt, he announced recognition of the Soviet Union that same day, thus spanning in ten days a gulf of sixteen years—"sixteen strangely wasted years," as Borah put it.

Roosevelt's conduct was cheered by more than three hundred telegrams of congratulations. One was from Borah: ". . . It was the fine, big, courageous thing to do." Beyond stating that Borah endorsed his action, the President refused to make the message public.[35] At any time, thought Borah, this move would have been of supreme moment in the cause of peace. At this time, it was nothing less than "a stroke of genius."

Litvinov left the country on November 25. Before sailing, he wrote Borah in Boise: ". . . You, I believe, were the first American to recognize the full implications of amicable relations between your country and mine . . . I therefore feel that you . . . have contributed a chapter in American-Soviet relations which will be remembered gratefully in both countries and I wish at this time to assure you of my own appreciation . . . warm respect and regard."[36]

Thus years of diplomatic hostility to one of the world's most energetic, aspiring, and powerful nations ended in recognition by the United States. Throughout those years Borah championed Russia's cause in the face of bitter opposition from many sections of the country and jeopardized his office by this campaign. At one time in the early twenties he was even black-listed by the D.A.R., aroused to heroic efforts to save the state. However, in favoring the restoration of diplomatic exchange, he was in the company of Norris, La Follette, Will Durant, John Dewey, Jane Addams, Roscoe Pound, and many others.[37]

The benefits Borah anticipated unfortunately did not result from the recognition of Russia in 1933 by President Roosevelt. The first major disappointment was the failure of the debt negotiations. This made operative the Johnson Debt Default Act, and no American loans could thereafter be extended to the Soviet Union. Without loans the expected trade boom did not materialize. As time passed, it also became apparent that Russia was not living up to her promises concerning propaganda activities. Roosevelt made an earnest effort to apply his inaugural pledge to be a good neighbor to Russia; however, as events unfolded, it was possible to perceive the wisdom in the warning: "If this country recognizes Russia, it should be able to take steps to recognize the difficulty of getting along with Russia."[38]

XVII Roosevelt and a Republican Maverick

A good cause is strengthened by opposition and a weak one justly destroyed by it.

—William Borah

The Roosevelt administration marked a decisive turning point. The wreckage of a bankrupt isolationist attitude was to be cleared away, and a new foreign policy constructed on the old foundations. Borah's course would continue to be wayward and incalculable, but he persistently urged economic, if not political, co-operation with other nations, and could, if he would, bring lagging public opinion up to any advanced stand he cared to take.

Borah regarded Franklin D. Roosevelt as a resourceful man whose initiative and courage impressed him. He found the atmosphere in March 1933 heady with the excitement of an impending era of reform. That he would find some policies to fight was inevitable, but his opposition was not expected to take on more formidable proportions than it had under Hoover. How effective his fighting strength would be as part of the Republican minority remained to be seen. One fact was certain: there was an urgent necessity for some kind of program, for the country was in a state of economic prostration.

It was Borah's nature to hold his fire until every doubt was dispelled from his mind. He waited until issues were clearly drawn before taking decisive steps. Usually he studied, pondered, and analyzed before he condemned or approved. He delayed his criticism of the New Deal until its aims and methods were clear. There was another reason why Borah took no active part in the legislating of the "hundred days." During the months following the inauguration he was a sick man.

In July 1932 he had submitted to an examination at the Mayo Clinic in Rochester, Minnesota, in an effort to diagnose some serious intermittent hemorrhages. The examination and X-rays revealed an internal obstruction, but no evidence of malignancy.[1] In the months following his visit to Rochester he spent much of his time in doctors' offices, an unhappy development for one who always said a man moves ten years closer to his grave when he comes in contact with a physician. With the passing of time, his condition grew steadily worse. Two doctors advised immediate surgery, but he balked at the very mention of an operation and tried every other form of treatment as a substitute. The fear of malignancy obsessed him. Finally the pain became so intense that he was left with no alternative. By June he was no longer able to go to the doctor's office and was attended at home. It was at this point that he wrote out in his own hand his last will and testament, making Mary Borah his sole heir and executrix.

In the midst of the National Recovery Act debate he entered Johns Hopkins' Brady Institute in Baltimore, reportedly for an annual checkup. Dr. Hugh Young, a noted urologist, performed the forty-minute operation and removed what proved to be a benign hypertrophy from the prostate with no difficulty. By the time Mrs. Borah arrived from Washington, the patient was reported in good condition; however, for such an active man the recuperation period was slow and tedious. Newspapers ran pictures showing a lined face and thin body. It was months before he regained his strength, but he then felt better than he had in years.

The special session ended before his release from the hospital. For the month of August, on doctors' orders, he went to Poland Springs, where he was cut off from all activity. After a brief stopover in Washington, Borah and his wife departed for Idaho, where they toured the state by motorcar with their friends, the C. C. Andersons. All through October and November "Idaho's biggest potato" traveled, making short, effortless speeches in Parma, Meridian, Lewiston, Wieser, Caldwell, Idaho Falls, and Boise. By November 1 he was feeling fit again. He wrote his general physician in Baltimore that he had gained ten pounds since his operation: "You know what Caesar said about Cassius—'Let me have men about me that are fatter.'" November found him back in Washington.

The time had come for Borah to go into action against the New Deal. A progressive Republican who had spurned the advances of Roosevelt in 1932 when others capitulated, he viewed the unfolding of the program with skepticism. His first attack took the form of a telegram to Governor Herbert Lehman of New York, congratulating him on resisting the proposal of Mayor La Guardia for greater federal control over municipal finances.[2] Borah liked the liberalism of FDR but not the N.R.A. He wanted the tariff reduced, but he resented the sweeping authority delegated to the executive in the Hull program. Borah favored changes in the country's monetary policy, but he did not like the administration's methods. He opposed the gradual centralization of power and government activities in Washington. Slowly he became convinced that the tendencies of the New Deal threatened the form of constitutional government that he understood, and warned that precedents set by capable hands would remain for incapable hands.[3]

An exchange on N.R.A. between Robert Wagner of New York and Borah attained a rare plane of reason and eloquence. Borah's argument was sustained by sound economic points and a long juridical bibliography. He maintained that this legislation protected any kind of monopoly; destroyed the independents in industry; turned over to the President, in the permissive business codes, material for laws which only Congress had the power to make; and could be used in a price-fixing conspiracy against the consumer. More than nine thousand letters came from small businessmen all over the country supporting his arguments. To the plea that the bill would have a two-year testing period, Borah replied it would be impossible at the end of any two-year period to change such a program. He fought vainly to strike from the Recovery Act the sections exempting compliant companies from the operation of the antitrust laws.

Borah was severely criticized for "playing politics with national recovery." He and Senator Nye were singled out as the real troublemakers. Hugh Johnson, chosen by Roosevelt to direct the administration of the Recovery Act, invited both men to join a Senate committee with sweeping authority to correct any evils in the administration of N.R.A. They refused to accept. The newspaperman, Paul Y. Anderson, excused Nye on the ground that he did not know any better, but he found no excuse for Borah, who was too good a lawyer to believe an industry could be kept under the codes of fair competition and still be subject to the full operation of the antitrust laws. For the government to induce industries to place themselves under the codes in consideration of certain legal immunities and then revoke those immunities would be a colossal act of dishonor.[4]

As the N.R.A. ran its course, Borah waited sardonically. His attitude could best be summarized in the words of Harry Hopkins to Johnson: "Hugh, your codes stink!" It was with considerable satisfaction that he read the decision in the Schechter case, which held the N.R.A. unconstitutional. Borah's blast at the New Deal put him back in the national spotlight and gave courage to timid Republicans, many of whom were hypnotized by Roosevelt. He fired them with a will to move up to the line of attack. Republican campaign managers also took comfort in his remarks. No other legislator so effectively exposed the Roosevelt administration's failure to control big business.

One of the marked tendencies of the early New Deal was to curtail the powers of the legislature and increase the authority of the executive. When the National Economy Act of 1933 was given precedence over all other legislation, opposition developed over the provision delegating to the President the power to make retrenchments in government expenditures. The debate brought from many members of Congress what Simeon D. Fess of Ohio called a "humiliating confession" that the body was powerless to make economies because of organized minorities. Senator Borah led the fight against the measure because, as he said: "I am unwilling . . . in the midst of this awful calamity . . . to single out the Congress . . . and say that that body, of all who were concerned in the matter, has been the signal failure and therefore we are called upon to abandon our function of seriously considering and passing such measures as we in our judgment feel are necessary for the situation."[5]

Borah attacked the policy of crop destruction while millions went without needed food. When Secretary Henry Wallace tried to persuade him to support the beet sugar bill, he charged that the administration was trying to preserve the domestic market for Cuban sugar by limiting western production; he also bantered the Democratic leaders about their inability to overcome Cuban opposition, over which the administration was supposed to have some influence. The problem, he said, was not overproduction but underconsumption and the lack of a proper method of distribution. Ogden Mills phrased it picturesquely when he protested against "removing plenty simply because there was want in the midst of it." In a radio address Borah branded Roosevelt's agricultural policies as fallacious in principle and a failure in practice.

Borah wanted to restore silver to the place it occupied before foreign demonetization in 1925, thus throwing open to debate the question which had bedeviled politics during the 1890's. In his opinion the efforts made in 1925 to force the gold standard upon the silver-using countries of the world was a fearful mistake, and he could not understand why it would be unsafe or unsound to restore conditions as they were prior to 1925.[6] Borah's money views resembled those of Daniel Webster. Both believed that the government should keep the banks under firm control in unified relationships. Neither senator was a paper-money expansionist or an advocate of a managed currency with nothing of intrinsic value behind it. Borah criticized the Roosevelt administration for its failure to provide a thoroughly unified banking system. As the representative of a state which ranked second only to Montana in silver production, he believed in the rehabilitation of silver and wanted other governments to join in this program.[7]

Before and during the London Economic Conference he approved Roosevelt's course and the Treasury's plans to buy newly mined silver; however, he joined the "silver bloc" with Senators King of Utah and Wheeler of Montana and was the first to disassociate himself from proposals which proved unsatisfactory to him. The silver bloc insisted that the Treasury's proposals were not enough and that the government could make much greater use of the inflationary possibilities of the metal. After several unsuccessful attempts he resolved that he would never again go to the White House with hat in hand asking for silver legislation, but would urge Congress to "pass it up to the President" as enacted legislation that was not subject to compromise. He did as much as anyone to force the hand of the administration on the issue.[8] The Silver Purchase Act of June 1934 passed with the aid of the silver bloc, but the effect was hardly the moderate reflation for which the planners prayed.[9] When the silver bill was signed, Borah was present at the White House. The President beamed and said: "Senator, we will get you yet." Borah smiled back: "I think you've had too much of me already."[10]

Borah was the real hero of the seven-day battle over the Glass-Steagall Banking Reform Bill in June 1933. On the verge of collapse, he continued to work quietly and patiently in the background until he finally brought together the overheated contenders long enough to get an agreement putting an end to the filibuster. Huey Long held out because he wanted to have Borah announce the agreement to the Senate. This meant nothing to Borah. When administration leader Joe Robinson finally gave up, Borah breathed a sigh of relief and remarked: "This is the last time I'll intrude in a family quarrel."

In his fireside chat of March 1933 the President appealed to the people to bring their money out of hiding. To this plea Borah responded: "I don't think the government has a scintilla of power to prosecute me for putting my money where I want to put it." He said we were off the gold standard and the government could not force people to deposit money in banks where there was no assurance they would get it back. "If I had over five thousand dollars in gold I would defy the government to come and get it. We are proceeding under pure bluff and we have no authority except for the fact that people fear to come into contact with the federal government."[11] During the Senate debate Borah rose from his chair in the third row, fixed his glasses on his nose, and shouted his angry defiance. He said the only remedy for financial unrest was to guarantee bank deposits and bring back gold into circulation, releasing money then held frozen in banks. Senator Norris joined him in supporting the revised system.

Influenced, undoubtedly, by Huey Long's "share the wealth" campaign, Congress finally passed a bill increasing the income tax in the higher brackets, as well as the corporation excess-profits tax, estate tax, and gift tax. However, opportunities for evasion were available owing to an earlier repeal of publicity provisions and the defeat of Borah's amendment to lift the tax exemptions from federal securities wherein, as estimated by the President, at least one third of all the millions in large American fortunes found a safe refuge from any income tax.[12]

The opening offensive in his summer campaign was a radio speech for the Washington *Evening Star* forum, delivered in July in the sweltering heat of his Washington office. Reporters found him putting in long hours on his sixty-ninth birthday. These were the years before air conditioning. His only relief came from a palm-leaf fan and his only complaint was the weather: ". . . and I don't see any way to change it." Borah took comfort in his knowledge of Gladstone's Midlothian campaign at the age of seventy. "Physically," he said, "I feel as big as Gladstone. Further than that I wouldn't presume to go. It isn't a question of how long one lives, anyway, it's a question of what you do while here."[13]

With an election approaching, Borah had to think about a trip home during the later summer of 1934 to take part in the campaign. He rented an office in the First National Bank building and took Henry L. Falk's house at 109 West Idaho Street for the month and a half he planned to stay. He worked out a very strenuous tour, with speeches at Idaho Falls, Boise, Meridian, Salmon City, Caldwell, Nampa, and Pocatello. At the annual Basque celebration he had his silhouette done by a sidewalk artist, patronized the fortune-teller, and bought a tambourine. In a speech at Genesee he endorsed the Liberty League; at Cambridge on October 3 he hit monopolies; at Wieser he made a plea that the Republican party face the issues. He went on to north Idaho and spent the last ten days of the campaign in the panhandle, speaking at Wallace, Coeur d'Alene, and Sandpoint.

The Democratic landslide of 1934 was no surprise to Borah. He expected it and interpreted it as meaning that the administration was in the middle of a program and the people wanted to see its outcome. After the Republicans were almost wiped out, he remarked: "There was a vast amount of reaction against the New Deal but what were the people offered in its stead? They can't eat the Constitution." In Chicago he announced that the Republican party must reorganize or die. Evidently he felt that the party might be dead already but, like the Irishman who fell over the precipice, the party was not conscious of it. When reporters asked him under what leadership the party should be reorganized, he declared: "I shall not assume leadership." He cautiously suggested Senator Vandenberg, who had been re-elected in Michigan.

As the lawmakers prepared for the next term of Congress, Borah released some fusillades he had been saving for the administration. He demanded the restoration of the 15 per cent pay cut to government employees, which he called hypocritical in view of the administration's policy to increase purchasing power. Eventually the wage cuts were restored either by executive order or congressional action. By March 1934 the administration abandoned its economy program and all former efforts to balance the budget.

Borah demanded a congressional investigation into the expenditure of funds by the Federal Emergency Relief Administration. He charged that there was shameful waste in its administration and implied that relief money was being spent for political purposes. These charges might have been more sensational were it not for the fact that Harry Hopkins, an administrator of first-rate ability and character beyond reproach, was in charge of the FERA.

Borah was careful not to attempt to impeach Hopkins, his chief objective being to make the FERA responsible for the expenditures of state authorities. He claimed that the use of relief funds for political influence, which was widespread, had not been managed through Hopkins but through state officials who were accessible to the Farleyites. Borah pressed to have the gap between state and federal relief eradicated either by new legislation or by reinterpretation of the existing statute. Hopkins, the relief administrator, assured Borah that ". . . no conditions which you say exist will be tolerated for a moment." Hopkins later noted that Borah submitted no specific cases on which his charges were based. He merely submitted evidence that administration costs were too high and that some people were holding jobs through the influence of the FERA, which ceased to exist in December 1935.

He stood amid New Deal revolutionizing as one of the chief defenders of the American form of government, maintaining that it had so usefully served its purpose in the past. He was not a die-hard opponent of everything in the New Deal. Because he discriminated, he was one of its most effective critics. When the four-billion-dollar relief bill was up for approval, Borah introduced an amendment restoring to their full effectiveness the antitrust laws, thus dismantling the NRA. His amendment failed to pass by a vote of 33 to 43. During the debate Borah announced: "I greatly dislike voting for this bill without knowing a little something about what the money will be spent for." Huey Long jumped up and replied: "The Senator will find out when he makes his campaign for reelection next year."

"Why bring that up?" asked Borah.[14]

In September he left for Idaho, just as the Ethiopian crisis worsened. He told reporters in Chicago that we would never go into a European war. The oil concessionaires there could fend for themselves. While in Illinois, he drove down to Fairfield for a short visit with his sisters. After a pleasant day with them, he departed for Idaho.

He arrived in Boise looking dapper in his tan suit, gray shirt, and blue tie after the long trip west. His departure had been noted in the East on the front page of the New York *Times,* so unusual was it for the Idaho senator, customarily garbed in dark colors, to sport a tan suit! That summer the Borahs rented a hotel suite because of its convenient location. On returning east, he stopped over in Chicago and held conferences in Ohio. When he arrived in the capital on November 14, reporters questioned him about plans for 1936. He told them: "I can't say I won't enter the primaries," which meant to them that he would. Immediately he set to work preparing for the next session and writing an article on the farm problem for *Colliers.* He wrote that the AAA might have had its virtues as an emergency proposition, but it offered no permanent solution to the tragedy of American farmers. He reiterated that the farmers had wanted the export debenture which the Grange had been urging for fifty years. With its failure the farmer had consented to reducing acreage and killing pigs. If the farmer were given a fair market, said Borah, he could realize his cost of production with a reasonable profit. Until then he would be forced to accept regimentation. He thought the demand could be created and the market found for the American farmer. This market was not abroad; in normal times only 18 per cent of farm income was derived from exports. Under a sound economic system the home market was ample, he said, to insure the prosperity of American agriculture.

At the core of the problem was the unequal distribution of wealth in the United States, where only 20 per cent of the income-earning population enjoyed 98 per cent of its savings. He called this a libel upon civilization. Purchasing power must be restored, he claimed, and never can be while private interests through combination and agreement fix prices. Nor should the home market be shared with foreigners by the American farmer so long as he is capable of supplying it. A prospering American agriculture was the best market for American manufactures.[15]

He introduced an amendment designed to reduce the interest rates on Home Owners' Loan Corporation mortgages from 5 to 3 per cent. Opponents suggested that the change would cost the government $500,000,000, demoralize the nation's private loan business, artificially increase the value of some homes, and lower the value of others in proportion. Borah's only reply was: "Fiddlesticks!" He insisted the 5 per cent rate was too heavy a burden on distressed home owners, who were the corporation's principal clients. He believed his amendment would have no disastrous effect on government or private business.[16]

On May 31, 1935, four days after the N.R.A. was held unconstitutional, Roosevelt told a press conference the decision took the nation back to the "horse and buggy" days. He summoned Felix Frankfurter and Hugh Johnson to a meeting where he told them the country was with him, and threatened to bring the Court into line if he had to "pack it" or deny it appellate jurisdiction. This attack on the Court elicited a sharp rebuke from Borah.[17] He told an NBC radio audience Roosevelt had ample power to deal with exigencies under the Constitution. In reply to Daniel Richberg, Rexford Tugwell, and Hugh Johnson, who had recently referred to life under a written constitution as the "ox-cart system," he said: "the ox-cart should and will have a high place at the bar of history." Borah could understand the President's impatience but he asked what could be thought of those "chirping satellites" who win favor by decrying the handiwork of Washington, Jefferson, and Madison, who have not the patience to frame a statute that shows careful thought within the Constitution, and who seek to cover their failure by talking loudly about the outmoded Court? He challenged Roosevelt to keep within the bounds of the Constitution or amend it, for the Court had no choice but to uphold the supreme law of the land. After this speech the press hailed Borah as the first to dare the President to come out and fight.[18]

The Democrats avoided every Republican effort to make the Constitution an issue in the campaign, and Roosevelt withheld further comment until after the election. By that time in rapid succession the Court had knocked out the Guffey Coal Bill, the AAA, and the New York Minimum Wage law. Interpreting the landslide of 1936 as a mandate to deal with the Court's obstruction, Roosevelt then astonished Congress, including the leaders of his own party, with his message of February 5 accompanied by a bill to reorganize the federal judiciary, giving him the power to appoint a judge to the High Court and inferior courts for every sitting member over seventy who refused to resign or retire within six months. This would have resulted in enlarging the Court from nine to fifteen justices. Walter Lippmann regarded the plan as no real proposal for judicial reform but a bloodless coup at the vital center of constitutional democracy.[19] Senator Ashurst, chairman of the Judiciary Committee, called it "a prelude to tyranny." Roosevelt's message precipitated one of the sharpest constitutional crises in seventy years.

Soon after his message Senators McNary, Vandenberg, and Borah, three of the most powerful men in the upper chamber, met quietly at the Capitol. They agreed that Republicans should lie low, avoid partisan suggestions, and quiet their own Senate following and such other loquacious Republicans as John Hamilton, Bertrand Snell, and Hoover. There was some trouble with the latter, who resented the idea of "muzzling him," especially when he learned Borah and McNary were at the meeting determining Republican policy. Vandenberg finally convinced the ex-President that silence was the best tactic to defeat the bill.[20]

The Democrats, led by Burton Wheeler of Montana, spearheaded the opposition aided by the liaison between Wheeler and Borah, who met almost daily and mapped out each move in their strategy. Two slier veterans never plotted the destruction of an overconfident president.

Senate hearings on the Court plan began March 10. At the outset the Judiciary Committee was divided—seven for, seven against, and four undecided. Delays gave the opposition time to rally public opinion. On June 14 a bipartisan majority issued their report condemning the plan as an attempt to subjugate the courts to the will of Congress and the President, thus destroying the independence of the judiciary. Borah and Wheeler shared the task of writing this report, fully aware that it would become a historic document. Seldom has so effective a summary come from a Senate committee. With devastating logic and moral passion it thoroughly destroyed the impact of the President's message and demonstrated that a hitherto compliant Congress was in revolt. Thus Roosevelt faced his first major legislative defeat.

The primary reason, however, for the failure of the Court plan was the sudden change which took place in the Court's outlook, resulting directly from the proposed reorganization. In rapid succession the Court upheld the Railway Labor Act, the Frazier Lemke Act, the Wagner Connery Act, and the Social Security Act. This change of front gave the death blow to the President's proposal. It went back to the Judiciary Committee, which then reported out a harmless measure for the reform of judicial procedure in the lower federal courts, leaving the Supreme Court unmodified.

Borah had been fighting for effective antitrust legislation since 1908. He remained the spokesman for old-fashioned competitive economics. If he were forced to accept centralized control of our economic life, with the competitive bloodstream blocked by the clot of monopoly, he said he would favor public rather than private control.[21] In 1935 he had introduced a bill providing for national charters and the regulation of big corporations by a federal commission under standards prescribed by Congress. In 1937 Harold Ickes noted in his diary: "I also told Borah, as the President had asked me to do, that at the next session he hoped to come to grips with the issue of monopoly; that he and Borah see this whole question eye to eye; that they recognize the futility of trying to prevent monopoly or break it up by long and futile court trials. Borah said he would be glad to cooperate in this matter . . ."[22]

That same year Borah joined forces with Senator Joseph O'Mahoney in writing a bill subjecting all corporations engaged in interstate or foreign commerce to a licensing authority, combining the powers once held by the NRA, NLRB, SEC, FTC, and a half dozen other federal agencies. Their bill represented Madison's earlier proposal to include in the Constitution express authority for federal incorporation of business organizations. It applied to corporations whose gross assets within the three preceding years exceeded $100,000. The government would reserve the right to withdraw the license of any corporation which in the opinion of the FTC violated fair labor and trade practices. Revocation would be subject to judicial review. Other features of the bill included enlarging the powers of the FTC, outlawing child labor, preventing wage discrimination against women, and requiring the distribution of surplus profits among employees unless it could be shown that such profits were needed for corporate purposes or maintaining the minimum-wage and maximum-hours standards established by law.[23]

Some senators felt that the controls in this bill were too far-reaching; others thought checks on corporations should be effected by direct regulatory measures. The licensing bill was reintroduced in 1939 and a committee created to investigate conditions in big business. Borah did not serve on it; in fact, he thought the move unnecessary. He did, however, accept membership as the only Republican on the Temporary National Economic Committee named on the President's recommendation in 1938; through public hearings and extensive research this committee assembled data on the degree of concentration of control in the American economic system. The TNEC reports prepared the ground for new antitrust legislation, but the onset of war postponed further action.

Early in January 1938 the Roosevelts were hosts to Vice-President and Mrs. Garner at a White House dinner. Borah, as dean of the Senate, was the highest-ranking guest seated one place from the President. Mrs. Borah, who wore a flesh-colored gown sprinkled with sequins, sat next to the Garners. In the course of the conversation Roosevelt leaned over and joked with the Idaho senator about his campaign for the presidency which was approaching.

"I'll tell you what I'll do, Bill," Roosevelt said, laughing. "If you're elected president, you take me for a ride on the Potomac in the presidential yacht. If I'm reelected, I promise to take you on a ride." Borah replied: "It's a deal, Mr. President. Only don't forget your part of the bargain."

XVIII Ten-Dollar Campaign: 1936

An institution is the lengthened shadow of one man.

—Ralph Waldo Emerson

A distinguished Washington correspondent once observed of Borah, "He winds himself up but he never strikes twelve!" This may once have been valid, but it was certainly not apt in 1936. In that year Borah's emergence as a hardheaded political strategist was the wonder of the capital. Advancing age, failing health, and the triumphant onrush of the New Deal had cast the shadows of political twilight on Borah, but he made an astonishing recovery from an operation and at seventy-one seemed ready to wage the hardest battle of his career. Early in the year observers noted the renewed vigor of Borah, who a few years before had to lie down on his office couch two or three times a day.

Several possibilities were open to the Republicans in the approaching campaign. The support of big business and conservatives was assured, but it would be necessary to win western farmers and eastern laborers away from the administration. For many progressive Republicans, particularly from the farm states, the strongest figure for the presidential nomination was Borah.[1] He assuredly had the qualifications to challenge Roosevelt. The Republicans evidently agreed on selecting a man from the West, and none could boast longer political experience than the dean of the Senate. He had a record relatively free from criticism. Over the years he had usually supported progressive principles and measures. Yet he was universally recognized as conservative on the Constitution, an asset he could capitalize on in the campaign. At the same time he had been careful to set himself apart from the reactionary element which had dominated the convention and campaign of 1928. He was a veteran campaigner who could boast of a loyal following and a nationwide audience.

For those dissatisfied with the Republican party as it was, Borah offered hope as an outspoken advocate of party reform. In April 1935 he recommended that an independent Republican convention be held in Chicago to adopt a progressive declaration of principles, and he proposed a four-point program, including avoidance of foreign entanglements, elimination of all forms of monopoly, maintenance of tariff protection, and abandonment of the policy of economic scarcity.[2] He did not want a third party but a new Republican party. He thought the young Republican clubs throughout the country could form the nucleus of such a movement, send representatives to a convention, elect a chairman, and complete a national organization. Charles Hilles, the national chairman, warned party leaders to guard against proposals for reorganization which would result in factional chaos. Borah challenged him to hold a plebiscite to determine the will of party members. From 1934 on Borah warned that the Republican party would be disastrously defeated under the leadership of the old guard, but nothing was done.

There was a streak of the elfin in Borah, though he managed to suppress it for fear it would mar his reputation as a statesman. When he was up to mischief, his eyes twinkled and the dimple in his chin grew deeper. The telltale signs were there during 1934 and 1935. The senator derived a boyish pleasure from reading mail that testified to the discomfort he caused among the old guard. He chuckled over letters berating him as "the Al Smith of the Republican party." What most disturbed the regulars was his friendliness with President Roosevelt and his refusal to promise to support the choice of the Republican convention. Ray Tucker predicted that Borah and Roosevelt would become even chummier as the months neared June, for he found signs that the two men were deliberately putting on a Damon and Pythias act, making a two-man threat to the G.O.P. It seemed clear to some observers that the President preferred the Idahoan as his opponent in 1936. No doubt he could make political capital of the fact that Borah had supported eleven out of seventeen major New Deal measures. In his self-assurance the President may have seen no real threat in a Borah candidacy, and in fact there was none, but Democratic leaders feared Borah's influence in the Senate and his reputation for liberalism.

Walter Lippmann averred that the real key of the future would lie between the kind of liberal individualism which Borah represented and the kind of regulated monopoly in which Roosevelt seemed to believe. Many Republicans, especially in the East, thought there was no real difference between Borah and Roosevelt, but there was a very deep difference. The two men were alike in their general feeling that large corporate wealth exercised too much power; but they differed on methods of dealing with the problem. Apart from certain aberrations, such as free silver, Borah was in the main a lineal descendent from the early American liberals, an individualist who opposed all concentration of power, political or economic. He was against private privilege and private monopoly, political bureaucracy, and centralized government. This was the tradition of Jefferson, Lincoln, Bryan, and Wilson. Lippmann thought that the alternative to the New Deal was not old guard Republicanism but a different kind of progressiveness. "Mr. Borah," he wrote, "or a candidate who represented his general point of view, might defeat Mr. Roosevelt." Borah believed in the principle of the Sherman Act, in widely distributed private property, in competition, in a government of limited powers, and in the distinctly American theory that the government is under the law and must be held to the law. According to Lippmann, this general philosophy was always the true alternative to a socialist order and an authoritarian state.

Roosevelt, on the other hand, had no such instinctive appreciation of American liberalism in its oldest and most authentic sense. He was disposed to think that these old liberal principles no longer fitted the modern world, that they belonged to a horse-and-buggy age, and that the future would bring a highly organized society controlled by a very powerful government. He was not greatly concerned about the old safeguards of liberty. What he was really concerned about was sufficient governmental power to provide welfare and security for everybody. He approached social problems in the manner of a Tory philanthropist, whose sympathy expressed itself in the desire to help people rather than let them help themselves. Thus he tried to present the farmers with monopolistic privileges equal to those enjoyed by certain industrialists, and to present wage earners with government-fostered labor unions. Generally his method of reform was to create new privileges to balance old ones, not to liquidate old privileges in order to provide more equal opportunity.

The issue symbolized by the philosophy of Borah and Roosevelt ran across all existing party lines. In his ultimate political faith

Borah was far closer to Secretary Hull and Senator Glass than to a Republican progressive like La Follette or a Democratic progressive like Senator Wagner. Borah moved away from rather than toward a collectivist order and an increasingly powerful government.[3]

The strong bond between Borah and Carter Glass is revealed in a letter from the Virginian which stated: ". . . nothing which relates to my public service has given me more satisfaction than the respect and . . . friendship which you have manifested toward me. On my side I have never known a man . . . for whom I have felt a more intimate attachment or . . . have ever held greater admiration. Both of us seem now to be walking a lonely road; but just as sure as there is a God in heaven there is coming a day of reckoning when those who are now engaged in transforming the government will wish they had never been born."[4]

The frequent meetings between Roosevelt and Borah continued to baffle Republican leaders. Few knew that occasionally Borah asked for a White House appointment which turned into a one-hour luncheon conference. Another meeting took place at the dinner given Vice-President Garner in the fall of 1935. As dean of the Senate, Borah led the congressional guests and afterwards talked privately with the President. On February 7, 1936, he lunched again with the President, sharing the meal brought to his office from the White House kitchen. They discussed the second AAA, the soil conservation program, the campaign, and neutrality legislation. Perhaps one reason for the President's affability was his expectation that the Idahoan would fail in his attempt to liberalize the Republican party and then shift his support to the Democrats.[5]

In August the Republican National Committee conducted a nationwide poll of county chairmen on their preference for the presidential candidate. They placed Borah in the lead with 247 votes, Colonel Knox second with 167, and Hoover sixth. The secret of Borah's popularity was thought to lie in the fact that he had been busy for over a year strengthening his relations with young Republican clubs. Another poll of delegates to the Northwestern Conference of Young Republicans at Yellowstone Park again gave Borah the lead.[6] By early September Mark Sullivan was writing that the preference for Borah was plain, its extent undeniable and its spontaneity convincing.

Borah must have done a great deal of soul-searching before embarking on an open candidacy. When he finally decided to enter the primaries, his one hope was to sew up enough delegates to force his party's selection of a liberal candidate and platform. Naturally he hoped the nomination would be his. What weighed heavily in favor of his decision was the fact that the Idaho primaries were held before the national convention. He could enter the primary and be nominated to succeed himself in the Senate. Since no candidate's name appears on the ballot for president, he could enter the presidential primary too. Then, if nominated for president, his name would still appear on the general election ballot for senator, and he could be elected to that office. Similarly, Idahoans could vote for him for president by voting for the Republican electors. If elected, he could simply resign from the Senate as Garner resigned from the House to become vice-president in 1932.

On December 20, 1935, he gave a hint of his intentions by approving a plan to enter a Borah-instructed delegation in the Wisconsin primary in April. He announced: "I am going to do what I can to get liberal delegations from as many states as possible. If the liberal forces wish to put my name at the head of the ticket I have no objection. If they want to put the name of some other liberal at the head of the ticket, that will be all right with me."[7]

The Wisconsin Republicans had come to Washington to ask him if they could enter his name. At seventy-one Borah stepped forth somewhat recklessly, changed his tactics, and took a final fling at the nomination. He announced he was inflexible as to his objective but flexible as to tactics. He intended evidently to conduct a "receptive" rather than an aggressive campaign for the nomination in June.[8] The big question was whether he could raise a campaign fund, personally direct the creation of state organizations, enter the primaries, and wage an active drive for the nomination.

In New York Hamilton Fish, Republican congressman for Roosevelt's Hyde Park district, opened a drive for a Borah delegation and voluntarily assumed the position of unofficial campaign adviser for Borah, whom he greatly admired. He repeatedly urged Borah to declare himself publicly so friends could start working for him in earnest.[9] Fish kept telling newspapermen Borah would announce his candidacy on or about January 1; then the date was postponed to February 1. With a show of impatience Borah told reporters that he planned making some speeches in February, but gave no assurance he would then announce his candidacy. A riddle of the day queried: "When is a candidate not a candidate? When his name is William E. Borah."

Fish was responsible for selecting Carl Bachmann, an attorney from Wheeling, West Virginia, and former Republican House whip, to act as Borah's campaign manager. Bachmann was reported to have rented a three-room suite in the Willard Hotel as national headquarters of "Borah for President." Borah had by then authorized "Young Republican" groups in Ohio, Idaho, Minnesota, Illinois, Wisconsin, Pennsylvania, New York, and South Dakota to try to pledge their states' delegations to him at the Cleveland convention. He began what some observers considered his campaign in the East with a speech in Brooklyn on January 28. A crowd of three thousand filled Kismet Temple that icy, windy January night. Few prominent New York Republicans attended the meeting. Borah was accompanied by William Ziegler, Jr., and W. Kingsland Macy, the latter part owner of a small New York newspaper chain. A moderate liberal and a former chairman of the New York State Republican Committee, Macy lacked national contacts and was inexperienced nationally, but Borah made no important decisions without him. As Borah stood on the platform, the lights accentuated the grayness of his hair, the greater bulk of his figure, and the wrinkles in his face. He told the audience:

> I do not flatter myself that I can bring you any new or startling message. I am not going to indulge in what must be a pleasant pastime, that of regaling people with one's personal qualifications for the Presidency . . . But that brings up the most important pre-convention question that we can consider, and that question is, who is going to determine the candidate's fitness, and how is it going to be determined?

Having spent a lifetime shunning partisan alignments, Borah was afraid that the Republican nominee would be chosen in a smoke-filled room long after midnight. "This is not a very good year . . . for exclusiveness in the matter of selecting a candidate for the Presidency," he warned. The rank and file must have a voice in his selection. He informed his audience that New York voters and others had had no voice in selecting their presidential candidate in more than thirty years. For himself, he had no faith in uninstructed delegations.

He then tackled two of the most controversial issues of the day, the Townsend program and lynching. He favored old-age pensions and had introduced an amendment to the Social Security Act increasing the monthly allotment for old people to $60. He thought the Townsend plan impracticable, particularly because he did not approve of pensioners having to spend the proposed monthly allotment of $200. He defended his antilynching stand. He had read all the debates on antilynching legislation since 1922. The constitutional questions raised then were identical with those raised in 1935, he said. He would support any measure which was constitutional to end this evil, but he knew of no power which the national government had to reach into the states and take hold of a violation of the law. "If the states cannot enforce law, who can?" He said the Negro above all should be interested in maintaining the integrity of the Constitution, and asserted that the Thirteenth, Fourteenth, and Fifteenth amendments had nothing to do with the Wagner-Costigan Antilynching bill.

He spoke out for neutrality. The basis of our foreign policy should be aloofness and divorcement. He attacked monopolies, declared for an independent judiciary, and branded legislating outside Congress (by commissions or bureaus) as illegal. Washington had warned long ago that usurpation (whether by Congress or the President) is the customary weapon by which governments are destroyed. The power of the purse (in tariff regulation) should not be in the hands of the executive. He concluded by saying: "We cannot go back. We cannot compromise. We must move forward . . . the political party which does not advance . . . will drop out and some other party will take its place."

Finally Borah broke the ice with a thumping announcement which made the headlines on February 4: "I'LL RUN." He made it in connection with his decision to enter the Ohio primaries, saying: "It is my intention to place at least 8 candidates for delegates-at-large in the field." After a four-hour conference in his office with Ohio's progressive leaders, Borah leaned forward in his chair and announced grimly: "We are going into Ohio to protect liberal principles." He signed the necessary papers and challenged all presidential aspirants to go into the Ohio primary with him. He intended to make a number of speeches in Ohio and present the issues as he saw them.[10]

Borah was the first of the 1936 presidential aspirants to toss his hat into the ring. Colonel Knox promptly followed with his announcement that he would fight for Ohio's eight delegates-at-large. After Knox entered, Borah asked for the entire fifty-two delegates from Ohio. A few days later Borah was asked what reply he would make to a demand from the Illinois State Committee that he pledge loyalty to the party. He replied: "I have no occasion for considering any question of loyalty to the party because I expect to be the nominee myself."[11]

Borah became a candidate because he could not detect a reflection of the liberal attitude in the faces of Hoover, Landon, or Knox. Unfortunately for his plan to make the Republican preconvention campaign a testing ground for his principles, the other candidates, when they finally declared themselves, were so anxious to avoid Republican dissension that they refused to engage in a rough-and-tumble contest with Borah or anyone else. Moreover, standpat Republicans were determined to give Borah a battle in every important primary he decided to enter. At a secret conference in New York there was drawn up a complete list of favorite-son candidates who could be put in the field with a fair chance. If Borah couldn't be defeated outright, his opponents would split the delegations, taking as many away from him as could be won.

The opposition within Republican ranks made his age a great obstacle. A man of seventy-one, who had recently undergone a serious operation, was unfit for the greatest responsibility his party could bestow. He would be nearly seventy-five at the end of one term. Opponents circulated such slogans as: "Senator Borah leaves us cold; he's a bonus man and he's pretty old."[12] A second important obstacle was the fact that he represented a small state. A story was revived about Franklin Pierce. Somebody once asked a New Hampshire man about him; the man replied that Pierce was pretty big in New Hampshire, but when they spread him all over the United States, he would be pretty thin in spots.[13] A third obstacle was the fact that only minor figures in politics eventually declared for him. His party was so faction-ridden that most eastern strength was dissipated on a variety of candidates. Some of the keenest political observers thought Borah was merely playing a game to insure his re-election in Idaho. With what support he had through lack of any real competition and his recognized flair for publicity, he was assured of most of the western states. The big question was: could he control them after the first ballot?[14]

Only thirteen of the forty-eight states held primaries. Even in these, the state organizations turned their backs on delegates who were instructed to support certain candidates. Normally they preferred to choose an uninstructed delegation or a favorite son ("hitching posts," as Borah called them). Then, once the delegates assembled, the real choice could be made by a few leaders at the convention. This was what Borah hoped to prevent by entering the primaries.

His campaign organization was comparable to that of a small-town mayoralty candidate. He carried the strategy of his campaign inside the rim of his broad black hat. In three converted bedrooms of the Willard Hotel, Carl Bachmann collected the change which fell in a scanty shower from admirers of the aging statesman. Bachmann diverted this rivulet of cash to stationery, postage, posters ("Let's Go With Borah, A Real Progressive"), rent, campaign buttons, telegrams, and advertising. By March 1936 the Borah campaign fund reached $3,000. The largest single contributions were $500 each from Fred Cole of Pasadena, Hamilton Fish, Salmon Levinson, Congressman Royal Johnson, and Oliver Haga of Boise. A contribution of $100 came from Borah's secretary, Cora Rubin. The remainder consisted of five- and ten-dollar donations from admirers in Idaho and other states.[15] Borah couldn't expect to win over his party's wheel horses in a ten-dollar campaign.

He spent little of this money on himself, paying travel expenses out of his own pocket. On the train he engaged a lower berth, never a compartment. He could not sleep well on the trains, but he refused to fly. In the hotels he engaged an ordinary bedroom with bath for five or six dollars. His meals were simpler still. Some newspapermen never forgot the experience of seeing him break crackers into milk and eat an apple from his pocket at lunch. He used none of the money in the primary states, depending upon his supporters there to furnish the halls and advertising while he paid his own expenses to appear. Usually he traveled alone.[16]

Late in March a lone figure passed through Washington's Union Station, with a porter carrying his bag, to board a six o'clock train to New York. Taking his seat in the parlor car, he appeared to be just another passenger. However, on the political scene he was Borah of Idaho embarking on the greatest adventure of his life. After thirty years of uncertainty he was for the first time starting out to try to make himself President. A long detour around the Pennsylvania floods brought him to Youngstown, Ohio, where he was greeted by seven inches of snow and a welcoming crowd of seventy-five. That night he attended a dinner followed by his speech at Stanbaugh Auditorium. This Youngstown meeting on March 19 was important but hardly inspiring. The snow kept away many who had reserved seats; of the four thousand expected, twenty-four hundred appeared. Borah was in need of a night's rest lost on the train. Those who expected to be deeply stirred by the fervor of his words left the auditorium disappointed.[17] To reassure the hard money East, he announced: "I am not in favor of inflation and never have been. Neither do I favor deflation. I should like to see a stable dollar." Later he was quizzed on his attitude toward the Frazier-Lemke Farm Mortgage Bill, designed to provide for refinancing three billions in farm mortgages by the government's issuing greenbacks. He was evasive, remarking: "It should be allowed to reach the floor of the House."[18]

In Ohio, Frank Gannett, a New York newspaper owner and publisher, was named Borah's running mate. Gannett did not like to drop his editorial work, but he thought the times called for the sacrifice. The Ohio State Central Committee announced Robert Taft would be the organization candidate to oppose Borah in the primaries. This did not disturb Borah, who thought that the populous Cleveland-Akron area would be his stronghold against Taft.[19]

Two days after his Youngstown speech Borah was in Chicago, severe winter weather following him en route. A wealthy Chicago lawyer, Edgar J. Cook, hired the Civic Opera House for his Illinois opening. Only a thousand turned out to hear him, but he spoke more effectively than in Youngstown. He assured his audience that he had no intention of bolting the party if he lost the campaign; however, he expressed confidence that if he carried the primary in Illinois on April 14, he would be the nominee of the Republican party in June.[20] Then he went on to deliver a blistering attack on big business and the old guard leadership in the Republican party. He made no apologies for having agreed more than once with the

Democrats. There were certain other issues, however, on which he uncompromisingly disagreed with the administration: the farm problem, the Constitution, and the courts. He discussed all three candidly. He paid his usual respects to neutrality and took his traditional shot at monopoly.[21]

Speaking on April 9 in Peoria, Borah again assailed big business. His targets were the Du Ponts and the Standard and Sun oil companies. While prosperity was returning, he said, it was failing to seep from the uppermost industrial strata. "Why isn't it spring?" he demanded before the overflow audience. "Because monopoly fixes the price of 80 percent of the things you must have to live, and because monopoly during the boom days destroyed the purchasing power of 70 percent of all American citizens. You'll likely hear that I am a radical. That is because I say the greatest question before us is how to save the independent small businessman, and the only way to do it is to destroy monopoly."

"One of the Du Ponts . . . said the other day that I am a dangerous man. He said he'd take anybody but me for President. Thank God, I haven't lived in vain."[22]

After speeches at Springfield, Decatur, Champaign, Urbana, and Danville he swung down to Fairfield, the little farm town where he was born. He spent the night at the home of his sister, Mrs. Mattie Rinard. The following morning all Fairfield came to greet him at a reception in the Fogle Hotel Annex. Taken in a flag-draped open car to the courthouse, he talked for about twenty minutes in a nonpartisan vein because he had promised his father he would never deliver a Republican speech in his home town. He described the first political meeting he ever attended in the Garfield campaign, and attributed his interest in politics to these early experiences.

After dinner with his sister he set out for Chicago, stopping to address a crowd in Carbondale. When asked what he would do at the Cleveland convention, he replied: "I have no chain about my neck. I shall be entirely free to make up my mind then. That has been my position since I was twenty-one years old. I make no agreements in advance."[23]

Soon the primary results began to come in. In Pennsylvania, where he had not campaigned, he carried the primary unopposed, but only 20 of the 75 delegates were pledged to abide by the result.

The Republican organization, of course, triumphed in New York. Borah had candidates in nine of the forty-three congressional districts, or 18 out of a total of 86, but all of them went down to defeat. The senator attributed this to "big business."[24] His candidacy was given impetus, however, in the Wisconsin primary, where he carried 22 of the 24 delegates. This victory assured him of a western bloc at Cleveland. In Wisconsin Borah had the only effective organization he seemed to possess anywhere in the country, comprising expert politicians who once worked for Senator La Follette. From the Emporia *Gazette* came congratulations from an old friend: ". . . 'Ere's to you, fuzzy wuzzy . . . You're a poor benighted 'eathen but a first class fighting man."[25] Returns from Ohio gave Borah 5 delegates while Taft won 47. New Jersey preferred Landon to Borah by four to one. In Nebraska Borah was the only candidate entered officially against Roosevelt, who received two thirds of the votes. There Knox and Landon received many write-in votes. In West Virginia Roosevelt received seven times as many votes as Borah in the two-party primary. In North Dakota, Republicans preferred an uninstructed delegation, favoring Landon over Borah.[26]

In Illinois Borah was opposed by another favorite son, Frank Knox, who was owner of the Chicago *Daily News*, was acceptable to Landon and Hoover, and had a well-financed organization. He made hundreds of speeches, spent an estimated $25,000, and made every effort to win, especially in Chicago. Knox carried Cook County by 79,000 votes, largely because a quarter of a million Negro voters were persuaded by the organ of the NAACP, the *Crisis*, to lend no aid whatever to Borah. However, he carried the 101 downstate counties by a margin of 30,000 or more votes over Knox, whose state-wide plurality was around 70,000. Thus while Knox won 8 delegates-at-large, Borah won 26 of the 49 district delegates and could count on almost half of Illinois' 57 delegates.

On the basis of the primary results Borah expected to enter the convention with not less than one hundred delegates. This included 22 from Wisconsin, 10 from Oregon, 8 from Idaho, and scattered delegates from western states all claimed as Borah territory. Landon forces claimed at least two hundred. Eastern bosses and managers could add about four hundred votes to Landon's two hundred. As long as these groups were allied against Borah, he could not be nominated. The Landon forces were certain not to make a deal with Borah. The only way he could win would be to gain enough members from the Landon or eastern delegations so that after the first few ballots he could add thirty or forty more delegates to his western strength. The discipline of the convention might then crack, and the delegates might nominate Borah in the excitement.[27]

As May wore on, Borah's attitude of intense hostility to Landon underwent a change. Six weeks earlier he had denounced him as a candidate of Standard Oil in states like Oklahoma. Since then emissaries from the Landon camp had worked diligently to soften Borah. Their most important mediator was William Allen White. They admitted tacitly that Borah could ruin Landon's chances by his continuous attacks, and the consequence would be the nomination of someone like Frederick Steiwer of Oregon. The possibility impressed Borah deeply. However, Borah disliked Landon's eastern supporters and wanted a progressive platform. In a New Jersey speech he threatened: "No party alignment will control me for a minute."[28] On May 28 Borah was scheduled to make a nationwide radio broadcast. He remarked in advance that he was not interested in the platform. "If I am the candidate, I will be the platform. If I am not the candidate, I won't need a platform."[29] In his radio speech he repeated: "In this campaign, the candidate of the respective parties will be the platform . . . It is undoubtedly right and proper and according to custom to make platforms but these platforms have no standing at the present time in the minds of the American people . . . This campaign will be a campaign of candidates."[30]

Borah's face had not been seen at a national convention since 1928. He had never permitted a delegation from Idaho to present his name to a convention, maintaining that such a performance would be a "mere flourish." He once said: "If those now in control would wake up some morning and find I had been nominated for president of the Republican party, they would groan, roll over and die." After fifty years of service to Republicanism many thought he deserved the party's highest honor, but as early as January 1936 standpatters and big-business men were opening their "stop Borah" drive.

While many agreed with the Philadelphia *Record* that the convention was certain to name some "reactionary nonentity such as

Landon," for "Borah is too good for it,"[31] he was still hopeful when he arrived at Cleveland two days before the convention. When offered a place on the Resolutions Committee, he turned it down. He was in no mood to co-operate. Following his refusal the Landon group invited Hoover to address the convention, dominated by the very men Borah wanted turned out. Leaders of the old guard, such as National Chairman Hilles, Connecticut wheel horse J. Henry Roraback, and Ohio State Chairman Walter Brown, Hoover's postmaster general (celebrated for having ordered a specially high-roofed government limousine to accommodate his plug hat), were the men who would swing eastern votes to the nominee. Borah had warned that if these men sat in the front row at Cleveland, the party would lose millions of liberal voters who had supported Roosevelt in 1932 and would support him again.

On June 8 he attended a caucus of the Idaho delegates. This was to be a day of tribulation. Some of his friends bluntly told him what he probably already knew—that he had no chance to be the nominee and would be able to deliver only about twenty of his own delegates to any other candidate of his choice. Even among his most loyal Idaho supporters he found strong sentiment for Landon. Borah denied having interest in any coalition against any candidate, and scorned a "stop Landon" faction which looked hopefully to him to furnish a rallying point and explode a bomb under the Landon band wagon. "They are willing for me to become the spearhead of a drive," he noted, "but they say nothing about what will happen to me after the opposition has been destroyed."[32]

He told the Idaho delegation he was ready to go forward as a candidate, but made it clear he would not bolt if Landon was nominated. His main interest was now in the platform; he wanted a strong plank against monopoly. Once he had indicated his altered position, all hope of a successful coalition against Landon faded. As Borah recalled his efforts over the years to revitalize the party and make it representative of the ideals of the average man, his voice broke and tears trickled down his cheek. The strain had been greater than even this rugged old mastiff could bear. Hurt more deeply than any but his closest friends ever imagined, he ended his remarks and retired to his room.

The highlight of the preconvention gathering was a press conference Borah was scheduled to give that same day. Four times it was postponed while he rested, and, as he put it, "tried to find out where I am." Another cause for delay was the necessity of finding a room large enough to hold two hundred reporters. Finally an empty dining hall was reserved for the meeting, which developed into a small convention. Delegates, scouts from other camps, and newspapermen crowded in to witness a climax in a gallant career, frustrated but unblemished by deviation from principle. The writing on the wall spelled LANDON. The prize was slipping from his grasp, and Borah would never get another chance at it. Withal, he was still the dominant figure of the convention. As one commentator predicted: "Governor Alf M. Landon may be nominated, but the shadow of this solitary man, who has been fighting all his life for causes in which he believed, will be long enough next November to reach from Idaho to the Atlantic on the east and the Pacific on the west."[33]

At four o'clock that afternoon, the crowd, practically sitting on each other, formed a hollow square which Borah entered amid a burst of applause. He sat in the midst of photographers and newsmen on a spindly gold chair barely capable of holding his weight. Normally shaggy and unkempt, his clothes were a symphony of brown, his long hair was brushed smooth, and he appeared to be in the best of spirits. He read a prepared statement and then submitted to questions. One of the first was: "If you get your platform, will you support the nominee?" "The nominee will have to fit the platform, if I get the platform I want," he answered with a chuckle. If his planks were adopted and Landon was named, would he support him? He said: "Let's cross that bridge when we come to it." They pressed him still further. If Landon were nominated, would he consider there had been such a change in party control as would satisfy him? "No," he said, deliberately after a moment's silence. "I don't think anything of that kind would do in view of what is going on in the election of the national committee."

He laid down his terms in a blistering statement, including demands which it seemed impossible for the convention to meet: a strong antimonopoly plank, a foreign affairs plank against entangling alliances, and an endorsement of the administration's silver policy. He wanted no mention of the gold standard. He challenged Landon to declare his views on these planks. He was willing to submit his terms on condition that he be assured the opportunity of addressing the whole convention if they were rejected. John Hamilton, Landon's manager, later said this was a matter for the whole convention to decide.

At the news conference Borah was witty and precise in his replies. Asked "Where did he find he was at?" he quickly replied, amid laughter, "I am about where I was." He was still a candidate though less fiery than usual. A hint of the old power still emanated somehow from his leonine appearance, with a casual air of humility that derived from inner confidence. He was still able to draw a crowd.[34] In the political arena he was a "shopworn angel," but in a larger realm he was a moral force to be reckoned with. Landon's managers were ready to go as far as Borah wished on the monopoly plank. As for the currency plank, John Hamilton readily admitted: "All I know about money is that it's damned hard to get." Eager for harmony, Republican leaders refrained from attacking Borah for his veiled threats to make speeches after the convention if his views were disregarded.[35]

The convention met in Cleveland's vast lake-front auditorium on June 9. Steiwer of Oregon was selected as keynoter. Republican notables crowded the platform and sat with the delegations. Borah remained in his hotel room. He took a walk along Lake Erie, read Steiwer's speech, praised it, and spent the rest of his time in conferences and meetings with delegates. The Landon forces assured him a hearing in the Resolutions Committee on his platform planks, and Landon, by phone from Topeka, expressed his willingness to have his friends meet with Borah. However, Borah told reporters: "If they'll accept my platform, that's one thing. But I will not go before any committee and plead for its acceptance."[36]

The platform was brought to Borah's hotel room where he was told that if dissatisfied with any of its provisions, he could present his suggestions to the committee. Borah, however, was now insisting that the committee agree in advance to submit his proposals as a minority report if they were not included in the platform draft. William Allen White frantically appealed to Borah to withdraw this demand. Borah refused. White spent most of the night trying to reach Borah without success; his phone was disconnected so he could sleep. Finally White burst into Borah's rooms and asked to see him. Two secretaries in the outer room remonstrated; the senator was asleep. However, White knocked on his bedroom door anyway. Sleepy-eyed and pajama-clad, Borah opened it. He donned a striped gown, White later recalled, which somehow emphasized the gaunt lines of his figure. They sat on the edge of the bed talking about trivial things for awhile; then they got down to business and agreed on two or three points. As White got up to leave, Borah walked along beside him with his arm around his shoulder, stood for a moment at the doorway, and said: "Well, goodbye, Will. I'm glad you came." Borah held White's hand affectionately for a moment, then smiled that old quizzical smile, and said something about the busy years that had passed and the ways they had walked to find themselves there. After a moment of silence White said: "Funny, isn't it?" Borah answered: "It certainly is." Then they both sighed and White left to return to the committee's grind. This was all they could say, two old, momentarily inarticulate gentlemen who had once walked together along the path of youth with their heads in the clouds.[37]

Emerging from Borah's room, White brushed past reporters and told them: "The wheels are turning." In the corridor he met John Thomas of Idaho and stuffed sheets of paper in his pocket. Thomas returned to Borah's suite. They talked for another ten or fifteen minutes and then Borah went back to bed.[38]

The subcommittee accepted Borah's demands, but in the larger Resolutions Committee a contest developed over his monopoly plank. Emissaries passed frequently back and forth between the subcommittee room and Borah's quarters, but Borah withheld approval of their plank. White implored him to reconsider. Landon urged by telegraph that every effort be made to satisfy the protesting senator. Borah penciled objections on the tentative drafts. As the day wore on, he showed more willingness to co-operate and finally agreed on the foreign relations plank. It was clear that Landon needed Borah more than Borah needed Landon. Borah had his way on monopoly too, and by midnight he accepted the currency plank, which represented a victory over Hoover, who wanted the gold standard. Borah then refused to make any statement with reference to the campaign. He had not had enough time to study the entire platform, and, he complained, he was extremely weary. He merely expressed his satisfaction that the platform was completed.[39]

On June 11 Landon was nominated on the first ballot. The Idaho delegates, released by Borah, flocked to the Landon bandwagon. Then the roll was called; West Virginia cast 15 votes for Landon and 1 for Borah; Wisconsin cast 6 votes for Landon and 18 for Borah. The total stood: Landon 934; Borah 19. During the turmoil there were shouts: "We want Borah! Where is Borah?"

Where was Borah? He had already left for Washington. Without setting foot in the convention hall, he packed his hand satchel and left Cleveland—alone. He had fought tooth and nail through four weary nights for the planks he wanted. Before reaching Washington, however, he learned that the Kansas governor had put his own interpretation on the currency plank, changing it to a sound money plank. This altered the whole situation again. Borah was furious. "What the hell did he mean by that?" he roared when he arrived in Washington. He insisted that the plank be approved as written. "If they don't do it, I don't know what I can do in the convention but I know damned well what I will do in the campaign." "Will you bolt?" a reporter asked. "Wait and see," was the reply.[40]

Borah kept Republican leaders on tenterhooks, wondering whether he would support Landon or bolt. He admitted having been given a square deal at Cleveland, but remained aloof from the national campaign. John Hamilton attempted for a time to bring him and Landon together and finally gave up. Borah knew Hamilton was piloting a sinking ship, and he did not care to get aboard.[41] Moreover, according to Arthur Krock, in the "shotgun platform," so full of industrial, agrarian, and Borah compromises, the contradictions were too many and no president elected on it could discharge its final requirements.[42]

After the Cleveland convention correspondents accused Borah of doing nothing but nursing his wounded pride. After a decent interval Borah advised the G.O.P. that he would campaign for reelection in Idaho, but he demanded the right to express his views on the money question as he saw fit.[43]

Old-timers in Idaho still love to repeat the story of the farm boy who returned home one day from a trip to the capital and breathlessly related to his father that he had seen the great Senator Borah. As proof the lad said he had heard a number of people calling him "senator."

"Son," the father drawled, "those city slickers were just joshin' you. Now what in hell would a man like Senator Borah be doin' in a place like Boise?"

It is true Borah had spent very little time in Idaho during the preceding six years; the last time he had been home was 1935. But he returned to Boise in the summer of 1936, ready for the crucial test of his political career. This fight was for nothing less than his absentee political landlordship. He knew that if he were not to end his years in the quiet of Boise or as an unlistened to "used to be" in Washington, he had to be re-elected. He wondered if the folks back home would consider his political craftsmanship worth a sixth term.

The 1932 Democratic landslide had crumbled the Republican dynasty in Idaho to its very foundations. Representatives Burton L. French and Addison T. Smith had established political records which compared favorably with those of other congressmen. Moreover, it was primarily to these other members of Idaho's congressional delegation that farmers, miners, sheepmen, and timber interests turned for federal assistance once Borah became the spokesman for purely national issues and devoted so much of his time to work on the Foreign Relations Committee. Able men like Smith and French, unlike Borah, found it necessary to pay more attention to the conventional pattern of congressional conduct in order to win re-election. Idaho could afford the luxury of only one Borah—and that as long as other congressmen cared for her material wants.

Solidly entrenched in the House, French had behind him twenty-six years of service, and Smith had served twenty years. Democratic upheavals in 1912 and 1918 had left them unscathed, but the 1932 election returns brought both their careers to an abrupt end. It seems unbelievable, but it is true—the race was not even close. Borah's term did not expire until 1936, but political observers wondered what would happen to him if the New Deal were still in full strength at that time.[44]

In 1934 rumors circulated that Jim Farley and the Democratic National Committee planned to launch a two-year drive to get Borah out of the Senate, and would fight him through Idaho's Democratic governor, C. Ben Ross. Farley was reported to be strengthening state, county, and precinct committees and to have announced that Borah would be defeated for re-election in 1936 if the Democrats had to move the treasury of the United States to Idaho. After reviewing this matter with Mr. Farley, the author was assured that no special effort was made in Borah's case. As chairman of the National Committee, it was Farley's job to attempt to defeat Republican rivals in every state campaign. He would have been justified in doing all he could to get Borah out of the Senate, but he denied taking part in any conference of high-powered leaders for that end. Evidently some imaginative journalist invented the threatening statements attributed to Farley about moving the treasury. Mr. Farley hinted that Roosevelt had certain favorites, including Borah, and preferred their re-election to Senate seats regardless of party affiliations; but Farley found it untenable, as chairman, to discriminate in his battle to defeat Republican candidates.[45]

In his biography of Roosevelt, James McGregor Burns reports that mutual friends of Borah and Roosevelt tried to induce Farley to withdraw administration support altogether from Borah's Democratic opponent in Idaho in exchange for Borah's support for the Democratic ticket. By then the Idahoan showed little enthusiasm for Landon. The proposed deal was backed by a Democratic faction in Idaho opposed to the Democratic candidate, Ross. We are told Borah was willing to go along with the idea, although no authority for this is offered. The scheme sounds plausible, and it was already clear that Borah had no use for Landon, but under no circumstances would he bolt to support F.D.R. His threats were designed to have a calculated effect. His detestation for the New Deal was well known. Moreover, Farley reported to the Democratic go-betweens that the Democratic candidate was in the fight to stay. Borah never took a stand as between Roosevelt and Landon.[46] Jim Farley bet Roosevelt five dollars that Borah would not come out for him during the campaign, and Farley won the bet!

At the threat of strong Democratic opposition Borah's friends rallied to his support. There was a warm letter from Bernard Baruch, who admired him because he never dealt in personalities. Burton Wheeler said he would go into Idaho "at the drop of a hat" and do all he could to re-elect Borah. Similar offers came from Norris, La Follette, and former N.R.A. administrator Hugh Johnson, who wrote Borah: "About all I know of politics is that I am a Democrat by inheritance but it doesn't go so far as wanting to see a national asset taken out of the Senate. I am small potatoes and few in a hill, but if ever I can do anything on that score, I am yours to command."[47]

The contest in 1936 was the first one in which Borah ever faced any real competition. C. Ben Ross, native-born Idaho governor, was the only Democrat ever elected to that post for three terms. Sixty-year-old Ross was a trick rider, had been a cowboy on the Oregon range, spoke the language of the farmers, had carried every county in the state, and had received more votes than were ever cast for any candidate in Idaho. He was the kind of campaigner who could speak on any given subject. With the winning personality of a man who could wash dishes at ladies' aid societies, this canny politician planned to criticize Borah for spending too much time on international affairs and not enough on Idaho. He knew how to make political capital of the Main Street delusion that senators are sent to Washington to gain pork-barrel favors.

Ross was convincing. He was so sure he would be elected he didn't want the aid of Jim Farley. He chose rather to go it alone, relying on his own campaign methods and personal brand of humor. He converted some, but another group in Idaho believed with equal fervor that Borah couldn't lose an election if he came out for Maine potatoes, the League of Nations, and more power to Wall Street. Old-timers still hung their hopes on their seventy-one year old idol. All the regulars combined had tried at one time or another to shatter the Borah myth and failed. "As long as Bill holds together," said one old Boisean, "Idaho will hold with him." He had triumphed when his strongest opposition was to be found in the inner circles of the state Republican organization. This had been the case in 1918, and had been so to an even greater degree in 1924, yet he won both elections by an enormous majority. Organization support has been normally essential for success in any state, but Borah was one notable exception.

Returning to Idaho early in July, Borah began on the twenty-fifth the first of a series of extended automobile tours of the state. After an early victory in the primaries, he concentrated his efforts upon defeating Ross. His followers distributed an effective list of his achievements:

WHAT BORAH DID FOR IDAHO AS A SENATOR

Law regulating and licencing commission men buying farm products, losing their licence in event of fraud.

Legislation for construction of Arrowrock Dam.

Bill providing for construction of American Falls Dam.

Extension of payments for water rights in Boise project thru 40 years.
Moratorium for settlers during depression.
Bills providing federal buildings at:
Bonners Ferry, St. Anthony, Montepelier and Grangeville
Author of Children's Bureau Bill and Labor Department Bill.
Bill to reduce salaries of Congressmen.
Threw $16,000 of his own salary back into the Treasury during depression.
Three Year Homestead Law.

It had been difficult for Republican leaders to be patient with Borah, as his course during convention proceedings was certainly irritating. In the campaign he was even more exasperating. His venom was aimed not at the New Deal but at the individuals in the Republican party he did not like. Early in October he announced emphatically that he would make no speeches for Landon. "I am not supporting him. Beyond that, my actions and my views I am voicing in my talks to the people of Idaho speak for themselves."[48]

He had been asked by the National Committee to make several nationwide radio broadcasts for Landon but refused. He warned Republican leaders that if they forced him to take a stand publicly on the national race, he would make it known that he preferred Roosevelt. This threat evidently grew out of a secret meeting of Republican leaders in Idaho who planned to smoke him out and attack him. His interview was reported from Republican sources in the Philadelphia *Record* (October 4, 1936), and it produced a national political sensation. Borah was bombarded by long-distance calls in a frantic effort to get him to retract the interview, but he merely insisted that he was tending to his own knitting and taking no part in the presidential contest.

At Cottonwood he attacked the gold standard. "We might as well go back to the ox age as talk about going back to the gold standard," he said. At Genesee he said: "There is nothing left for me in the way of glory in the Senate." He wanted only to help in the fight against monopoly and to improve the monetary situation. At Moscow he advocated the formation of a monetary authority under the control of Congress. He wound up the long, strenuous swing through Idaho with speeches in Burley, Buhl, Idaho Falls, Parma, Malad, and Coeur d'Alene, where he closed his campaign.

Driving back to Boise, he voted in the sixth precinct at 11th and Bannock streets with Mrs. Borah.

Toward the close of the campaign, candidate Ross's self-assurance waned perceptibly. Earlier he had boasted that he would "take Borah for a cleaning." By the end of October he summed up his expectations by merely saying: "I am an optimist." Like most Democrats he was hoping to ride into office on F.D.R.'s coattails. Borah remained in Boise to watch the election returns come in at the *Statesman* office.

There were plenty of split ballots in Idaho that year. Borah was the lone G.O.P. victor in the Gem State. He led Ross in the voting by two to one and even forged ahead of F.D.R.'s tremendous majority by four thousand. The extent of Borah's victory was not apparent until a final count revealed he polled 126,000 votes, almost double the Ross figure of 71,500 and more votes than any Idaho candidate had ever received (the total population was 445,000). He was the sole survivor amid an avalanche that swept the Democrats into state offices and gave Idaho's four electoral votes to Roosevelt. Ross then admitted that there had never been any doubt in his mind about Borah's ability.

Right after the election Borah went to bed sick in the Owyhee Hotel. He nevertheless prepared a statement for the Idaho papers:

> The vote I received has filled my cup of gratitude to overflowing. The people of the state, regardless of party, have put me under an obligation which will summon to its discharge all that I have to give. There was a time when I felt that I wanted to retire. The people of the state had done so much for me that I felt I had better risk a discharge than to quit. So I chose to go into the contest. I am going back to serve the people to whom I am affectionately devoted.[49]

He said that Roosevelt's victory placed on the President a great responsibility: "I shall work with him whenever I can." In a letter to a friend he declared Landon was buried because the masses believed he would, if elected, be the representative of the interests "of the few as against the many." The party is out of power, he predicted, for an indefinite period.[50]

The Idaho *Statesman,* which had not approved of Borah's conduct, printed an editorial which accused him of riding into office on the New Deal bandwagon. He took the course not of courage but of safety, it said. With his name on the Republican ballot he did not raise his voice to defeat the party that had placed in jeopardy the Constitution. "It is inevitable," commented one editor, "that Mr. Borah will come to know, if not to acknowledge, that the price of his tremendous majority was too high."[51]

From the standpoint of the regulars this was a valid statement, but Borah rarely got the support of regulars. He was really an independent with a mystic loyalty to the party which never seemed to live up to the ideals he conceived for it. He was a Republican by inheritance and a Democrat by inclination. He tried to stand for the best in the two parties and was inevitably accused of straddling. It was not cowardice, however, which prompted him to act as he did. It took courage for him to wage an unending battle against the old guard in the party which he really loved, even though he scourged it.

The New York *Times* concluded that Borah was both a lion and a fox. A man of courage, he knew when to be brave and also when to lie low. Borah placed his case before the voters on a strictly nonpartisan basis and was elected by a very large vote, which was a tribute both to him and to the discrimination of Idaho voters. Telegrams poured in congratulating him on his sixth straight victory—whole fistfuls of messages from the lowly and the prominent. Wires came from Amos Pinchot, Bernard Baruch, Walter Lippmann, William Green, Salmon Levinson, Joseph Tumulty, Ward Morehouse, and a host of Idaho friends. They all gave testimony to the truth of the old saying: "You can't beat a thorobred [*sic*] with a cold-blooded quarter horse over distance of ground."[52]

Only sixteen Republicans were left in the Senate after the election of 1936, and nearly all of them were progressives like Capper, Frazier, McNary, Vandenberg, and Borah, who was entering his thirtieth year as lawmaker. The Idaho veteran continued to exert an influence in the Senate because many of the New Dealers liked him and were willing to listen to him. Some of them were new at the job, and others were political accidents.

Borah returned to Idaho in September 1937 for a month's rest.

His attention during that summer had been focused on the war in China, which he called "an aggressive war of conquest." Arriving at Boise on the "Portland Rose," he soon learned that F.D.R. was scheduled to cross the big potato commonwealth the following week. Borah was pleased; in fact, he was accused of rushing home simply because Roosevelt was coming.[53] Their meeting was certainly no accident. It was preceded by several days of negotiations and a telegraphic invitation which Borah accepted. The favor shown him was intended to effect the political situation in Idaho, where Borah seemed to hold the balance of power between two Democratic factions vying for the Senate seat held by Jim Pope, a 100 per cent New Dealer whom Roosevelt wanted re-elected. Although Roosevelt had carried the state by a vote of two to one in 1936, Borah had polled thirty thousand more votes than the President. A few words of recommendation from him, it was thought, would insure Pope's re-election in 1938.[54]

F.D.R. arrived on September 28 and addressed the Boise crowd briefly from his car near the Capitol steps. For Borah there was a hearty handshake at the station and a place in the second car of the motorcade. Introducing Roosevelt, Borah said: "This is a great day for Idaho. We all join in welcoming our great President." Roosevelt said he felt like Antaeus: "I regain strength by just meeting the American people." He liked to think of America achieving "a wider distribution of the control of industrial activities, and that sounds like Borah," he said. Later he added: "I try to think about the influence the United States can have on the rest of the world for peace, and that sounds like Borah, too."

On the train Borah ate lunch and had a private talk with the President. He was the only Republican asked aboard the train since it had left Hyde Park. Beaming with satisfaction as he passed photographers on the platform, he explained that while he expected to have no part in the proceedings, he couldn't let any President of the United States come to Boise without paying his respects.[55]

Back in Washington, however, the smiling and handshaking were soon forgotten in the heat of political debate. In a ninety-minute speech Borah charged that the philosophy of crop reduction in the new farm bill was driving the country to national suicide. It could only mean a constant reduction of purchasing power. He favored the ever-normal granary but found no authority for production control. With its cost, he said, our farm surplus could be bought and distributed to the needy, thus supporting agricultural prices and helping the country. "Let's get over the fool idea that the farmers of the United States don't know how to run their farms," he urged. He was trying to cure the malady of underconsumption with the milder wrong of overproduction.

While Mrs. Borah was in the West visiting relatives, Borah fell ill in the summer of 1938 and was attended by a nurse until his wife's return. They went directly to Poland Springs, where he spent three weeks in bed with a severe case of influenza. The October trip to Idaho was canceled that year, and as soon as he was able, he became absorbed in foreign affairs as world conditions worsened. In the Senate he warned the United States to keep its hands off Europe. He opposed an arms build-up but supported increases in the air force. Though hostile to a third term for the President, he said the Constitution should be left alone. "Let anyone who undertakes to break the tradition answer to the people who will settle the matter," he advised.[56]

Early in February 1939 overwork caused another collapse. Complaining of a cold, he left the office and during that night he had to be rushed to the hospital to be treated for lung congestion, probably pneumonia. Recurring influenza was reported as the cause for his condition, which was described as serious. Letters poured in from a score of anxious friends: Hiram Johnson, Joe Bailey, Henry Cabot Lodge, Jr., Walter George, J. Hamilton Lewis, and Arthur Capper. However, by February 16 he was back at work again, though much thinner, having spurned the doctor's advice to go south for a short rest. Before his illness he had announced that it was imperative to form a new bloc in the Senate to check the "foreign ambitions," as he put it, of President Roosevelt. In recent months he had grown very suspicious of administration policy.[57] Shortly after that the old team of Borah and Johnson reappeared. A series of informal conferences with senators on the international situation preceded the debate on national defense and neutrality. Battle-scarred, Borah took down his old weapons and made ready for a last-ditch stand for neutrality as war clouds gathered over Europe.

XIX The Troubled Thirties

Dictators ride to and fro upon tigers which they dare not dismount. And the tigers are getting hungry.

—Winston Churchill

Japanese aggression in China, Italian expansion into Ethiopia, civil war in Spain, and dictatorships and annexationist ambitions in fascist Italy and Germany occupied the headlines of the troubled thirties. As in Wilson's time, foreign affairs interrupted the domestic reform program and presented a new and sharper challenge to the United States as a world power. No policy, no prudence, no energy, no generosity could, it appeared, restore the old, peaceful, secure days of the recent past. There was a growing nostalgia for the days when all America, not merely Oklahoma, felt that everything was going her way. For the first time the republic was forced to share with others the disabilities of fear, tension, and sacrifice imposed by that eternal vigilance that is the price of liberty. Like Macbeth, the United States could sleep no more; as with all insomniacs, nerves became fretted and judgment was uneven.[1]

With Hubert Herring and Edwin Borchard, Borah belonged in the peace party with the neutralists who occupied time gathering proof that all but three American lives were lost in strict accordance with international law during Germany's submarine war on the Allies during 1914-17. Like many other Americans, they believed our entry into World War I was a grave mistake; we must never repeat it. They seemed convinced that Britain had needed the United States to protect her vast empire. Denying that they were isolationists, they claimed to be the true internationalists, for they could assure peace while the "Sir Galahad philosophy of collective security" led only to war, imperialism, vast armaments, sanctions, and national economic self-sufficiency. They favored a rigid adherence to the traditional doctrine of neutrality which exacts impartiality toward all belligerents. If neutral rights were violated, they advocated protecting them, if necessary, by force. This was in line with Borah's remark: "I do not consider neutrality as synonymous with cowardice."[2] In part, at least, this explains his otherwise bewildering attitude on the Spanish Civil War. We should take no sides, he advised. When we have exhausted the methods of peace, we have done our full duty to the cause of peace and to the world.

Throughout the twenties Borah had called for a vigorous foreign policy aimed at revision of the Versailles Treaty, disarmament, and outlawry of war, but he maintained that our primary interest would remain domestic reform. He did not believe that attention should be diverted from fundamental problems at home, and he became more urgent about this as conditions abroad steadily deteriorated. While he never ignored world issues and tried to view them in their proper perspective, he reiterated his faith in American moral superiority and his wish to exercise that moral influence in carrying out the American mission. To do this required staying at home to develop more fully the democratic way of life. His was not a policy of complete withdrawal from world affairs, but it was characterized by a consistent refusal to make any political commitments infringing on the nation's freedom of action, no matter how desirable the final goal. Wilsonian internationalism stood completely rejected. Borah pledged that the United States always stood ready to fulfill its obligations to mankind, but he insisted that the nation must always act independently—neither at the bidding nor through the permission of other countries. Senator Arthur Vandenberg of Michigan, who succeeded to Borah's leadership in the Senate, thought so too.

Not until 1940, when France fell and Britain stood alone, confronting the grim prospect of blood, sweat, and tears, did a sense of the implacable necessities of the situation really begin to overcome the suspicion that somebody was trying to put something over on us. Vandenberg lived to see the unfolding of events; Borah died in the midst of the transition. While he lived, he continued to cling to his bankrupt philosophy of hopeless independence, stating as late as October 1937: "I do not think the way to keep us out of war is to undertake to curb aggressors." He was frank to admit that he could see no effective peaceful means either. He was therefore in favor of keeping absolutely aloof from European embroilments.

Borah might have gleaned some of his ideas on the nature of the European struggle from the diplomatic historian, Samuel Flagg

Bemis, from whom he requested a copy of a speech in which the isolationist Yale professor said: "I suggest we look after the United States first and not go on another crusade for democracy in Europe, where the issue is not altogether democracy, but primarily another contest of power politics and imperialism." Bemis actually disliked isolation but preferred it to identification with "the senseless repetition of the cyclical struggle between dynamic and static forces." He thought, along with Borah, that it would be better to keep our young men home than to send them overseas to lose their lives in another of Europe's endless quarrels which had been going on for centuries and would continue into the future. Emotionally we were unready for a commanding role in world affairs. Borah represents one of the best examples of this emotional immaturity. His speeches during the thirties bespoke the sentiment of millions of honest, sincere, robust Americans whose inherited and acquired instincts told them that they belonged to the United States and that their proper role was looking after their own affairs. America was, indeed, the reluctant world power.[3]

At the dedication of the Borah Foundation for the Outlawry of War in Moscow, Idaho, in September 1931, Idaho's senior senator charged that Japan's invasion of Manchuria was a violation of the Kellogg Pact, the League Covenant, the Versailles Treaty, and international law.[4] Hoover's secretary of war, Henry Stimson, was also convinced that Japanese militarists had violated treaties and destroyed the security system set up at the Washington Conference. Although loud in his condemnation of Japan, Borah advised the withdrawal of Americans from China to prevent any provocative act.

For more than two months Stimson maintained his nonrecognition of the new situation in Manchuria with no support from the British Foreign Office. On February 23, 1932, his one-man offensive took the form of an open letter, said to be the joint work of Hoover and Borah, addressed to Senator Borah as chairman of the Foreign Relations Committee; in this letter he gave his nonrecognition policy vehement expression and extended it to cover violations of the Nine Power Pact and the Kellogg Pact. The United States insisted on its treaty rights in the Far East. Stimson hoped this letter would rally American public opinion to support his position and at the same time show the world how far we were willing to go. Borah responded by praising the nonrecognition plan. Then the two men made arrangements for delivering to the Senate certain documents on Manchuria as a step toward eventual settlement of the problem by negotiation. Events proved that the Stimson doctrine had no deterrent effect on Japan. It amounted to opposing aggression with weapons that were irritating but ineffectual. Borah acquiesced because he was opposed to the use of force.[5] There is some evidence that the Stimson policy, expressed in this letter and generally praised by the American press, played a role in influencing Japan to effect a compromise with China resulting in the withdrawal of troops from Shanghai in May 1932.

Early in 1933, when the failure of the League to solve the Manchurian problem had become evident, Borah introduced a resolution (S.J. 229) patterned on the Embargo Acts of 1912 and 1922 empowering the President to stop arms shipments to Latin American countries. This resolution probably originated in the State Department, then in the midst of an effort to reprimand Japan. Borah regarded the proposal mainly as a blow at munitions makers. This and an identical measure proposed by Senator McReynolds, which also failed, did something to establish a bridge of policy between the Hoover and Roosevelt administrations.[6]

In a speech on the Naval Construction bill of 1934, Borah called the great manufacturers of arms "international criminals." We were selling large quantities of war materials to Japan. He warned that American soldiers might be torn limb from limb by them if war with Japan ever came. So long as munitions firms exercised an influence over the government, he said, no progress in disarmament could be made; despite the depression, he charged, they were realizing profits up to 30 per cent. By inference Borah was asking the Senate to initiate an investigation of the munitions industry.[7]

Peace became more and more an emotional issue. In 1934 Senator Gerald Nye led the shouting as the new antiwar chorus swelled. The Senate gave him carte blanche and $50,000 to head an investigation of the role bankers and munitions makers had played in bringing the United States into World War I. The committee adduced information of some significance concerning the influence of J. P. Morgan's fiscal activities with Britain in the prewar period, but it made absurd attempts to convict Wilson of duplicity. However, it concentrated on branding American munitions makers as "Merchants of Death." The work of this committee paved the way for the neutrality legislation of 1935.[8]

On March 23, 1935, Borah had lunch with the President—his first visit to the White House since the inauguration. Roosevelt later told a press conference, with no further elaboration, that the Idaho leader had "an extremely interesting mind." Commenting freely to the press on the principles rather than the details of their discussion of German rearmament, Borah said Germany would do as she pleased and the Allies would submit. "I have a very strong conviction," he added, "that there is not going to be any war in Europe within the near future or for any reasonable time." Europe would never have *real* peace, however, until the Versailles Treaty was revised. "This may lead to a re-writing of the Treaty on such terms as will give much greater assurance of peace and stability in Europe." The administration as yet showed little disposition to condemn or even protest against the aggressive steps take by Hitler: the repudiation of the Versailles and Locarno treaties, the re-occupation of the Rhineland, the persecution of the Jews, and the rearming of Germany. Nor did Borah lift his great voice in protest.[9]

Two of the best sources we have for Borah's attitude toward fascism are an address and an article dated 1937. Celebrating the one hundred fiftieth anniversary of the Constitutional Convention in September, he spoke at the Masonic services in Washington, where he was introduced by Representative Sol Bloom. Then followed a scathing attack on Nazism and its adherents in this country who would undermine our system of government. He held out the threat of electrocution to von Neurath for planting Nazi meddlers, "evangels of the swastika," here. In an article on fascism which was prepared for, but not accepted by the *Nation,* he submitted that fascism and communism were whelps from the same kennel, both barking at the same thing—constitutional government. Both had for their principal tenet hate. He struck out at the complacency found everywhere which would witness the transplanting to this democracy of the Nazi brand of fascism in all its hideous deformity—race antagonism, religious intolerance, and cruelty. He found the fascists more active and adroit than the communists. Though they worked in different ways, both sought the same ends.

He said he was not interested in fascism as it related to foreign countries, but only as it might eventually affect this one. We cannot afford to be unconcerned, he said, about the attempt by foreign countries to stir up racial feelings here. He called for an end to the continuing activities of armed and uniformed groups of fascists. The vast majority of German-Americans, said Borah, are opposed to the Nazi movement. His article was rejected because he failed to list positive steps to control Nazi activities in this country without limiting civil rights. Borah explained in a letter to the *Nation's* editor that he had more specific information, but had not included it in his article for the simple reason that it would embarrass sources which were constantly supplying him with new information.[10]

Borah wrote German *Bund* leader Fritz Kuhn stating that he had facts and data in his possession showing that Nazi organizations were teaching doctrines wholly at war with our theory of government. In his reply Kuhn not only denied this but stated that there was no official connection between the German-American *Bund* and the National Socialist party in Germany. The *Bund* received no subsidies from the fatherland and was engaged in no indoctrination program here.[11]

Hitler's assaults on the property, position, and finally the person of thousands of Jews in Germany drew quick response in this country. Borah's grandfather was of German origin, and the onetime Illinois farm boy had always entertained a quiet pride in his forebears, who pioneered in building the Midwest. Borah had applauded Hitler's repudiation of the war guilt and territorial clauses of the Versailles Treaty, which he himself had often condemned. The Idaho senator saw much to admire in the social reforms ushered in on a grand scale by the Nazis after 1933, but he was repelled by the Nazi persecution of the Jews. Though he was determined to use all his influence to prevent Nazi theories of government from being introduced into this country, his morality in politics evidently stopped at the water's edge. So long as foreign countries confine themselves to their own areas, he implied, he would have nothing to say in the way of criticism. Every country has a right to put its own house in order according to its own ideas.

Borah received letters from all over the country protesting against his refusal to speak out against Nazi persecutions. Rabbi Stephen Wise, active in the Zionist cause, wrote him in an effort to enlist his participation in the Senate debate on the plight of the Jews in Poland. Senator Wagner of New York had introduced a bill to admit ten thousand Jewish refugee children to this country from Germany. Activated by narrow nationalism and a fear of economic collapse, Borah opposed any repeal or modifications of the immigration laws to give Jewish refugees of Nazi terror asylum here. He wrote: ". . . as I look at it, . . . this country belongs to the people of this country. I am not willing, myself, while hundreds of thousands in this country are hungry, perhaps millions of children underfed . . . and hordes of young boys and girls coming into active life seeking jobs without ability to get them, to let down the bars. That, to my mind, could not be justified on any theory of patriotism or humanity."[12]

He maintained that we could not go back to the old system of making the United States a haven for the dissatisfied and oppressed people of all lands, not with twelve million unemployed in this country. Moreover, he sensed an effort to draw us into a controversy with Europe over the colonial question. In spite of repeated urgings from Rabbi Wise, he refused to protest against Britain's handling of her mandate and her attempts to limit the migration of Jews into Palestine. Zionists like Wise were up in arms, but Borah stated that unless we were willing to go farther than England and assume obligations in this matter ourselves, we had to trust the patience and wisdom of the mandatory power. The colonial problem was purely a European question. He was full of sympathy for the Jews, he said, but once we established such a precedent, we would be forced to take the refugees of all countries. While he sympathized with efforts of Zionists to establish a homeland in Palestine, he was opposed to this country's assuming any responsibility. Unsatisfied with the stand Borah had taken thus far, Levinson wrote him early in 1938:

> The brutal treatment by Nazi Germany of the labor unions, of all the religious and liberal groups, and the deprivation of all semblance of rights on the part of the people would seem to call from a great humanitarian like yourself for severe condemnation rather than the semblance of a strained defense of a brazen breach of our Treaty.[13]

Borah paid scant heed to this and other pleas. The strong statements friends sought from him never came. He was certainly no sympathizer with the Nazi cause, but he gave the curious impression that it was immune from attack on the rather indefensible ground that it was purely a German "family affair." On the colonial problem he added this enlightened bit of information: Germany had the same right to take back her colonies in peace that England had to take them in World War I!

In the summer of 1935 Congress passed the first Neutrality Act, granting the President discretionary power to impose an embargo in the event of a declared war. Roosevelt termed the purpose of the law "wholly excellent," but he was unhappy about certain weaknesses in the legislation which he hoped would be remedied in the future. Secretary of State Hull and other internationalists deplored the legislation as certain to encourage aggressors, but Borah declared it "a milestone in our return to a long established policy." In a radio speech he left his audience guessing with this curious statement: ". . . this nation will remain at peace with all nations who want peace; and if there be those who do not want peace, and will not have peace, we, under such circumstances, need have no fear." If Borah really believed that in another major European war we could hope to continue our maritime commerce with neutral nations uninterrupted even under the terms of the Neutrality Act, without being drawn into the conflict, then the lessons of history had no meaning for him.[14]

Roosevelt came slowly to a realization that the United States could not afford to sit back while totalitarian despots struck down one free nation after another, and said as much in his Quarantine Speech of 1937, for which he was denounced by Senators Wheeler, Nye, and Borah as a "warmonger."[15] This speech marked the beginning of the administration's retreat from isolation. By then the Italians had overrun Ethiopia, the Nazis were helping Franco conquer Spain, and Hitler had defied the Locarno Pact. In this year of heightening tension Congress, still controlled by isolationist sentiment, decided to pass a permanent neutrality measure. The chief innovation in the measure was the Pittman resolution or the "cash and carry" clause, which Borah had opposed from the start.

During his speech of March 1, 1937, a crowded Senate chamber listened to the word picture he drew of American factories and ports suffering from aerial bombardment while the country attempted to preserve its neutrality. "I am one of those," he said, "who believe there are some things you have to fight for." The cash-and-carry provision, which Senator Vandenberg called the doctrine of transferred risk, would make this country the ally of the nation having the greatest navy—Great Britain. It would be inevitable, Borah said, that the nation attacking Britain, if brought to a desperate pass, would bomb American factories. He advocated attaching to our policy of building up our foreign trade a decisive announcement of our intention to protect that trade.[16] No one attempted to answer his arguments. Despite one last plea, the Senate adopted the cash-and-carry feature, 62 to 6. Borah stood in the rear of the chamber, smiling sadly as the majority vote rolled on to its unexpectedly crushing total.[17] Then he fell back on his somber meditations.

When the American gunboat "Panay" was sunk by the Japanese, Borah brushed aside proposals for sending Tokyo an ultimatum; he saw no cause for drastic action. "The facts show," he asserted, "that the *Panay* was in a war region and what happened may be expected . . . in a war zone." He was sure we could protect our nationals in China without becoming involved in war.[18]

In February 1938 Borah led the opposition to the administration's foreign policy, charging that the country was being deliberately exposed to the very influences that brought on World War I. In Anthony Eden's speech in the House of Commons on December 21, 1937, Borah found evidence for the existence of an understanding between England and the United States with regard to the situation in the Far East. He attacked British lecturers who came here "to spread their propaganda" that world peace could not be preserved except through a close working alliance. "All these things cannot be whistled down the wind," said Borah. "They are what make foreign policies . . . put nations into action . . . brought on the World War . . . Our policy will be affected by them in spite of anything we may do." He was willing to support the program for naval increases if convinced that they would be for the use of the United States alone, but he suspected that more than national defense was contemplated.[19]

Eventually Borah censured Hitler for his refusal to halt persecution in Germany. At the same time he found the main issue in dispute to be Germany's former colonies. He predicted that the *Third Reich* would eventually get them back, although England would try to hold them as long as possible. Imperialism was the cause of the frantic armaments race, drawing the "have-not" nations (Germany, Italy, and Japan) together. The Versailles Treaty produced these dictatorships. He said: "Subtract Versailles and there is nothing extraordinary in the European situation."[20]

Through the early part of 1938 Borah kept insisting that there was no such thing as branding an aggressor. He also roasted certain people, whom he failed to identify, for speaking ex cathedra: their remarks were calculated to make all kinds of trouble. The only sensible speech, he submitted, was that of Ambassador Joseph Kennedy from London in April 1938. We may suppose, on the face of things, that Borah placed great store in what Kennedy told him. That same month Kennedy wrote Borah:

> The more I see of things here, the more convinced I am that we must exert all of our intelligence and effort toward keeping clear of any involvement. As long as I hold my present job, I shall never lose sight of this guiding principle. I find that Mr. Chamberlain, Lord Halifax, and other high officials here understand thoroughly the state of public opinion at home. They have assured me, in private conversation, that they are going ahead with their plans without counting on the United States to be either for or against them. They have never given me the slightest impression that they want or expect anything special from us. Having had this clearly understood from the beginning, I have been able to deal with them in a frank and business-like manner . . .[21]

In an interview in the spring of 1938 Borah told C. William Duncan: "The United States is getting worked up over the prospect of war. I'm not . . . You are a young man as compared to me and neither of us will live to see the day when the United States is invaded. With the Atlantic on one side and the vast Pacific on the other we are safe. It would be folly, from a military standpoint, for another country to try to invade us and they know it." Japan had no designs on the United States, he said. She wanted China only. He charged Britain and France with duplicity at the Geneva Conference of 1932 and condemned as a "shameless betrayal" their sanctioning the crushing of Haile Selassie's sovereignty in Ethiopia. What is the difference, he asked, between seizing a nation and accepting the seizure? The democracies of Europe have no more regard for treaty obligations than dictatorships, he asserted.[22]

Commenting on the *Anschluss* in a speech on March 28, 1938, Borah found it a sad and stirring thing to see the vast estate of Maria Theresa pass under the dominion of another power. "But if you begin your study of the event with the signing of the Versailles Treaty . . ." he said, "that which happened to Austria would appear natural, logical, inevitable, and a thing which is not of the slightest moment to the government of the United States." Austria had never been a genuinely independent nation since escaping from the operating table at Versailles. It was inevitable that some strong power would extend its dominions to this pivotal piece of territory. Even if Hitler had remained a hod carrier, Austria and Germany would have attempted another *Anschluss,* as in 1921. Declared Borah: "It is nothing less than a flimsy piece of transparent acting for these nations who joined in committing that first crime to . . . make a world tragedy of the fact that the nation thus outraged has come under a new master. Austria cannot possibly receive harsher treatment."[23]

Before an agreement was reached settling any of the Nazi demands at the Munich conferences in September 1938, the French government made an urgent appeal for American intervention in the crisis. Borah castigated the French premier: "It would have been more in harmony with that national honor so often exemplified in French history had Mr. Blum [Daladier] given his attention to the fact that France had a solemn treaty with Czechoslovakia to come to her rescue and instead of advising the United States as to her duty, had advised his own people to courageously stand by their treaty."[24] As Hitler threatened war, Daladier and Chamberlain made their supreme effort to appease him, compelling Czechoslovakia to agree to the Four Power accord which gave him the Sudetenland.

In this, one of the most complex events of modern times, French weakness, British pacifism, Polish hatred of Russia, the recent Soviet purges, and American isolation all played their part. However, Borah was quick to render a verdict against Paris and London, glossing over Nazi aggression. After the event he commented: "The Munich Pact makes the violation of treaties a cardinal tenet of modern diplomacy . . . makes the mere name of treaty a byword and a hissing." While our government had urged an agreement, he claimed we were not responsible for its terms.[25] He called the Munich Pact the best illustration of cold-blooded betrayal of one nation by another in the history of modern times.

In a letter to Walter Lippmann he accused France and England of using the words democracy and dictatorship to promote sympathy for themselves and hatred for Germany, despite the fact that they had combined to destroy the one real democracy in Europe. Then they tried to throw the blame over on us. "As an American," wrote Borah, "I am quite willing that all the glory of that world surrender belongs exclusively to France and Great Britain acting as the amanuenses of Hitler."[26] Borah was convinced that Britain had made up her mind as early as May 1938 that she would help Germany in the dispute with the Czechs. If Britain had been frank with Czechoslovakia, informing her of British intentions in May, he felt certain that that small country could have made a far better settlement with Germany than she finally had to take. Borah blamed Britain for allowing Hitler to reach a position where Germany could violate the laws of men and nations. Imperialistic greed and not a clash of ideals was the main factor threatening war. He charged Britain with deliberately and selfishly encouraging Hitler in his eastward drive, hoping he would thus satisfy his appetite and leave her safe. At Munich, he declared, Britain conducted a policy of ostracizing Moscow, one of her main objectives being to dispose of Russia as a European power; yet within two months she was courting a close association with Russia.

These charges were not supported by evidence then available. We were as desperately anxious for peace as Britain or France. Our own President had joined Chamberlain and Daladier in a plea to Mussolini to persuade Hitler to accept a peaceful settlement, giving him substantially all he asked for. Hitler yielded only to the extent of meeting with the three other heads of state at Munich. By his incessant attacks on Britain, Borah was unwittingly reassuring the war party in Germany of American indifference. Listening to Borah in Berlin, no German could seriously believe that the United States had any intention of following the President's lead in his determination, by methods stronger than words but short of war, to lend moral and material support to the hard-pressed democracies of Europe.[27]

Just before the debate began on amending the Neutrality Act, Borah expressed the wish to visit Germany and talk with Hitler about the plight of the Jews and other matters related to world peace. He entertained hopes that the conference might produce a plan for international peace. Early in 1938 William K. Hutchinson, a staff correspondent for the International News Service, had urged him to make a personal appeal to Hitler to cease his attacks on Jews in Germany. "I am willing to do anything . . .," said Borah, "but it must be effective, otherwise it may bring only greater unhappiness down on the heads of those poor people." The State Department sent an appeal on March 24, 1938, to all major powers for co-operation in financing the emigration of political refugees from Germany. Jewish organizations preferred this action to an appeal from Borah.

Shortly after the Munich Pact an even more violent Jewish purge was precipitated by the assassination of a German official in Paris. In mid-November Roosevelt ordered Ambassador Hugh Wilson home from Berlin and expressed shock that such outrages could occur in a twentieth-century civilization.

On November 23 Borah told Hutchinson he would still like to visit Germany if he could only be certain of having an interview with Hitler. Hutchinson quoted Borah as saying: "There are so many great sides to him, I believe I might accomplish something . . . if I only could talk to him face to face. There's always the possibility I might get Hitler to relax a bit. I just can't get that thought out of my mind." Hutchinson encouraged him to go, believing that once Borah was on German soil Hitler would be glad to talk to him.

Next Hutchinson called on Kurt Sell, Washington correspondent for the German News Agency, relating Borah's wish. He explained Borah insisted on having a personal talk with Hitler and suggested that the *Third Reich* offer him transportation, for he was not a rich man and might find it embarrassing if unable to finance the trip himself. Sell was far from enthusiastic, but he finally agreed to sound out his government.

On November 22, 1938, German Ambassador Dieckhoff sent the following confidential telegram to the reichsminister in Berlin:

Senator Borah has been introduced to me through an intermediary, and has intimated that he would like to travel to Germany and have an audience with the Fuehrer . . . Borah has great sympathy for Germany and it is well known that he has for years attacked the reparations settlement and he has especially raged over the Versailles Treaty. Well known also is his aversion for an American alliance with England or France. Recently he has advocated precautions against more Jews emigrating here . . . he believes that the very fact of his trip to Germany would operate to calm the situation there . . . Borah intimated he would like to do all in his power to knit together the torn threads as between Germany and the United States, and he would be greatly troubled if the Fuehrer would refuse him this audience. He would like to travel in December. As was indicated, he would not refuse, if free passage as the guest of the North German Lloyd were offered him.

Dieckhoff betrayed less enthusiasm about the journey than Sell. He continued:

I believe that no good purpose could be served by having Borah come now. The very fact that he has in the last few years repeatedly spoken out sharply against the Third Reich would perhaps be no unconditional hindrance, for he is himself a man of integrity, who . . . though without any large political following, is nevertheless esteemed throughout the country. However, I do not believe that the trip of a single senator, especially one belonging to the opposition, could swiftly alter the foreign policy of President Roosevelt. With such weak implements, as the activities of Herr Kennedy in London show, the relations between the United States and Germany are not to be righted. I reserve further comment for my oral communication.[28]

The Foreign Office in Berlin telegraphed a coded reply on November 26, addressed to their chargé, Hans Thomsen:

Please communicate to Senator Borah concerning his question, in an appropriate manner, that the Fuehrer and Foreign Secretary are prepared to receive him any time . . . For your personal information the doubts suggested by the ambassador were not considered here as important.[29]

Borah was informed by telephone on November 28 that the German embassy in Washington had received this message, inviting him to visit Germany for talks with Hitler and von Ribbentrop. A few days later Thomsen informed the Berlin officials: "Senator Borah has received the ready acceptance of his proposition with great joy. He will acquaint the State Department of his purpose and seek their backing, which I consider expedient, so that there can be no ultimate objection to his plan from the circle around the President. The cost of the trip Borah himself wants to undertake to avoid the suspicion of having accepted a gift from Germany. Final decision is expected within a few days."[30]

Borah delayed action until Secretary Hull returned from the eighth Pan-American Conference at Lima in December 1938. He would go to Germany only if the attitude of the State Department was friendly or neutral. Ruefully, he remarked: "I must take my chances anyway of being a complete failure and achieving nothing. I would have to live with that for the rest of my life."

Hutchinson pressed Borah for a decision, but learned that he planned a trip to Baltimore first for a checkup by his doctors and a talk with Judge R. Walton Moore, former assistant secretary of state. By the time he returned to his office, relations with Germany had worsened. Borah learned that Hull frowned upon the idea of a trip to Germany, and after President Roosevelt declared at his press conference with the Senate Military Affairs Committee, "Our frontier is on the Rhine," Borah concluded: "They've tipped him off. He's going to keep me from seeing Hitler."

The debate on the Neutrality Act was pending in the January session of Congress, and Borah was preparing to oppose the administration's recommendation for repeal of the arms embargo. He foresaw how embarrassing it would be for him if he were to have recently visited Hitler. So he postponed his trip indefinitely. In February illness overtook him. At no time during the busy session that spring or summer was there any opportunity for a trip abroad. Congress adjourned August 5; by mid-August the government began evacuating Americans from European ports; and by September England and Germany were at war. Once more circumstances thwarted Borah's plan for a trip abroad.

Observers have pointed out how conciliatory Hermann Goering was in conversations with William Rhodes Davis. On the other hand, numerous other visitors, including Sumner Welles, Hamilton Fish, and Charles A. Lindbergh, tried last-minute talks with Hitler and von Ribbentrop, all of which proved futile. Borah, however, betrayed naïve confidence that a talk with Hitler might have produced some fortunate results. Shortly after war broke out, he said to Hutchinson: "Lord, if I could only have talked with Hitler, all this might have been avoided." It was fortuitous that the march of events prevented Borah from joining those pacifists and liberals like George Lansbury and David Lloyd George, who trudged up the hill to Berchtesgaden to lay before the Fuehrer their plans for world peace.[31]

Partially recovered from his illness, Borah led the fight in the Senate against expanding the air corps, surmising that the proposed increases were based on "bluff and jitterism." He found another example of this in the move "to decorate that sand dune on the other side of the Pacific"—referring to the plan to fortify Guam and improve her harbors. The cost, he warned, would bankrupt the nation, while the improvement would be obsolete before the program was completed.[32]

When Hitler's troops entered Prague in March 1939, Borah was asked if this meant war. He replied: "If Hitler is as wise as I believe him to be, he has no designs whatsoever on France. He would gain nothing by attacking France but would so imperil the economic and financial stability of all Europe as very likely to bring about the collapse of his own regime. He has enough on his hands now to consolidate his gains and keep him busy for some time." He went on: "I know it to be a fact as much as I ever will know anything . . . that Britain is behind Hitler . . . Britain wants Hitler to become supreme in all Central Europe . . . Britain will give Hitler a free hand in Europe so long as he makes no move that can be interpreted as a threat to the British lifeline or imperial British possessions." After the Slovakian annexation Borah exclaimed: "Gad, what a chance Hitler has! If he only moderates his religious and racial intolerance, he would take his place beside Charlemagne. He has taken Europe without firing a shot." Like so many others, Borah had been mesmerized by the German spellbinder.[33]

When Hitler answered Roosevelt's appeal for peace by asking for a general revision of the Versailles Treaty, Borah said: "If only the noisy brats over here would keep their mouths shut, Hitler will settle his problems and do it with Chamberlain's consent and help. These two men are going to dominate Europe . . . Chamberlain is never going to let Stalin take the place of Hitler." Borah eventually developed some misgivings about the German dictator, fearing he would become corrupted by power, for he wielded more power in 1939 than Napoleon possessed in 1812.[34]

By mid-July the House had passed a bill containing the arms embargo and a provision empowering the President to define combat areas into which American vessels could not proceed. The Senate Foreign Relations Committee decided, by a vote of 12 to 11, to postpone the question of amending the Neutrality Act or repealing the arms embargo until the next session. Speaking for those who wished to retain the arms embargo and remain neutral, Borah was the key man in the debate preceding the vote. The day before the final Foreign Relations Committee meeting he called the leaders of the isolationist bloc to his office and told them that they must not pocket the bill in committee but should allow the issue to go before the Senate for debate and a vote. No decision was reached at this meeting, but Borah renewed his talks with individual members of the group during the day. The die-hards went into hasty consultation because Borah was scuttling their plan to pigeonhole the measure. Bennett Champ Clark was chosen to bring Senators George and Gillette into line so that the antiadministration forces would be assured of a close majority. They agreed to vote with Clark on condition that there would be no leak to the White House.[35] When it became clear that Congress was about to recess until the following January without taking action, the President, in a final effort, held a conference in the oval room of the White House on July 18. Present were Hull, Garner, Pittman, Barkley, Austin, McNary, Knox, Stimson, McCormick, Rayburn, and Borah. While sandwiches were served, the European situation was discussed. For the first time in many months the administration was asking for Republican as well as Democratic counsel.

The President opened the meeting by saying: ". . . what we do here tonight may be of the greatest importance to the people of the United States, and probably to the world." He emphasized indications that war might break out "at any time, any day, any week."

There was great danger ahead, and he wanted to be prepared to meet the situation should war come. There were no interruptions until he finished, when he asked: "Cordell, what do you think about it?"

Hull confirmed the President's views, outlining the gravity of the situation and asking for a new neutrality law repealing the arms embargo. If our foreign policy were left up in the air, he reasoned, it would only act as a factor urging Germany to war at once. Hull felt he was making little headway, and, according to some, his manner faltered near the end of his presentation. His plan received its *coup de grâce* when Borah interrupted to announce: "I do not believe there is going to be any war in Europe, between now and the first of January or for some time thereafter. Of course, I may be mistaken . . . at least I would rather take the risk of the happening of war than to . . . risk . . . doing those things which will draw the United States into the controversies of Europe. I simply wanted to say it is my opinion, for what it is worth, that we will not have war."

In a burst of Tennessee mountain temper Hull spoke up: "I wish the Senator from Idaho would come down to the State Department and read the dispatches which come in from all over Europe from day to day and I am sure he would change his opinion." The Idahoan replied: ". . . I don't give a damn about your dispatches. They would not govern me in the matter of legislation. Too many things enter into the question of war and what will bring on war . . . We all have means of acquiring information. I myself have gone to great effort to secure information from different sources. I do not . . . simply read the newspapers . . . but I have since the signing of the Versailles Treaty studied Europe as closely as I would study the daily happenings in this country . . ." Other accounts report that Borah said his sources of information were more reliable than the State Department's. Hull restrained himself with great difficulty.

When another senator questioned Hull, he replied: "In view of the statement by Senator Borah that the State Department is inefficient . . . I shall not make any replies to any further questions." Borah protested: "Mr. Secretary, that is a very unfair statement. I have not questioned the efficiency of the State Department, or the Secretary . . . I have a very high regard for the Secretary . . . If I have said anything which reflects personally on the Secretary

. . . or his Department, I am anxious to withdraw it and apologize . . . But I do not withdraw the statement that I would not for a moment be governed simply, or primarily, by the dispatches in the State Department as to whether or not we are going to war."

Garner tried to smooth ruffled tempers by asking Alben Barkley if he had enough votes for revision. Barkley replied: "I don't think so. I'm sure we haven't." All present agreed. A pending bill, it was suggested, would make the Fuehrer think twice. Borah dismissed this theory with a wave of the hand. "What's the use of talking like that?" he asked. "Hitler doesn't give a damn what a committee of the United States Senate does. He is moved by deeper impulses than that, whether right or wrong."

Then the President delivered a long statement saying that if revision failed, it would be his duty to inform the country that the Senate had refused to act. Borah answered him with asperity: "You have your duties . . . I have never voted knowingly to take away from you the responsibility which under the Constitution belongs to you . . . But speaking for myself, and for the Senators who voted as I did on the matter of postponement, I feel sure that we have constitutional obligations resting on us . . . I do not propose knowingly to surrender these . . . One thing is sure; it is no part of your constitutional duty to tell the Senate when to act or how to act . . . I gladly assume this responsibility. We could not escape it if we desired to do so. The Constitution fixed the responsibility on us, and, after all, we are operating under a Constitution and not under Hitler."

Finally Garner said: "Well, Captain, we may as well face the facts. You haven't got the votes and that's all there is to it." Roosevelt took a scratch pad, wrote two statements which were then released to the press, and after more than three hours of heated discussion the senators left the White House.[36] On August 5 Congress adjourned without repealing the Neutrality Act, leaving Roosevelt and Hull in the position of having been repudiated on the highest matter of policy; by September the war which Senator Borah promised would not come burst upon the world. He lived long enough to discover how unreliable his sources of information were.

On the morning following the parley Borah was so hoarse that he could scarcely speak. He declined to comment on what was said the night before: "I don't propose to enter into any controversy with the President if it can be avoided but I do think these bans on White House conferences ought to be lifted."[37] Although the White House meeting was supposed to be secret and off the record, word of it was permitted to slip out indiscreetly by those isolationist senators who preferred to believe Borah was right. Some even thought his solemn pronouncement was enough to doom further efforts at repeal of the arms embargo, but Garner's statement indicates repeal was doomed in any case.

America's diplomatic reporting at the time was full and accurate. The State Department had confidential information that Hitler might move at any time and precipitate a general European conflict. If Borah had seen these dispatches or been apprised of their contents, he might not have made such an emphatic prediction. It developed, after his death, that the chief source of his information was a planographed left-wing magazine called *The Week*, published by Claude Cocburn in London. It was available to anyone who cared to subscribe for two dollars a year; Borah was one of the few American subscribers. Although this publication had been known to scoop its more conservative rivals on occasion, this was not one of the occasions. The article to which Borah had referred merely showed that not all of the ostriches in international politics were in Washington. In London the House of Commons had just recently voted a two-month recess over the protests of Winston Churchill. Most observers rated Borah's conduct at the White House conference as unbelievably arrogant and opinionated. While his presumption was inexcusable, it should not be allowed to obscure the fact that, as usual, his views were optimistically shared by thousands of Americans. The belief that war could be avoided was general, reinforced not only by newsletters in Washington and London but also by the views of American diplomats who disapproved of the President's policy. The question also has been raised as to whether in fact Roosevelt and Hull did not overstate the probability of war, in the light of information then at their disposal. Hitler's move into Poland rested on the outcome of von Ribbentrop's negotiations with Moscow, which were then unconcluded.[38]

After the adjournment the Borahs left for a brief sojourn in Poland Springs. After that they planned to "gypsy around" over the Maine coast and through New England until September 1, when a trip to Idaho was scheduled. The senator was preparing a series of speeches on foreign affairs when war broke out. From Poland Springs he predicted the entry of the United States into the war if the arms embargo were repealed. He announced:

> . . . I feel it is the duty of every public official . . . in this supreme crisis to assist people in realizing this great desire to remain free of the European struggle. We should remain calm and loyal to our own people and if we do so we can stay out . . . we cannot enter the struggle in part . . . If we should furnish arms to one side . . . we would have taken sides . . . if the demands of that side called on us to send our boys into the slaughter pens of Europe to save democracy again our boys would follow our guns into the trenches . . . Let us in good faith and with great tolerance . . . do all we can to save our people from the sacrifice of this imperialistic war.[39]

In a letter to an Idaho constituent he explained his opposition to the cash-and-carry provision of the Neutrality Act: "I feel . . . once we begin furnishing arms, munitions and implements of war, it will place us in such relation to the situation that we will be acting practically as if we were ourselves in the war—and in my judgment, the chances of our getting in are very great." In a radio address on October 23, 1939, he accused Lord Lothian, the British ambassador to this country, of trying to drag the United States into the war on England's side. At a press conference he accused Britain and France of pulling their punches against Germany on the western front. "There is something phony about this war," said Borah, thus coining a famous phrase. "You would think that they would do what they are going to do while Germany and Russia are still busy in the East, instead of waiting until they have cleaned up . . . there."[40]

Congress met in special session on September 21 to consider the repeal of the arms embargo. Three Senate leaders, Overton, Pat McCarran, and Borah, announced they were prepared to fight the President's appeal to lift the embargo from "hell to breakfast."[41] Borah was ready to expedite consideration of the Neutrality Act in committee in exchange for unrestricted floor debate. He needed time only for study and organizing the opposition. Ammunition for the debate against lifting the embargo was continually supplied to Borah by Edwin Borchard, professor of international law at Yale University, and Thomas Healy, who was in the School of Foreign

Service at Georgetown University. Little public interest was shown in the debate since everything had been said many times before, but the galleries filled up when the seventy-four-year-old Borah rose from his chair to answer Key Pittman, who led the fight for the administration. Borah spoke twice as long as Pittman, his remarks ranging from precise citations on international law to an eloquent arraignment of Europe's bloody power politics. He pleaded for the nation to stand by its previous decision to cease trade in instruments of mass murder. He could see nothing in the administration's program to advance the cause of peace. Toward the end of his speech his voice dropped almost to a whisper. Applause swept the galleries as he sat down, exhausted. All the old vehemence, ardor, determination, and eloquence were manifested in this effort. Fellow senators, even those who disagreed with everything he said, flocked to congratulate him. No one felt like taking the assignment of rebuttal, so the Senate adjourned.[42]

After the long debate the opposition gradually broke down. War had begun to shake their resolution. The arms embargo was repealed, and Congress approved the trade in arms on a cash-and-carry basis by a vote of 55 to 24 in the Senate and 243 to 172 in the House. We moved to a position of nonbelligerency, of giving all aid short of war. But as late as April 1940 the attitude of the neutralists remained unshaken. As long as he lived, Borah held firmly to his conviction that this country should take no official interest in the outcome of the war in Europe, even if it meant a Nazi victory. This attitude was buttressed by the comfortable thought that this was a "phony war" and that Britain and France could win it by their allegedly superior resources.

When Britain imposed a blockade on all German exports, Borah roundly denounced it. Pittman admitted the blockade violated international law, but said it was provoked by a previous German wrong—the sowing of wild mines around Britain. Seated on a stone wall in the small park outside the Capitol and wrapped in an army blanket hung over his shoulders like a toga, Borah endorsed what Pittman said but concluded that we were limited in our capacity to do anything about the mines, while we had something to do with the blockade and ought not to have submitted to it. It was enough that we had revised the neutrality laws to aid Britain; no government should be asked to do more. "Add to this the British requirement of a certificate as to the nature of our cargoes shipped to Europe," he said, "and we no longer have any business on the high seas."[43]

In January 1940 Borah urged a "reasonable trade agreement" with Japan to replace the 1911 treaty which was due to expire on January 26. Stimson, in a forceful letter, argued for an American embargo on the shipment of supplies to Japan, which enabled that country to make war on China. He called Japan's action a clear case of unprovoked aggression and asserted it would be within our rights to impose an embargo on the shipment of war materials to Japan "and take ourselves out of a dirty business." Meanwhile, Senator Pittman was preparing to introduce a bill replacing an embargo on American exports to Japan. Borah was opposed to any embargo or boycott of Japanese goods. "We are fooling with dynamite," he said. He warmly endorsed the advice of William R. Castle, former American ambassador to Tokyo, as stated in an article, that our abrogation without warning of our commercial treaty with Japan and the proposed embargo would lead to war. According to Borah, we could not afford to lose Japan's four-hundred-million-dollar annual trade except for a very sound reason. He did not consider recent incidents, such as had occurred at Tientsin, serious enough to break off trade relations with our third largest customer. Joined by Senator Vandenberg, he wanted a new agreement framed from a purely commercial standpoint and in no way sanctioning the "new order in East Asia." Borah was desperately afraid European dislocations would induce a prolonged depression and paralysis of American trade. More fearful over the prospects of economic collapse at home than of the war in Europe, he never swerved from his conviction that the United States could continue to rely on her own resources for national security.

Dr. Wellington T. Kong, Chinese vice-minister of publicity, took issue with Borah over his indulgent position with regard to Japan:

> Unless the democratic countries led by the United States stand for their principles and collective security against aggressive tendencies, even more disasters will be in store for us. There must be something wrong

with any person who still hopes to get blood money by selling munitions and war materials to Japan in order to further her aggression and kill tens of thousands of innocent Chinese.[44]

The "phony war" lasted another four months followed by the blitzkrieg on the Low Countries and the attack on France. As the threat to Britain mounted, Americans were shocked from their complacency. An age was dying—the age of international optimism, Kellogg Pacts, disarmament drives, and goodwill pilgrimages. The world, too absorbed in its woes, did not comprehend the impending tragedy.

XX The Last Roll Call

It is a grave thing when a State puts a name among her jewels.

Washington's social life reached full swing in mid-January 1940, when a mammoth benefit for the Finnish victims of Russia's invasion was arranged to include the Washington *première* of "Gone with the Wind." At Mrs. Garner's party for cabinet wives and Senate ladies in the Rose Room of the Washington Hotel a reporter heard laughter coming from one of the tables where Mary Borah had convulsed some friends with an amusing story. She was dressed in black velvet with several strands of pearls at the neck. On her blonde hair she wore a small pillbox with a white wimple.[1] "Mrs. Borah," her husband once wrote a friend, "has a keen sense of humor, and she has retained it through all these years of gloomy companionship."[2]

"Little Borah," as she was called, had become almost a social institution in Washington. She was a popular figure at teas, luncheons, and receptions. When her husband refused to give up the time to accompany her, she attended these affairs alone or with another escort. She took great interest in her work at the veterans' hospital (St. Elizabeth's). She had learned, since her first lonely days in Washington, to love the city which was to be her home for the rest of her days. Idaho now stood second in her affections.

The day after Mrs. Garner's party, Mrs. Borah attended a reception for Mrs. Charles Edison, wife of the new secretary of the navy. The Senate confirmed his nomination that same day, after Senator Borah finished denouncing Edison's proposal to empower the President to commandeer industry in peacetime. Any such action, claimed Borah, would be a violation of the Bill of Rights and a move toward totalitarianism. He made no objection to Edison's nomination but merely wished it to be understood that he did not endorse this proposal. He insisted that only such power as is found in the Constitution, which was itself adopted in a period of emergency, could be exercised because of an emergency. All around him were evidences that faith in democratic principles and processes was dying, but Borah said that "the little democracy of Finland," then engaged in a life and death struggle with Russia, "had demonstrated to the world the falsity of this cowardly lie."

In this short speech he added that it was vitally important at that time to expose and punish the activities of those whose "isms" ran counter to the principles of our government. "The most vicious enemies of human liberty," he asserted, "the most dangerous to free institutions, are the treacherous foes who seek shelter under the laws and institutions which assure free speech, free press and personal liberty, and then make use of this shelter to destroy the government which protects them." If doubts concerning the Constitution were to be indulged, he declared, they should be resolved against all possible encroachments. He concluded:

> The glory of the Bill of Rights is that it is a restraint upon government as well as upon individuals . . . not only is this Bill of Rights a sacred document of the American people, but when the time comes, as please God, I am sure it will . . . that the oppressed people of the world begin to fight their way back to civilization and away from the frightful 'isms' which engulf them in misery and slavery, they will look to this Bill of Rights as embodying their hopes and ideals . . . If human liberty is sacred, this document is sacred . . .[3]

The confirmation of Edison was unanimous. These were to be Borah's last words in the Senate, and the roll call confirming Edison recorded his last vote.

At that moment in history German troops were poised for the invasion of Belgium, putting an end to the "phony war." In Congress Roosevelt's requested loan to Finland, which Borah opposed, was tabled for a week. Its defeat was predicted, as a wary House and Senate wished to steer clear of the European war.

On Monday, January 15, Borah paid his monthly visit to the doctor, who found him in excellent physical condition. Later that day he went to his office as he had done every day since the special neutrality session had ended that previous fall. He attended the Senate session for a brief twenty minutes and then returned to the office to read his mail. Outside the windows of Room 139 in the Senate office building the trees were laden with ice. In the inner office Borah was alone, except for the familiar objects around him:

the big, untidy desk piled high with letters and papers; and the black leather couch with its two pillows and the old army blanket he sometimes wore around his shoulders like a toga as he sat outside on cold afternoons. Opposite his desk hung the big steel engraving of Daniel Webster; on the other wall hung a framed copy of Lowell's "Stanzas on Freedom"; on the mantel stood two wooden lamps and a cane carved from a tree on Mount Borah in Idaho. After finishing his mail, he asked the clerk to pick him up in the park outside at four-thirty and drive him home, making certain that the young law student would have time to prepare for his evening classes.[4]

Next morning he was up as usual at seven-thirty. Clad in his dressing gown, he paused at his wife's bedroom door to chat. "He always worried so about my own health," Mary Borah later recalled, and that morning he told her to be sure and see a doctor because she was sneezing. "I remember thinking," she later remarked, "he looks so well."[5] Then he went into the bathroom for his shower. When he failed to come out for a long time, his wife went in to find him on the floor unconscious, his head covered with blood.

On arrival the doctor declared that Senator Borah had suffered an unpredictable and irreparable brain hemorrhage as he was finishing his shower. His head had struck some object in his fall, leaving a deep gash in the temple. Immediately he went into a coma which lasted four days, broken only by intermittent fits of consciousness. Once he called for his wife and asked her to bring his slippers.

Nothing was reported to the newspapers at first, but an evening edition on Wednesday accounted for his confinement as a result of slipping on a rug in his apartment.[6] However, by Thursday headlines announced:

BORAH LOSING LAST FIGHT FOR HIS LIFE

Newspapermen gathered in the lobby of 2101 Connecticut Avenue, and the telephone in the Borah apartment rang incessantly. One call was from the President; another was from a little girl who played with him in the park. That day the Senate convened for a few minutes of silent prayer for his recovery. However, Dr. Worth

Daniels, speaking for the other physicians in attendance, told reporters: "There is no hope whatever." He survived until 8:45 Friday evening, January 19, when, without rallying from the coma, he died in the company of his secretary, Cora Rubin, and a nurse who placed a rosary which had been blessed by the Pope in his hands as the two women knelt in prayer.

President Roosevelt was among the first to issue a statement praising him as "a unique figure whose passing leaves a void in American public life." He wrote:

> The Senate and the nation are sadly bereft . . . We shall miss him, and mourn him and long remember the superb courage which was his. He dared often to stand alone and even at times to subordinate party interest, when he presumably saw a divergence of party . . . and national interest. Fair minded, firm in principle and shrewd in judgment, he sometimes gave and often received hard blows; but he had a great personal charm and a courteous manner which had its source in a kind heart. He had thought deeply and studied with patience all the great social, political and economic questions which had so vitally concerned his countrymen during the long period of his public service.[7]

Later, at the White House conference on children in a democracy, the President remarked that he spoke "with a heavy heart" because he had just received word of the death of "a very old friend of mine, a very great American."

Newspapers in Europe marked his death with mixed comment. The London *Daily Express* remembered him ". . . as a bitter critic of Britain." "In this country," it continued, "he was looked upon as an extremist. But we should not forget that all Americans shared his creed: 'America First.' They only differed with him on the best way to secure their country's interests . . . He was known to the average man in England better than almost any other United States politician barring the ruling President." In Berlin the *Lokal Anzeiger* noted: "Borah tried consistently after World War I to inform public opinion of the criminal nature of the Versailles *diktat* in which he saw the germs of a later conflict." And Joseph Goebbels' organ, *Der Angriff,* stated: "American life loses a personality valued by friend or foe on account of his courage, honesty, and decent method of fighting."

In Idaho the *Statesman,* which had often criticized his efforts, concluded that there probably never would be general agreement concerning the nature of his influence in national affairs but admitted that it had been enormous. "Millions of Americans looked upon him as their political savior and took as gospel his every political utterance." Another antagonist, Cordell Hull, declared: "The country loses a fearless stateman, ever faithful to his principles." William Gibbs McAdoo said: "You don't have to agree with every position taken to concede that he was an intellectual giant in the Senate and one of the truly great men of his time." Raymond Clapper thought he was a strong balance wheel in American opinion. Hugh Johnson recalled that in private life "he was gentle as a woman," while in debate "he could wield either a rapier or a cudgel. The galleries filled when he spoke on any subject . . ." Ernest K. Lindley thought his death too great a loss to be summed up in a column. His was the "most effectively liberal voice in the Republican party." Dorothy Thompson recorded that the nation mourned him with an intimate grief seldom felt for any public figure. The Washington *News* observed that long before Franklin Roosevelt, he had begun the battle for the underdog.

Most eloquent of all was the tribute paid him by William Allen White in three columns of his Emporia *Gazette,* which concluded with these words: ". . . If one sentence would sum up the service of his career, it would be this: here was a righteous man who was wise and unafraid, who followed his star, never lowered his flag and never lost his self respect. His greatness was purely personal . . . he was an honest man who dedicated his talents to his country's good, as selfless as ever a man had been in American public life . . ."

The funeral was held in the Senate chamber on Monday, January 22. Never within the memory of those present had there been such a gathering. Thousands who could not obtain tickets jammed the halls outside and the rotunda. In the chamber Borah lay in a steel coffin covered with gray broadcloth, lined with white satin, and enclosed to the waist by thick plate glass. In his hands he held a bouquet of faded violets placed there by his wife.

The President, cabinet, justices of the Supreme Court, the diplomatic corps, and the members of Congress filed into the Senate chamber. Congressmen had to stand six deep in the corners and along the walls. The only empty seat was the second from the aisle in the third row on the left, or Republican side, now covered with a spray of red roses. Borah had sat at its desk for nearly thirty-three years. Mary Borah entered, gazed at her husband for a brief moment, and then retired to the lobby where she remained with friends through the ceremony. There was no eulogy.

President Roosevelt led the formal procession from the Senate, followed by the many dignitaries and diplomats. From the galleries went Eleanor Roosevelt, Alice Longworth, Ruth Hanna McCormick, many Washington friends, and more than a hundred Idahoans. Then the swinging doors were closed and locked. While the chairs were cleared away, Borah's body was taken to lie in state in the well of the Senate, where thousands of mourners filed past. Into the stillness of the place came fellow senators, singly and in pairs. Carter Glass stood in silent tribute for a few moments, plucked a rose from the blanket on the coffin, and walked sadly away. Later a guard of honor accompanied the funeral cortege to a Pullman coach to begin the long journey to Idaho.

At Omaha a special train provided by the Union Pacific for "a man who had worked for the West and who should be given homage by the West" received the coffin. So it was that seven cars, drawn by a locomotive draped in black, crossed the western plains and brought Bill Borah home for the last time to Idaho. On its way to Boise, where he had grown to greatness, the train traveled the same route taken by an obscure country lawyer from Kansas fifty years ago when he arrived in the Idaho capital with fifteen dollars in his pocket. Now at almost every town along the way, bells tolled and people lined the tracks at all hours, fifteen hundred of them at Pocatello, to catch a glimpse of the funeral train. At intervals it was allowed to stop so that mourners could view the coffin and its honor guard. Snow had begun to fall during the night and continued into the cold dawn of that gray, wintry day when the train drew into the Boise station. Three thousand loyal citizens braved freezing temperatures to meet it. The chimes in the depot steeple tolled a muffled requiem as the hearse carried him up the broad, slippery avenue to the statehouse.

On the second floor rotunda of the Capitol building it was spring in midwinter. Every available space was banked with wreaths and bouquets. The perfume of lilies, roses, carnations, daffodils and irises filled the air. Thousands thronged the wide steps and filed past the bier, many of them having traveled great distances to pay homage to a man who had held their state of Idaho like a fief for thirty years—farmers, laborers, cowboys, lawyers, teachers, students, housewives, shopkeepers, the curious and the genuinely bereaved, those who had voted for and against him. Never had a citizen of Idaho come home to such a display of genuine sorrow.

Out at Morris Hill Cemetery, just within the Boise city limits, on a triangular plot eighty feet to a side, a veteran gravedigger performing his accustomed labor wept as he worked. He told a reporter: "I knew him for many years. But this is the prettiest spot in the cemetery; it will be a nice place for him to rest." Two days later, with Boise's depot chimes again tolling and echoing through the gloomy haze of a heavy snowfall, a long motorcade wound its way slowly out from the Capitol in the Boise valley to Morris Hill, where all that was mortal of William Edgar Borah was committed to Idaho earth.

He withstood his people for his Country
But his people did homage to the man
Who held his conscience higher than their praise
  And his country
Heaped her honors on the grave of the Patriot
  To whom living
His own righteous self respect sufficed
  Alike for motive and reward.[8]

Any fair estimate of Borah must recognize that the man—his spirit, character, and personality—transcended his acts. Borah was much more than the sum of what Borah said and did. What he did in the practical sense largely went unnoticed: no important congressional measure bears his name, and no great administrative policy carries his stamp. However, his influence was tremendous, and friends and opponents alike realized that it was a refreshing influence. He was a leader of complete sincerity, courage, patriotism, and a happy mixture of other qualities: directness, kindliness, and the type of passion that easily rose into eloquence. Above all, he was a man who had a special vision of America and who maintained it with determined independence. He often seemed so inconsistent—so much a nonconformist at times, so much a conformist in election years and other party crises—that many observers dismissed him as unfathomable, as Borah the enigma, Borah the inscrutable. However, if we grasp his vision of the republic and its proper aims, much of the inconsistency disappears.

To say that he was an old-fashioned liberal is to offer an inadequate explanation of his convictions and political philosophy. To say that he was a latter-day believer in state rights, or that he was a disciple of Jefferson and Adam Smith, or that he was an isolationist, is also inadequate. We need a more positive statement.

In his ideas he was the product of a special period, the era of Populism and Progressivism, with all the limitations as well as the thrust and crusading zeal of both these movements; moreover, he was the product of a special environment, the rural West of southern Illinois, Kansas, and southern Idaho. He was therefore bold and adventurous, but adventurous in a somewhat immature way. He believed that American civilization was the best in the world because it was founded on the best hopes. He believed that the most shining American achievement was not our wide diffusion of wealth, our businesslike efficiency, or our technological expertness; it was our political system, so free, so flexible, and so aptly devised to develop the capacities of the people. He believed, finally, that the greatest service we could perform for the world, as well as for ourselves, was to maintain our political institutions and aims in their pristine purity and vigor. Lincoln had said in his speech in Independence Hall that the nation's fathers had created a standard and an example for all mankind; Borah thought it wise statesmanship to shield and perpetuate the example.

He was thus an idealist, even a romantic. He fervently cherished the idea of an innocent America, an America too much devoted to the principles stated in the Declaration of Independence, Washington's Farewell Address, Jefferson's First Inaugural, and the Gettysburg Address to risk a compromise of its faith and a coarsening of its character by active entanglement with the Old World. His insistence on American aloofness was not selfish or mean-spirited. On the contrary, it was an exalted faith in an old national dream—the dream of a republic of unique quality which must not let its peculiar virtues suffer contamination. He constantly asserted the oldest American traditions, the simplest and most fundamental American tenets. His outlook was perhaps better understood abroad, where men saw how valuable the Jeffersonian and Lincolnian principles were, than it was by internationalists at home. At any rate, Borah's attitude had a rugged generosity which foreigners appreciated. As in his battles over home issues, so in debating foreign questions he was never prejudiced, vituperative, or vindictive; he defended his stand without the venomous rancor that characterized Henry Cabot Lodge, or the blustering misrepresentations to which Colonel Robert R. McCormick resorted.

In domestic affairs Borah's devotion to the older America, to his image of the innocent republic, is again the best explanation of much of his public conduct. Reverencing the political system of simpler days, he had no desire to multiply agencies and institutions, make life more complicated, and pile new bureaucracies on old ones. Subtraction often seemed to him more needed than addition. Hence it was that although a liberal, he opposed the child labor amendment, and although he esteemed justice in dealing with enemies, he was against the alien property administration. He liked neither the Harding-Coolidge legislation favoring special interests nor the George Norris legislation erecting safeguards against special interests. Fundamentally he often took Lord Melbourne's view: "Why can't they leave it alone?" Of course, he realized that national growth demanded new measures, but he was willing to leave these measures to men like his great colleague from the Pacific Northwest, Senator Charles L. McNary, the author of that fundamental legislation for forest conservation from which Borah's own Idaho profited so much. When he threw himself behind a bill or policy which he thought desirable, he was the most effective and inspiring of fighters—as Walter Lippmann wrote, a host in himself.

We may say much in criticism of Borah's ruling conceptions. His image of the innocent America lacked realism; he could well have caught from Theodore Roosevelt both a fuller understanding of the grim need for domestic readjustments and a larger vision of the country's necessary role in world affairs. Nevertheless, he was not so inconsistent as he seemed. For that matter, a charge of inconsistency would never have worried him, for he believed with Emerson that self-reliance is the first duty of man and that only the little mind will feel concerned if a determined independence involves reversals and contradictions.

Though his formal education was cut short, Borah had opportunity in college to acquaint himself with the best American literature, and of all the authors he read, Emerson most powerfully influenced him. Throughout life he continued reading the works of the great transcendentalist, and made the essays, "Culture," "Behavior," "Manners," "Power," and the rest, his continuing guide. He used to refer to the refreshment and strength they gave him. No doubt, Emerson's "Eloquence" had a special appeal for him, and he would have agreed with the statement that the best orators were "grave men, who preferred their integrity to their talent"; however, it was two other papers that inspired him most.

The disquisitions on "Self-Reliance" and "Courage" provided the maxims by which Borah chose to live. Ever since his college days under Professor Canfield, Borah had understood the value of nonconformity, of the refusal to be what later times termed an "organization man." Emerson had said: "Whoso would be a man must be a nonconformist," and Borah meant to illustrate the maxim. The Borah who was taunted abusively by political enemies disregarded them in the light of Emerson's declaration: "Nothing is at last sacred but the integrity of your mind." The Borah who was told that he must bow to public opinion was ready to quote the sentence: "What I must do is all that concerns me, not what the people think. This rule . . . may serve for the whole distinction between greatness and meanness." Borah the student, whose avoidance of social life aroused criticism in both Boise and Washington, would have defended himself by the comment: "I shun father and mother, wife and brother, when my genius calls me." Borah the fighter felt Emerson's great truth: "He has not learned the lesson of life who does not every day surmount a fear."

With his massive strength and his sharply marked shortcomings, Borah had the character of a force of nature. Like nature, he was spasmodic, perverse, unexpected—and impressive. This is what his friends meant when they said that as with the weather, with earthquakes, and with the universe, the only course to follow was to accept him. As long as he was active in public life, people could feel that at least one man was as proudly erect as the Washington monument. They could feel that among the swarms of self-seekers, compromisers, and evaders, one leader would say just what he thought was right and do just what he thought was best for the country. His vision might sometimes fail and his course might sometimes be erratic, but he could always be counted on for three of the rarest qualities of statesmanship: conscience, courage, and passion.

Notes

NOTES TO CHAPTER I

1. "The Settlement of the West: A Study in Transportation," *Century*, 63 (January, 1902), 362. For a glimpse into an emigrant car heading west, see Robert Louis Stevenson, *Across the Plains* (New York, 1906).
2. Christopher P. Connolly, "Presidential Possibilities: Borah of Idaho," *Colliers*, 55 (July 31, 1915), 6.
3. The settlement known as Borah's Ferry dwindled; in 1917 it had only twenty-five people. Today only the ferryhouse remains. Letter to the editor, Fenimore County (Wisconsin) *Times*, October 30, 1929; see also Senator Borah to Mrs. Ange Jackson, February 10, 1922, Box 219, Borah Papers, Ms. Division, Library of Congress, Washington, D.C.; see also "Borah's Kentucky Origins" in Louisville *Courier*, quoted in Borah *Scrapbook*, Vol. 10, p. 31 on microfilm in the Borah Papers. One critic later found it ironic that the Senator's ancestors once operated a ferry, which might explain why he often shifted his political allegiance from one faction to another.
4. Sue Borah Lasley to Senator Borah, January 23, 1925, Box 254, Borah Papers.
5. Senator Borah to Mrs. J. T. McMahon, May 6, 1927, Box 283, *ibid.*
6. Borah to G. Douglas Wardrop, November 13, 1914, Box 60, *ibid.*
7. The record book of Alf Scott's shop near Merriam shows Will Borah's patronage through 1885, Box 606, *ibid.*
8. "The Closing Argument of W. E. Borah in the Haywood Trial," a pamphlet in the Borah Papers, Idaho Historical Society, Boise (hereafter cited as Borah Papers, I.H.S.), pp. 27-28.
9. Washington *Herald*, April 17, 1910; Borah *Scrapbook*, Vol. 13, pp. 102-3.
10. Portland *Oregonian*, June 26, 1934; United States *News*, May 28, 1934, p. 10.
11. Samuel J. Woolf, *Drawn from Life* (New York, 1932), p. 120.
12. Jonathan Mitchell, "Borah Knows Best," *New Republic*, 85 (Jan-

uary 29, 1936), 333; Walter Johnson, *William Allen White's America* (New York, 1947), pp. 26-27; Borah *Scrapbook,* Vol. 2.

13. Borah *Scrapbook,* Vol. 13, pp. 102-3.
14. Charles F. Borah to Senator Borah, December 29, 1926, Box 283, Borah Papers.
15. Waldo S. Braden, "William E. Borah's Years in Kansas in the 1880's," *Kansas Historical Quarterly,* 15 (November, 1947), 360-67; Lyons *Republican,* December 13, 1883; Ben Jones, *Sam Jones: Lawyer* (Norman, 1947), pp. 4 ff.; Horace Jones, *The Story of Early Rice County* (Topeka, 1928).
16. Lyons *Republican,* June 17, 1884; University of Kansas *Register* (1885), p. 216. The Lyons school records were destroyed by fire. In order to get his teacher's certificate Borah had to pass an examination including history, geography, grammar, arithmetic, the Constitution, and bookkeeping. Braden, "Borah's Years in Kansas," 360-67.
17. *Catalogue* of the University of Kansas (Topeka, 1886).
18. Beverly Smith, "The Lone Rider from Idaho," *American Magazine,* 113 (March, 1932), 40; *Fighting Liberal: The Autobiography of George W. Norris* (New York, 1945), p. 47.
19. Weekly University *Courier* (Lawrence, Kansas), April 9, 1886, p. 1.
20. Johnson, *White's America,* p. 40.
21. *Ibid.,* pp. 40-41.
22. "Senator Borah Stole No Turkeys, but He Paid for Them," *Literary Digest,* 60 (March 29, 1919), 58-61.
23. *The Autobiography of William Allen White* (New York, 1946), p. 144; Dorothy Canfield Fisher to the author, March 4, 1954; James Canfield to the author, March 14, 1954.
24. Lyons *Republican,* August 9, 1888; Braden, "Borah's Years in Kansas," 360-67.
25. Lyons *Republican,* April 18, 1889, October 9, 1890; see also Lyons *City Record,* II, pp. 34, 36, 55.
26. Ezra Whitla to the author, January 16, 1957.

NOTES TO CHAPTER II

1. Ellis P. Oberholtzer, *A History of the United States Since the Civil War* (5 vols.; New York, 1928), II, p. 489.
2. Annie Laurie Bird, *Boise, the Peace Valley* (Caldwell, 1934), p. 268.

3. Mark Sullivan in Washington *Star,* April 5, 1906.
4. Borah's certificate as attorney bears the date cited, but he made a legal agreement for William Thompson at Boise in his own hand as early as October 29, 1890. Borah Papers, I.H.S.
5. Borah *Scrapbook* (April 17, 1910), Vol. 13, p. 104.
6. Washington *Herald,* April 17, 1910.
7. Borah *Scrapbook,* Vol. 13, p. 104.
8. Borah to Rev. S. T. Montgomery, March 5, 1917, Box 183, Borah Papers.
9. Boston *Herald,* July 8, 1922.
10. Idaho *Statesman,* April 23, 1895; Marriage Book, No. 4, p. 3 (the license was issued April 20, 1895), Ada County Records, Courthouse, Boise.
11. Christopher P. Connolly, "Presidential Possibilities: Borah of Idaho," *Colliers,* 55 (July 31, 1915), 28; Borah *Scrapbook,* Vol. 13, p. 104.
12. Typescript in the Borah Papers, I.H.S.
13. Transcript No. 449 on appeal from Fourth Judicial District, Cassia County, in Idaho State Supreme Court, 1898, State House, Boise.
14. Borah to Louis Schwartz, April 2, 1929, Box 301, Borah Papers.
15. When last heard from, Davis was conducting a profitable business from a Los Angeles hotel. He owned over one thousand acres of claims in Nevada and had ambitions of fitting out a buccaneering expedition to seize some South American country and install himself as king.
16. Philip Taft and Selig Perlman, *History of Labor in the United States, 1896-1932* (New York, 1935), IV, p. 169-70.
17. *Ibid.,* 184 ff.; Industrial Commission Report, XII, p. 393; James Hawley, ed., *History of Idaho: The Gem of the Mountains* (4 vols.; Chicago, 1920), I, p. 251-52.
18. Hawley, *History of Idaho,* I, p. 253; cf. Christopher P. Connolly, "The Moyer-Haywood Case," *Colliers,* 39 (May 11, 1907), 13-15.
19. Portland *Journal,* June 2, 1907.
20. Washington *Herald,* April 17, 1910; Borah *Scrapbook,* Vol. 13, p. 105.
21. Borah *Scrapbook,* Vol. 13, p. 105; see also Vol. 11, p. 82.
22. Portland *Journal,* June 2, 1907; *World's Work,* 57 (December, 1928), p. 141.
23. "Closing Argument of W. E. Borah for the Prosecution, the Great

Coeur d'Alene Riot-Murder Trial," July 27, 1899 (Wallace, Idaho), p. 26, in Borah Papers, I.H.S.

24. *Ibid.*, p. 49.
25. Stewart Holbrook, *The Rocky Mountain Revolution* (New York, 1956), pp. 63-64.
26. Idaho *Statesman*, May 25 and 26, 1903.
27. Dubois to Borah, December 6, 1899, Borah Papers, I.H.S.

NOTES TO CHAPTER III

1. Idaho *Statesman*, July 14, 1891. In his biography *Borah of Idaho* (New York, 1936), pp. 40-41, Claudius Johnson asserts that Borah really won the election, but because he was a newcomer in town the Republican boss had him counted out. The newspaper account states Borah withdrew because he was then only twenty-six and the age requirement was thirty.
2. Idaho *Statesman*, February 13, 1892.
3. Lewiston *Tribune*, July 1, 1896.
4. Johnson, *Borah of Idaho*, pp. 48-49; Borah *Scrapbook*, Vol. 11, p. 80.
5. Speech of August 26, 1896. A pamphlet in Borah Papers, I.H.S., p. 7.
6. *Ibid.*, p. 12. This diatribe was prompted by Britain's steadfast refusal to open her mints to silver on any terms satisfactory to the Americans and Borah's belief that she was at the bottom of an international conspiracy to keep gold above silver, thus causing the economic distress from which the American nation suffered.
7. Idaho *Statesman*, September 27, 1896.
8. Borah persisted in his fidelity to bimetallism, maintaining on the floor of the Senate as late as 1934 that had it not been for the discovery of new gold deposits in Alaska and South Africa, the free coinage of silver would have become a necessity.
9. Undated speech in Borah Papers, I.H.S.; Selig Adler, *The Isolationist Impulse, Its Twentieth-Century Reaction* (New York, 1957), p. 25.
10. Idaho Falls *Post*, February 17, 1929.
11. Speech before the Republican State Convention, Boise, August 20, 1902, a pamphlet in Borah Papers, I.H.S.; see also Boise *Evening Capital News*, July 19, 1902; cf. speech delivered by Borah on Roosevelt before the Republican Convention at Pocatello, Idaho, May 18, 1904, in Borah Papers, I.H.S.

12. Boise *Capital News,* August 14, 1902.
13. *Ibid.,* October 21, 1902.
14. *Ibid.,* September 12, 1902.
15. Idaho *Statesman,* November 5 and 13, 1902; for a survey of the campaigns of 1896 to 1906, see Claudius Johnson, "William E. Borah: The People's Choice," *Pacific Northwest Quarterly,* 44 (January, 1953), 15-22.
16. Idaho *Statesman,* January 8, 1902.
17. Caldwell *Tribune,* June 27 and July 11, 1894.
18. Walter Johnson, ed., *Selected Letters of William Allen White, 1899-1943* (New York, 1947), White to Hanna, November 29, 1902, pp. 50-51.
19. Lewiston *Tribune,* January 9, 1903.
20. Boise *Evening Capital News,* January 9, 1903.
21. Johnson, *Borah,* p. 56; Lewiston *Tribune,* January 9, 1903.
22. Boise *Evening Capital News,* January 28, 1936 (a reprint).
23. *Ibid.,* June 18, 1904.
24. *Ibid.,* August 15, 1905.
25. *Ibid.,* October 30, 1905.
26. *Ibid.,* February 19, 1906.
27. "Hon. W. E. Borah on the Nomination of Candidates for Senator," a pamphlet, Boise, July 7, 1906, in Borah Papers, I.H.S.
28. Boise *Capital News,* July 24, 1906.
29. *Ibid.,* July 26, 1906.
30. For Borah's acceptance speech, see Pocatello *Tribune,* August 3, 1906; Borah *Scrapbook,* Vol. 2.
31. Borah *Scrapbook,* Vol. 6.
32. Boise *Evening Capital News,* January 16, 1907; Borah *Scrapbook,* Vol. 6.
33. Boise *Evening Capital News,* May 9, 1907.
34. Idaho *Statesman,* January 18, 1907.

NOTES TO CHAPTER IV

1. Boise *Evening Capital News,* January 1, 1906.
2. From a typescript of the eulogy loaned to the author by Borah's secretary, Mrs. Cora Rubin Lane, Long Beach, California.
3. Interview with Harry Orchard at the Idaho State Penitentiary, Boise, June 29, 1952.

4. Borah to Frank Gooding, March 23, 1906, Borah Papers, I.H.S.
5. *Bill Haywood's Book: The Autobiography of William D. Haywood* (New York, 1929), p. 206.
6. Louis Filler, *Crusaders for American Liberalism* (New Springs, Ohio, 1950), pp. 225 ff.
7. Clarence Darrow, *The Story of My Life* (New York, 1932), pp. 147-48.
8. Report of the prosecuting attorney, May 18, 1907, in folder, "The Haywood Trial," Ada County Courthouse, Boise, Idaho.
9. Francis X. Busch, *Prisoners at the Bar* (Indianapolis, 1952), p. 28.
10. Leroy E. Froom, ed., *Harry Orchard: The Man God Made Again* (Nashville, 1952), Historical notes for chapter 9, pp. 132-33.
11. John W. Carberry in a dispatch to the Boston *Globe,* July 12, 1907; Luke Grant in the Chicago *Record-Herald* (same date).
12. Boston *Globe,* July 13, 1907.
13. Chicago *Record-Herald,* July 12, 1907.
14. *Bill Haywood's Book,* pp. 212-13.
15. Holbrook, *Rocky Mountain Revolution,* p. 251; Irving Stone, *Clarence Darrow for the Defense* (New York, 1943), pp. 235-42.
16. Darrow, *The Story of My Life,* p. 153.
17. *Ibid.,* pp. 153-54.
18. Boise *Capital News,* November 28, 1926.
19. "Haywood Trial: Closing Argument of W. E. Borah," pp. 128-29.
20. Washington *Post,* July 27, 1907.
21. Darrow, *The Story of My Life,* p. 153.
22. July 27, 1907.
23. For some interesting details on the instructions of Judge Fremont Wood to the jury in this case, see Oscar King Davis, *Released for Publication* (Boston, 1925), pp. 43-44. See also Historical notes for chapter 9 in Froom, *Harry Orchard,* pp. 121-36; cf. Judge Wood's Recommendation in folder, "The Haywood Trial," Ada County Courthouse, Boise, and Busch, *Prisoners at the Bar,* p. 45.

NOTES TO CHAPTER V

1. Borah *Scrapbook,* Vol. 5, p. 18.
2. *Ibid.,* p. 18.
3. *Ibid.,* p. 35.
4. Boise *Evening Capital News,* January 28, 1905; see dispatch No.

59512 in Record Group 60, March 15, 1907, Dept. of Justice records, National Archives, Washington, D.C.
5. Boise *Evening Capital News,* September 24, 1907.
6. Davis, *Released for Publication,* p. 34.
7. "A Little Drama out in Idaho," *Colliers,* 40 (December 7, 1907), p. 19.
8. Borah to A. E. McCartney, April 13, 1907, Borah Papers. I.H.S.
9. *Ibid.*
10. Davis, *Released for Publication,* p. 35.
11. Boise *Evening Capital News,* June 24, 1907.
12. *Appeal to Reason* (Girard, Kansas), April 20, 1907.
13. Davis, *Released for Publication,* p. 36.
14. *Minute Book* of the United States District Court, Southern Division, Boise, Idaho (April, 1907), pp. 233-34.
15. George H. Kester to Borah, April 14, 1907, Borah Papers, I.H.S. Kester was shortly thereafter convicted for embezzling funds of the Lewiston National Bank.
16. April 8, 1907, Borah Papers, I.H.S.
17. Borah to Bourne, April 13, 1907, *ibid.*
18. Borah to C. H. Lingenhalter, April 30, 1907, *ibid.*
19. Cash to Bonaparte, Record Group 60, March 25, 1907, Dept. of Justice records.
20. Boise *Evening Capital News,* April 19, 1907.
21. White to Borah, June 13, 1907, Borah Papers, I.H.S.
22. Borah to White, June 24, 1907, *ibid.;* cf. Borah to Bourne, July 6, 1907, *ibid.*
23. *The Autobiography of William Allen White* (New York, 1946), pp. 374-75.
24. *White's America,* p. 164; cf. Christopher P. Connolly, "The Moyer-Haywood Case," *Colliers,* 39 (May 11, 1907), 13-15; see also Connolly to Borah, January 25, 1927, Box 283, Borah Papers.
25. Connolly to Borah, August 26, 1907, Borah Papers, I.H.S.
26. White to Borah, August 18, 1907, *ibid.;* see also Joseph G. Dudley to Borah, August 12, 1907, *ibid.*
27. Connolly to Borah, August 26, 1907, *ibid.*
28. August 22, 1907, *ibid.*
29. Borah to A. E. McCartney, April 13, 1907, *ibid.;* Borah to O. K. Davis, August 24, 1907, *ibid.;* see also Boxes 8, 9, and 10, *ibid.*

30. Record Group 60, August 11, 1907, Dept. of Justice records; cf. Davis, *Released for Publication,* pp. 36-37.
31. Record Group 60, C.N. 115999, August 24, 1907, Dept. of Justice records.
32. Bourne to Borah, April 17, 1907, Borah Papers, I.H.S.
33. Bourne to Borah, July 11, 1907, *ibid.*
34. Taft to Borah, August 30, 1907, *ibid.*
35. Davis, *Released for Publication,* p. 37.
36. Borah *Scrapbook,* Vol. 5, p. 5.
37. Boise *Evening Capital News,* October 3, 1907; Borah *Scrapbook,* Vol. 5, pp. 2-3; see also Chicago *Evening Post,* October 4, 1907.
38. White to Borah, October 24, 1907, Borah Papers, I.H.S. (Borah never wrote the article.)
39. Borah *Scrapbook* (April, 1908), Vol. 11, p. 75. Ruick, after an investigation, was exonerated of misconduct.
40. Borah *Scrapbook,* Vol. 5, p. 24.
41. Dorothy Johnson and Charles Gates, *Empire of the Columbia* (New York, 1957), pp. 605-6.
42. Borah *Scrapbook,* Vol. 5, p. 38.
43. *Ibid.* (undated), Vol. 5, p. 10.

NOTES TO CHAPTER VI

1. Washington *News,* March 9, 1907; Borah *Scrapbook,* Vol. 6.
2. Borah *Scrapbook,* Vol. 6.
3. *Ibid.,* Vol. 1, Series 2.
4. George Norris, *Autobiography,* pp. 97-98.
5. Letter to the author, February 29, 1956.
6. Borah to J. A. H. Hopkins, April 11, 1923, Box 233, Borah Papers.
7. Clinton W. Gilbert, *The Mirrors of Washington* (New York, 1921), pp. 245-46; Richard Hofstadter, *The Age of Reform, from Bryan to Roosevelt* (New York, 1955), p. 283.
8. Walter Davenport, "Borah, the Man Who Grew Up," *Colliers,* 90 (September, 1932), 10-11.
9. Robert Huse, Jr., to the author, October 2, 1956.
10. Wilson Midgley, *Possible Presidents* (London, 1928), pp. 126-27.
11. Overdue list of librarian, Box 250, Borah Papers. Borah's library has been preserved by his widow in Washington and will go, on her death, to the University of Idaho, Moscow, Idaho.

12. Closing words of John Quincy Adams in *Lectures on Rhetoric and Oratory* delivered to the classes of senior and junior sophisters in Harvard University (Cambridge, 1810), II, pp. 396-97.
13. Samuel J. Woolf, *Drawn from Life,* pp. 121-23; Beverly Smith, "The Lone Rider from Idaho," *American Magazine,* 113 (March, 1932), 40.
14. Woolf, *Drawn from Life,* pp. 121-23; see also "Borah Looks to Emerson as a Guide," New York *Times Magazine,* November 27, 1927.
15. New York *Times,* November 27, 1927.
16. Washburn's *Washington Weekly* (*ca.* December, 1925), cited in Box 269, Borah Papers.
17. Personal Notebooks, Box 685, *ibid.*
18. Borah to William Bruce, November 14, 1938, Box 422, *ibid.*
19. December 31, 1925, Box 269, *ibid.*
20. Christopher P. Connolly to Henry Pringle, December 14, 1928, Box 307, *ibid.;* Washington *Herald,* January 10, 1933; Borah *Scrapbook,* Vol. 10, p. 75; Borah to Mrs. W. F. Emigh, no date, Box 618, Borah Papers; Borah to William Allen White, November 7, 1921, Box 208, *ibid.;* Peter Viereck to Borah, December 19, 1928, and Borah to Viereck, December 22, 1928, Box 307, *ibid.*
21. Claudius Johnson, "Borah's Bequest to Democracy," *Idaho Yesterdays,* 1 (Winter, 1957-58), 18; see also Boxes 198, 215, and 619, Borah Papers.
22. John Chamberlain, *Farewell to Reform* (New York, 1933), p. 138.
23. *World Almanac* (New York, 1902), pp. 135-46.
24. Borah *Scrapbook,* Vol. 4, Series 2.
25. George R. Brown, *The Leadership of Congress* (Indianapolis, 1922), p. 257; George Mowry, *The Era of Theodore Roosevelt* (New York, 1958), p. 244.
26. Ray Tucker, *Sons of the Wild Jackass* (Boston, 1932), pp. 4-19; Walter Johnson, *Letters of William Allen White,* p. 9; Alfred Lief, *Democracy's Norris* (New York, 1939), p. 124.
27. C. W. Fulton to Borah, December 20, 1907, Borah Papers. Other committee assignments later included Expenditures in the Navy Department, Public Lands, Claims, Irrigation, Standards, Weights and Measures, and the Revision of the Laws of the United States. At various times Borah was a member of eleven different Senate committees. During his entire career in the Senate he was a mem-

ber of the Committee on Education and Labor; from 1909 until his death he was a member of the Judiciary Committee; and from 1913 to 1940 he served on the Foreign Relations Committee.

28. Arthur W. Dunn, *From Harrison to Harding: A Personal Narrative Covering a Third of a Century, 1888-1921* (2 vols., New York, 1922), II, p. 107; see also Ray Tucker, "Borah of Idaho," *American Mercury,* 9 (December, 1926), 385-86.
29. Dunn, *Harrison to Harding,* II, p. 108.
30. *Congressional Record,* 60 Cong., 1 Sess. (April 20, 1908), Vol. 42, pp. 4962-70.
31. Borah *Scrapbook,* Vol. 2, p. 23.
32. Joseph Foraker, *Notes of a Busy Life* (2 vols., Cincinnati, 1916), II, chapters 41-43; Henry Pringle, *Theodore Roosevelt: A Biography* (New York, 1956), pp. 458-64; Boise *Evening Capital News,* April 20, 1908.
33. Boise *Capital News,* June 16, 1908; Borah to Taft, June 18, 1908, cited in Henry Pringle, *The Life and Times of Willam Howard Taft: A Biography* (2 vols., New York, 1939), II, p. 354.
34. Borah *Scrapbook* (May 28, 1908), Vol. 8.
35. Pringle, *Taft,* I, pp. 354-55.
36. Borah *Scrapbook,* Vol. 8; Charles Merz, "This Man Borah," *New Republic,* 43 (May 27, 1926), 9-13.

NOTES TO CHAPTER VII

1. New York *Times,* March 1, 1909.
2. *Ibid.,* March 4, 1909.
3. Borah *Scrapbook,* Vol. 13, p. 8.
4. *Congressional Record,* 61 Cong., 1 Sess. (May 24, 1909), Vol. 44, p. 2315.
5. *Ibid.* (May 10, 1909), p. 1683.
6. Boise *Evening Capital News,* May 25, 1910.
7. *Pollock* v. *Farmers' Loan and Trust Company,* 157 U. S. 429 (1895) and 158 U. S. 601 (1895).
8. William E. Borah, "Income Tax Amendment," *North American Review,* 191 (June, 1910), 760-61; see also his Senate speech in *Congressional Record,* 61 Cong., 1 Sess. (May 3 and 4, 1909), Vol. 44, pp. 1680-87, 1693-1701.
9. Phillip C. Jessup, *Elihu Root* (2 vols., New York, 1938), II, pp. 230-31.

10. *Congressional Record,* 61 Cong., 1 Sess. (June 29, 1909), Vol. 44, p. 3931.
11. *Ibid.* (June 30, 1909), pp. 3985-90.
12. Boise *Capital News,* January 25, 1901, contains an editorial diatribe against the existing method of electing senators.
13. *Congressional Record,* 61 Cong., 3 Sess. (January 13, 1911), Vol. 46, pp. 847-48.
14. *Ibid.* (January 19, 1911), pp. 1103-7.
15. *Ibid.* (February 16, 1911), p. 2657; New York *Herald,* February 17, 1911.
16. *Congressional Record,* 61 Cong., 3 Sess. (February 17, 1911), Vol. 46, pp. 2773-74.
17. *Ibid.* (February 24, 1911), p. 3307; Borah *Scrapbook,* Vol. 17, p. 12.
18. January 21, 1911.
19. Edward Lowry, *Washington Close-ups, Intimate Views of Some Public Figures* (Boston, 1921), pp. 227-28; "The People," *Outlook,* 163 (January, 1934), 13-14.
20. *Congressional Record,* 62 Cong., 1 Sess. (June 27, 1911), Vol. 47, pp. 2558-61, 2575.
21. Coe Crawford to Theodore Roosevelt, July 27, 1911, in Theodore Roosevelt Papers, MS Division, Library of Congress, Washington, D.C.; George Mowry, *Theodore Roosevelt and the Progressive Movement* (Madison, 1947), pp. 66-67.
22. Borah *Scrapbook,* Vol. 13, p. 51; Chicago *Tribune,* January 4, 1910; William Borah, "A Bond Issue for Reclamation," *Independent,* 67 (November 4, 1909), 1064-65.
23. *Congressional Record,* 60 Cong., 1 Sess. (May 4, 1908), Vol. 42, pp. 5983-84.
24. *Ibid.;* on the power of the executive to withdraw public lands, see his Senate speech of May 11, 1910, in *ibid.,* 61 Cong., 2 Sess., Vol. 45, pp. 6066-74; on the public land laws, see *Ibid.,* 62 Cong., 2 Sess. (January 17, 1912), Vol. 48, pp. 1011-26.
25. Borah *Scrapbook,* Vol. 15, p. 29; Overland *Press,* February 21, 1910.
26. Taft to Roosevelt, May 28, 1910, quoted in Pringle, *Roosevelt,* pp. 531-32.
27. *The New International Yearbook* (1911), p. 736.
28. Davis, *Released for Publication,* pp. 187-90.

29. *Congressional Record,* 62 Cong., 2 Sess. (April 18, 1912), Vol. 48, pp. 4969-70.
30. Borah *Scrapbook,* Vol. 15, p. 52. President Wilson named the first secretary of labor, William B. Wilson, a Pennsylvania congressman.
31. Lindsay Rogers, "American Government and Politics," *American Political Science Review,* 16 (February, 1922), 43 n.
32. Clinton Gilbert, *You Takes Your Choice* (New York, 1924), pp. 191 ff.
33. Ray Tucker, *Sons of the Wild Jackass,* pp. 70 ff.

NOTES TO CHAPTER VIII

1. Boise *Evening Capital News,* March 24, 1912.
2. Undated typescript in Box 97, Borah Papers.
3. Borah to Roosevelt, May 22, 1912, Roosevelt Papers.
4. New York *Tribune,* June 8, 1912; New York *Herald,* June 8, 1912; New York *Times,* June 8, 1912. The *Times* sounded out Roosevelt leaders at this point in reference to their prospective attitude in case of a bolt. William L. Ward of New York, Borah, and Frank Kellogg were described as "too staunch Republicans to relish the idea of facing the long future with the brand of irregularity upon them."
5. New York *Times,* June 9 and 11, 1912.
6. Borah *Scrapbook,* Vol. 16, p. 41.
7. New York *Herald,* June 11, 1912.
8. *Ibid.*
9. Gilbert E. Rose, "The Truth about the Contests," *La Follette's Weekly,* July 20 and 27, August 3, 1912.
10. Mowry, *Roosevelt,* pp. 239-40.
11. Victor Rosewater, *Backstage in 1912: The Inside Story of the Split Republican Convention* (Philadelphia, 1932), pp. 128 ff.; New York *Times,* June 12 and 13, 1912.
12. William Jennings Bryan, *A Tale of Two Conventions* (New York, 1912), pp. 22-26; New York *Times,* June 18, 1912.
13. New York *Herald,* June 19, 1912; *La Follette's Autobiography: A Personal Narrative of Political Experience* (Madison, 1913), pp. 647-57; Bryan, *Tale of Two Conventions,* pp. 29-36.
14. New York *Tribune,* June 17, 1912. There is evidence that Borah voiced Roosevelt's public position. The Chicago *Tribune,* under the same date, said: "There is no bolt contemplated by Colonel Roose-

velt . . ." The New York *Times,* same date, reported: "Roosevelt denies that a bolt is planned." "I have heard the report," Roosevelt is quoted as saying, and then he added without a moment's hesitation, "It is all nonsense." Evidently T. R. decided to bolt after Taft was nominated, as Borah later alleged.

15. New York *Times,* September 6, 1912; see also Olathe (Kansas) *Mirror,* undated clipping in Borah *Scrapbook,* Vol. 16, p. 56; Washington *Star,* September 26, 1935.
16. Borah *Scrapbook* (June 20, 1912), Vol. 16, p. 7.
17. Frank Harper to John Greenway, May 19, 1912, Roosevelt Papers; New York *Tribune,* June 21, 1912.
18. Typed account of the meeting in the folder marked "1912" in Box 97, Borah Papers; New York *Times,* June 21, 1912; *As I Knew Them: Memoirs of James E. Watson* (New York, 1936), pp. 160-61; Johnson, *Borah,* pp. 139-41.
19. Roosevelt to J. C. O'Laughlin, July 9, 1912, Roosevelt Papers.
20. Borah *Scrapbook,* Vol. 16, p. 87; George S. Viereck, "Can a Third Party Succeed? Borah Says No," *Liberty* (June 11, 1932), 41.
21. Borah *Scrapbook,* Vol. 16, pp. 87 ff.
22. *Ibid.,* p. 41.
23. Boise *Evening Capital News,* September 15, 1921; typescript of Borah's speech in Box 97, Borah Papers.
24. Charles Thompson, *Presidents I've Known and Two Near Presidents* (Indianapolis, 1929), pp. 132 ff. This account is based on Mr. Thompson's eyewitness report of the Boise meeting.
25. Borah *Scrapbook,* Vol. 16, p. 138.
26. "The Evening of Waterloo," editorial in Cincinnati *Times-Star,* June 21, 1912.

NOTES TO CHAPTER IX

1. U.S. Congress, 63 Cong., Special Sess., Senate Document, p. 3.
2. *Congressional Record,* 63 Cong., 2 Sess. (December 12, 1913), Vol. 51, p. 763.
3. *Ibid.* (December 17, 1913), Vol. 51, pp. 1065-72.
4. *Ibid.* (June 26, 27, and 29, 1914), Vol. 51, pp. 11186-87.
5. *Ibid.* (June 28, 1914), Vol. 51, pp. 11187 ff.
6. Borah to Gilson Gardiner, May 15, 1916, Box 174, Borah Papers.
7. Johnson, *Borah,* p. 156; Borah to Howard Kyle, June 10, 1922, Box 218, Borah Papers.

8. New York *Times,* February 27, 1914.
9. George Perkins to Borah, February 27, 1914, Box 166, Borah Papers.
10. Borah to Perkins, February 28, 1914, *ibid.*
11. Perkins to Borah, March 1, 1914, *ibid;* Dupont to Borah, March 4, 1914, *ibid.*
12. Borah to John Hart, July 28, 1914, Box 163, *ibid.*
13. Borah *Scrapbook,* Vol. 16, p. 140.
14. Borah to Charles Lisle, November 28, 1914, Box 163, Borah Papers.
15. *Current Opinion,* 56 (April, 1914), 266. For Harvey's prediction, see New York *Times,* November 1, 1914, III; Borah *Scrapbook,* Vol. 16, p. 140.
16. Boston *Transcript,* March 17, 1915.
17. Harvey to Borah, June 22, 1915, Box 91, Borah Papers.
18. *Congressional Record,* 64 Cong., 1 Sess. (January 13, 1915), Vol. 52, pp. 1495-1502; cf. Borah *Scrapbook,* Vol. 17; New York *Times,* January 15, 1915.
19. Borah *Scrapbook,* Vol. 17.
20. New York *Times,* June 8, 1916; Mary Grey Peck, *Carrie Chapman Catt: A Biography* (New York, 1944), pp. 244-48.
21. Mowry, *Roosevelt,* pp. 331-32; New York *Times,* June 7, 1916.
22. Charles Bonaparte to Theodore Roosevelt, June 13, 1916, Bonaparte Papers, Ms. Division, Library of Congress, Washington, D.C.; Nicholas Murray Butler, *Across the Busy Years* (2 vols., New York, 1939), I, pp. 258-64; New York *Times,* June 7, 1916; Mowry, *Roosevelt,* p. 350.
23. New York *Times,* June 7 and 9, 1916; William E. Dodd, *Woodrow Wilson and His Work* (New York, 1932), p. 186; *The American Year Book* (1916), pp. 30-31.
24. Borah *Scrapbook,* Vol. 17; Boise *Capital News,* June 19, 1916.
25. *Autobiography,* p. 527.
26. Borah *Scrapbook* (June 20, 1916), Vol. 17.
27. New York *Times,* May 9, 1915, and March 4, 1916.
28. *Congressional Record,* 64 Cong., 1 Sess. (January 5, 1916), Vol. 53, p. 506.
29. *Ibid.,* 65 Cong., 1 Sess. (February 7, 1917), Vol. 54, p. 2749; Borah to Ed Dewey, March 29, 1917, Box 180, Borah Papers.

30. *Congressional Record,* 65 Cong., 1 Sess. (April 2, 1917), Vol. 55, pp. 102-4.
31. *Ibid.* (April 4, 1917), pp. 252-53.
32. New York *Times,* July 27, 1917.
33. *Congressional Record,* 65 Cong., 1 Sess. (April 19, 1917), Vol. 55, pp. 831-37; Charles Merz, "The Idaho Minority of One," *New Republic,* 43 (June 3, 1925), 40-41; Johnson, *Borah,* pp. 198-99.
34. *Literary Digest,* 55 (September 29, 1917), 10. Borah purchased bonds in each of the four liberty loan drives but continued to oppose the principle.
35. Borah *Scrapbook,* Vol. 17; *Congressional Record,* 65 Cong., 1 Sess. (April 28, 1917), Vol. 55, pp. 1442-45.
36. Borah *Scrapbook,* Vol. 17.
37. April 28, 1917.
38. Borah to Ed Dewey, May 9 and June 28, 1917, Box 180, Borah Papers.
39. Borah to Bartlett Sinclair, May 1, 1917, *ibid.*
40. June 6, 1917.
41. March 20, 1918.
42. June 21, 1917.
43. Claudius Johnson, "William E. Borah, the People's Choice," *Pacific Northwest Quarterly,* 44 (January, 1953), 17.
44. Woodrow Wilson to Fred T. Dubois, August 1, 1918, Dubois Papers, Idaho State College, Pocatello, Idaho.
45. Hawley, *History of Idaho,* I, pp. 309-10; Johnson, "Borah, People's Choice," p. 18.
46. Clinton Gilbert, *Behind the Mirrors: The Psychology of Disintegration at Washington* (New York, 1922), pp. 251-52.
47. Belle Case and Fola La Follette, *Robert M. La Follette* (2 vols., New York, 1953), II, pp. 960-61.
48. *Ibid.*
49. When Senators Hitchcock and Williams accused Lodge of having packed the committee with antileague senators, Lodge refused to answer them. Karl Schriftgiesser, *Gentleman from Massachusetts: Henry Cabot Lodge* (Boston, 1944), p. 333; Eleanor Dennison, *The Senate Foreign Relations Committee* (Stanford, 1942), p. 10; New York *Times,* May 13, 1919; John Garraty, *Henry Cabot Lodge: A Biography* (New York, 1953), p. 364.

NOTES TO CHAPTER X

1. John C. Vinson, *William E. Borah and the Outlawry of War* (Athens, 1957), p. 11.
2. *All in a Life Time* (New York, 1922), pp. 130-31.
3. New York *Times,* November 12, 1918.
4. *Congressional Record,* 66 Cong., 1 Sess. (August 12, 1919), Vol. 58, pp. 3789-91.
5. Richard W. Leopold, *Elihu Root and the Conservative Tradition* (Boston, 1954), pp. 123 ff.; Baltimore *Sun,* December 26, 1922; Arthur Walworth, *Woodrow Wilson, World Prophet* (2 vols., New York, 1958), I, p. 78.
6. New York *Times,* January 27, 1917; Vinson, *Borah and Outlawry,* p. 22.
7. New York *Times,* November 28, 1918.
8. New York *Times,* February 1, 1919. Borah wrote to Senator J. Hamilton Lewis that he did not mean by this statement to give offense to Christians. Undated letter, Box 552, Borah Papers.
9. *Congressional Record,* 65 Cong., 3 Sess. (February 21, 1919, Vol. 57, pp. 3911 ff.; cf. Johnson, *Borah,* pp. 228-30; New York *Times,* February 22, 1919.
10. February 18, 1919, Box 552, Borah Papers; New York *Times,* February 19, 1919.
11. *Nation,* 108 (February 22, 1919), 273; Beveridge to Borah, February 23, 1919, Beveridge to Bross, February 23 and 26, 1919, Bross to Beveridge, February 25, 1919, Beveridge Papers, Ms. Division, Library of Congress, Washington, D.C.; "Borah Can Be Spared," editorial in Indianapolis *Times-Star,* February 19, 1919; Johnson, *Borah,* p. 228.
12. "Militarism in the League of Nations?" *Forum,* 61 (March, 1919), 297-306.
13. New York *Post,* February 22, 1919; Johnson, *Borah,* p. 232; New York *Times,* March 7, 1919.
14. Beveridge to Bross, March 9, 1919, Beveridge Papers; New York *Times,* March 9, 1919.
15. New York *Times,* March 10, 1919.
16. *Ibid.,* March 20, 1919.
17. Borah to John Hart, March 24, 1919, Borah to Albert Beveridge, January 28, 1919, Box 550, Borah Papers; New York *Times,* March 28, 1919.
18. Leopold, *Root,* pp. 135-37; Garraty, *Lodge,* pp. 357-58.

19. "The Peace League Launched," *Literary Digest,* 60 (February 8, 1919), 14.
20. *Ibid.,* 61 (April 26, 1919), 9; Borah to Albert B. Hart, April 21, 1919, Box 550, Borah Papers.
21. Vinson, *Borah and Outlawry,* pp. 27-29.
22. Henry Cabot Lodge, *The United States and the League of Nations* (New York, 1925), pp. 146-47; Garraty, *Lodge,* pp. 321 ff.
23. When the delegation from the Irish Nationalist convention presented their demands to Wilson in 1918, he made promises beyond his power to fulfill but refused to receive Cohalan with the rest of the group.
24. The role of the hyphenates in the anti-League campaign is treated in detail in Selig Adler's *Isolationist Impulse,* pp. 75-92.
25. New York *Times,* May 15 and June 30, 1919.
26. *Ibid.,* June 4, 6, and 9, 1919; Boise *Capital News,* June 9, 1919.
27. *Congressional Record,* 66 Cong., 1 Sess. (June 9, 1919), Vol. 58, pp. 558 ff.; Detroit *Journal,* June 10, 1919; New York *Times,* June 10, 1919; Walworth, *Wilson,* I, pp. 340-41.
28. Garraty, *Lodge,* p. 366; James C. Malin, *The United States after the World War* (New York), 1930), pp. 43-44.
29. Alan Cranston, *The Killing of the Peace* (New York, 1945), pp. 62 ff.
30. New York *Times,* August 19, 1919.
31. David Lawrence, *The True Story of Woodrow Wilson* (New York, 1924), pp. 270-73; Walworth, *Wilson,* I, pp. 351 ff. Borah believed that when the American delegation learned of the secret agreements at Paris, if not earlier, its members should have demanded their rejection or, if necessary, quit the conference.
32. Borah to James T. Williams, September 9, 1919, Box 550, Borah Papers.
33. New York *Times,* September 11, 1919; Cranston, *Killing of the Peace,* pp. 174-75.
34. Thomas Bailey, *Woodrow Wilson and the Great Betrayal* (New York, 1945), chapters 6 and 7.
35. Cranston, *Killing of the Peace,* p. 196; Vinson, *Borah and Outlawry,* p. 26; Borah to Francis Owens, January 23, 1920, Borah to Walter B. Hinneman, January 16, 1920, Box 551, Borah Papers.
36. *Congressional Record,* 66 Cong., 1 Sess. (November 19, 1919), Vol. 58, pp. 8781-84.
37. Beveridge to Borah, November 25, 1919, Beveridge Papers; Will

Griffith, *Idols of Egypt* (Carbondale, 1947), p. 69; Johnson, *Borah,* pp. 244-45.

38. Frank Simonds, *Can America Stay at Home?* (New York, 1932), pp. 105-6.
39. November 24, 1919, Beveridge Papers.
40. New York *Times,* July 26, 1919.
41. William A. Williams, "The Legend of Isolationism in the 1920's," *Science and Society,* 18 (Winter, 1954), 8-20.
42. Adler, *Isolationist Impulse,* p. 103; Vinson, *Borah and Outlawry,* p. 17.
43. Boston *Transcript,* May 10, 1919.
44. January 23, 1920, Box 551, Borah Papers.
45. Schriftgiesser, *Lodge,* p. 349; cf. Garraty, *Lodge,* p. 386; Lodge, *United States and the League,* pp. 193-95; Washington *Post,* January 24, 1920; Johnson, *Borah,* pp. 246-48. Ray McKaig, an Idaho friend of Borah's, told the author that Borah once related how Lodge had to be restrained by force to prevent compromise. He said Lodge was registered in a Washington hotel under another name and locked in his room for the weekend!
46. Frederick M. Alger to Borah in New York *Times,* April 2, 1920; William T. Hutchinson, *Lowden of Illinois: The Life of Frank O. Lowden* (2 vols., Chicago, 1951), II, pp. 430, 452, and 462.
47. Watson, *As I Knew Them,* pp. 213 ff.; Karl Schriftgiesser, *This Was Normalcy: An Account of Party Politics during Twelve Republican Years, 1920-1932* (Boston, 1948), p. 8.
48. New York *Times,* June 12, 1920; Gilbert, *Mirrors of Washington,* pp. 254-55; Hutchinson, *Lowden,* II, pp. 430 ff.
49. Watson, *As I Knew Them,* pp. 213 ff.; Fola La Follette, *La Follette,* II, pp. 996-98; Charles Merz, "Idaho Minority of One," *New Republic,* 43 (May 27, 1925), 38.
50. Borah to Beveridge, September 6, 1920, Borah Papers; New York *Times,* October 2, 5, and 16, 1920; Schriftgiesser, *Lodge,* p. 75; Thompson, *Presidents I've Known,* pp. 229-30.

NOTES TO CHAPTER XI

1. Simonds, *Can America Stay at Home?,* pp. 129-30.
2. *Nation,* 113 (July 20, 1921), 61.
3. New York *Times,* February 21, 1921.
4. Henry Pringle, "The Real Senator Borah," *World's Work,* 57 (December, 1928), 134; Borah *Scrapbook,* Vol. 6.

5. Gilbert, *Behind the Mirrors,* pp. 150-51.
6. *Ibid.,* p. 34.
7. Merlo J. Pusey, *Charles Evans Hughes* (2 vols., New York, 1951), II, pp. 440-44; Vinson, *Borah and Outlawry,* pp. 56-57.
8. *Congressional Record,* 67 Cong., 1 Sess. (September 26, 1921), Vol. 61, pp. 5794-5802; New York *Times,* April 13, May 1, July 2, September 21-28, October 3, 1921.
9. *Congressional Record,* 67 Cong., 1 Sess. (October 18, 1921), Vol. 61, pp. 6414-16; New York *Times,* March 22, 1922.
10. *Congressional Record,* 67 Cong., Special Sess. (April 20, 1921), Vol. 61, pp. 474-78; Borah to James T. Williams, March 28, 1921, in Boston *Transcript,* April 21, 1921; New York *Times,* April 15, 1921.
11. Charles Merz, "Borah's One Man Party," *New Republic,* 43 (June 10, 1925), 66.
12. Robert E. Osgood, *Ideals and Self-Interest in America's Foreign Relations* (Chicago, 1953), p. 330.
13. *Ibid.,* p. 333.
14. "Disarmament Winning at Washington," *Literary Digest,* 69 (June 11, 1921), 8; *Congressional Record,* 66 Cong., 3 Sess. (March 11, 1921), Vol. 60, p. 4169.
15. Vinson, *Borah and Outlawry,* pp. 31 ff.; for the Walsh resolution, see New York *Times,* December 12, 1920.
16. *Congressional Record,* 66 Cong., 3 Sess., Vol. 60, p. 310.
17. Vinson, *Borah and Outlawry,* pp. 31 ff.; see also John C. Vinson, *The Parchment Peace* (Atlanta, 1956), p. 51; for the debate on the resolution, see *ibid.,* chapter 6; cf. C. Leonard Hoag, *Preface to Preparedness: The Washington Disarmament Conference and Public Opinion* (Washington, D. C., 1941), pp. 35 ff.; Borah *Scrapbook,* Vol. 1; Schriftgiesser, *This Was Normalcy,* p. 134.
18. Hoag, *Preface to Preparedness,* pp. 35-36; New York *Times,* March 30, 1922; Osgood, *Ideals and Self-Interest,* pp. 337-38.
19. *Congressional Record,* 66 Cong., 3 Sess. (January 25, 1921), Vol. 60, p. 1996; New York *Times,* January 26, 1921.
20. Hughes' biographer claims that the secretary of state favored arms limitation all along but thought the time was not yet ripe; Pusey, *Hughes,* II, pp. 454-55; cf. *New Republic,* 25 (February 2, 1921), 271.
21. New York *Times,* January 27, 1921.
22. Vinson, *Borah and Outlawry,* pp. 28-29; New York *Times,* May 10 and 26, 1921; Borah *Scrapbook,* Vol. 1, Series 2; Hoag, *Preface to*

Preparedness, pp. 60-61; *Literary Digest*, 69 (June 11, 1921), 8-9; Borah to William J. O'Brian, June 16, 1924, Box 237, Borah Papers.

23. Samuel Hopkins Adams, *Incredible Era: The Life and Times of Warren Gamaliel Harding* (Boston, 1939), pp. 245 ff.; *Literary Digest, ut supra.*

24. "Snags in the Way of Disarmament," *Literary Digest*, 70 (July 30, 1921), 12.

25. New York *Times*, July 12, August 12 and 30, November 12-13, 1921; Vinson, *Borah and Outlawry*, pp. 40-41.

26. 67 Cong., 2 Sess., Vol. 62, pp. 3232 ff., 3555 ff., 3776 ff., and 3787 ff.; John C. Vinson, "The Drafting of the Four Power Treaty of the Washington Conference," *Journal of Modern History*, 25 (March, 1952), 40-47.

27. February 19 and 21, March 21-23, 1922.

28. *Ibid.;* Borah to Doremus Scudder, April 21, 1922, Box 215, Borah Papers; Baltimore *Sun*, March 20, 1922; John C. Vinson, "The Parchment Peace," *Mississippi Valley Historical Review*, 39 (September, 1952), 303-14; Vinson, *Parchment Peace*, chapters 6, 7, and 8; Vinson, *Borah and Outlawry*, pp. 44-47; Osgood, *Ideals and Self-Interest*, pp. 342-46.

29. Borah to George Krogness, July 2, 1919, Box 550, Borah Papers; cf. Oswald G. Villard's editorial, "The Madness at Versailles," *Nation*, 108 (May 17, 1919), 778-80.

30. *Congressional Record*, 67 Cong., 1 Sess. (September 26, 1921), Vol. 61, pp. 5800-5801.

31. New York *Times*, January 26, February 16, 1922; Osgood, *Ideals and Self-Interest*, pp. 298-300.

32. William E. Borah, "The Ghost of Versailles at the Conference," *Nation*, 113 (November 9, 1921), 525-26; New York *Times*, December 9, 1921.

33. *Congressional Record*, 67 Cong., 3 Sess. (November 23, 1922), Vol. 63, pp. 55; cf. New York *Times*, November 23-24, 1922; Vinson, *Borah and Outlawry*, pp. 50-52.

34. *Nation, ut supra.*

35. New York *Times*, January 26, 1922.

36. *Ibid.*, December 11, 1921.

37. Osgood, *Ideals and Self-Interest*, pp. 298-300.

38. Borah to Henry M. McCracken, September 26, 1922, Box 215, Borah Papers.

39. Washington *Post,* January 23, 1923; *Literary Digest,* 76 (January 27, 1923), 11.
40. New York *Times,* January 24, 1923.
41. New York *Times,* VII, December 11, 1921, February 14, 1923; *Literary Digest, ut supra;* New York *Evening Post,* December 18, 1922; London *Times,* January 19, 1933.
42. New York *Times,* December 30, 1922; Washington *Post,* December 28, 1922.
43. Vinson, *Borah and Outlawry,* pp. 54-58; Springfield *Republican,* December 23, 1922; Detroit *News,* December 30, 1922; Seattle *Star,* January 9, 1923; New York *Times* editorial, February 16, 1923; letter to the editor, New York *Times,* March 11, 1923.
44. *Congressional Record,* 67 Cong., 1 Sess. (June 23, 1921), Vol. 61, pp. 2958 ff.; *ibid.* (July 14, 1921), Vol. 61, pp. 3764 ff.; *ibid.* (February 13, 1922), Vol. 62, pp. 2491 ff.; New York *Times,* June 24, July 15, August 23, 1921.
45. New York *Times,* April 23, 1922.
46. *Ibid.,* October 2, 1922; cf. *Nation,* 115 (October 18, 1922), 399.
47. New York *Times,* March 12, 1923.
48. Box 219, Borah Papers; cf. Johnson, *Borah,* pp. 260-61; Borah to Mark Austin, July 11, 1921, Box 201, Borah Papers.
49. New York *Times,* July 8 and 18, August 20, 1922; Florida *Times-Union,* August 25, 1922.
50. New York *Times,* February 8, 1923; Johnson, *Borah,* p. 261.
51. *Congressional Record,* 67 Cong., 2 Sess. (July 6, 1922), Vol. 62, pp. 10015-20; New York *Times,* June 30, July 6, November 15, 1922.
52. New York *Times,* November 3 and 10, 1922; Boxes 219 and 220, Borah Papers.
53. Johnson, "Borah, People's Choice," *ut supra;* Boyd A. Martin, *The Direct Primary in Idaho.* (Stanford, 1947), pp. 66 ff. and 78 ff.; New York *Times,* October 13, 1922; Annie Pike Greenwood, "Bill Borah and Other Home Folks," *Nation,* 116 (February 28, 1923), p. 236.
54. Cincinnati *Inquirer,* March 22, 1923; *Literary Digest,* 77 (April 7, 1923), 11.
55. New York *Times,* March 28, 1923.
56. Borah *Scrapbook* (August 11, 1923), Vol. 4, Series 2.

NOTES TO CHAPTER XII

1. Charles Merz, "Borah's One Man Party," *New Republic,* 43 (June 10, 1925), 66-69.
2. Borah *Scrapbook,* Vol. 5, new series, p. 17.
3. Charles Merz, "Androcles and the Lion: The Silent President and the Roaring Borah," *Century,* 111 (April, 1926), 699-700; Robert B. Smith, "Borah: Friend and Foe: Sidelights on a Peace That Passeth Understanding," *Independent,* 114 (May 9, 1925), 522-23.
4. Merz, "Androcles and the Lion," *ut supra,* 700-701.
5. Borah to H. S. Van Alstine, May 21, 1926, Box 262, Borah Papers.
6. Typescript of speech, October 18, 1926, Box 272, *ibid.*
7. New York *Times,* June 18, December 2, 1926; Borah to B. F. Neale, June 30, 1926, Box 262, Borah Papers; Gilbert Fite, *George N. Peek and the Fight for Farm Parity* (Norman, 1954), pp. 217 and 226; Bruce Minton and John Stuart, *The Fat Years and the Lean* (New York, 1940), pp. 59-61.
8. Borah to Will Tyson, July 17, 1926, Box 262, Borah Papers.
9. Borah *Scrapbook,* Vol. 23; New York *Times,* June 16, 1928.
10. Fite, *Peek,* p. 217.
11. New York *Times,* December 7, 1923.
12. *Ibid.,* November 16, 1923.
13. Borah to Gleed Miller, January 25, 1924, Box 247, Borah Papers.
14. Claude M. Fuess, *Calvin Coolidge: The Man from Vermont* (New York, 1940), pp. 338-41.
15. *Ibid.,* p. 332; Johnson, *Borah,* pp. 288-89.
16. Fuess, *Coolidge,* pp. 338-39.
17. What seems to be the most authentic account of this meeting appears in the Borah *Scrapbook,* Vol. 17; cf. Fuess, *Coolidge,* pp. 339-40; Duff Gilfond, *The Rise of St. Calvin: Merry Sidelights on the Career of Mr. Coolidge* (New York, 1932), pp. 178-84.
18. Johnson, *Borah,* pp. 289-90.
19. New York *Times,* February 24, 1924.
20. Thomas L. Stokes, *Chip off My Shoulder* (Princeton, 1940), p. 155.
21. Harry M. Daugherty, *The Inside Story of the Harding Tragedy* (New York, 1932), pp. 166 ff., 207 ff., and 287-89; Gilbert, *You Takes Your Choice,* p. 36.

22. Stanley Frost, "Capping the Mad Gusher," *Outlook*, 136 (April 16, 1924), 647-48.
23. Borah *Scrapbook* (April 7, 1924), Vol. 4, Series 2; Baltimore *Sun*, April 7, 1924.
24. Philadelphia *Inquirer*, May 12, 1928; Borah *Scrapbook*, Vol. 7, p. 13.
25. Borah *Scrapbook*, Vol. 7, p. 13.
26. Borah to John Hart, March 1, 1924, Box 238, Borah Papers.
27. "Borah as Presidential Timber," *Literary Digest*, 77 (April 7, 1923), 9.
28. Ten years later Couzens commented: "We heard nothing from it." He said he was obligated to Borah for refusing the offer, for it would have resulted in a "terrible catastrophe" for the country! Washington *News*, December 5, 1934.
29. "The Call for Borah and La Follette," *Nation*, 118 (February 20, 1924), 194; see also "The Duty to Revolt," *Nation*, 115 (August 9, 1922), 140; cf. "Borah and a Third Party," *Literary Digest*, 74 (August 26, 1922), 14.
30. Kenneth C. Mackay, *The Progressive Movement of 1924* (Columbia University Ph.D. thesis, 1947), p. 195; cf. Johnson, *Borah*, pp. 302-3. In February 1923 Borah proposed that 7 out of 9 judges be required to concur in pronouncing an act of Congress unconstitutional.
31. *Nation*, 150 (January 27, 1940), 87; Borah to Harvey, May 15 and 31, 1924, Box 243, Borah Papers.
32. New York *Times*, June 9, 1924.
33. Fuess, *Coolidge*, p. 343.
34. The account of this meeting is based on Nicholas Murray Butler's report in *Across the Busy Years*, I, pp. 280-81. There are other accounts, which differ on details, but Butler was a witness to all that took place and was a reliable, though caustic, reporter.
35. Borah *Scrapbook*, Vol. 4, Series 2, and Vol. 22, Series 1; Gilbert, *You Takes Your Choice*, pp. 44-47.
36. New York *Times*, June 18, July 17, 1924.
37. New York *Times*, September 4 and 5, 1924; cf. Borah *Scrapbook*, Vol. 4, Series 2.
38. Boise *Capital News*, Ocotber 8, 1924; Borah *Scrapbook*, Vol. 4, Series 2.
39. At that time the Idaho State Supreme Court handed down a ruling

that a candidate's name could appear on the ballot of only one party, which forced Borah to make a choice. He chose the Republican party. See New York *Times,* October 8, 1924.

40. Borah *Scrapbook* (October 10, 1924), Vol. 17, Series 1.
41. Boise *Capital News,* December 7, 1924. The official vote was 99,846 for Borah and 25,199 for Martin.
42. November 5, 1924, Box 244, Borah Papers.
43. Levinson to Cora Rubin (Lane), September 9, 1924, Box 243, *ibid.*
44. Borah to Senator Moses, November 29, 1924, Box 244, *ibid.*
45. Moses to Borah, December 1, 1924, *ibid.*
46. "The Republican Victory: What Shall We Do with It?," *Scribner's Magazine,* 77 (January, 1925), 3a-4a.
47. Idaho *Statesman,* December 24, 1924.
48. Borah to Murray Brookman, March 6, 1925, Box 259, Borah Papers.
49. Borah to Henry M. Huxley, December 16, 1924, *ibid.*
50. Borah to Charles Pace, March 24, 1925, Box 249, *ibid.;* New York *Times,* February 24, 1925.

NOTES TO CHAPTER XIII

1. 119 (December 31, 1924), 719.
2. For a more detailed comparison of Lodge and Borah, see Washburn's "Washington Weekly" in Boston *Transcript,* May 3, 1933.
3. Walter Lippmann, *Men of Destiny* (New York, 1928), pp. 148 ff. Mr. Lippmann explains, with cogent reasons, why the effort of the Senate to control the conduct of foreign affairs was bound to be ineffective and obstructive.
4. J. L. Garvin, London *Observer,* January 25, 1925.
5. Borah *Scrapbook* (December 21, 1924), Vol. 2, Series 2.
6. Manchester *Guardian Weekly,* February 2, 1923.
7. William S. White, *Citadel: The Story of the United States Senate* (New York, 1956), pp. 15-16.
8. Midgley, *Possible Presidents,* p. 129; Manchester *Guardian Weekly,* February 2, 1923.
9. Interview with William R. Castle, former undersecretary of state, December 1956.
10. Rodney Dutcher, Washington *News,* March 22, 1927.
11. Johnson, *Borah,* pp. 316-18; Allan Nevins, "Borah and World Politics," *Current History,* 37 (February, 1933), 518; *Newsweek,* 11 (January 24, 1938), 9.

11a. Letter, Manchester *Evening News* (ca. May 20, 1930).
12. June 21, 1932, Box 583, Borah Papers; Chicago *Progressive,* May 1, 1927.
13. Dennison, *Senate Foreign Relations Committee,* pp. 20 ff.
14. Pusey, *Hughes,* II, p. 612.
15. Borah *Scrapbook,* Vol. 23. By March 1925 nearly twenty treaties had been ratified in Borah's short term as chairman.
16. New York *World,* January 14, 1925.
17. Washington *Times,* October 21, 1925; see also Borah *Scrapbook,* Vol. 23, Series 1.
18. New York *Times,* October 21, 1925.
19. Washington *Herald,* November 5, 1925.
20. New York *Times,* December 21, 1925.
21. *Ibid.,* December 24, 1925.
22. Speech to students at the University of Michigan at Ann Arbor, reported in New York *Times,* May 19, 1925; speech in St. Louis, in *ibid.,* May 19, 1923; *Congressional Record,* 69 Cong., Special Sess. (December 18, 1925), Vol. 67, pp. 1071-77.
23. Speech before the Saturday Club of New York, in New York *Times,* March 20, 1923.
24. Speech before the Unitarian Laymen's League, in New York *Times,* May 12, 1925; see also Chicago *Evening Post,* October 21, 1925.
25. Brittanicus Viator, "Representative Men: Senator Borah," *English Review,* 62 (January, 1936), 29.
26. *World's Work,* 58 (June, 1929), 34; New York *Times,* May 12, 1925.
27. *Nation,* 121 (December 30, 1925), 751.
28. Editorial in New York *Times,* January 28, 1926.
29. Manley O. Hudson to the editor, *ibid.,* May 14, 1925.
30. *Ibid.,* May 6, 1925.
31. Walter Lippmann, "The Outlawry of War," *Atlantic Monthly,* 132 (August, 1923), 249. For Borah's reply, see *ibid.* (September, 1923), 431.
32. Borah *Scrapbook* (November 30, 1925), Vol. 5, Series 2, p. 18. The letter was signed by such notables as John Grier Hibben, William Allen White, James R. Angell, Alton Parker, Cyrus McCormick, Josephus Daniels, Carrie Chapman Catt, and Ray Lyman Wilbur.
33. Borah to John Grier Hibben, November 30, 1925, *ibid.;* see also Box 263, Borah Papers.

34. Washington *Post,* December 19, 1925; New York *Times,* December 19, 1925; Borah *Scrapbook,* Vol. 23, Series 1.
35. *Congressional Record,* 69 Cong., 1 Sess. (January 27, 1926), Vol. 67, pp. 2824-25.
36. Worcester *Evening Gazette,* February 15, 1926; New York *Times,* January 24, 28, and 29, February 10, 1926.
37. *Nation,* 122 (March 10, 1926), 243-44; Worcester *Evening Gazette,* February 22, 1926.
38. New York *Times,* February 25 and 26, 1926.
39. Schriftgiesser, *This Was Normalcy,* pp. 232-33.
40. *Congressional Record,* 71 Cong., 3 Sess. (December 10, 1930), Vol. 74, pp. 504-5.
41. *Time,* 25 (February 11, 1935), 13. Borah and Johnson had been erstwhile enemies since the campaign of 1920 (see Chapter X).
42. "What the Monroe Doctrine Really Means," *Colliers,* 75 (January 31, 1925), 25.
43. Foster Rhea Dulles, *America's Rise to Power, 1898-1954* (New York, 1954), p. 154.
44. *Ibid.*, p. 155.
45. New York *Times,* December 30, 1926; Washington *Herald,* January 8, 1927.
46. New York *World,* February 24, 1927.
47. Dulles, *America's Rise to Power,* p. 155.
48. Borah to President Calles, Mexico City, January 22, 1927, Box 280, Borah Papers.
49. January 24, 1927, *ibid.*
50. A law of 1799 which forbade any U.S. citizen to communicate with a foreign government in relation to any disputes or controversies with the United States.
51. New York *Times,* March 21, 1927; *Nation,* 124 (April 13, 1927), 392-94.
52. Dulles, *America's Rise to Power,* p. 155.
53. Baltimore *Sun,* August 18, 1925.
54. New York *Times,* November 17 and 18, 1926.
55. Thomas Millard to Borah, June 18, 1925, Borah to Millard, June 20, 1925, September 15, 1925, Box 259, Borah Papers; Washington *Post,* June 28, 1925; New York *Times,* June 28, August 3, 1925; Borah to C. T. Wang, September 28, 1925, quoted in C. C. Tansill, *Back Door to War: The Roosevelt Foreign Policy, 1933-*

1941 (Chicago, 1952), p. 65; Borah statement to the press, October 19, 1925, Box 259, Borah Papers.

56. *Foreign Relations* (1928), I, pp. 799-802; Tansill, *Back Door to War,* pp. 63-66; Idaho *Statesman,* June 30, 1927.
57. August 16, 1927, Box 284, Borah Papers.
58. August 18, 1927, *ibid.*
59. Telegram to Borah from Committee Headquarters, Boston, August 20, 1927, *ibid.*
60. August 20, 1927, *ibid.*
61. *Ibid.*
62. August 22, 1927, *ibid.*
63. Holmes to Borah, August 25, 1927, *ibid.*
64. Borah to Jane Addams, September 3, 1927, *ibid.*
65. Midgley, *Possible Presidents,* pp. 130-31.

NOTES TO CHAPTER XIV

1. John E. Stoner, *S. O. Levinson and the Pact of Paris: A Study in the Techniques of Influence* (Chicago, 1942), pp. 72-73; Robert H. Ferrell, *Peace in Their Time: The Origins of the Kellogg-Briand Pact* (New Haven, 1952), pp. 31-32 and 36; John C. Vinson, *Borah and Outlawry,* pp. 59 ff.
2. John Dewey, "Outlawry of War," *Encyclopedia of the Social Sciences,* II, pp. 508-10; "Morals and the Conduct of States," *New Republic,* 14 (March 23, 1918), 232-34.
3. *Congressional Record,* 67 Cong., 4 Sess. (February 13, 1923), Vol. 64, pp. 12-13; see also Ferrell, *Peace in Their Time,* pp. 33-34; Vinson, *Borah and Outlawry,* pp. 62-77; Donald Drummond, *Passing of American Neutrality, 1937-41* (Ann Arbor, 1955), pp. 26-27; Drew Pearson and Constantine Brown, *The American Diplomatic Game* (New York, 1935), pp. 12-13.
4. New York *World,* March 18, 1923; Borah *Scrapbook,* Vol. 23, Series 1; New York *Times,* April 1, 1923.
5. *Historical Outlook,* 16 (February, 1925), 58-60; Borah *Scrapbook,* Vol. 23; New York *Times,* April 1, 1923.
6. William E. Borah, "How to End War," *Nation,* 119 (December 31, 1924), 738-39.
7. April 3, 1926, Box 269, Borah Papers.
8. Borah to Samuel Colcord, January 9, 1925, Box 257, Borah Papers.

9. Drummond, *Passing of Neutrality,* p. 28; Vinson, *Borah and Outlawry,* pp. 114 ff.
10. Ferrell, *Peace in Their Time,* p. 72.
11. Joseph Agan to Borah, May 7, 1927, Box 282, Borah Papers.
12. Borah to Professor Jerome Davis, May 3, 1927, *ibid.;* Pearson, *American Diplomatic Game,* p. 19; Dewey, "Outlawry of War," *up supra.*
13. Ferrell, *Peace in Their Time,* pp. 80-81.
14. Borah to Levinson, July 12, 1927, Box 282, Borah Papers.
15. Borah to Raymond Fosdick, in New York *Times,* May 6, 1927.
16. New York *Times,* November 26, 1927.
17. Borah to Levinson, July 26, 1927, Box 282, Borah Papers.
18. Borah to Rev. Sidney Gulick, in New York *Times,* November 11, 1927.
19. James T. Shotwell, *War as an Instrument of National Policy and Its Renunciation in the Pact of Paris* (New York, 1929), pp. 112-15; Ferrell, *Peace in Their Time,* p. 161.
20. Pearson, *American Diplomatic Game,* pp. 27-28; Ferrell, *Peace in Their Time,* pp. 138-40; Gilfond, *Rise of St. Calvin,* pp. 262-66.
21. New York *Times Magazine,* February 5, 1928; cf. Ferrell, *Peace in Their Time,* pp. 161-62.
22. New York *Times,* February 6, 1928.
23. Borah to Kellogg, March 31, 1928, Box 218, Borah Papers: Kellogg to Borah, July 22 and 27, August 2 and 10, 1928, and Borah to Kellogg, July 28, 1928, gives their exchange of views during the period preceding the signing of the Kellogg-Briand Pact, Box 542, Borah Papers. For a good account of the ceremony at the signing, see Ferrell, *Peace in Their Time,* pp. 215 ff.
24. Ferrell, *Peace in Their Time,* p. 207; Borah to Robins, August 6, 1928, Box 218, Borah Papers.
25. Borah to Levinson, August 2, 1928, quoted in Ferrell, *Peace in Their Time,* pp. 200-207; Osgood, *Ideals and Self-Interest,* pp. 348-49.
26. New York *Times,* November 14, 1928; Ferrell, *Peace in Their Time,* pp. 234-35; *Nation,* 127 (November 28, 1928), 561; cf. *Nation,* 128 (January 23, 1929), 91.
27. New York *Times,* January 2, 1929.
28. *Congressional Record,* 70 Cong., 2 Sess. (January 3, 1929), Vol. 70, pp. 1069-70; Osgood, *Ideals and Self-Interest,* p. 348.

29. Charles G. Dawes's diary, January 15, 1929, in *Notes as Vice President, 1928-9* (Boston, 1935), p. 236; Ferrell, *Peace in Their Time*, pp. 250-51.
30. *Congressional Record*, 70 Cong., 2 Sess. (January 15, 1929), Vol. 70, p. 1728.
31. *Ibid.*, p. 1731.
32. New York *Times*, November 18, 1925.
33. *Congressional Record*, 70 Cong., 2 Sess. (January 3, 1929), Vol. 70, p. 1065; Tansill, *Back Door to War*, pp. 217 ff.; Edgar Kemler, *The Deflation of American Ideals* (Washington, D.C., 1941), p. 143; Osgood, *Ideals and Self-Interest*, pp. 346-50.
34. George W. Wickersham, "The Pact of Paris," *Foreign Affairs*, 9 (January, 1931), 364; Ray Tucker, "Borah of Idaho," *American Mercury*, 9 (December 1, 1926), 388; Edwin Borchard and William P. Lage, *Neutrality for the United States* (New Haven, 1937), p. 298.
35. *Freeman*, 6 (February 28, 1923), 580.
36. *Men of Destiny*, pp. 152-83.
37. Osgood, *Ideals and Self-Interest*, pp. 349-50.

NOTES TO CHAPTER XV

1. Glenn D. Whisler, "Our Next President," *Forum*, 79 (June, 1928), 935.
2. Wallace *Miner*, August 25, 1927; Borah *Scrapbook*, Vol. 5, Series 2, p. 109.
3. March 18, 1926, Box 270, Borah Papers.
4. March 23, 1926, *ibid.*
5. Hoover to Borah, February 23, 1928, Box 293, *ibid.*
6. Borah *Scrapbook*, Vol. 5, Series 2, p. 148.
7. *Colliers*, 82 (August 4, 1928), 38.
8. Borah *Scrapbook*, Vol. 24, Series 1; New York *Sun*, June 16, 1928.
9. Edwin C. Hill, in New York *Sun*, June 15, 1928; cf. Borah *Scrapbook*, Vol. 7, Series 2.
10. Henry Pringle, *Alfred E. Smith: A Critical Study* (New York, 1927), p. 370.
11. New York *Times*, September 20, 1928.
12. The Farm Bureau bill was the result, and it went much farther along the lines of state socialism than the McNary-Haugen bills,

which Hoover had formerly opposed. W. H. Liggett, *The Rise of Herbert Hoover* (New York, 1932), p. 340.

13. *Nation,* 127 (October 3, 1928), 307.
14. Oswald Garrison Villard, *Fighting Years: Memoirs of a Liberal Editor* (New York, 1939), pp. 468-69; *Nation, ut supra.*
15. Radio speech delivered in Chicago, October 18, 1928.
16. *The Memoirs of Herbert Hoover* (3 vols., New York, 1952), II, p. 208.
17. November 5, 1928, Box 293, Borah Papers.
18. "Herbert's Godfather," *Colliers,* 82 (August 4, 1928), 40.
19. New York *Evening Post,* November 8, 1928.
20. Borah to Ed Dewey, November 13, 1928, Box 293, Borah Papers.
21. Salt Lake City *Tribune,* February 17, 1929.
22. New York *Times,* January 19, 1929.
23. Herbert Hoover to the author, February 2, 1957.
24. Borah's White House conferences, from typescripts in the possession of his secretary, Mrs. Cora Rubin Lane, loaned to the author. This conference was reported under the date January 18, 1929.
25. *Ibid.*
26. February 21, 1929, *ibid.;* Harris G. Warren, *Herbert Hoover and the Great Depression* (New York, 1959), p. 54.
27. White House Conference, January 18, 1929; *Colliers,* 84 (September 14, 1929), 65.
28. Hoover, *Memoirs,* II, p. 292.
29. Warren, *Hoover,* pp. 60-61.
30. Robert S. Allen, *Why Hoover Faces Defeat* (New York, 1932), pp. 58-82; Warren, *Hoover,* pp. 168-72.
31. Borah *Scrapbook* (May 12, 1929), Vol. 9, p. 59.
32. W. S. Myers and W. H. Newton, eds., *The Hoover Administration: A Documented Narrative* (New York, 1936), p. 392; New York *World,* editorial, June 19, 1929; Schriftgiesser, *This Was Normalcy,* pp. 268-69; *Congressional Record,* 71 Cong., 1 Sess. (June 17, 1929), Vol. 71, 2947; Warren, *Hoover,* pp. 88-89.
33. William C. Murphy, Jr., "Mr. Borah Turns Practical," *Commonweal,* 11 (February 19, 1930), 446-47.
34. Myers and Newton, *Hoover Administration,* p. 397.
35. Hoover, *Memoirs,* II, pp. 292-93.
36. New York *World,* September 28, 1929.

37. *Commonweal, ut supra.*
38. Borah to Robert Washburn, April 18, 1931, Box 329, Borah Papers; see also Boston *Post,* May 25, 1931.
39. Washington *Post,* December 30, 1930.
40. Savannah *Morning News,* September 14, 1930.
41. Springfield *Weekly Republican,* September 14, 1930.
42. Johnson, *Borah,* p. 445. This account of the Idaho campaign of 1930 is based on Borah *Scrapbook,* Vol. 9, Series 2. Campaign expenses totalled $333.50. Statement of receipts, etc., November 4, 1930, Box 317, Borah Papers.
43. New York *Times,* November 23, 1930.
44. Washington *Herald,* November 17, 1930.
45. Washington *Star,* February 2, 1931.
46. *Ibid.,* June 8, 1931.
47. Borah to Charles Wood, July 6, 1931, Box 322, Borah Papers.
48. Akron *Times Press,* September 9, 1931.
49. Hoover, *Memoirs,* III, p. 101.
50. Undated clipping (*ca.* November, 1932), in Borah *Scrapbook,* Vol. 9, Series 2.
51. *Ibid.*
52. Chicago *Daily News,* October 17, 1932; *Nation,* 133 (August 5, 1932), 117.
53. Idaho *Statesman,* September 2, 1932.
54. William E. Borah, "Bigger Guns or Better Homes?," *Colliers,* 84 (December 7, 1929), 10-11.
55. Borah *Scrapbook,* Vol. 17, Series 1; see also Borah's article, "Call Money and Stock Gambling," *World's Work,* 58 (June, 1929), 33-34.
56. Borah *Scrapbook,* Vol. 17, Series 1.
57. Akron *Beacon Journal,* February 11, 1932.
58. Chicago *Daily News,* August 2, 1933.
59. Chicago *World Examiner,* October 24, 1931.
60. *Literary Digest,* 111 (November 7, 1931), 7; Baltimore *Sun,* October 24, 1931; New York *Herald Tribune,* October 25, 1931; Robert Ferrell, *American Diplomacy in the Great Depression* (New Haven, 1957), pp. 201 ff., gives an unflattering account of Borah's role in the Laval visit. We are told Borah possessed a long nose

for publicity and summoned the French press, when actually it was the other way around.

61. Washington *Post,* October 25, 1931; stenographic report, October 26, 1931, loaned to the author by Cora Rubin Lane.

62. Borah *Scrapbook,* Vol. 9, p. 277; *Nation,* 133 (September 23, 1931), 293.

63. Washington *Star,* October 1, 1931.

64. Typescript, May 30, 1926, Box 272, Borah Papers; New York *Times,* May 31, 1926.

65. Interview, November 26, 1955.

66. Albert Tennyson, "Public Career of United States Senator William E. Borah, with specific reference to his activities . . . on domestic policies," University of Iowa, M.A. thesis, 1938; Washington *Post,* April 9, 1927; New York *Times,* April 9, 1927; Warren, *Hoover,* p. 213; New York *World,* December 26, 1929; *Outlook,* 143 (June 9, 1926), 195; *Literary Digest,* 104 (January 11, 1930), 7-9.

67. Washington *News,* June 21, 1932; Hoover, *Memoirs,* III, pp. 318-20; Warren, *Hoover,* pp. 209-23.

68. Chicago *Evening Post,* August 2, 1932.

69. Chicago *Daily News,* September 19, 1932.

70. New York *Times,* November 12, 1932.

71. Allan Nevins, "Borah and World Politics," *Current History,* 37 (February, 1933), 513-19, gives a brilliant analysis of Borah's service on the Foreign Relations Committee.

72. *Ibid.*

73. *Outlook,* 159 (November 11, 1931), 333.

74. Nevins, "Borah and World Politics," *ut supra,* pp. 518-19.

NOTES TO CHAPTER XVI

1. Max Beloff, *Foreign Policy of Soviet Russia, 1929-41* (2 vols., New York, 1947), I, p. 116.

2. William A. Williams, *The Shaping of American Diplomacy* (Chicago, 1956), pp. 655-59.

3. New York *Times,* July 27, 1917.

4. *Ibid.,* December 2, 1917, VII, p. 3.

5. *Ibid.,* July 14, 1918, I, p. 4.

6. March 6, 1920, Box 198, Borah Papers.

7. Bainbridge Colby to Baron Camillo Romano Avezzeno, August 10,

1920, cited in Louis Fischer, *The Soviets in World Affairs* (2 vols., New York, 1951), I, pp. 300-302.

8. May 17, 1922; review of Winston S. Churchill's *The Aftermath* in New York *American,* March 31, 1929.
9. *Congressional Record,* 67 Cong., 2 Sess. (May 31, 1922), Vol. 62, pp. 7904-9; New York *Times,* May 18, 1922.
10. Borah to Jacob Newman, July 25, 1927, Box 221, Borah Papers.
11. From an article by Borah in La Follette's *Magazine* (1922) reprinted in the Idaho *Free Press,* Box 221, Borah Papers.
12. New York *Times,* March 19, 1923. For an account of the Boston meetings, see Box 234, Borah Papers; cf. New York *Times,* December 3, 1922.
13. Fischer, *Soviets,* I, pp. 312-14.
14. William A. Williams, *American-Russian Relations, 1789-1947* (New York, 1952), pp. 179 and 201-3; *Literary Digest,* 80 (January 14, 1924), 10-11; *Colliers,* 76 (September 12, 1925), 6.
15. Reply dated December 16, 1923, in Williams, *American-Russian Relations,* p. 203.
16. *Ibid.;* Pusey, *Hughes,* II, p. 528; Borah to Robins, December 20, 1923, Box 245, Borah Papers.
17. Borah to Albert F. Coyle, January 30, 1924, *ibid.*
18. New York *Times Magazine,* December 30, 1923.
19. Edward Carr, *The Interregnum, 1923-4* (7 vols., New York, 1954), IV, pp. 246-47; *George Wharton Pepper, Philadelphia Lawyer: An Autobiography* (Philadelphia, 1944), p. 184; see also the folder "Russia," Box 245, Borah Papers; cf. New York *Times,* December 22, 1923; *New Republic,* 37 (February 6, 1924), 284-85.
20. New York *Times,* January 26, 1924; *Literary Digest,* 81 (March 8, 1924), 21.
21. Borah to Irvin Rockwell, September 30, 1925, Box 249, Borah Papers; cf. Borah's speech before the Philadelphia Forum, December 17, 1925, Box 259, *ibid.*
22. Fischer, *Soviets,* II, pp. 567-70; Arthur U. Pope, *Maxim Litvinov* (New York, 1943), pp. 257-59.
23. Pope, *Litvinov,* p. 217; Fischer, *Soviets,* II, p. 569.
24. Washington *Post,* January 10 and 11, 1929.
25. Borah to Colonel Robert McCormick, April 9, 1932, Box 332. Borah Papers.
26. Stimson to Borah, April 8, 1929, *ibid.*

27. Report from American Embassy in Berlin to U.S. State Department, transmitted in a letter to Borah, August 8, 1929, File #EE 811.44 BORAH, William E./22, State Department Records, National Archives, Washington, D.C.; see also Box 307, Borah Papers, which contains all the correspondence about this affair including the letter from Knickerbocker to Julian Mason, editor of the New York *Post,* dated April 18, 1929; cf. Fischer, *Soviets,* II, p. 496.
28. April 9, 1932, Box 322, Borah Papers. Interview with Hamilton Fish, November 28, 1956.
29. Borah to Rev. Henry Dexter, November 21, 1930, Box 318, Borah Papers.
30. Borah to Thomas Kennedy, December 15, 1928, Box 307, *ibid.* This letter shows Borah entertained hopes that Hoover would take a liberal view of the matter.
31. Borah to Stimson, August 25, 1932, File 861.01/1789, State Department Records, National Archives.
32. Stimson to Borah, September 8, 1932, *ibid.*
33. Louis Fischer, *Men and Politics: An Autobiography* (New York, 1941), pp. 213-14.
34. Beloff, *Foreign Policy of Soviet Russia,* I, pp. 116 ff.
35. Borah to Franklin D. Roosevelt, November 19, 1933, in Borah *Scrapbook,* Vol. 10, p. 163.
36. Litvinov to Borah, November 11, 1933, *ibid.*
37. Ernest Bates, *This Land of Liberty* (New York, 1930), p. 254.
38. Editorial in San Diego *Union,* 1933, quoted in Thomas Bailey, *America Faces Russia: Russian-American Relations from Early Times to the Present* (Ithaca, 1950), p. 262.

NOTES TO CHAPTER XVII

1. Mayo Clinic Report, August 6, 1932, Box 343, Borah Papers.
2. Raymond Clapper, *Review of Politics,* 89 (February, 1934), 28-29.
3. *Ibid.*
4. "Chiselers at Work and Play," *Nation,* 138 (February 7, 1934), 154-55.
5. Dwight Dumond, *Roosevelt to Roosevelt: The United States in the Twentieth Century* (New York, 1937), p. 254.
6. "Borah's Three Plank Prosperity Program," *Literary Digest,* 113 (May 21, 1932), 7.

7. *Golden Book,* 20 (September, 1934), 302-10.
8. *Literary Digest,* 120 (August 3, 1935), 7.
9. Dixon Wecter, *The Age of the Great Depression, 1929-41* (New York, 1948), pp. 65-70.
10. Washington *Star,* June 29, 1934.
11. Camden *Courier Post,* April 29, 1933.
12. Ernest Bates, *The Story of Congress* (New York, 1936), p. 436.
13. Washington *Evening Star,* June 29, 1934.
14. Borah *Scrapbook,* Vol. 13, Series 2, p. 185.
15. William E. Borah, "The Farmer's Enemy," *Colliers,* 97 (February 1, 1936), 12-13.
16. Washington *News,* January 16, 1936.
17. Chesly Manly, *The Twenty Year Revolution, from Roosevelt to Eisenhower* (Chicago, 1954), pp. 64-65.
18. "The Supreme Court Decision," *Vital Speeches,* 1 (June 2, 1935), 586-89.
19. New York *Herald Tribune,* February 9, 1937.
20. Joseph Alsop and Turner Catledge, "The 168 Days," *Saturday Evening Post,* 210 (September 18 and 25, October 16, 1937), 8 ff., 20 ff., 20 ff.
21. Springfield *Republican,* September 1, 1936.
22. *The Secret Diary of Harold L. Ickes* (3 vols., New York, 1954), II, p. 214.
23. New York *Herald Tribune,* December 1, 1937.

NOTES TO CHAPTER XVIII

1. Basil Rauch, *The History of the New Deal, 1933-1938* (New York, 1944), pp. 234-35.
2. Washington *Herald,* April 23, 1935.
3. Walter Lippman, in New York *Herald Tribune,* April 18, 1936.
4. Carter Glass to Borah, July 3, 1934, Borah *Scrapbook,* Vol. 24, p. 115.
5. New York *Times,* February 8, 1936.
6. *Christian Science Monitor,* August 12, 1935.
7. Washington *News,* December 20, 1935; New York *Times,* December 20, 1935.
8. New York *Times,* December 21, 1935.
9. Interview with Hamilton Fish, November 28, 1956.

10. Mark Sullivan, in Washington *Star,* February 1, 1936; *Time,* 27 (February 10, 1936), 16. For a full account of the Brooklyn speech, see New York *Times,* January 29, 1936, and *Vital Speeches,* 2, pp. 296-302; see also *Time,* 28 (February 17, 1936), 14.
11. Washington *Post,* February 16, 1936.
12. When his advancing age was mentioned, Borah's supporters countered with statistics: Masaryk was eighty-five, Von Hindenburg eighty-six, and Gladstone eighty-four at the height of their effectiveness.
13. Christopher P. Connolly to Borah, November 27, 1926, Box 283, Borah Papers.
14. Frank Kent, in Baltimore *Sun,* January 2, 1936.
15. *Time,* 27 (March 30, 1963), 21-22; *Newsweek,* 7 (April 18, 1936), 9.
16. *Time, ut supra.*
17. *Ibid.*
18. Borah voted for the Thomas Amendment to the AAA, for unlimited coinage of silver, for the Silver Purchase Act of 1934, for the Patman Bonus Bill, and also to override the veto of this bill.
19. Box 606, Borah Papers; see also Washington *Post,* February 27, 1936.
20. Washington *Star,* March 21, 1936; *Time, ut supra.*
21. *Vital Speeches,* 2 (March 22, 1936), 412-15.
22. Wayne County *Press,* April 9, 1936; another version quotes him as saying, "When Standard Oil and the DuPont dynasty says anybody but Borah, I know what that means . . ." (Chicago *Tribune,* April 11, 1936).
23. New York *Times,* April 5, 1936.
24. Washington *Evening Star,* April 3, 1936.
25. William A. White to Borah, April 9, 1936, Box 400, Borah Papers.
26. *Review of Reviews,* 94 (July, 1936), 36.
27. *New Republic,* 86 (March 18, 1936), 164.
28. *Ibid.,* 87 (May 20, 1936), 44; *Newsweek,* 7 (May 23, 1936), 16.
29. Philadelphia *Public Record,* May 28, 1936.
30. New York *American,* May 29, 1936.
31. Philadelphia *Public Record,* January 2, 1936; see also "Storm Warnings in Idaho," *Colliers,* 97 (April 4, 1936), 28-30.

32. Pocatello *Tribune,* June 8, 1936.
33. Ralph J. Donaldson, in Cleveland *Plain Dealer,* June 9, 1936.
34. Ernest K. Lindley, in New York *Herald Tribune,* June 9, 1936; *Christian Science Monitor,* June 9, 1936.
35. *Christian Science Monitor, ut supra.*
36. Washington *Herald,* June 10, 1936.
37. Editorial by William A. White, "Friendship's Garland," in Emporia *Gazette, ca.* January 21, 1940.
38. Washington *News,* June 10, 1936.
39. Washington *News,* June 12, 1936.
40. Washington *Post,* June 14, 1936.
41. Stokes, *Chip off My Shoulder,* pp. 434-35.
42. New York *Times,* June 17, 1936.
43. Washington *News,* June 19, 1936.
44. *Time,* 28 (August 24, 1936), 22; Thomas C. Donnelly, ed., *Rocky Mountain Politics* (Albuquerque, 1940), pp. 180-82.
45. Harry J. Brown, Salt Lake City *Tribune,* November 18, 1934; Blackfoot (Idaho) *Daily Bulletin,* quoted in Borah *Scrapbook,* Vol. 8, p. 93; interview with Jim Farley, October 30, 1957.
46. James McGregor Burns, *Roosevelt, the Lion and the Fox* (New York, 1956), p. 279.
47. Hugh Johnson to Borah, July 29, 1935, in Borah *Scrapbook,* Vol. 13, pp. 170 ff.
48. New York *Post,* October 5, 1936.
49. Boise *Capital News,* November 4, 1936.
50. Borah to Thomas Whitten, December 5, 1936, Box 400, Borah Papers.
51. Idaho *Statesman,* November 5, 1936.
52. Box 401, Borah Papers. For a detailed account of Borah's 1936 campaigns, see Orde S. Pinckney, "William E. Borah and the Republican Party," Univ. of California Ph.D. theses, pp. 84-140.
53. Washington *Star,* September 22, 1937; Washington *Herald,* August 31, 1937.
54. Spokane *Spokesman Review,* September 28, 1937; Burns, *Roosevelt,* p. 317.
55. Washington *Post,* and Spokane *Spokesman Review,* September 29, 1937.

56. New York *Times,* December 21, 1938.
57. Washington *Times-Herald,* February 1, 1939; Washington *Post,* February 2, 1939.

NOTES TO CHAPTER XIX

1. Denis Brogan, *The Price of Revolution* (New York, 1952), p. 220.
2. Charles O'Donnell, "American Foreign Policy," *Review of Politics,* 1 (July, 1939), 333-37.
3. Borah to the editor of *Philadelphia Public Record,* October 9, 1937, Box 405, Borah Papers; Foster Rhea Dulles, *America's Rise to World Power,* pp. 144-48; Frederick Lewis Allen, *The Big Change* (New York, 1954), p. 161; Tacoma *News Tribune,* March 29, 1939.
4. New York *Times,* September 25, 1931; *Foreign Affairs,* 10 (1931), 220-30.
5. February 23, 1932, Stimson Papers, Ms. Division, Yale University Library, New Haven; Richard N. Current, *Stimson: A Study in Statecraft* (New Brunswick, 1954), pp. 85-98.
6. Donald Drummond, *Passing of American Neutrality,* p. 33; *Congressional Record,* 72 Cong., 2 Sess. (January 11, 1933), Vol. 76, pp. 1151 and 2096.
7. New York *Herald Tribune,* March 6, 1934.
8. Manly, *Twenty Year Revolution,* pp. 51-52; *Time,* 34 (July 17, 1939), 17-19.
9. When the National Socialists took power, all we did was to imply in veiled terms that we did not approve. For Borah's remarks, see Washington *News,* March 25, 1935.
10. Borah to Oswald G. Villard, July 2, 1937, and typescript of the article, Box 404, Borah Papers; speech on "fascism" in New York *Times,* September 17, 1937; cf. *Vital Issues,* 3 (May 6, 1937), 482-84.
11. Fritz Kuhn to Borah, September 20, 1937, Box 411, Borah Papers.
12. Borah to James P. Roe, November 25, 1938, Box 416, Borah Papers; for his position on religious persecution in Mexico, see Harold H. Hinton, *Cordell Hull: A Biography* (New York, 1942), pp. 287 and 333.
13. For the correspondence on the Jewish refugee problem, see Boxes 405 and 416; Levinson to Borah, February 22, 1938, Box 422, Borah Papers.

14. Speech broadcasted by CBS and reprinted in *Vital Issues,* 2 (September 22, 1935), 36-38; *New Republic,* 86 (March 4, 1936), 97-98.
15. Alben Barkley, *That Reminds Me* (New York, 1954), p. 168.
16. New York *Times,* March 2, 1937.
17. *Ibid.,* March 5, 1937.
18. Washington *Herald,* December 14, 1937.
19. *Ibid.,* February 2, 1938.
20. *Ibid.*
21. Ambassador Joseph Kennedy to Borah, April 28, 1938, Box 423, Borah Papers.
22. Borah *Scrapbook,* Vol. 23, p. 154; New York *Herald Tribune,* May 11, 1938.
23. Washington *Star,* March 30, 1938; William E. Borah, "Our Imperative Task: To Mind Our Own Business," in L. R. Sarett and W. T. Foster, eds., *Modern Speeches on Basic Issues* (Boston, 1939), pp. 279-85.
24. Washington *Times,* September 13, 1938.
25. Washington *Star,* October 30, 1938; Washington *News,* September 28, 1938.
26. October 18, 1938, Box 544, Borah Papers.
27. Washington *Star,* March 28, 1939; see also Box 544, Borah Papers.
28. Translation of instructions of the German ambassador in Secret Archives of Foreign Secretary, Serial No. B21, from a photocopy of the original in the German Foreign Office, Bonn.
29. Dispatch of Undersecretary Woermann, *ibid.*
30. November 30, 1938, *ibid.*
31. The authority for this account is William K. Hutchinson, "News Articles on the Life and Works of Hon. William E. Borah," Senate Document 150 (Washington, D.C., 1940), pp. 29-40; Tansill, *Back Door to War,* p. 563.
32. Washington *News,* February 28, 1939.
33. Hutchinson, "News Articles," pp. 38-40.
34. *Ibid.*
35. Tucson *Daily Citizen,* July 17, 1939; Joseph Alsop and Robert Kintner, *American White Paper* (New York, 1940), pp. 43-44.
36. Washington *Star,* July 21, 1939.
37. *Ibid.*

38. Stenographic report of the meeting, Box 426, Borah Papers; Chicago *Tribune,* July 19 and 20, 1939; Barkley, *That Reminds Me,* pp. 260-61; Baltimore *Sun,* July 19, 1939; Kintner and Alsop, *White Paper,* pp. 44-47; Hinton, *Hull,* pp. 339-40. Borah took exception to Senator Barkley's references to the conference. His resentment was especially directed at lifting his remarks out of context. The statement predicting no war in Europe, he claimed, was wholly disconnected from the question whether or not there would be a war. "It was upon an entirely different subject . . ." See *Congressional Record,* 76 Cong., 2 Sess. (October 20, 1939), p. 640.
39. Borah to International News Service, September 1, 1939, Box 426, Borah Papers. In a letter to Borah (September 26, 1939, Box 427, Borah Papers) Dorothy Thompson said he was right in his hatred of war but wrong in his analysis of it.
40. Washington *News,* September 18, 1939; Borah to Cleve Groom, September 18, 1939, Box 426, Borah Papers.
41. Washington *News,* September 22, 1939.
42. New York *Times,* October 3, 1939; Washington *News,* October 2, 1939.
43. Statement to Albert Warner of CBS, Box 544, Borah Papers.
44. New York *Times,* December 15, 1939, January 11, 1940; undated clippings, Box 544, Borah Papers.

NOTES TO CHAPTER XX

1. Washington *Times-Herald,* January 10, 1940.
2. Undated letter from Borah to Fred Bixby, Box 270, Borah Papers.
3. "Borah—the Last Word," *Christian Century,* 57 (January 31, 1940), 143-44.
4. *Time,* 35 (January 29, 1940), 18-19.
5. Idaho *Statesman,* January 26, 1940.
6. Washington *Times-Herald,* January 17, 1940.
7. Boise *Capital News,* January 20, 1940.
8. Epitaph on tombstone of Unionist James Petigru, St. Michael's churchyard, Charleston, quoted in Walter Lippmann, *Interpretations, 1931-2* (2 vols., New York, 1932), I, pp. 210-11.

Bibliography

MANUSCRIPTS

WILLIAM E. BORAH PAPERS, IN MANUSCRIPT DIVISION, IDAHO STATE HISTORICAL SOCIETY, BOISE.

This collection of papers lay unnoticed for many years in the basement of a Boise office building. The collection was the gift of Mrs. W. E. Borah to the Historical Society in 1956. It contains Borah's office correspondence as an Idaho attorney from 1890 to 1907, legal papers, drafts of addresses, court records mainly of civil cases tried by him, and some notes relating primarily to his law practice. Included are papers relating to the Republican party, the Western Federation of Miners' conspiracy cases (Paul Corcoran, William D. Haywood), and the assassination of Frank Steunenberg, the Edward H. Dewey mining and railroad enterprises, the Barber and Potlatch lumber companies, and the Pacific and Idaho Northern Railway.

WILLIAM E. BORAH PAPERS, IN MANUSCRIPT DIVISION, LIBRARY OF CONGRESS, WASHINGTON, D.C.

This larger collection of Borah Papers, consisting mainly of his Senate office files, was the gift of his widow to the Congressional Library shortly after his death. The papers fill more than seven hundred boxes. Essentially, the most important are the letters to and from Senator Borah, 1912-40. The office files covering the years from 1907 to 1912 were discarded when Borah's office was moved from the basement of the Capitol to the Senate office building. The letters are arranged chronologically within topical folders in alphabetical order. In most cases, carbons of replies accompany incoming letters. The range of subjects is bewildering and the absence of all but a few personal letters precludes gaining much insight into Borah's private life or inner thoughts.

In addition to the letters, there are several other broad subdivisions which include a number of boxes on appointments, patronage, government departmental matters, reprints and drafts of speeches, speech materials, stenographic notebooks, all Borah's household bills and receipts filed monthly, notebooks with recorded quotations, and copies of Senate bills or resolutions.

Deposited with the Borah Papers were ten boxes of 1936 campaign material from the office of Hamilton Fish. Five volumes of Borah's major Senate speeches were privately printed in a limited edition to supplement the more complete *Congressional Record.*

Approximately fifty volumes of scrapbooks compiled by the senator and his office staff covering a wide range of Borah activities and publicity, valuable especially for his Idaho campaigns, were deposited by Mrs. Borah at his request in the library of the University of Idaho in Moscow. Microfilm copies of the contents of these scrapbooks were made for the Library of Congress' collection.

In addition to these materials, Borah's wife and secretary supplied me with a variety of useful materials including additional scrapbooks (now in the Library of Congress), typescripts of his White House conferences, copies of speeches unprinted elsewhere, personal notebooks, and letters. An interesting collection of Borah cartoons in the original, relating to many phases of a long political career, were deposited in the College of Idaho at Caldwell.

OTHER MANUSCRIPTS

Ray Stannard Baker Papers, Library of Congress (hereafter LC); Albert J. Beveridge Papers, LC; Charles J. Bonaparte Papers, LC; Frederick C. Dubois Papers, Idaho State College, Pocatello; Robert M. La Follette Papers, LC; Franklin D. Roosevelt Papers, Hyde Park, New York; Theodore Roosevelt Papers, LC; Henry L. Stimson Papers, Yale University Library, New Haven; William Allen White Papers, LC; Woodrow Wilson Papers, LC.

INTERVIEWS

Lloyd Adams, Margaret Cobb Ailshie, Mr. and Mrs. C. C. Anderson, Scott Anderson, James T. Babb, Sam Blaine, J. C. "Chet" Borah, Mary McConnell Borah, Harold Burton, William R. Castle, Charles C. Cavanah, Frank Chalfant, Angelina Church, Senator Frank Church, Chase Clark, D. Worth Clark, Mrs. Nellie K. Clark, Mrs. Ralph Crews, Mrs. J. W. Cunningham, Angela Curran, Joseph Dallas, Dr. Worth Daniels, Frederick Davenport, Ralph Davis, H. G. Doddridge, Lynn Driscoll, Senator Henry Dworshak, Ernest Eagleson, Agnes Emery.

Dr. and Mrs. Ralph Falk, James A. Farley, Hamilton Fish, Mrs. E. J. Frawley, James Gipson, Raymond Givens, William Hard, Hudson Hawley, James Hawley, Jess Hawley, Jr., William K. Hutchinson, Joseph Imhoff, Charles Koelsch, Fola La Follette, James Lampert, Cora Rubin Lane, Alice Roosevelt Longworth.

M. Pearl McCall, Frank McCoy, Ray McKaig, Frank Martin, Ira Masters, Allan Nevins, B. W. Oppenheim, Harry Orchard, Robert W. Overjorde, Karl Paine, Mary Louise Perrine, Otto Peterson, G. G. Power, Mary Quirk, Taylor C. Robertson, Irvin C. Rockwell, Kate Rosenheim, Mary Rubin, Mrs. Norman Ruick.

C. J. Schooler, Harry Shellworth, Ruth Shoup, Addison T. Smith, Edwin Snow, Archibald Steele, Louis Thrailkill, Samuel L. Tipton, James Twogood, Earl Venable, Burton K. Wheeler, Ezra Whitla, Sir Arthur Willert, Pliny Williamson, Lyle C. Wilson.

NEWSPAPERS

Baltimore *Sun*
Boise *Capital News*
Boise *Evening Capital News*
Boston *Transcript*
Chicago *Daily News*
Chicago *Tribune*
Idaho *Free Press*
Idaho *Statesman*
Lewiston *Tribune*
Lyons *Republican*
New York *Herald*
New York *Herald Tribune*
New York *Times*
New York *World*
Philadelphia *Public Record*
Pocatello *Tribune*
Portland *Oregonian*
Salt Lake City *Tribune*
Springfield *Republican*
Washington *Evening Star*
Washington *Herald*
Washington *News*
Washington *Post*
Washington *Star*

PERIODICALS

American Historical Review
American Magazine
American Mercury
American Political Science Review
Atlantic Monthly
Century
Christian Century
Colliers
Commonweal
Current History
Foreign Affairs
Forum
Historical Outlook
Idaho Yesterdays
Independent
Journal of Modern History
Kansas Historical Quarterly
Literary Digest
Mississippi Valley Historical Review
Nation
New Republic
Newsweek
North American Review
Outlook
Pacific Northwest Quarterly
Review of Reviews
Saturday Evening Post
Scribner's Magazine
Sunset
Time
United States News and World Report
Vital Speeches
World's Work

BOOKS AND PAMPHLETS

Adams, John Quincy. *Lectures on Rhetoric and Oratory, Delivered to the Classes . . . in Harvard University* (2 vols., Cambridge, 1810).

Adams, Samuel Hopkins. *Incredible Era: The Life and Times of Warren Gamaliel Harding* (Boston, 1939).

Adler, Selig. *The Isolationist Impulse: Its Twentieth Century Reaction* (New York, 1957).

Bibliography

Allen, Frederick Lewis. *The Big Change* (New York, 1954).

Allen, Robert S. *Why Hoover Faces Defeat* (New York, 1932).

Alsop, Joseph, and Robert Kintner. *The American White Paper* (New York, 1940).

Bailey, Stephen K., and Howard Samuel. *Congress at Work* (New York, 1952).

Bailey, Thomas A. *America Faces Russia: Russian-American Relations from Early Times to the Present* (Ithaca, 1950).

———. *Woodrow Wilson and the Great Betrayal.* (New York, 1945).

Barkley, Alben. *That Reminds Me* (New York, 1954).

Bates, Ernest. *This Land of Liberty* (New York, 1930).

———. *The Story of Congress* (New York, 1936).

Beal, W. D. *A History of Southeastern Idaho: An Intimate Narrative of Peaceful Conquest by Empire Builders* (Caldwell, 1942).

Beloff, Max. *Foreign Policy of Soviet Russia, 1929-41* (2 vols., New York, 1947).

Bird, Annie Laurie. *Boise, the Peace Valley* (Caldwell, 1934).

———. *Seeing Idaho* (Pocatello, 1937).

Blum, John Morton. *The Republican Roosevelt* (Cambridge, 1954).

Bonchek, Herman S. *Borah and American Ideals* (Youngstown, 1936).

Borah, William E. *Closing Argument . . . for the Prosecution in the Great Coeur d'Alene Riot Murder Trial . . .* (Wallace, 1899).

———. *Closing Argument of W. E. Borah, Haywood Trial* (Boise, 1907).

———. *Roosevelt Club Borah-Butler Debates* (Boston, 1927).

———. *Wherefores of Borah* (Washington, D.C., 1926).

Borchard, Edwin, and William Lage. *Neutrality for the United States* (New Haven, 1937).

Bowers, Claude G. *Albert A. Beveridge and the Progressive Era* (New York, 1932).

Brogan, Denis. *The Price of Revolution* (New York, 1952).

Brosnan, Cornelius J. *History of the State of Idaho* (New York, 1948).

Browder, Robert Paul. *The Origins of Soviet-American Diplomacy* (Princeton, 1953).

Brown, George R. *The Leadership of Congress* (Indianapolis, 1922).

Brush, Daniel Harmon. *Growing up in Southern Illinois . . . the Memoirs of Daniel Harmon Brush,* edited by Milo M. Quaife (Chicago, 1944).

Bryan, William Jennings. *A Tale of Two Conventions . . . an Account of the Republican and Democratic National Conventions of June, 1912 . . .* (New York, 1912).

Bryn-Jones, David. *Frank Kellogg: A Biography* (New York, 1937).

Burns, James McGregor. *Roosevelt: The Lion and the Fox* (New York, 1956).

Busch, Francis X. *Prisoners at the Bar* (Indianapolis, 1952).

Butler, Nicholas Murray. *Across the Busy Years* (2 vols., New York, 1939-40).

Carr, Edward H. *The Interregnum, 1923-1924* (7 vols., New York, 1954).

Chamberlain, John. *Farewell to Reform: The Rise, Life and Decay of the Progressive Mind in America* (New York, 1933).

Colgrove, Kenneth. *American Senate and World Peace* (New York, 1944).

Cooper, Russell M. *American Consultation in World Affairs . . .* (New York, 1934).

Cox, James M. *Journey Through My Years* (New York, 1946).

Cranston, Alan. *The Killing of the Peace* (New York, 1945).

Current, Richard N. *Secretary Stimson: A Study in Statecraft* (New Brunswick, 1954).

Darrow, Clarence. *The Story of My Life* (New York, 1932).

Daugherty, Harry M. *The Inside Story of the Harding Tragedy* (New York, 1932).

Davenport, Walter. *Power and Glory: The Life of Boies Penrose* (New York, 1931).

Davis, Oscar King. *Released for Publication: Some Inside Political History of Theodore Roosevelt and His Times, 1898-1918* (Boston, 1925).

Dawes, Charles G. *Notes as Vice President, 1928-9* (Boston, 1935).

Dennison, Eleanor E. *The Senate Foreign Relations Committee* (Stanford, 1942).

Dentler, Clara Louise. *Katherine (v. B.) Luther of the Wittenberg Parsonage* (Philadelphia, 1924).

Dodd, William E. *Woodrow Wilson and His Work* (New York, 1932).

Donaldson, Thomas C. *Idaho of Yesterday* (Caldwell, 1941).

Donnelly, Thomas C., ed. *Rocky Mountain Politics* (Albuquerque, 1940).

———. *The 1932 Campaign: An Analysis* (New York, 1935).

Drummond, Donald. *Passing of American Neutrality, 1937-41* (Ann Arbor, 1955).

Dulles, Foster Rhea. *America's Rise to World Power, 1898-1954* (New York, 1954).

Dumond, Dwight. *Roosevelt to Roosevelt, the United States in the Twentieth Century* (New York, 1937).

Dunn, Arthur W. *From Harrison to Harding, a Personal Narrative Covering a Third of a Century, 1888-1921* (2 vols., New York, 1922).
Dunne, Peter Finley. *Mr. Dooley Says* (London, 1910).

Ferrell, Robert. *American Diplomacy in the Great Depression* (New Haven, 1957).
———. *Peace in Their Time: The Origins of the Kellogg-Briand Pact* (New Haven, 1952).
Filler, Louis. *Crusaders for American Liberalism* (New Springs, 1950).
Fischer, Louis. *Men and Politics: An Autobiography* (New York, 1941).
———. *The Soviets in World Affairs* (2 vols., New York, 1951).
Fite, Gilbert C. *George N. Peek and the Fight for Farm Parity* (Norman, 1954).
———. *Peter Norbeck, Prairie Statesman* (Columbia, Missouri, 1948).
Foraker, Joseph Benson. *Notes of a Busy Life* (2 vols., Cincinnati, 1916).
Froom, Leroy E., ed. *Harry Orchard: The Man God Made Again* (Nashville, 1952).
Fuess, Claude. *Calvin Coolidge, the Man from Vermont* (New York, 1940).
Fuller, George W. *A History of the Pacific Northwest* (New York, 1931).

Garraty, John. *Henry Cabot Lodge: A Biography* (New York, 1953).
Gilbert, Clinton. *The Mirrors of Washington* (New York, 1921).
———. *Behind the Mirrors: The Psychology of Disintegration at Washington* (New York, 1922).
———. *You Takes Your Choice* (New York, 1924).
Gilfond, Duff. *The Rise of St. Calvin: Merry Sidelights on the Career of Mr. Coolidge* (New York, 1932).
Goldman, Eric. *Rendezvous with Destiny* (New York, 1952).
Griffith, Will, ed. *Idols of Egypt* (Carbondale, 1947).

Haines, Lynn. *The Senate from 1907-1912 . . .* (Washington, 1912).
Hard, William. *Raymond Robins' Own Story* (New York, 1920).
Hawley, James H. *History of Idaho: The Gem of the Mountains* (4 vols., Chicago, 1920).
Haworth, Paul L. *America in Ferment* (Indianapolis, 1915).
Haynes, George H. *The Senate of the United States: Its History and Practice* (Boston, 1938).
Haywood, William. *Bill Haywood's Book: The Autobiography of William Haywood* (New York, 1929).
Hechler, Kenneth W. *Insurgency: Personalities and Politics of the Taft Era* (New York, 1940).

Hinton, Harold B. *Cordell Hull: A Biography* (New York, 1942).
Hoag, C. Leonard. *Preface to Preparedness: The Washington Disarmament Conference and Public Opinion* (Washington, D.C., 1941).
Hofstadter, Richard. *The Age of Reform, from Bryan to Roosevelt* (New York, 1955).
Holbrook, Stewart. *The Rocky Mountain Revolution* (New York, 1956).
———. *Far Corner: A Personal Narrative of the Pacific Northwest* (New York, 1952).
Holt, W. Stull. *Treaties Defeated by the Senate* (Baltimore, 1933).
Hoover, Herbert. *Memoirs* (3 vols., New York, 1951-2).
Huff, Warren and Edna. *Famous Americans* (Los Angeles, 1941).
Hugh-Jones, E. M. *Woodrow Wilson and American Liberalism* (London, 1947).
Hutchinson, William K. *News Articles on the Life and Works of Honorable William E. Borah . . .* (Washington, D.C., 1940).
Hutchinson, William T. *Lowden of Illinois: The Life of Frank O. Lowden* (2 vols., Chicago, 1951).
Hutton, Mary A. *The Coeur d'Alenes, or a Tale of the Modern Inquisition in Idaho* (Wallace, 1900).

Ickes, Harold. *Secret Diary* (3 vols., New York, 1943).

Jessup, Philip C. *Elihu Root* (2 vols., New York, 1938).
Johnson, Claudius. *Borah of Idaho* (New York, 1936).
Johnson, Dorothy, and Charles Gates. *Empire of the Columbia* (New York, 1957).
Johnson, Walter. *The Battle Against Isolation* (Chicago, 1944).
———. *William Allen White's America* (New York, 1947).
———, ed. *Selected Writings of William Allen White* (New York, 1947).
Jones, Ben. *Sam Jones, Lawyer* (Norman, 1947).
Jones, Horace. *The Story of Early Rice County* (Topeka, 1928).

Kaltenborn, Henry V. *Fifty Fabulous Years* (New York, 1950).
Kemler, Edgar. *The Deflation of American Ideals: An Ethical Guide for New Dealers* (Washington, D.C., 1941).
Kennan, George. *Soviet-American Relations, 1917-20* (2 vols., Princeton, 1956-8).
Kent, Frank. *Political Behavior . . .* (New York, 1928).
Kohlsaat, Herman H. *From McKinley to Harding: Personal Recollections of Our Presidents* (New York, 1923).

La Follette, Belle Case and Fola. *Robert M. La Follette* (2 vols., New York, 1953).

La Follette, Robert M. *La Follette's Autobiography: A Personal Narrative of Political Experience* (Madison, 1913).

Langer, William L., and S. E. Gleason. *The Challenge to Isolation, 1937-40* (New York, 1952).

———. *The Undeclared War, 1940-1* (New York, 1953).

Lawrence, David. *The True Story of Woodrow Wilson* (New York, 1924).

Leopold, Richard W. *Elihu Root and the Conservative Tradition* (Boston, 1954).

Lief, Alfred. *Democracy's Norris: The Biography of a Lonely Crusade* (New York, 1939).

Liggett, William H. *The Rise of Herbert Hoover* (New York, 1932).

Lippmann, Walter. *Interpretations, 1931-5* (2 vols., New York, 1932, 1936).

———. *Men of Destiny* (New York, 1928).

———. *Preface to Politics* (New York, 1913).

Lodge, Henry Cabot. *The United States and the League of Nations* (New York, 1925).

Lowry, Edward G. *Washington Close-ups: Intimate Views of Some Public Figures* (Boston, 1921).

Lubell, Samuel. *The Future of American Politics* (New York, 1952).

MacKay, Kenneth C. *The Progressive Movement of 1924* (New York, 1947).

Malin, James C. *The United States after the World War* (New York, 1930).

Manly, Chesly. *The Twenty Year Revolution: From Roosevelt to Eisenhower* (Chicago, 1954).

Marshall, Thomas. *Recollections of Thomas R. Marshall: Vice President and Hoosier Philosopher* (Indianapolis, 1925).

Martin, Boyd A. *The Direct Primary in Idaho* (Stanford, 1947).

May, E. R. *The World War and American Isolation, 1914-1917* (Cambridge, 1959).

Midgley, Wilson. *Possible Presidents* (London, 1928).

Millis, Walter. *Road to War, America, 1914-1917* (New York, 1935).

Minton, Bruce, and John Stuart. *The Fat Years and the Lean* (New York, 1940).

Morgenthau, Henry. *All in a Life Time* (New York, 1922).

Morlan, Robert L. *Political Prairie Fire: The Non-Partisan League, 1915-1922* (Minneapolis, 1955).

Mowry, George. *The Era of Theodore Roosevelt, 1900-1912* (New York, 1958).

———. *Theodore Roosevelt and the Progressive Movement* (Madison, 1947).

Moyer, George S. *Attitude of the United States toward the Recognition of Soviet Russia* (Philadelphia, 1926).

Myers, Henry Lee. *The United States Senate, What Kind of a Body* (Philadelphia, 1939).

Myers, William, and Walter Newton. *The Hoover Administration, a Documented Narrative* (New York, 1936).

Neuberger, Richard. *Our Promised Land* (New York, 1938).

Norris, George. *Fighting Liberal: The Autobiography of George W. Norris* (New York, 1945).

Nye, Russell B. *Midwestern Progressive Politics: A Historical Study of Its Origins and Development, 1870-1950* (East Lansing, 1951).

Oberholtzer, Ellis Paxson. *A History of the United States since the Civil War* (5 vols., New York, 1928).

Osgood, Robert E. *Ideals and Self-Interest in America's Foreign Relations* (Chicago, 1953).

Pearson, Drew, and Robert S. Allen. *Washington Merry-go-round* (New York, 1931).

Pearson, Drew, and Constantine Brown. *American Diplomatic Game* (New York, 1935).

Peck, Mary Gray. *Carrie Chapman Catt: A Biography* (New York, 1944).

Pepper, George. *George Wharton Pepper, Philadelphia Lawyer: An Autobiography* (Philadelphia, 1944).

Pope, Arthur Upham. *Maxim Litvinov* (New York, 1943).

Pringle, Henry. *Alfred E. Smith: A Critical Study* (New York, 1927).

———. *The Life and Times of William Howard Taft* (2 vols., New York, 1939).

———. *Theodore Roosevelt: A Biography* (New York, 1931).

Pusey, Merlo J. *Charles Evans Hughes* (2 vols., New York, 1951).

Rauch, Basil. *The History of the New Deal, 1933-1938* (New York, 1944).

Rosewater, Victor. *Backstage in 1912: The Inside Story of the Split Republican Convention* (Philadelphia, 1932).

Sarett, L. R., and W. T. Foster, eds., *Modern Speeches on Basic Issues* (Boston, 1939).

Schriftgiesser, Karl. *The Gentleman from Massachusetts: Henry Cabot Lodge* (Boston, 1944).

———. *This Was Normalcy: An Account of Party Politics during Twelve Republican Years, 1920-32* (Boston, 1948).

Seldes, Gilbert. *Years of the Locust, America 1929-32* (Boston, 1933).

Shideler, James H. *Farm Crisis, 1919-1923* (Berkeley, 1957).

Shotwell, James T. *War as an Instrument of National Policy . . .* (New York, 1929).

Simonds, Frank H. *Can America Stay at Home?* (New York, 1932).

Stevenson, Robert Louis. *Across the Plains* (New York, 1906).

Stoddard, Henry L. *As I Knew Them: Presidents and Politicians from Grant to Coolidge* (New York, 1927).

Stokes, Thomas L. *Chip off My Shoulder* (Princeton, 1940).

Stone, Irving. *Clarence Darrow for the Defense: A Biography* (New York, 1943).

Stoner, John E. *S. O. Levinson and the Pact of Paris: A Study in the Techniques of Influence* (Chicago, 1942).

Taft, Philip, and Selig Perlman. *History of Labor in the United States* (New York, 1918-35).

Tansill, C. C. *America Goes to War* (Boston, 1942).

———. *Back Door to War, the Roosevelt Foreign Policy, 1933-41* (Chicago, 1952).

Thompson, Charles. *Presidents I've Known and Two Near Presidents* (Indianapolis, 1929).

Tucker, Ray. *Mirrors of 1932* (New York, 1931).

Tucker, Ray, and Frederick Barkley. *Sons of the Wild Jackass* (Boston, 1932).

Villard, Oswald Garrison. *Fighting Years: Memoirs of a Liberal Editor* (New York, 1939).

Vinson, John Chalmers. *The Parchment Peace* (Atlanta, 1956).

———. *William E. Borah and the Outlawry of War* (Athens, 1957).

Walworth, Arthur. *Woodrow Wilson, World Prophet* (2 vols., New York, 1958).

Warren, Harris Gaylord. *Herbert Hoover and the Great Depression* (New York, 1959).

Watson, James. *As I Knew Them: Memoirs of James E. Watson* (New York, 1936).

Wecter, Dixon. *The Age of the Great Depression, 1929-41* (New York, 1948).
White, William Allen. *The Autobiography of William Allen White* (New York, 1946).
———. *The Changing West: An Economic Theory about Our Golden Age* (New York, 1939).
White, William S. *Citadel: The Story of the United States Senate* (New York, 1956).
Wilbur, Ray Lyman, and A. M. Hyde. *The Hoover Policies* (New York, 1937).
Williams, William Appleman. *American-Russian Relations, 1789-1947* (New York, 1952).
———. *The Shaping of American Diplomacy* (Chicago, 1956).
Woolf, Samuel J. *Drawn from Life* (New York, 1932).

Young, Roland. *This is Congress* (New York, 1943).

UNPUBLISHED MATERIAL

Perrine, Mary Louise. "Elephants and Donkeys," the memoirs of Mary Borah.
Pinckney, Orde S. "William E. Borah and the Republican Party, 1932-40," a doctoral dissertation, University of California, Berkeley, 1957.
Tennyson, Albert. "Public Career of United States Senator William E. Borah, with specific reference to his activities on domestic policies," M.A. thesis, University of Iowa, 1938.

Acknowledgments

It would be a pleasure to mention, if it were possible, the names of all those who have had any share at all in the preparation of this book. The list would certainly be long. To those who have given me a sizeable measure of assistance, mere mention here cannot express my appreciation.

The idea of a Borah biography originated with Margaret Clapp, who would have done greater credit to this subject had she not been vested with her responsibilities as president of Wellesley College.

Allan Nevins, who supervised my doctoral study at Columbia concerning Borah's early career, continued to take an interest in the book's progress after it was no longer his responsibility. The manuscript has benefited vastly as a result of his expert editing.

Examining the Borah Papers necessitated long months of work in Washington, D.C., and Idaho. To facilitate this, Columbia University awarded me the Erb Fellowship in American history in 1953. Research for this book was completed with this aid and a grant from the American Philosophical Society in 1957.

Friends, including the late Dr. H. Richard Charlton, his associates, Phil M. Smith and William Cullan, with Mrs. Roy Garofano, gave me much needed assistance in the early stages of this study. Unfailing counsel and assistance were always forthcoming from my professors at Columbia: John Krout, Richard B. Morris, William Leuchtenburg, and Herman Ausubel.

Dr. Percy Powell and Katherine Brand helped me to thread my way through the Borah Papers in the Library of Congress. At the Idaho Historical Society my work was made pleasant by Mr. Jerry Swinney and Dr. Merle Wells. At Hunter College George N. Shuster and Dean Mina S. Rees rendered cheerful assistance, and Professor Dorothy Fowler, who read an early draft, gave me the benefit of her experience.

Long interviews with Mrs. William E. Borah, who gave me the first opportunity to use the Borah Papers for a biography, with

Mrs. Cora Rubin Lane, the senator's lifelong secretary, with Dr. and Mrs. Ralph Falk, in whose home I was always refreshed and renewed for my task, and with all the friendly people of Idaho helped me to acquaint myself better with Borah.

Former Justice Harold Burton and John Lord O'Brian helped me to resolve some legal questions. The late Dorothy Canfield, her brother James Canfield, Porter Fones, and Hudson Hawley put their interviews in the form of a series of letters.

A special word of thanks is due all those who helped with the typing of the manuscript: Susan Daland, Dorothy Levitin, Barbara Haslam Cusack, Yvonne Chang, and Shirley Handman.

I also wish to acknowledge here the debt I owe Mary Louise Perrine, who first intervened with her aunt, Mrs. Borah, on my behalf. Finally, it seems scarcely adequate to mention the long enduring patience and interest of my friends and family.

Index